My nephew is so cute... I can hardly stand it!
    —**Katsura Hoshino**

Shiga Prefecture native Katsura Hoshino's hit manga series
D.Gray-man has been serialized in *Weekly Shonen Jump* since 2004.
Katsura's debut manga, "Continue," appeared for the first time in
Weekly Shonen Jump in 2003.

Katsura adores cats.

D.GRAY-MAN
VOL. 16
SHONEN JUMP ADVANCED
Manga Edition

STORY AND ART BY
KATSURA HOSHINO

English Adaptation/Lance Caselman
Translation/John Werry
Touch-up Art & Lettering/HudsonYards
Design/Matt Hinrichs
Editor/Gary Leach

VP, Production/Alvin Lu
VP, Sales & Product Marketing/Gonzalo Ferreyra
VP, Creative/Linda Espinosa
Publisher/Hyoe Narita

D.GRAY-MAN © 2004 by Katsura Hoshino. All rights reserved.
First published in Japan in 2004 by SHUEISHA Inc., Tokyo. English translation rights arranged by SHUEISHA Inc.

The rights of the author(s) of the work(s) in this publication to be so identified have been asserted in accordance with the Copyright, Designs and Patents Act 1988. A CIP catalogue record for this book is available from the British Library.

Printed in the U.S.A.

Published by VIZ Media, LLC
P.O. Box 77010
San Francisco, CA 94107

10 9 8 7 6 5 4 3 2 1
First printing, February 2010

THE WORLD'S MOST
CUTTING-EDGE MANGA

SHONEN JUMP
ADVANCED
www.shonenjump.com

www.viz.com

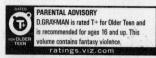

SHONEN JUMP ADVANCED MANGA EDITION

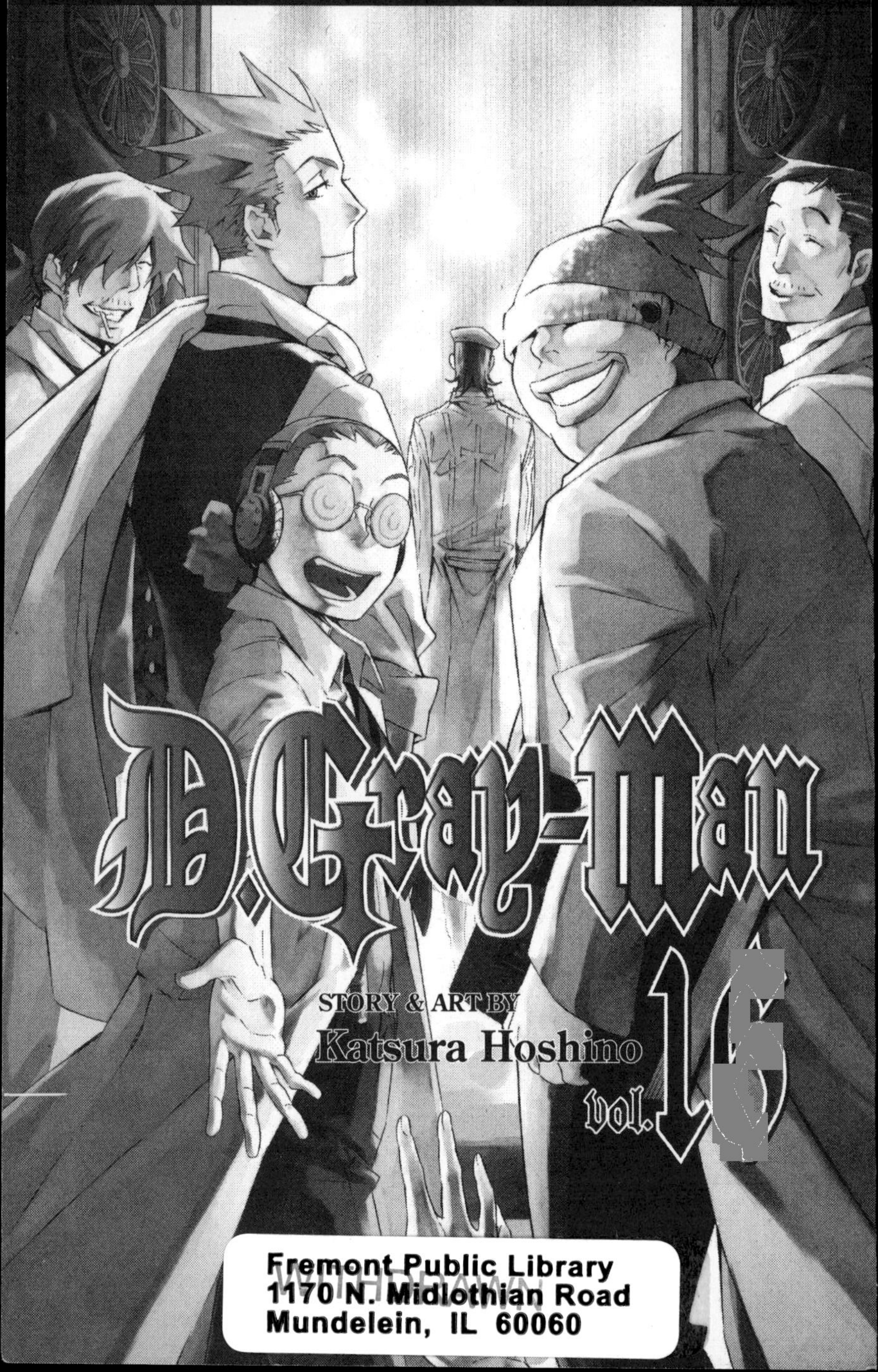
D.Gray-man
STORY & ART BY
Katsura Hoshino
vol. 16

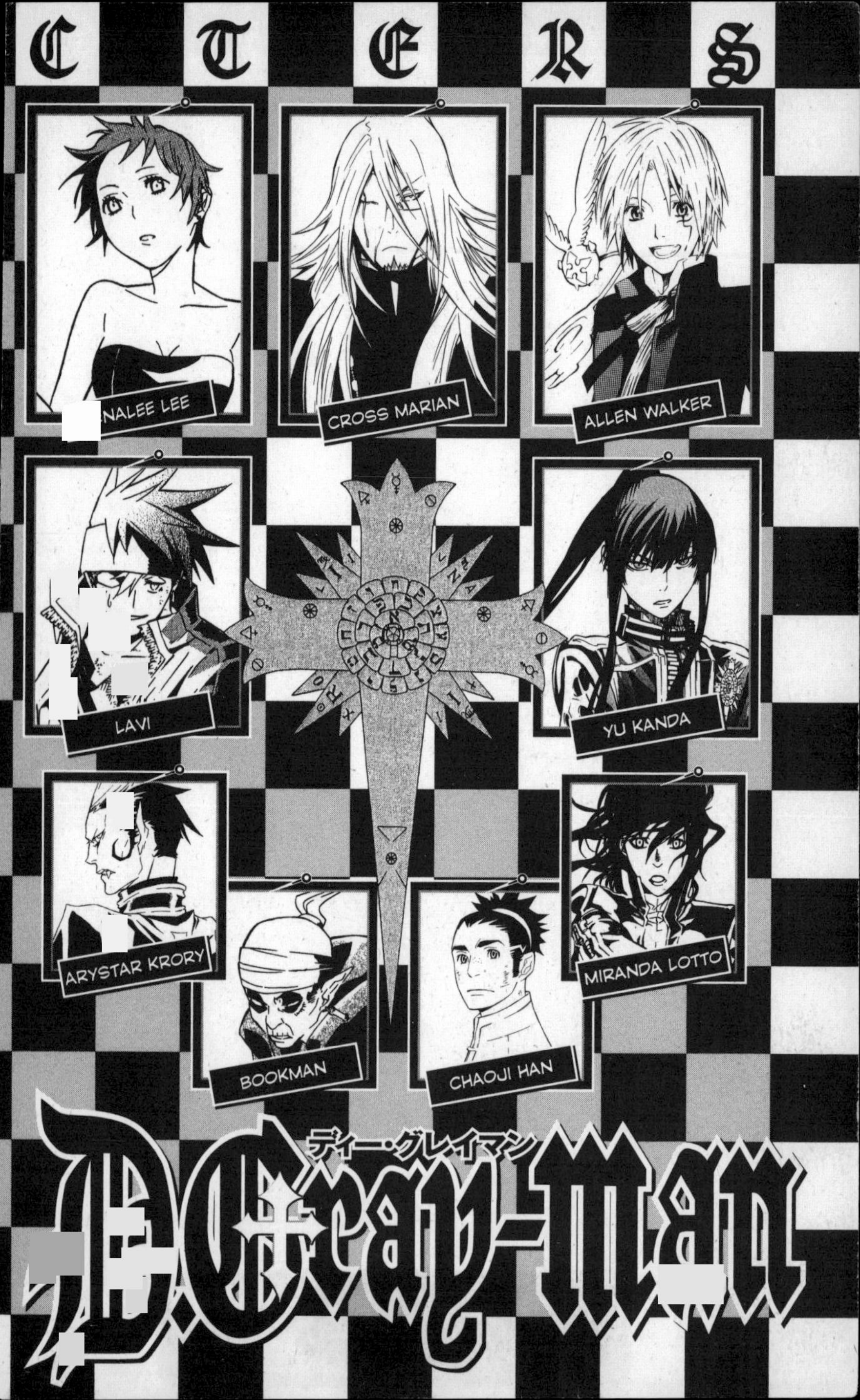
C T E R S
NALEE LEE
CROSS MARIAN
ALLEN WALKER
LAVI
YU KANDA
ARYSTAR KRORY
BOOKMAN
CHAOJI HAN
MIRANDA LOTTO
ディー・グレイマン
D.Gray-man

CHARA

JOHNNY GILL

BAK CHAN

KOMUI LE

MALCOLM C. ROUVELIER

REEVER WENHAM

MILLENNIUM EARL

LEVEL 4

HOWARD LINK

STORY

IT ALL BEGAN CENTURIES AGO WITH THE DISCOVERY OF A CUBE CONTAINING AN APOCALYPTIC PROPHECY FROM AN ANCIENT CIVILIZATION AND INSTRUCTIONS IN THE USE OF INNOCENCE, A CRYSTALLINE SUBSTANCE OF WONDROUS SUPERNATURAL POWER. THE CREATORS OF THE CUBE CLAIMED TO HAVE DEFEATED AN EVIL KNOWN AS THE MILLENNIUM EARL BY USING THE INNOCENCE. NEVERTHELESS, THE WORLD WAS DESTROYED BY THE GREAT FLOOD OF THE OLD TESTAMENT. NOW, TO AVERT A SECOND END OF THE WORLD, A GROUP OF EXORCISTS WIELDING WEAPONS MADE OF INNOCENCE MUST BATTLE THE MILLENNIUM EARL AND HIS TERRIBLE MINIONS, THE AKUMA.

WITH THE EARL'S MINIONS DEFEATED AND THE ARK IN THE HANDS OF THE BLACK ORDER, ALLEN FINDS HIMSELF UNDER SUSPICION AND ASSIGNED A GUARD BY THE CENTRAL AGENCY. BUT THE EXORCISTS SOON FIND THEMSELVES UNDER ATTACK YET AGAIN, THIS TIME IN THEIR OWN HEADQUARTERS. AND TO MAKE MATTERS WORSE, ONE OF THE ATTACKERS IS THE MILLENNIUM EARL'S NEW SECRET WEAPON—A LEVEL 4 AKUMA!

D.GRAY-MAN
Vol. 16

CONTENTS

The 150th Night: Blood & Chains   7

The 151st Night: The God I Hate   23

The 152nd Night: Until We Meet Again   39

The 153rd Night: Ready for Red   55

The 154th Night: The Battle Lines Shift   71

The 155th Night: Echoes in the Long Morning   87

The 156th Night: The Next Stage   103

The 157th Night: Recitativo   123

The 158th Night: Evil Flower   139

The 159th Night: A Stormy Move in the Wee Hours   155

The 160th Night: The Second Destruction of the Black Order   171

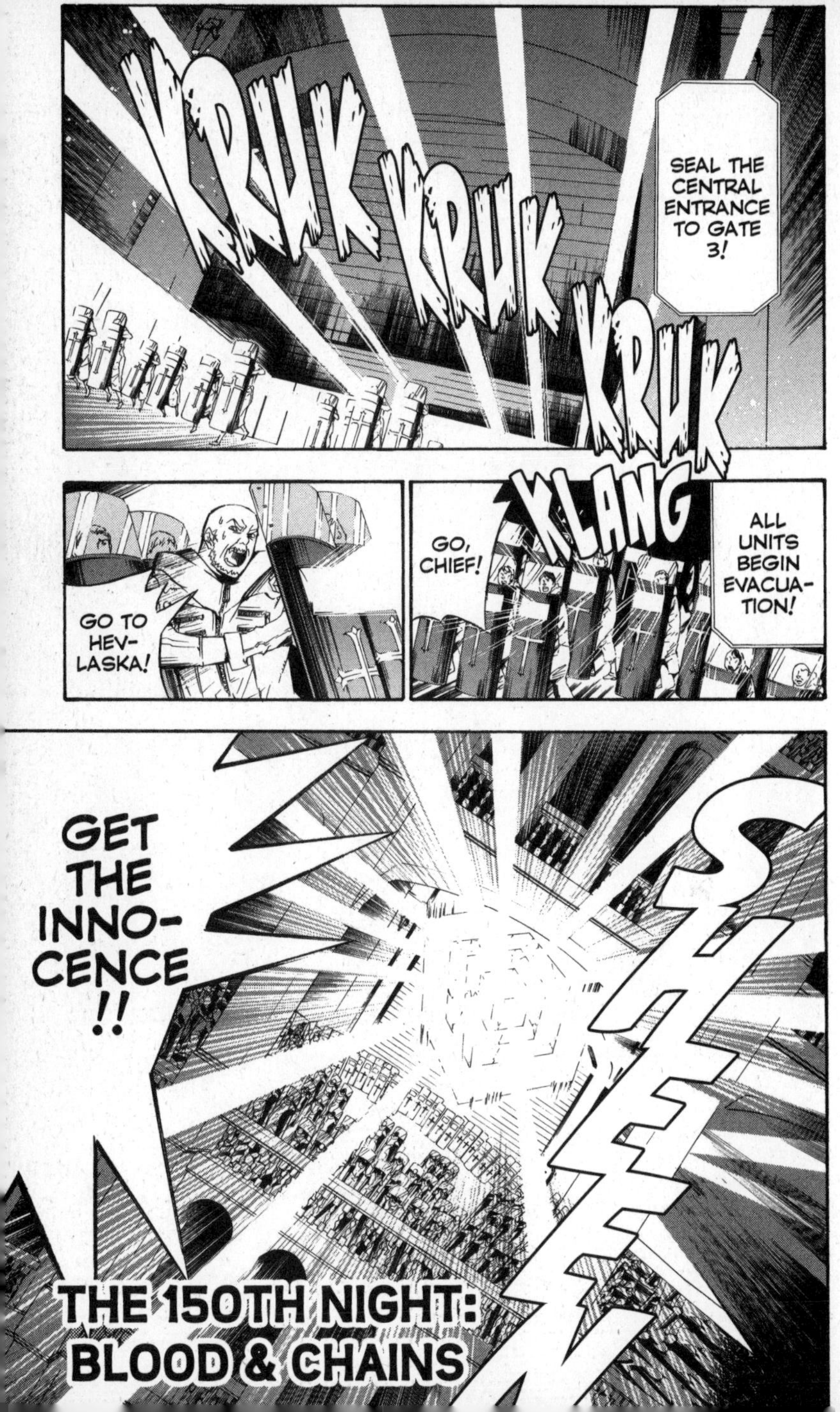
SEAL THE CENTRAL ENTRANCE TO GATE 3!
KRUK KRUK KRUK
ALL UNITS BEGIN EVACUATION!
KLANG
GO, CHIEF!
GO TO HEV-LASKA!
GET THE INNOCENCE!!
THE 150TH NIGHT: BLOOD & CHAINS

BEEP
BEEP
BEEP
BEEP
BEEP
BEEP
BEEP
BEEP
HEY...
WHERE DO YOU THINK YOU'RE GOING...
... "CHIEF"?

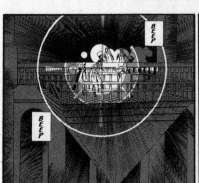

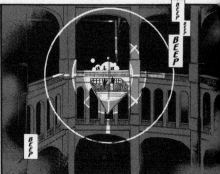

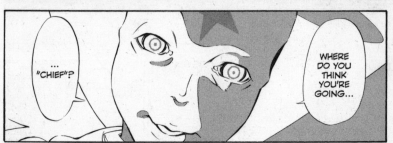

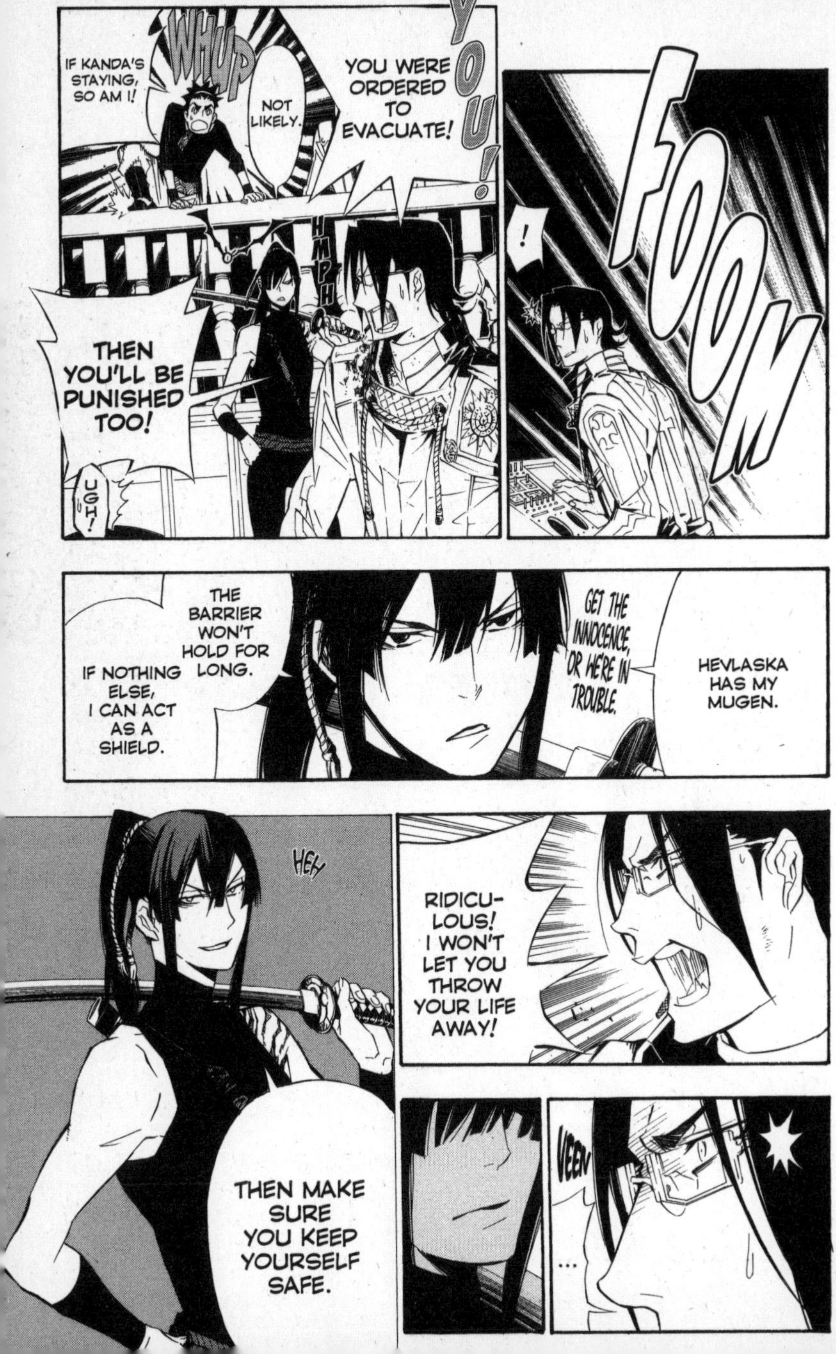
FOOM
!
YOU!
YOU WERE ORDERED TO EVACUATE!
NOT LIKELY.
WHUP
IF KANDA'S STAYING, SO AM I!
HMPH
THEN YOU'LL BE PUNISHED TOO!
UGH!
HEVLASKA HAS MY MUGEN.
GET THE INNOCENCE, OR WE'RE IN TROUBLE.
THE BARRIER WON'T HOLD FOR LONG.
IF NOTHING ELSE, I CAN ACT AS A SHIELD.
RIDICULOUS! I WON'T LET YOU THROW YOUR LIFE AWAY!
VEEN
...
HEH
THEN MAKE SURE YOU KEEP YOURSELF SAFE.

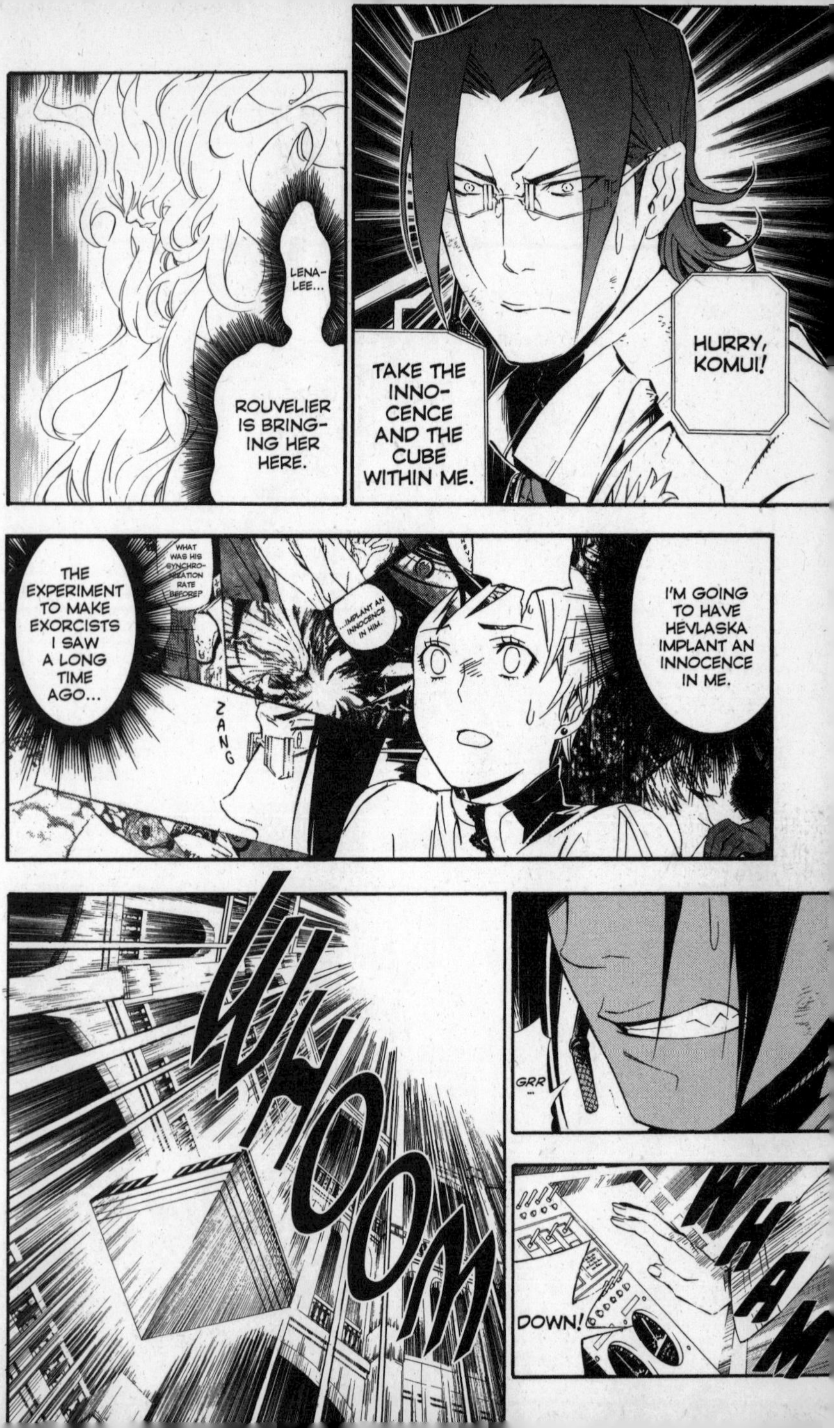
HURRY, KOMUI!
TAKE THE INNOCENCE AND THE CUBE WITHIN ME.
LENALEE...
ROUVELIER IS BRINGING HER HERE.
I'M GOING TO HAVE HEVLASKA IMPLANT AN INNOCENCE IN ME.
...IMPLANT AN INNOCENCE IN HIM.
WHAT WAS HIS SYNCHRONIZATION RATE BEFORE?
THE EXPERIMENT TO MAKE EXORCISTS I SAW A LONG TIME AGO...
ZANG
GRR...
WHAM
DOWN!
WHOOM

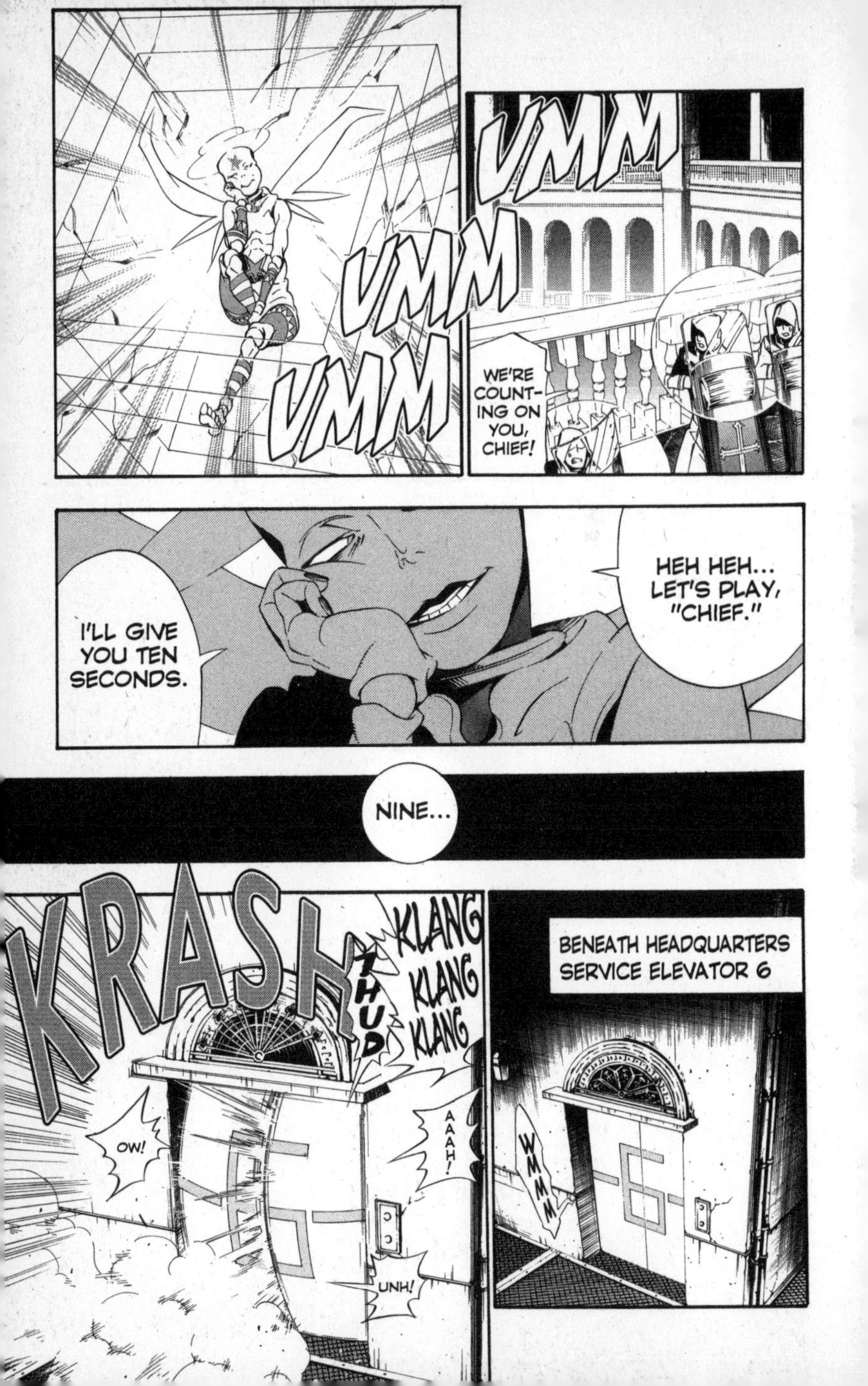
UMM
WE'RE COUNTING ON YOU, CHIEF!
UMM
UMM
HEH HEH... LET'S PLAY, "CHIEF."
I'LL GIVE YOU TEN SECONDS.
NINE...
BENEATH HEADQUARTERS SERVICE ELEVATOR 6
WMMM
KLANG KLANG KLANG
THUD
KRASH
AAAH!
OW!
UNH!

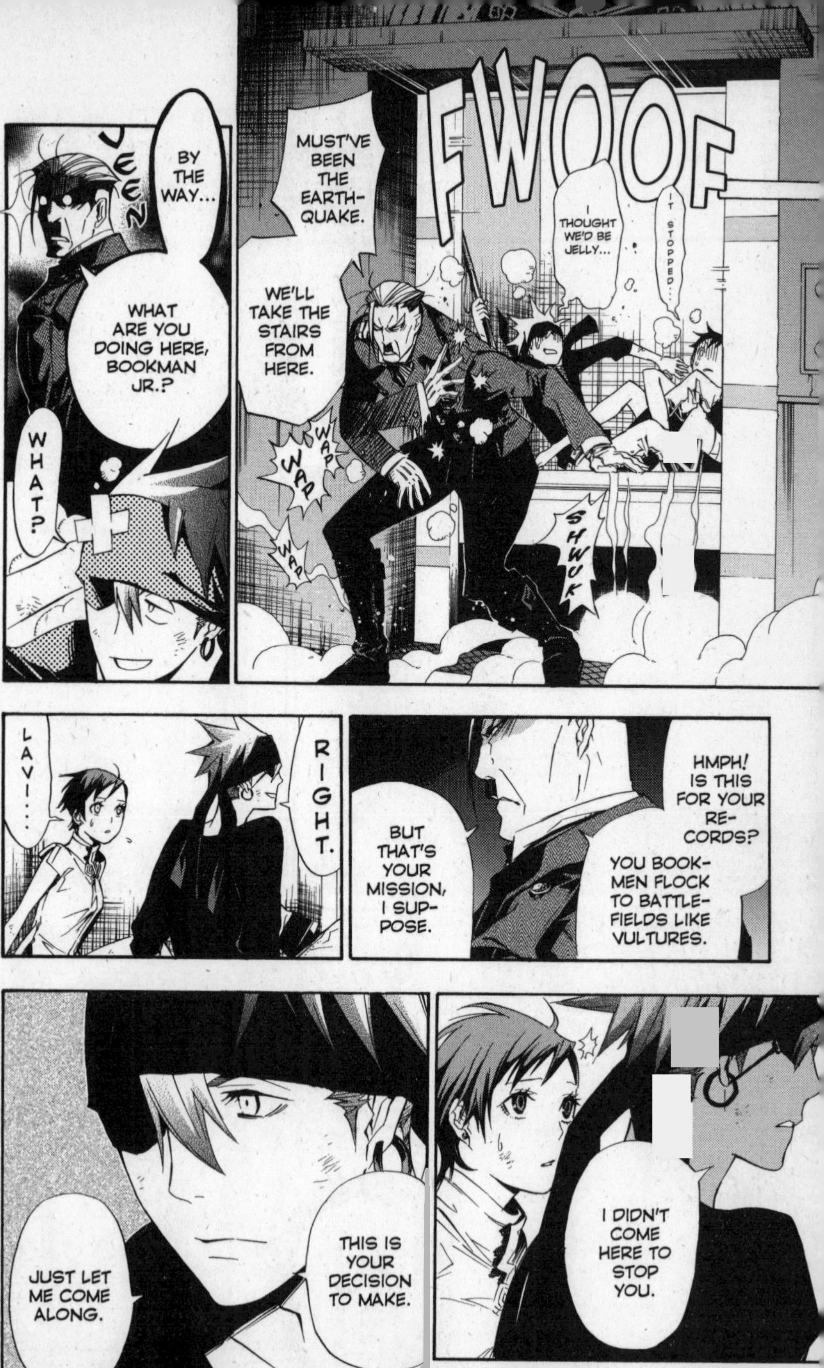
FWOOF
IT STOPPED...
I THOUGHT WE'D BE JELLY...
MUST'VE BEEN THE EARTHQUAKE.
WE'LL TAKE THE STAIRS FROM HERE.
WAP
WAP
WAP
SHWUK
BY THE WAY...
VEEN
WHAT ARE YOU DOING HERE, BOOKMAN JR.?
WHAT?
HMPH! IS THIS FOR YOUR RECORDS?
YOU BOOKMEN FLOCK TO BATTLEFIELDS LIKE VULTURES.
BUT THAT'S YOUR MISSION, I SUPPOSE.
RIGHT.
LAVI...
I DIDN'T COME HERE TO STOP YOU.
THIS IS YOUR DECISION TO MAKE.
JUST LET ME COME ALONG.

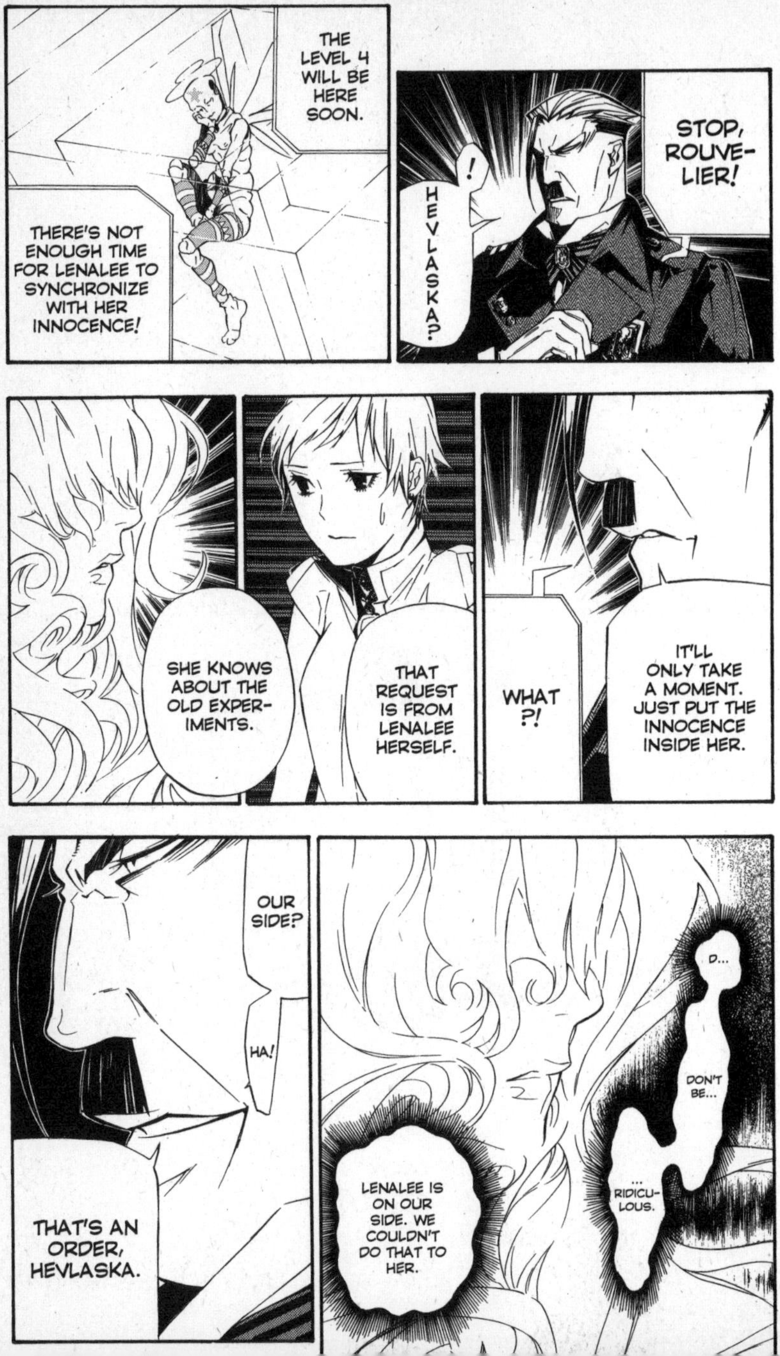
STOP, ROUVE-LIER!
!
HEVLASKA?
THE LEVEL 4 WILL BE HERE SOON.
THERE'S NOT ENOUGH TIME FOR LENALEE TO SYNCHRONIZE WITH HER INNOCENCE!
IT'LL ONLY TAKE A MOMENT. JUST PUT THE INNOCENCE INSIDE HER.
WHAT?!
THAT REQUEST IS FROM LENALEE HERSELF.
SHE KNOWS ABOUT THE OLD EXPER-IMENTS.
D...
DON'T BE...
...RIDICU-LOUS.
LENALEE IS ON OUR SIDE. WE COULDN'T DO THAT TO HER.
OUR SIDE?
HA!
THAT'S AN ORDER, HEVLASKA.

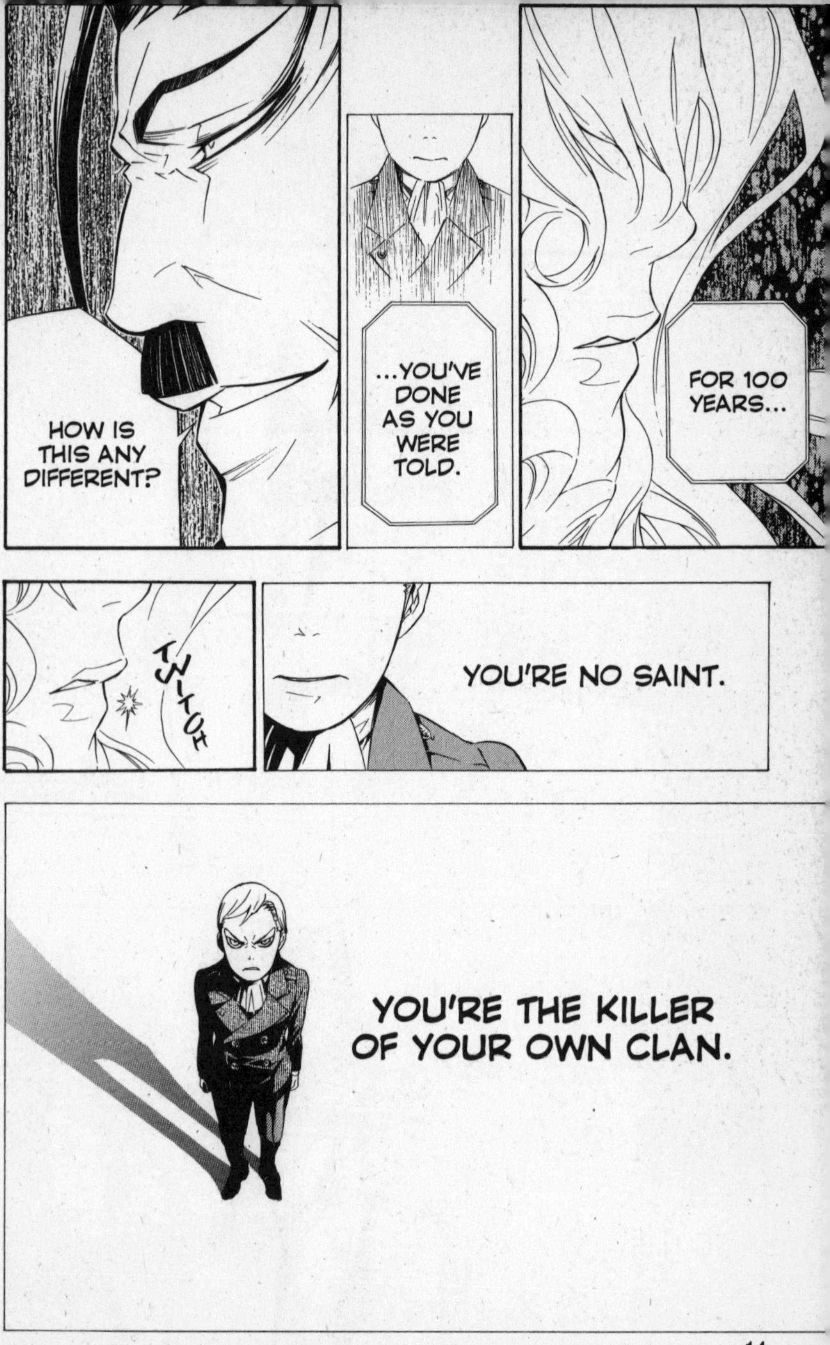
FOR 100 YEARS...
...YOU'VE DONE AS YOU WERE TOLD.
HOW IS THIS ANY DIFFERENT?
YOU'RE NO SAINT.
TWITCH
YOU'RE THE KILLER OF YOUR OWN CLAN.

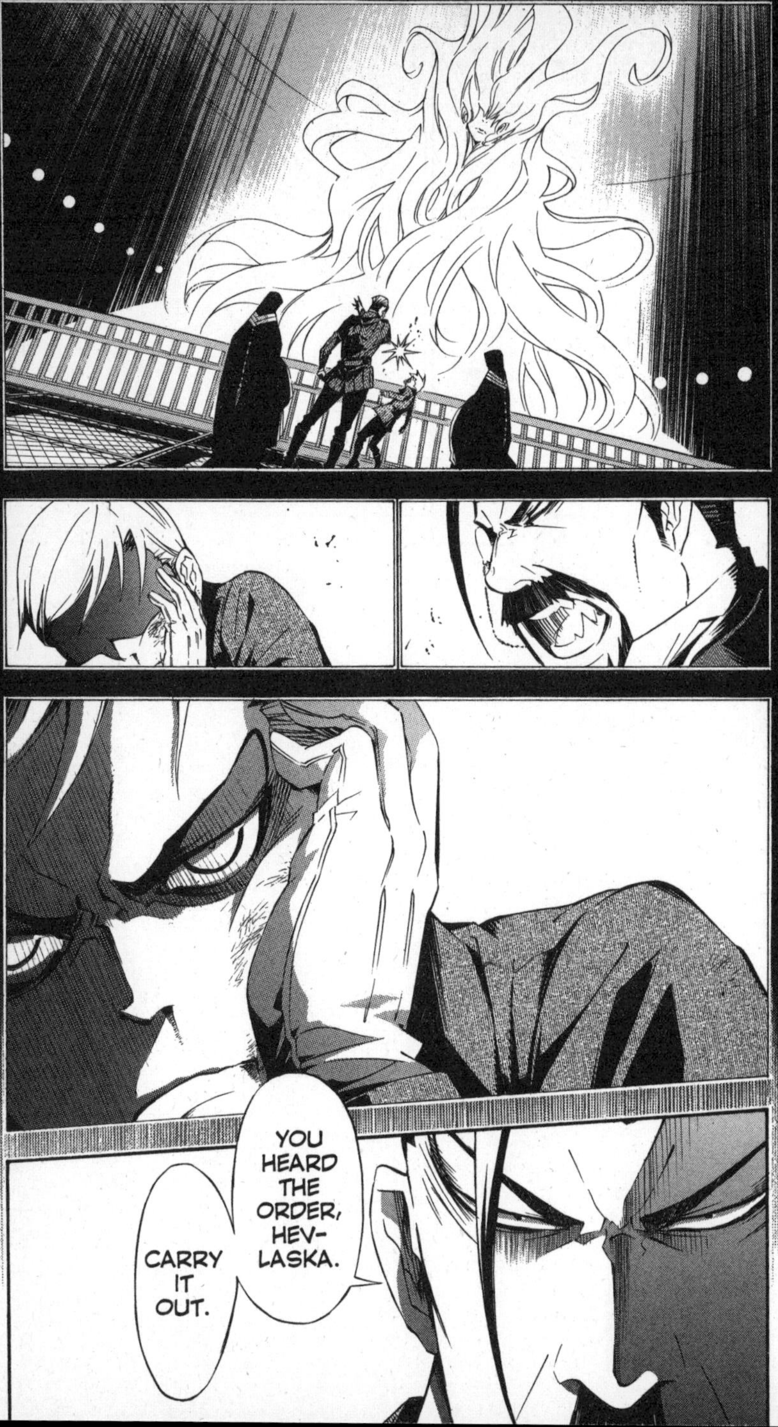
YOU HEARD THE ORDER, HEV-LASKA.
CARRY IT OUT.

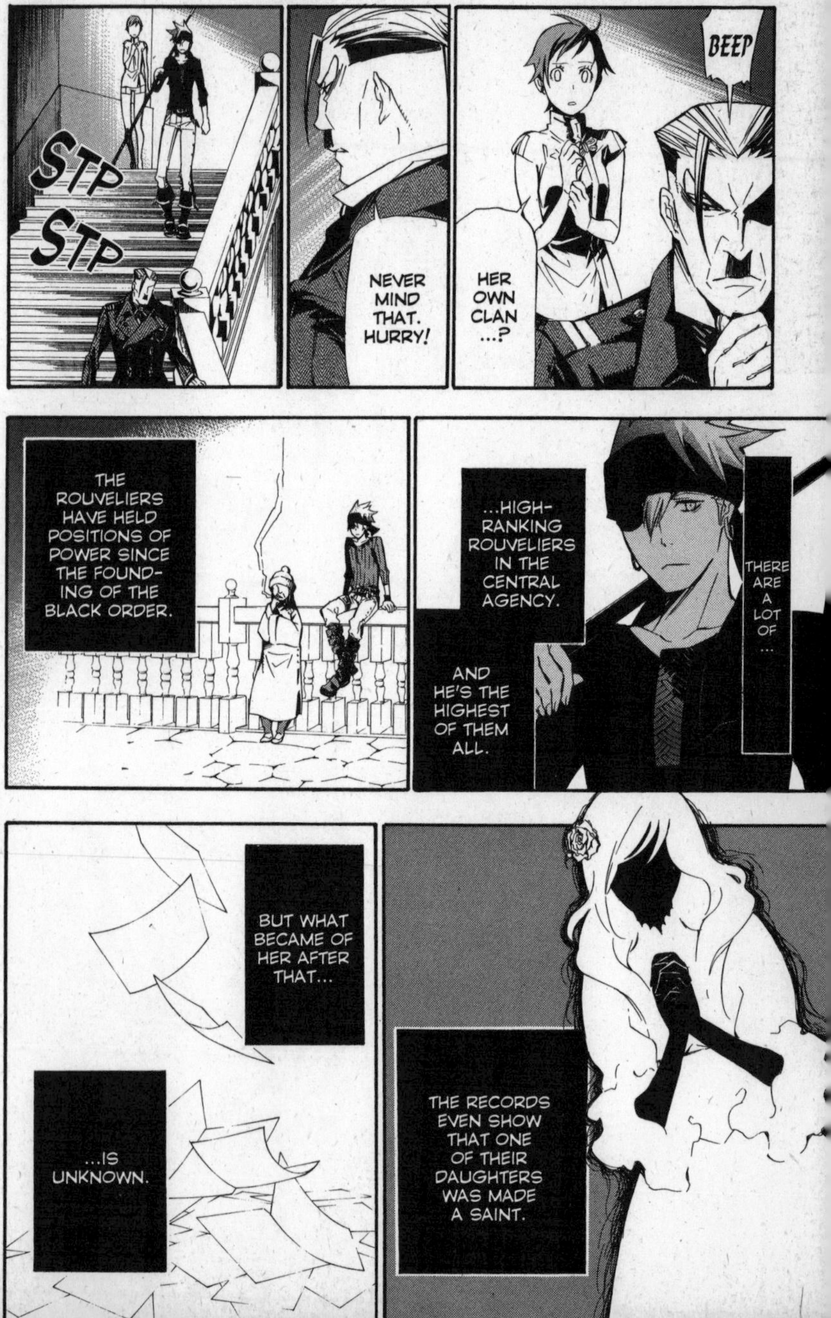
BEEP
HER OWN CLAN ...?
NEVER MIND THAT. HURRY!
STP
STP
THERE ARE A LOT OF ...
...HIGH-RANKING ROUVELIERS IN THE CENTRAL AGENCY.
AND HE'S THE HIGHEST OF THEM ALL.
THE ROUVELIERS HAVE HELD POSITIONS OF POWER SINCE THE FOUNDING OF THE BLACK ORDER.
THE RECORDS EVEN SHOW THAT ONE OF THEIR DAUGHTERS WAS MADE A SAINT.
BUT WHAT BECAME OF HER AFTER THAT...
...IS UNKNOWN.

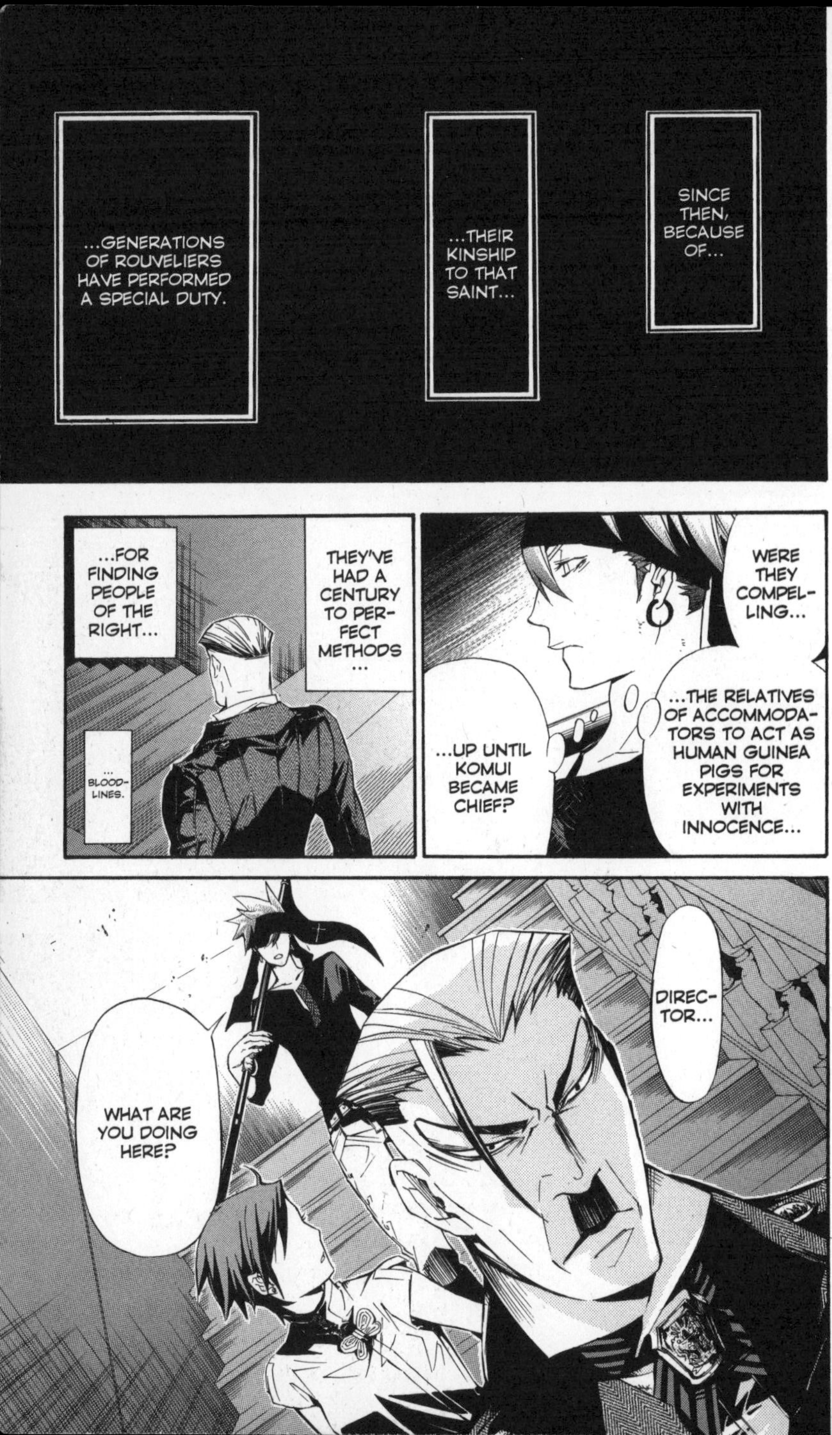
SINCE THEN, BECAUSE OF...
...THEIR KINSHIP TO THAT SAINT...
...GENERATIONS OF ROUVELIERS HAVE PERFORMED A SPECIAL DUTY.
WERE THEY COMPEL-LING...
...THE RELATIVES OF ACCOMMODA-TORS TO ACT AS HUMAN GUINEA PIGS FOR EXPERIMENTS WITH INNOCENCE...
...UP UNTIL KOMUI BECAME CHIEF?
THEY'VE HAD A CENTURY TO PER-FECT METHODS...
...FOR FINDING PEOPLE OF THE RIGHT...
...BLOOD-LINES.
DIREC-TOR...
WHAT ARE YOU DOING HERE?

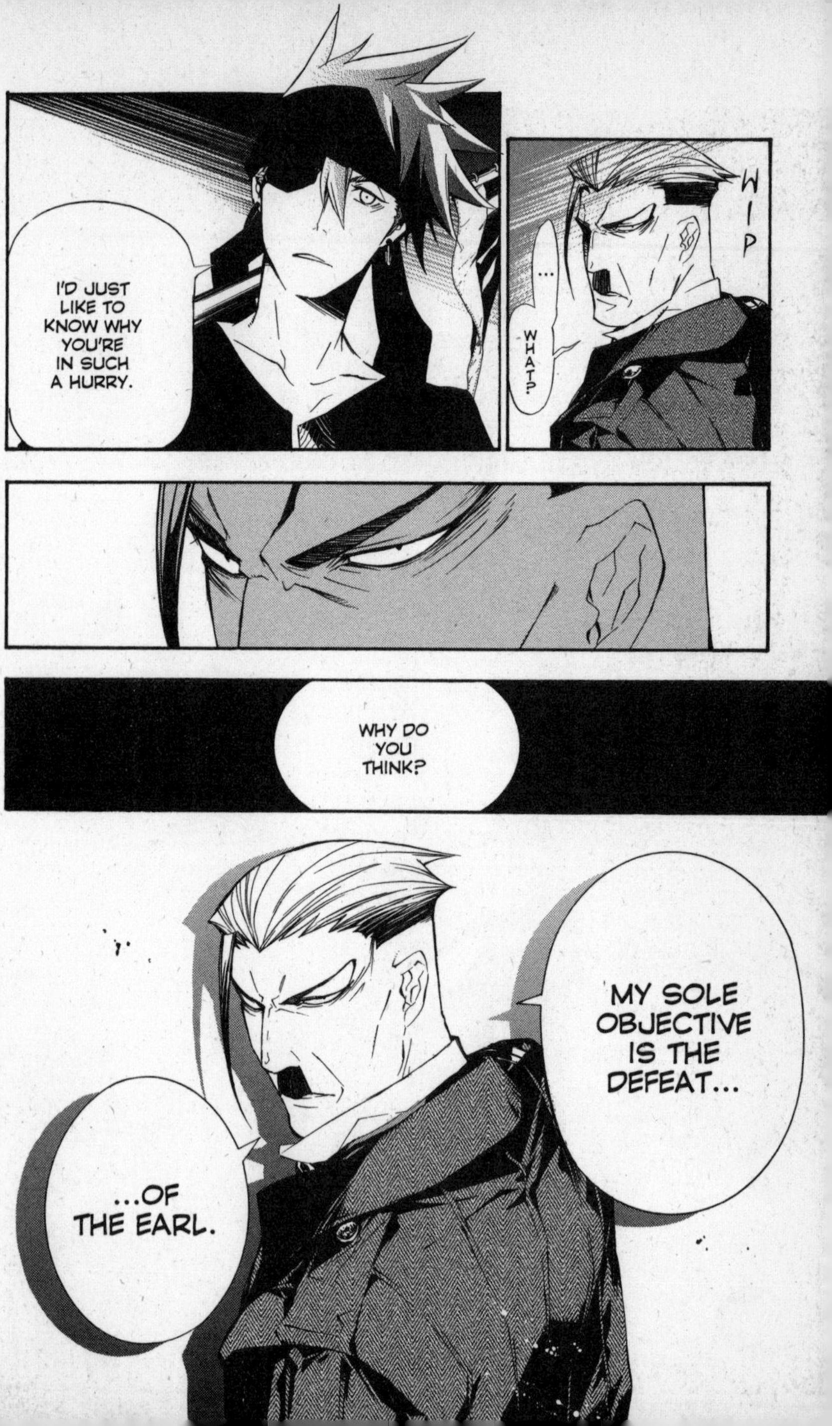
WHIP
...
WHAT?
I'D JUST LIKE TO KNOW WHY YOU'RE IN SUCH A HURRY.
WHY DO YOU THINK?
MY SOLE OBJECTIVE IS THE DEFEAT...
...OF THE EARL.

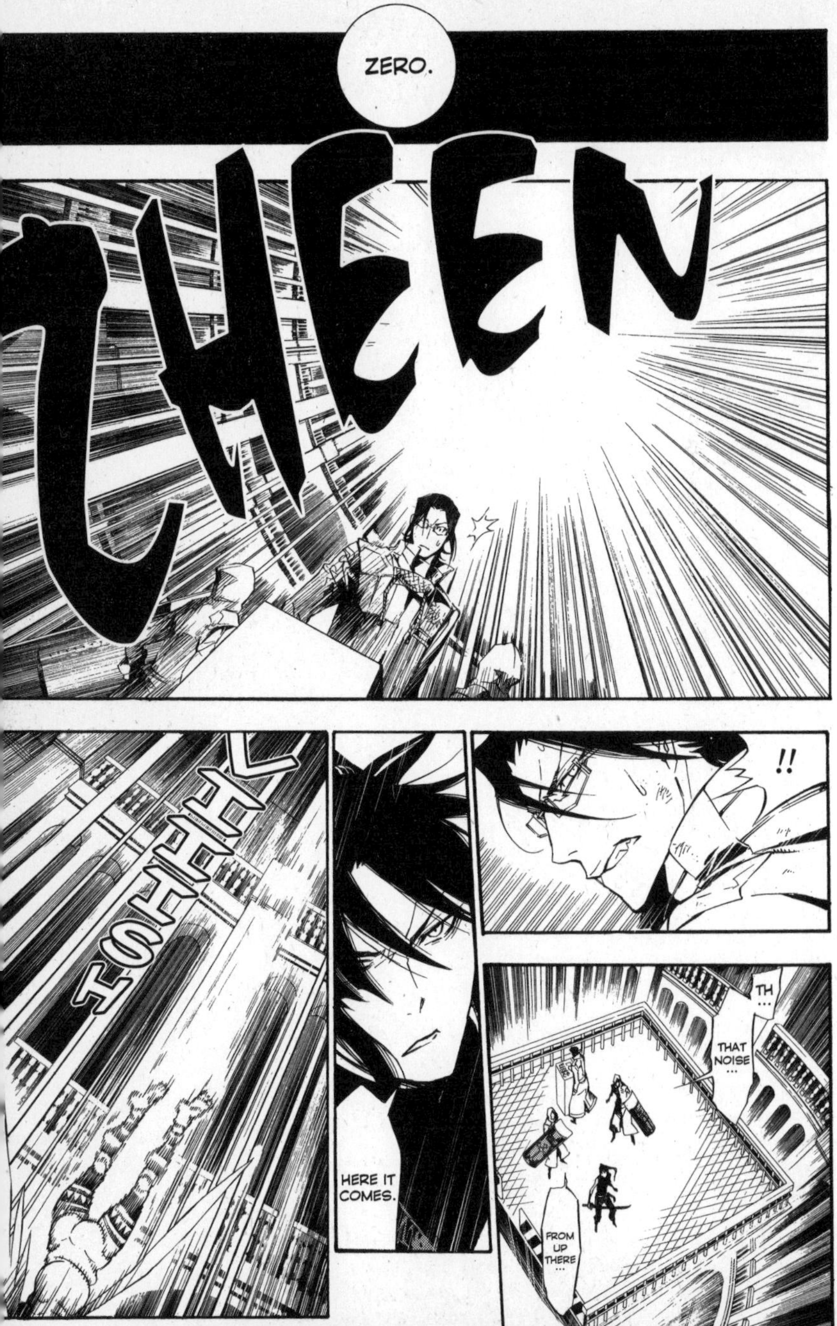
ZERO.
CHEEN
!!
TH...
THAT NOISE...
FROM UP THERE...
HERE IT COMES.
SHHHK

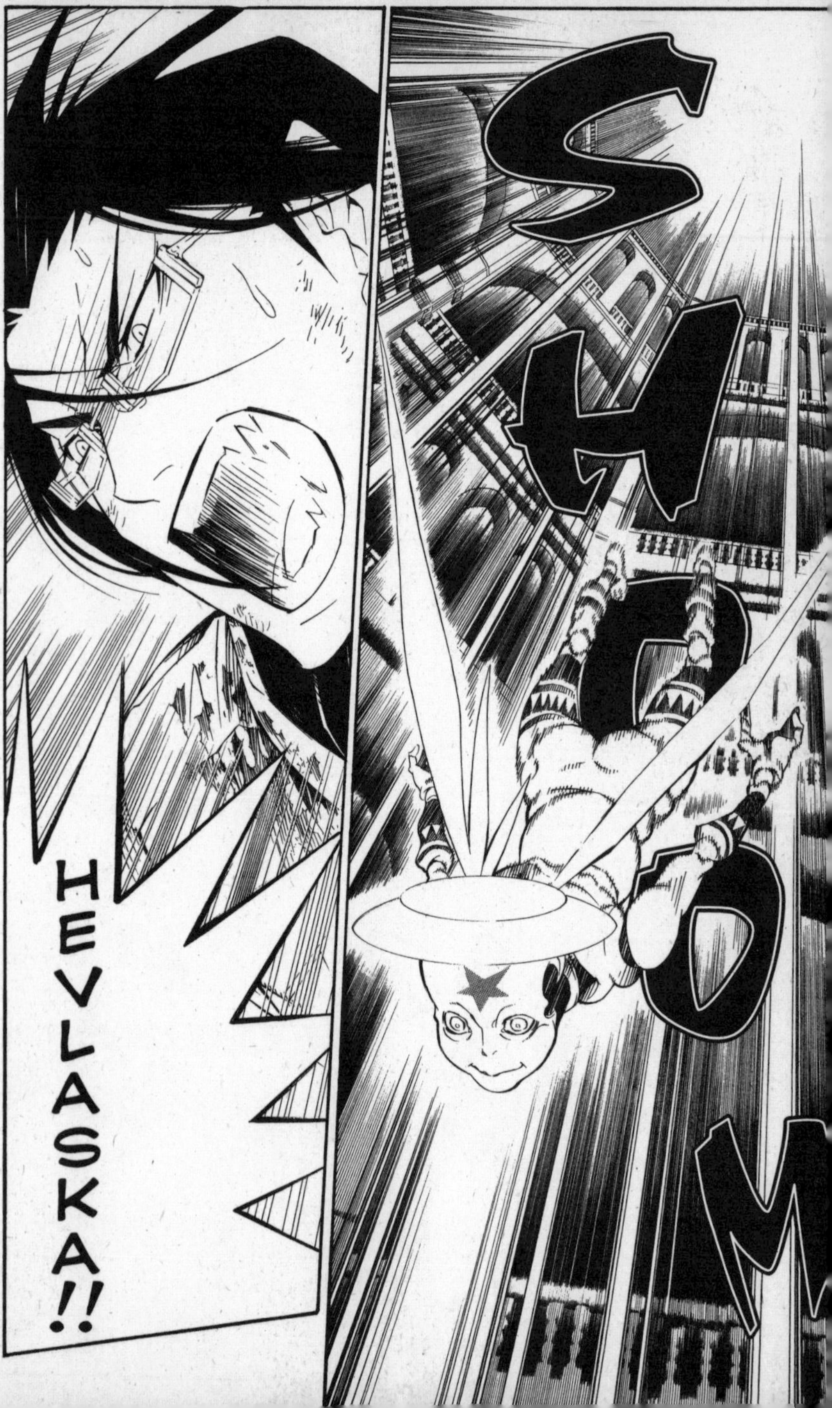
SHOOM
HEVLASKA!!

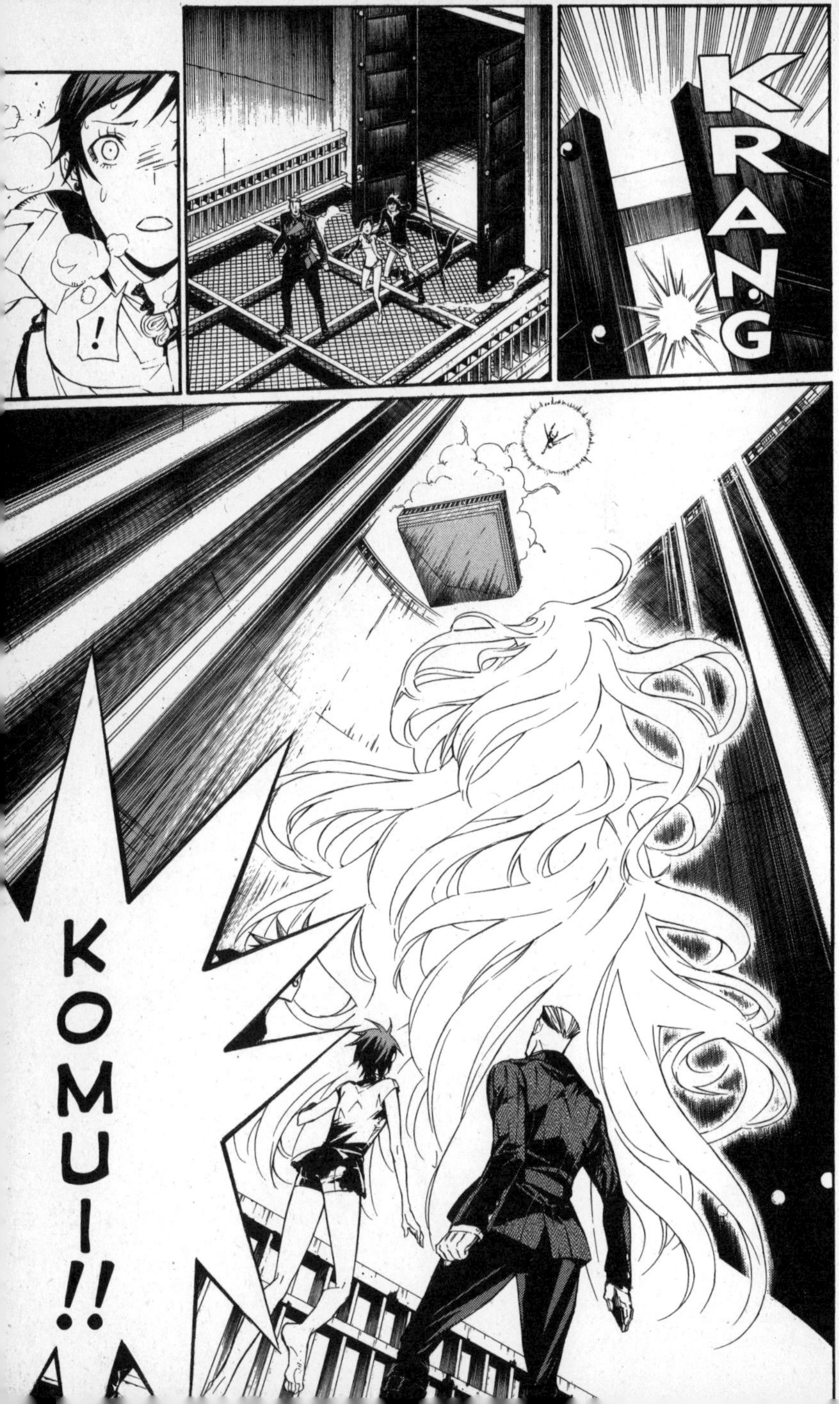
KRANG
!
KOMUI!!

THE PEOPLE OF D.GRAY HOUSE

A FATHER'S FEELINGS ☆

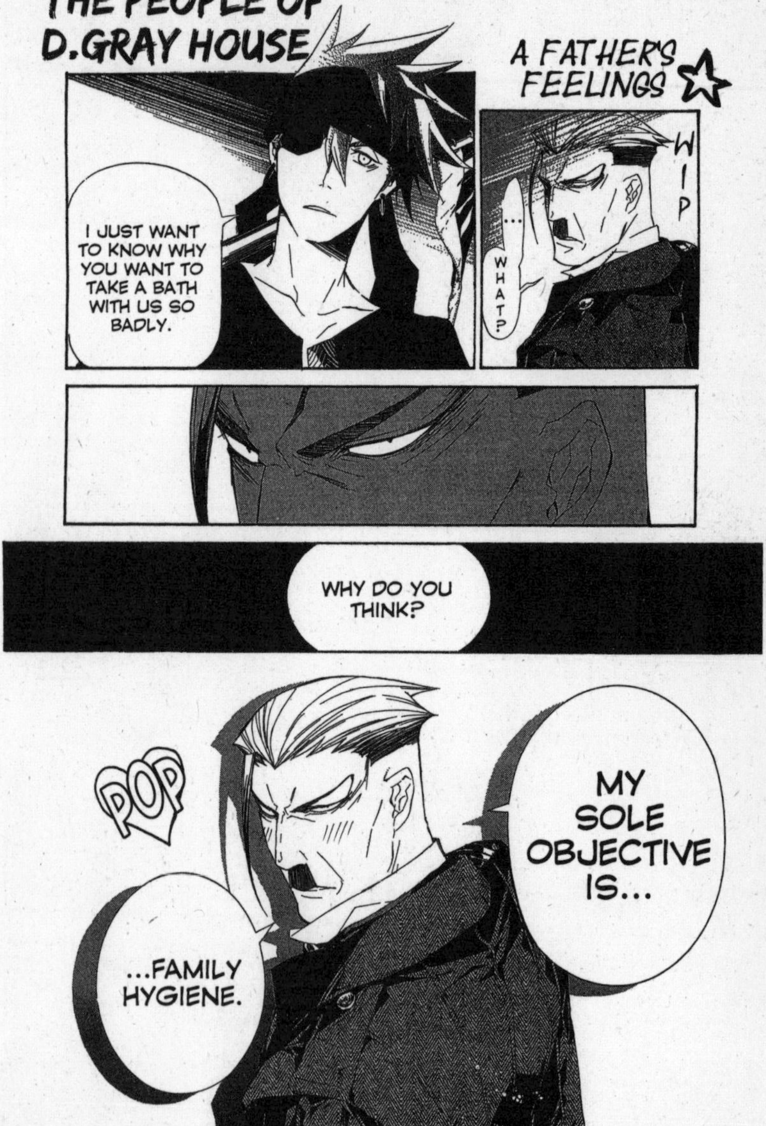
WHIP
...WHAT?
I JUST WANT TO KNOW WHY YOU WANT TO TAKE A BATH WITH US SO BADLY.
WHY DO YOU THINK?
MY SOLE OBJECTIVE IS...
POP
...FAMILY HYGIENE.

FATHER IS LONELY.

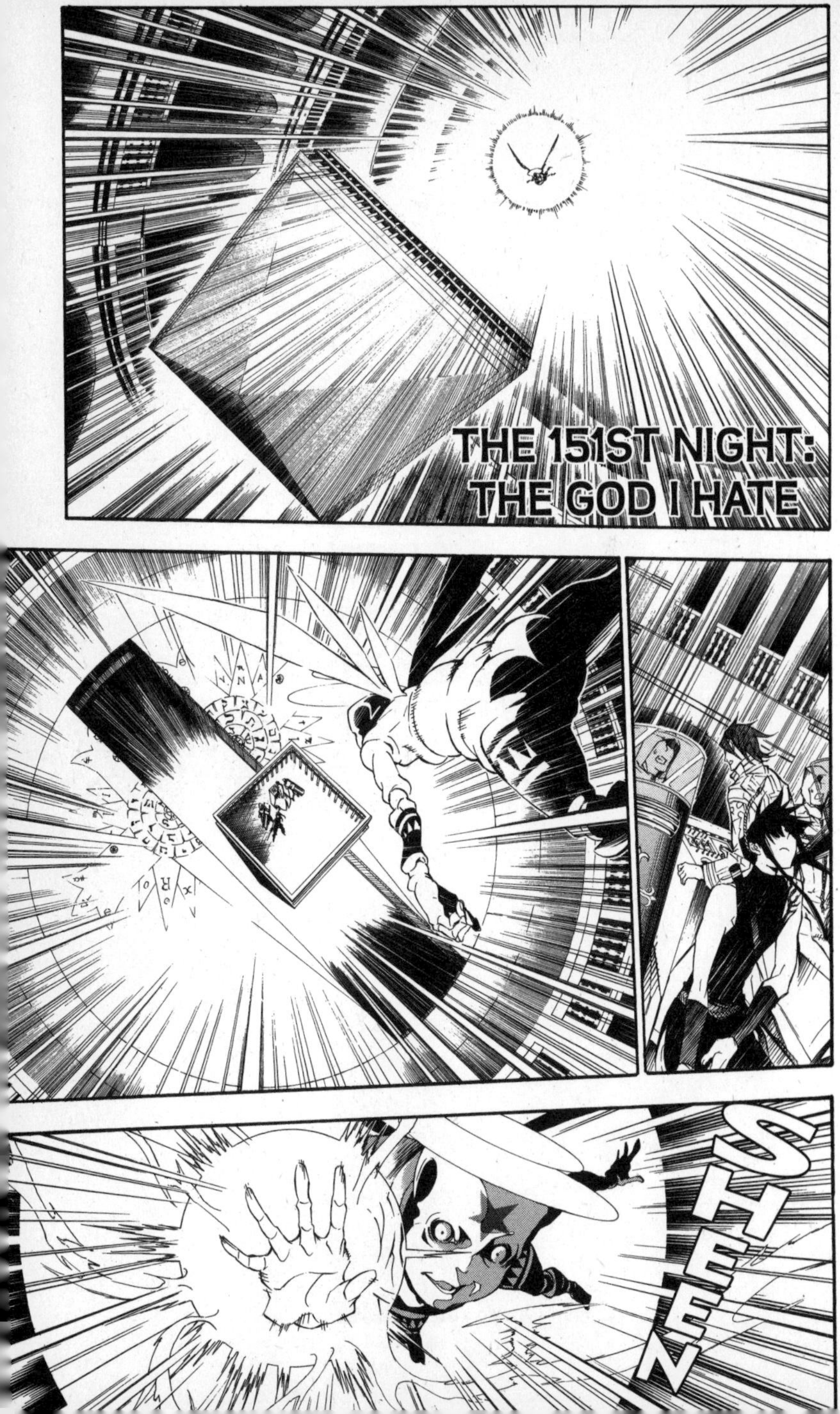
THE 151ST NIGHT:
THE GOD I HATE
SHEEN

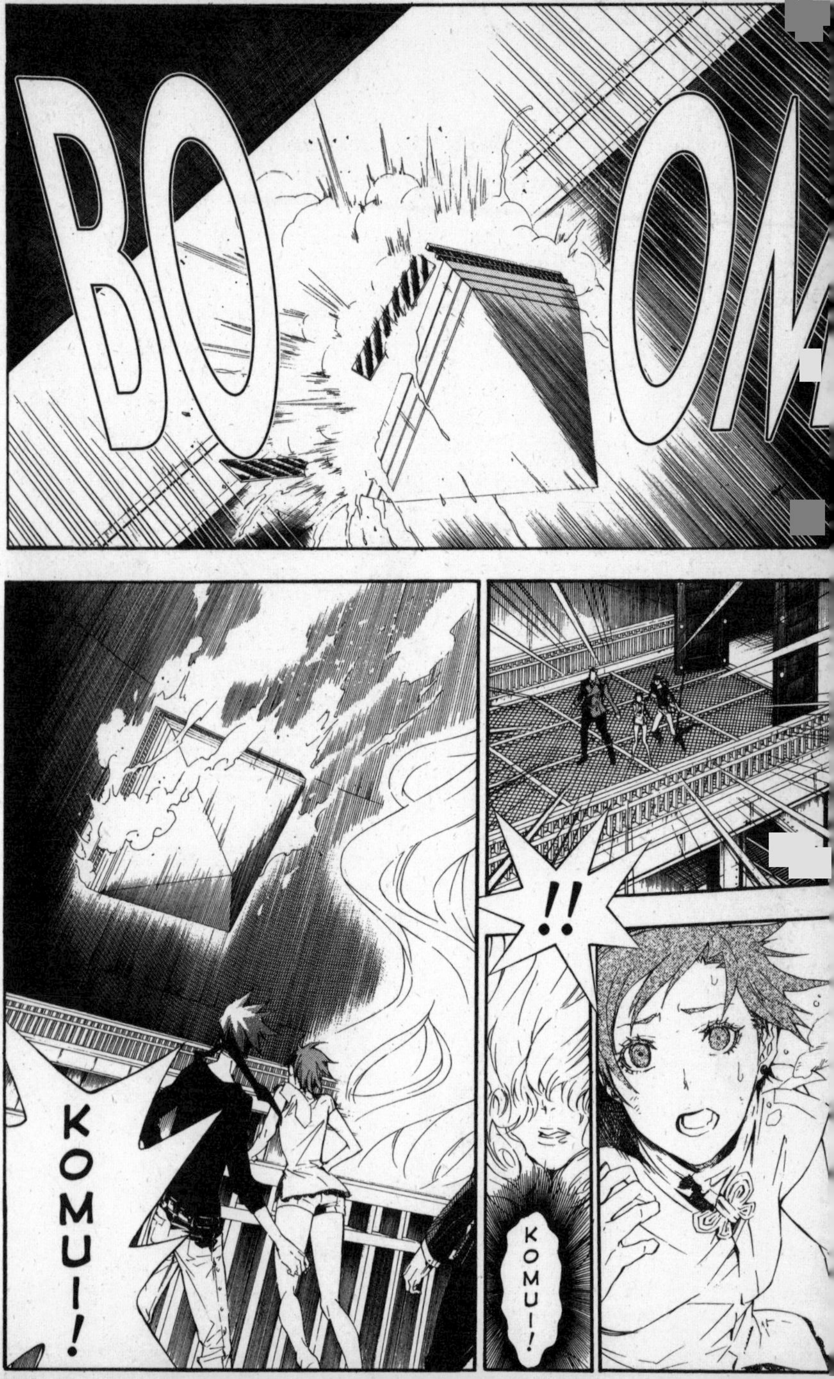
BOOM
!!
KOMUI!
KOMUI!

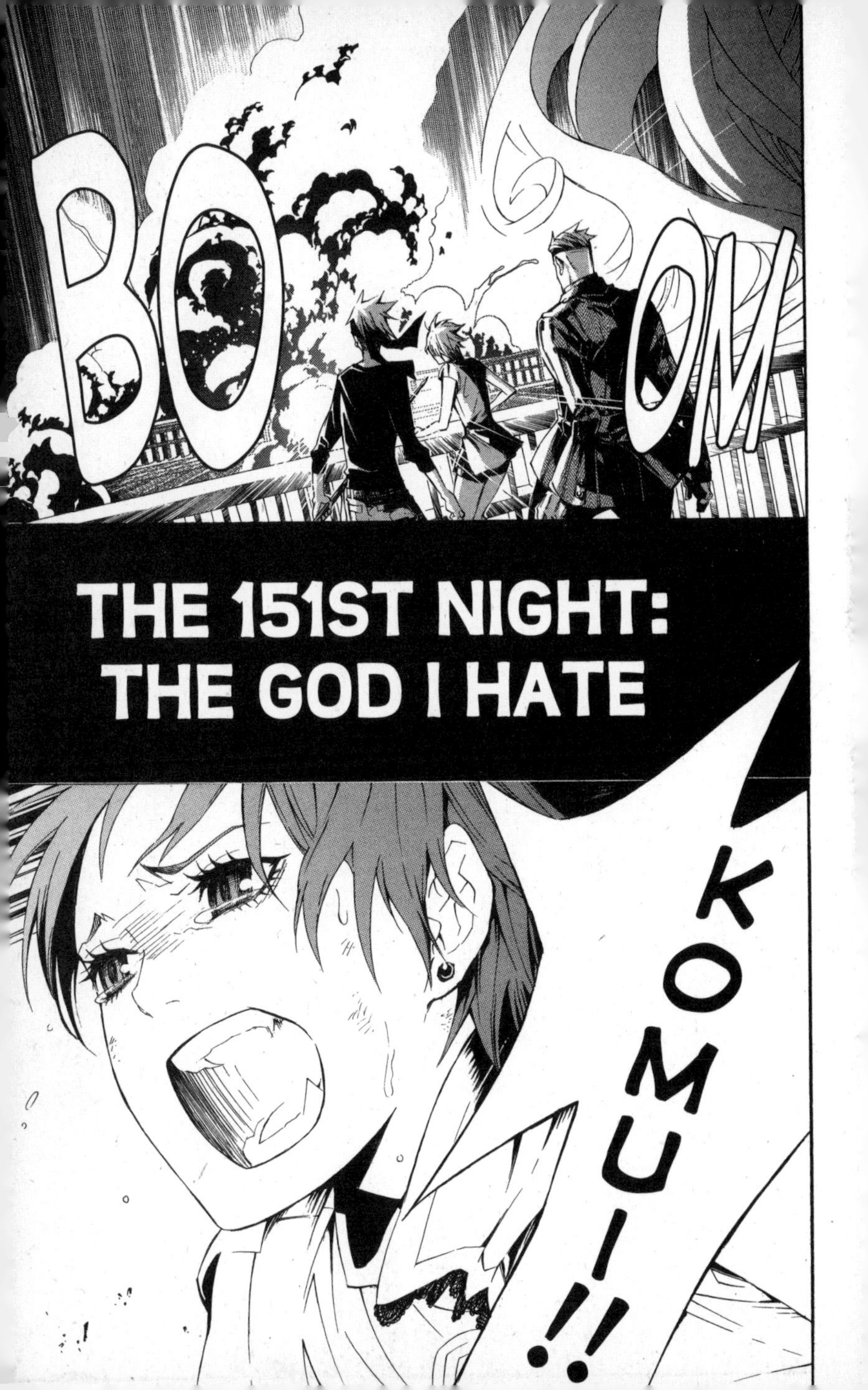
BOOOM
THE 151ST NIGHT: THE GOD I HATE
KOMUI!!

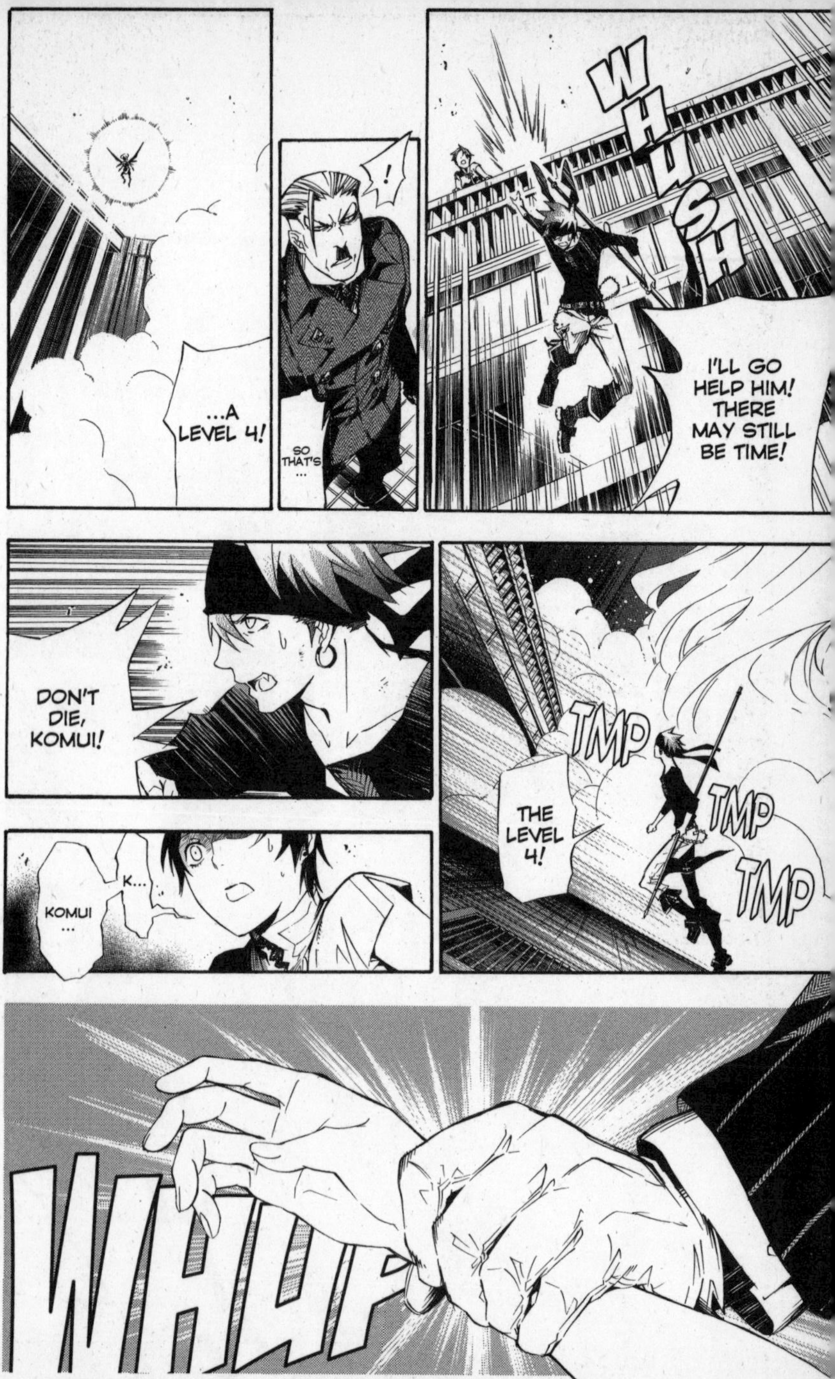
WHUSH
I'LL GO HELP HIM! THERE MAY STILL BE TIME!
!
SO THAT'S...
...A LEVEL 4!
TMP
TMP
TMP
THE LEVEL 4!
DON'T DIE, KOMUI!
K...
KOMUI...
WHAP

THE ELEVATOR'S BROKEN. HE WON'T BE ABLE TO GET THE INNOCENCE.

HEVLASKA, PUT THE INNOCENCE INTO LENALEE!

NOW!!

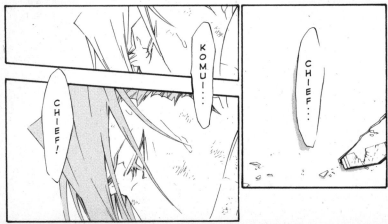

KOMUI...

CHIEF...

CHIEF!

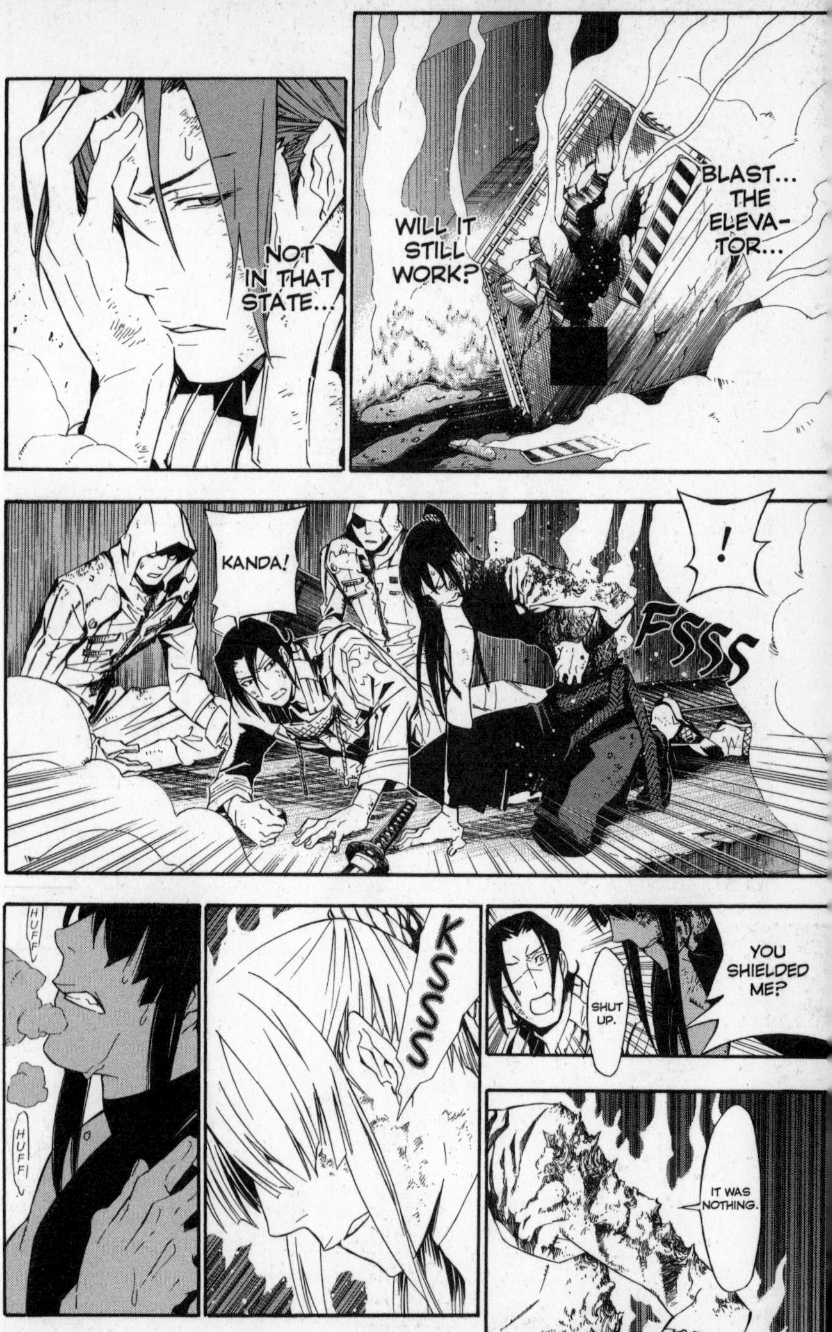
BLAST... THE ELEVATOR...
WILL IT STILL WORK?
NOT IN THAT STATE...
!
FSSS
KANDA!
YOU SHIELDED ME?
SHUT UP.
IT WAS NOTHING.
KSSSSS
HUFF
HUFF

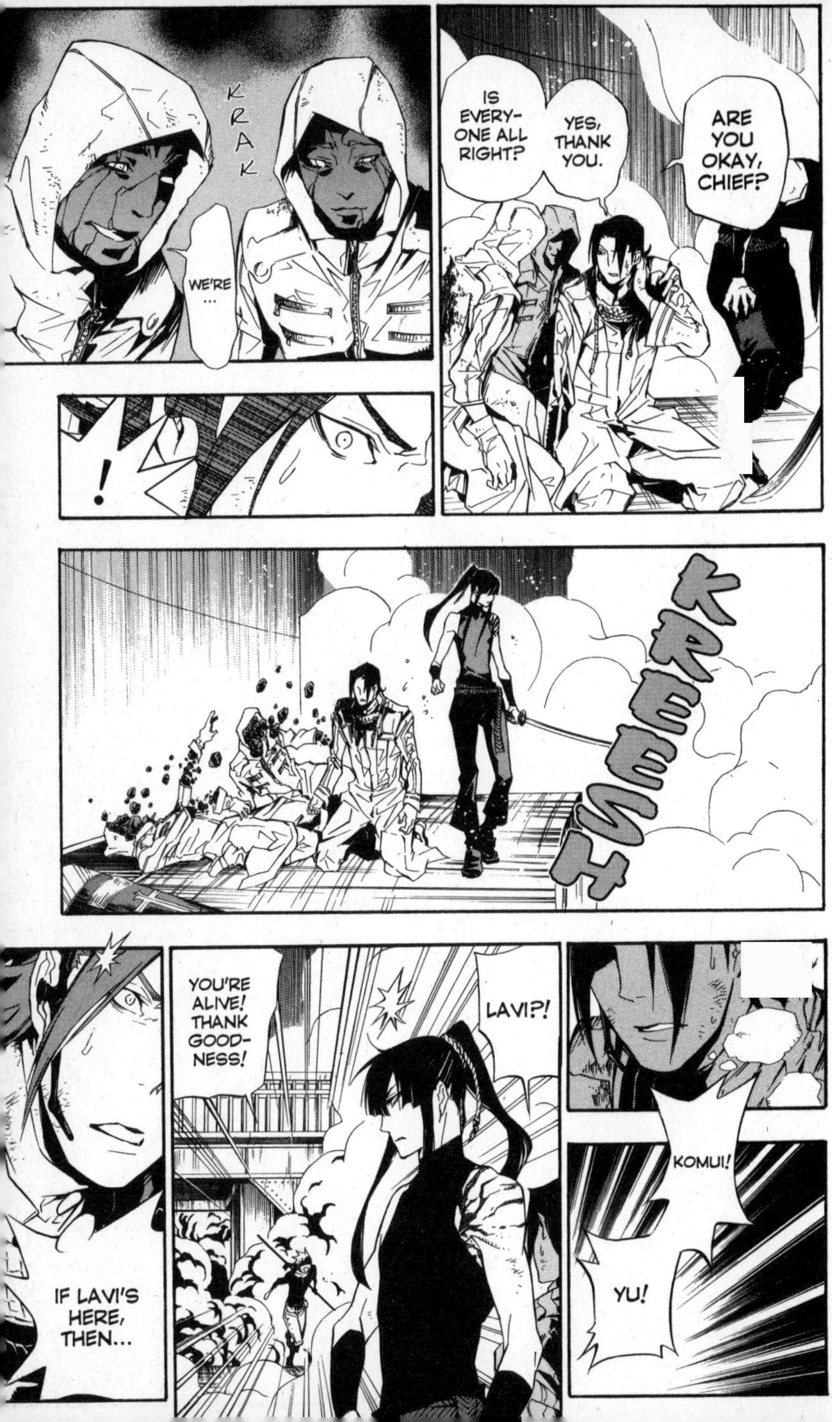
ARE YOU OKAY, CHIEF?
YES, THANK YOU.
IS EVERYONE ALL RIGHT?
KRAK
WE'RE ...
!
KRESH
KOMUI!
YU!
LAVI?!
YOU'RE ALIVE! THANK GOODNESS!
IF LAVI'S HERE, THEN...

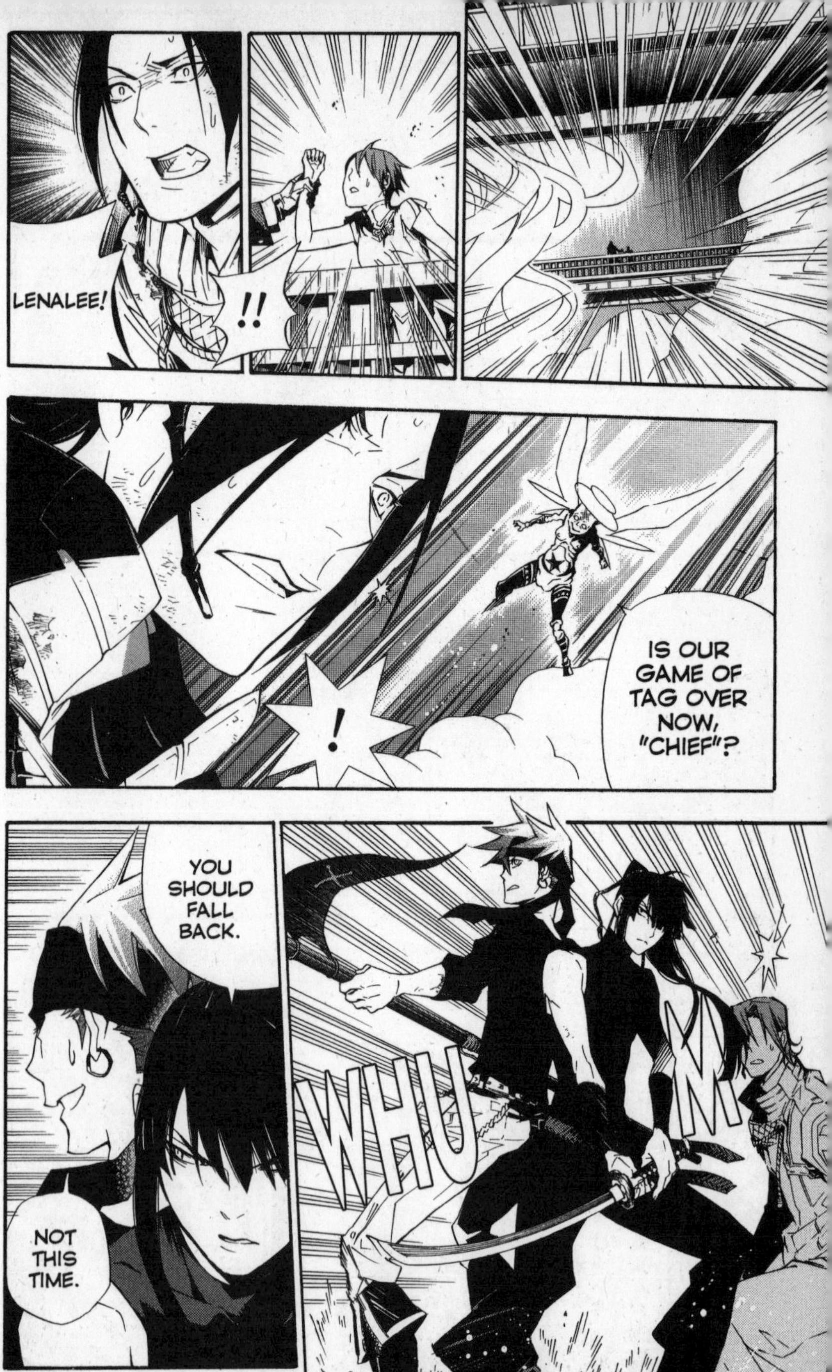
!!
LENALEE!
IS OUR GAME OF TAG OVER NOW, "CHIEF"?
!
WHUM
YOU SHOULD FALL BACK.
NOT THIS TIME.

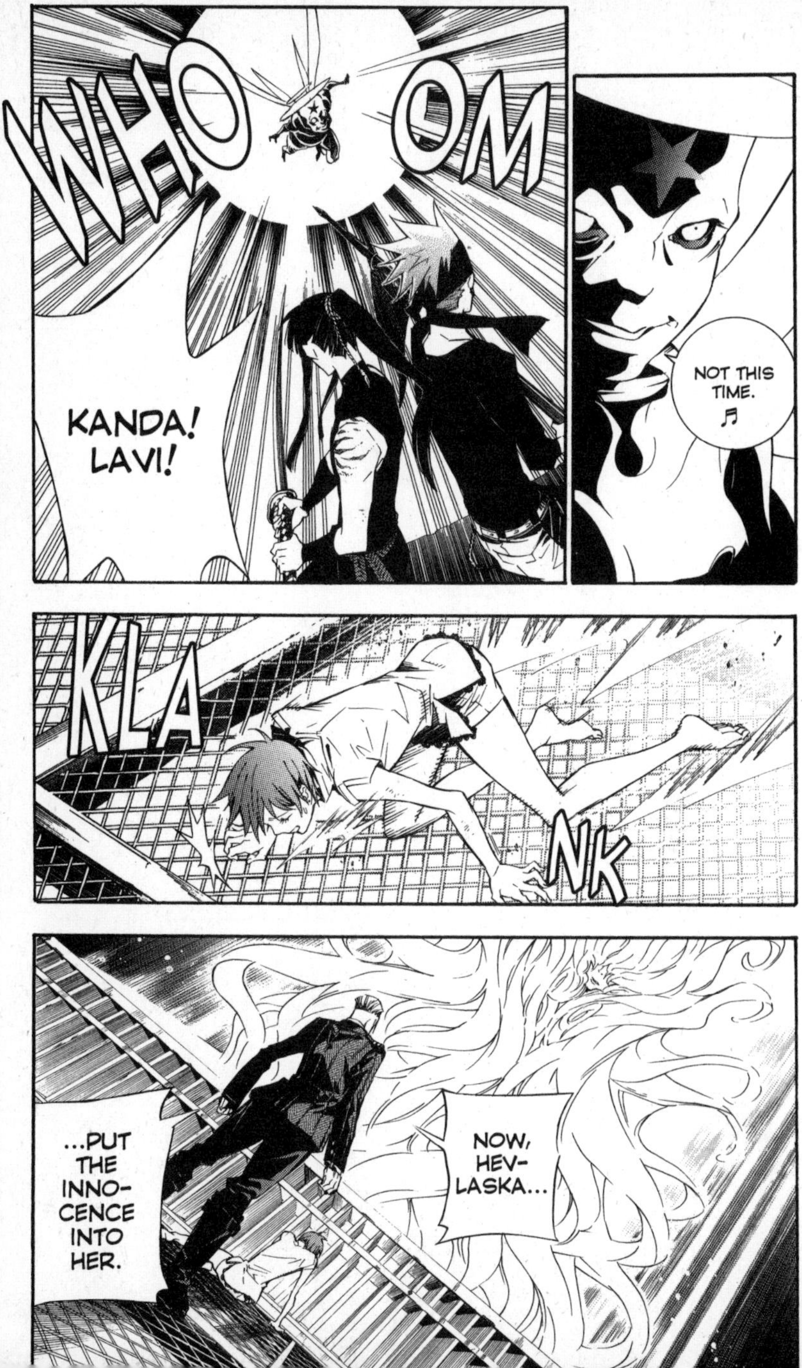
NOT THIS TIME. ♬
WHOOM
KANDA! LAVI!
KLANK
NOW, HEV-LASKA...
...PUT THE INNO-CENCE INTO HER.

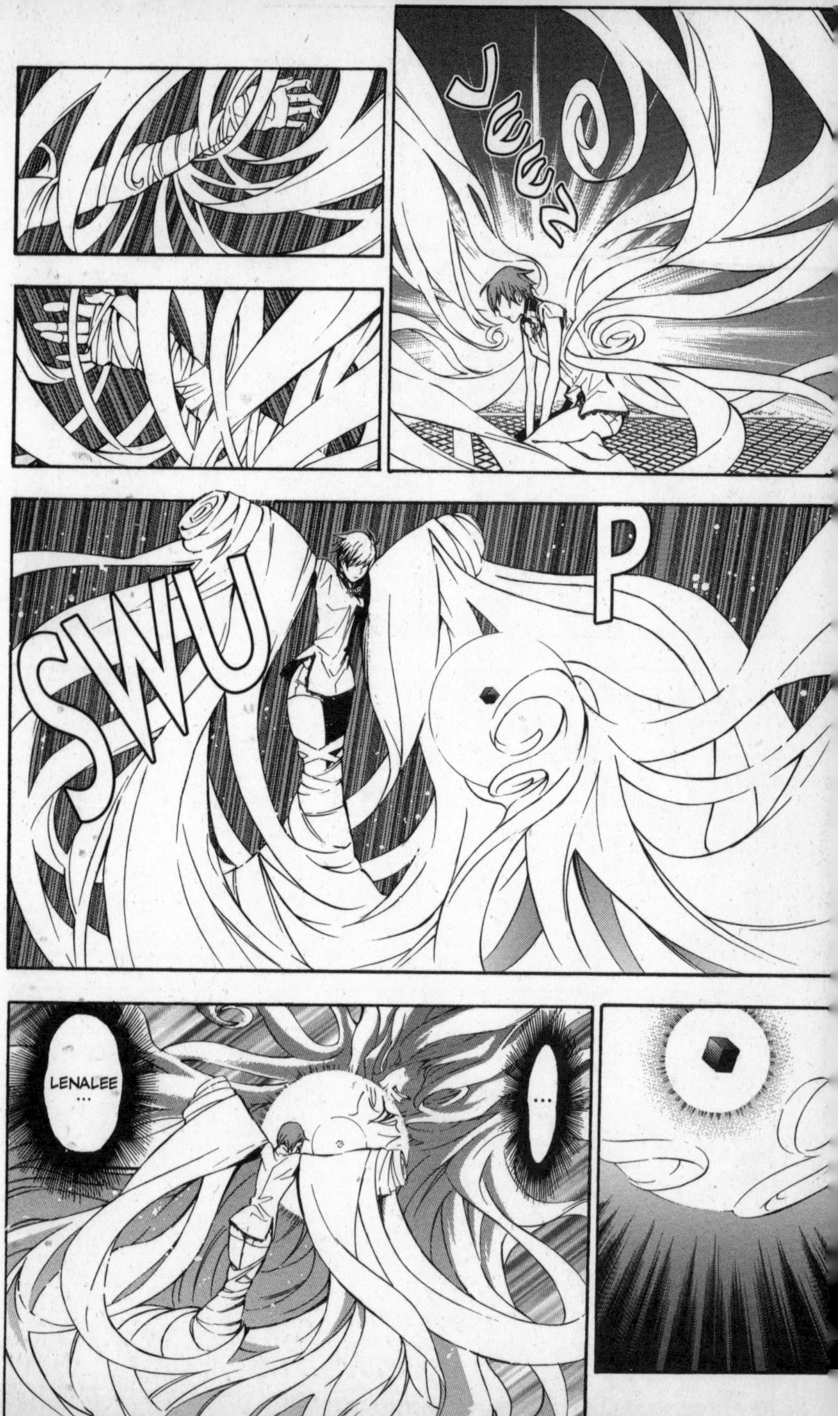
JWEEN
SWUP
LENALEE ...
...

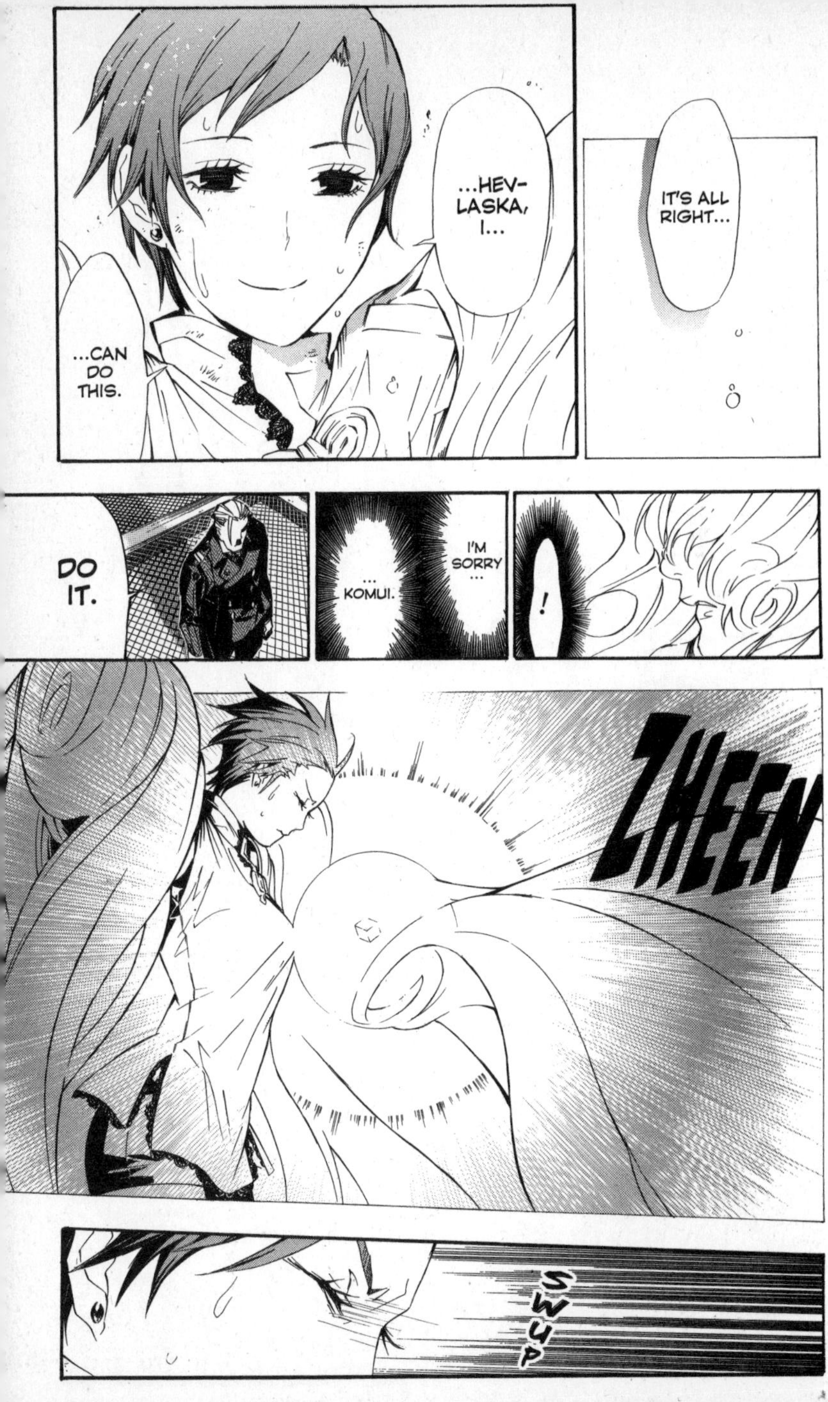
IT'S ALL RIGHT...
...HEV-LASKA, I...
...CAN DO THIS.
!
I'M SORRY...
...KOMUI.
DO IT.
ZHEEN
SWUP

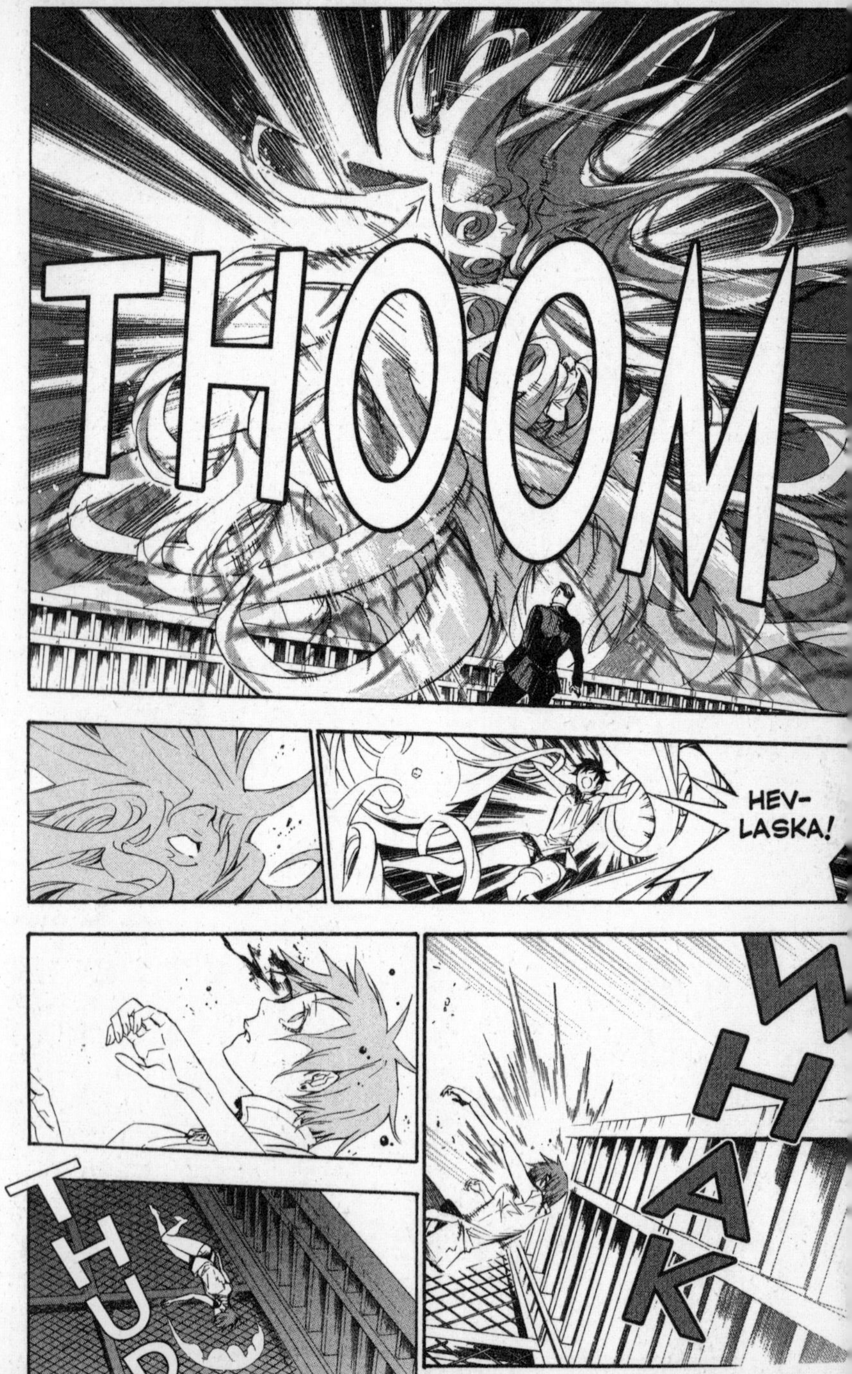
THOOM
HEV-
LASKA!
WHAK
THUD

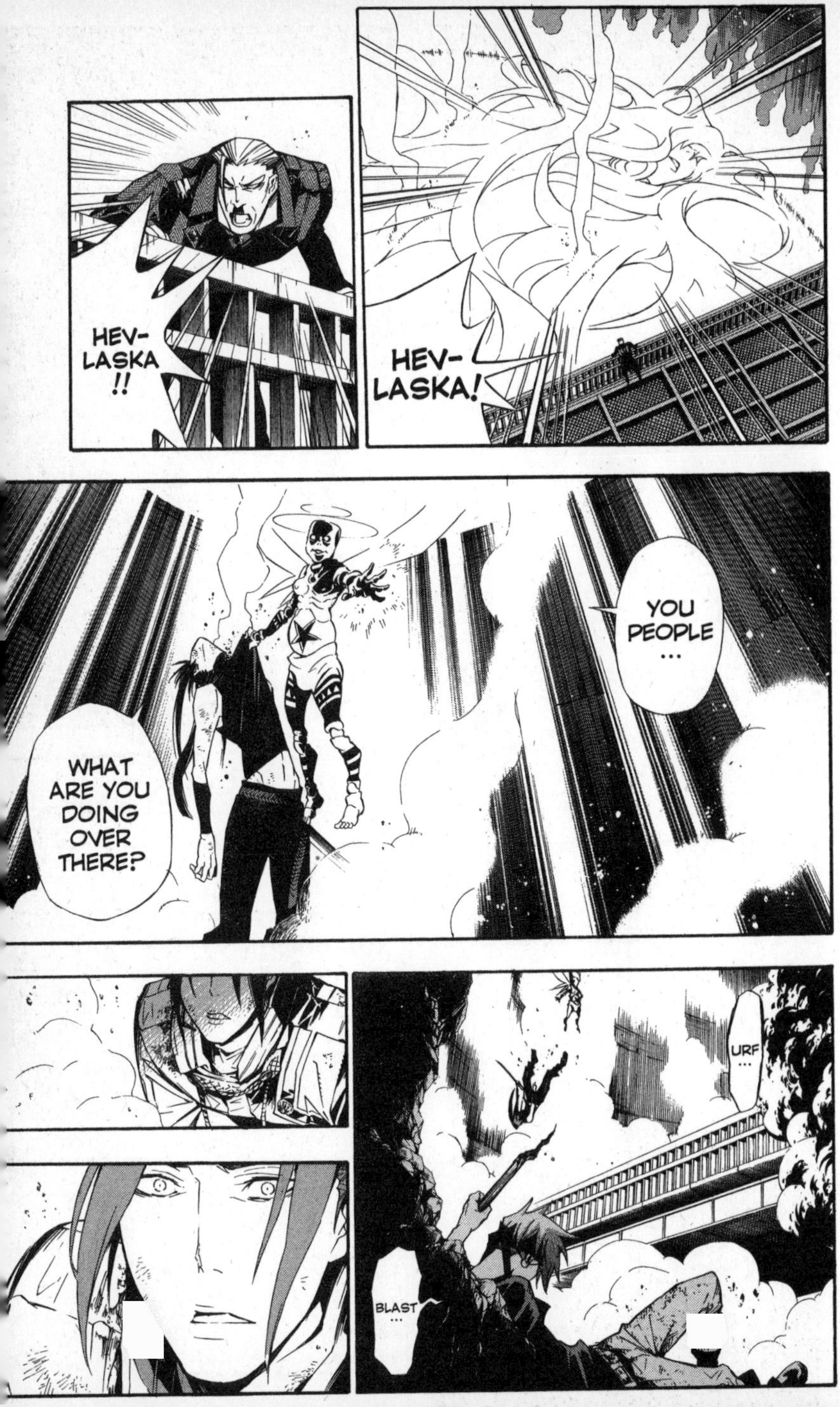
HEV-LASKA!
HEV-LASKA!!
YOU PEOPLE...
WHAT ARE YOU DOING OVER THERE?
URF...
BLAST...

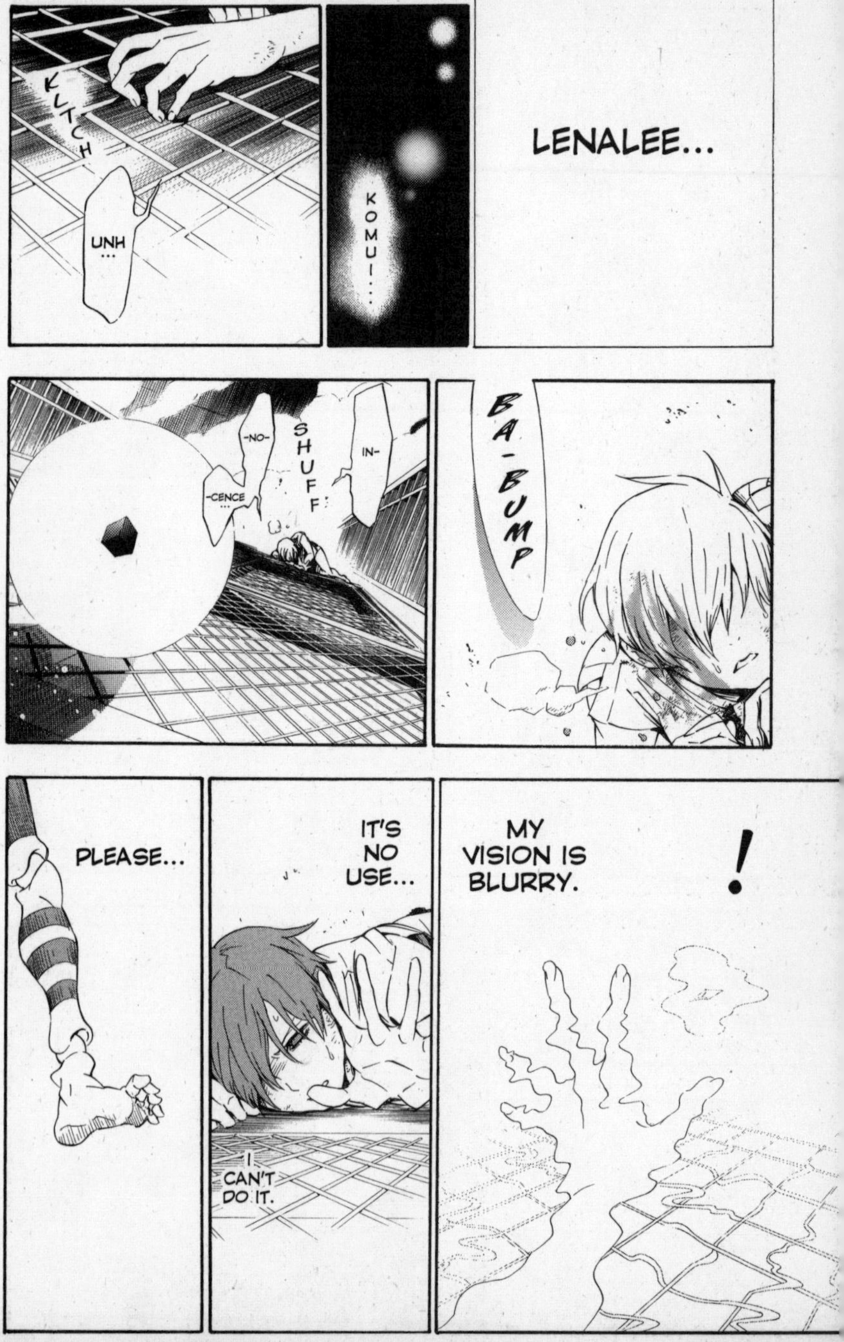
LENALEE...
KOMUI...
KLTCH
UNH...
BA-BUMP
IN-
SHUFF
-NO-
-CENCE...
MY VISION IS BLURRY.
!
IT'S NO USE...
I CAN'T DO IT.
PLEASE...

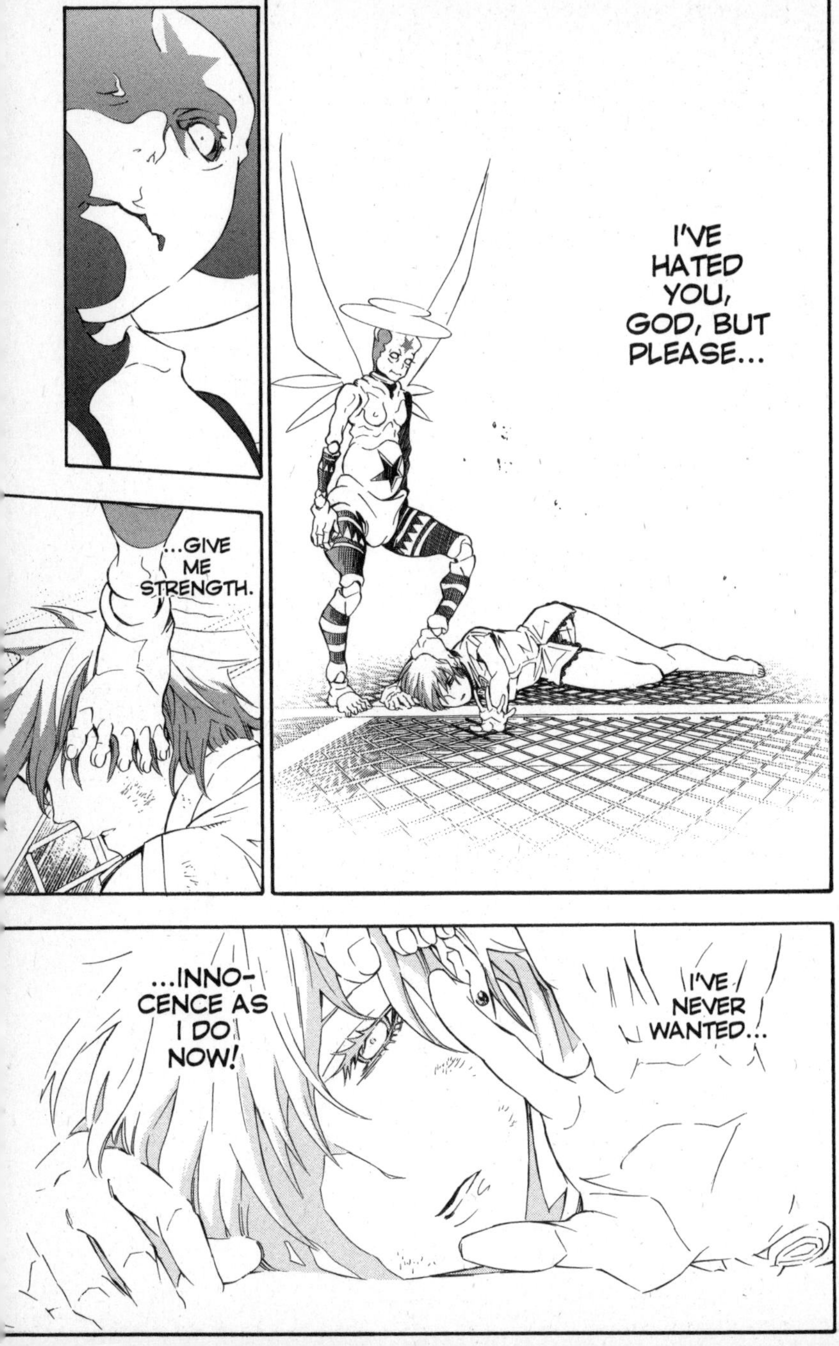
I'VE HATED YOU, GOD, BUT PLEASE...
...GIVE ME STRENGTH.
I'VE NEVER WANTED...
...INNO-CENCE AS I DO NOW!

A LEVEL 4 THAT MY
LITTLE BROTHER
DREW.

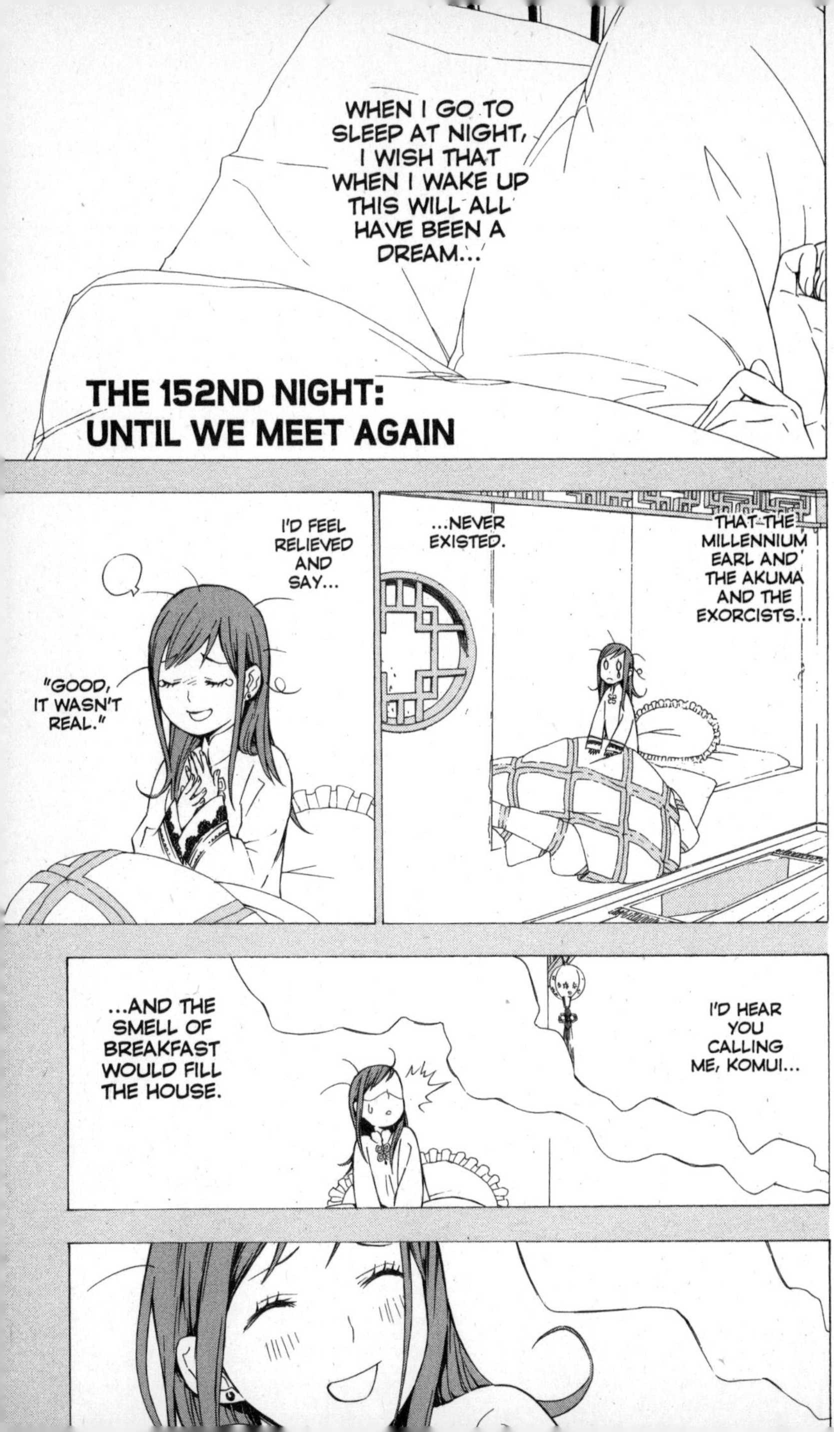
WHEN I GO TO SLEEP AT NIGHT, I WISH THAT WHEN I WAKE UP THIS WILL ALL HAVE BEEN A DREAM...
THE 152ND NIGHT: UNTIL WE MEET AGAIN
THAT THE MILLENNIUM EARL AND THE AKUMA AND THE EXORCISTS...
...NEVER EXISTED.
I'D FEEL RELIEVED AND SAY...
"GOOD, IT WASN'T REAL."
I'D HEAR YOU CALLING ME, KOMUI...
...AND THE SMELL OF BREAKFAST WOULD FILL THE HOUSE.

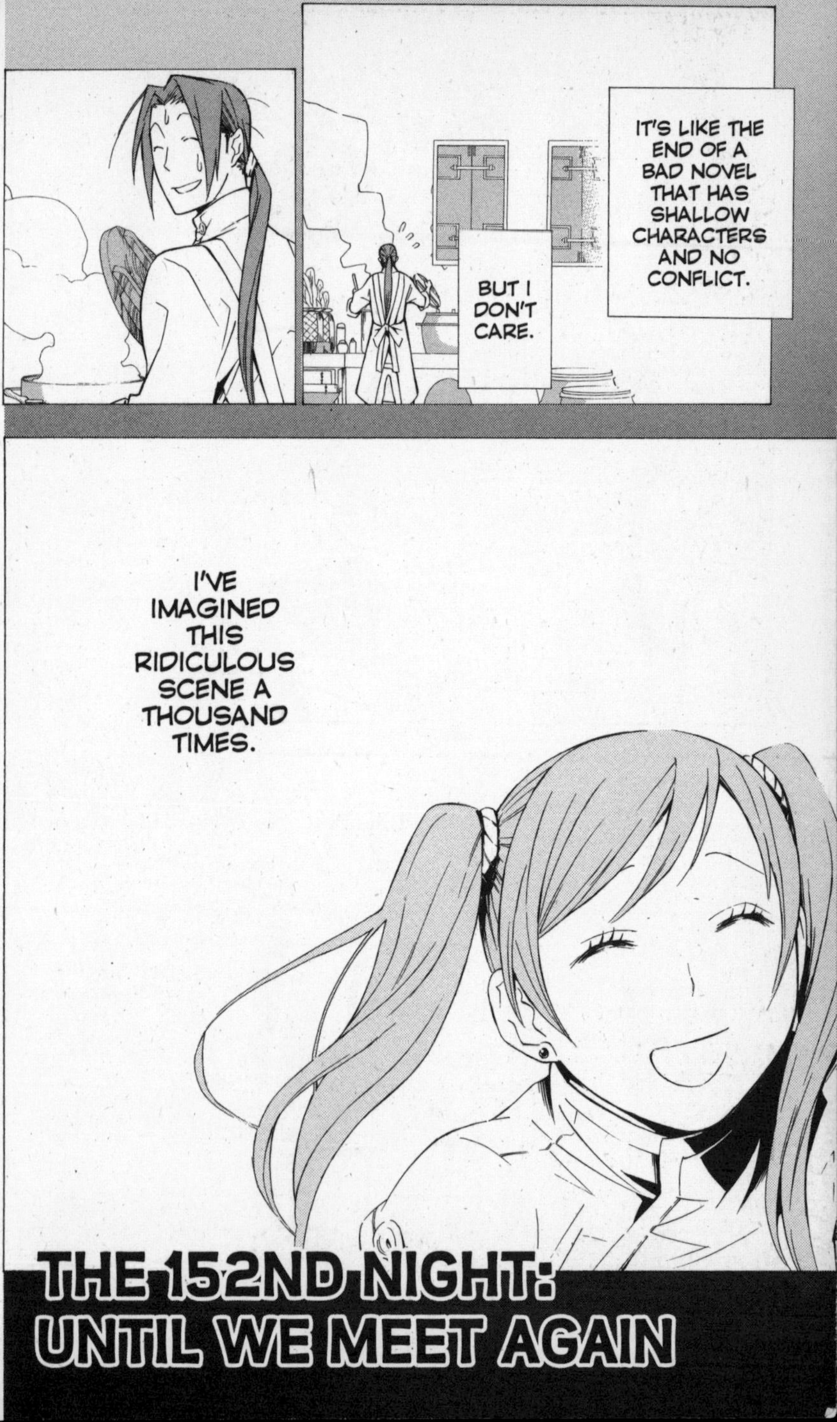
IT'S LIKE THE END OF A BAD NOVEL THAT HAS SHALLOW CHARACTERS AND NO CONFLICT.
BUT I DON'T CARE.
I'VE IMAGINED THIS RIDICULOUS SCENE A THOUSAND TIMES.
THE 152ND NIGHT: UNTIL WE MEET AGAIN

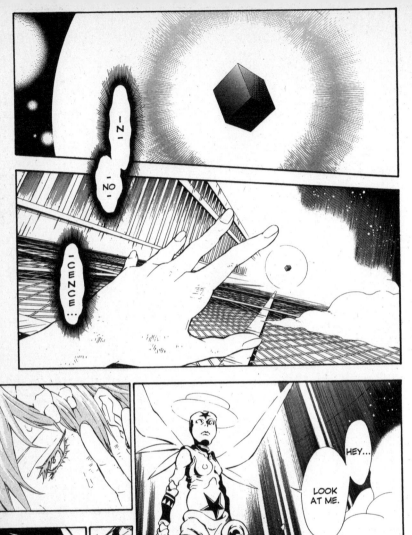

-IN-

-NO-

-CENCE...

HEY...

LOOK AT ME.

HEY...

!

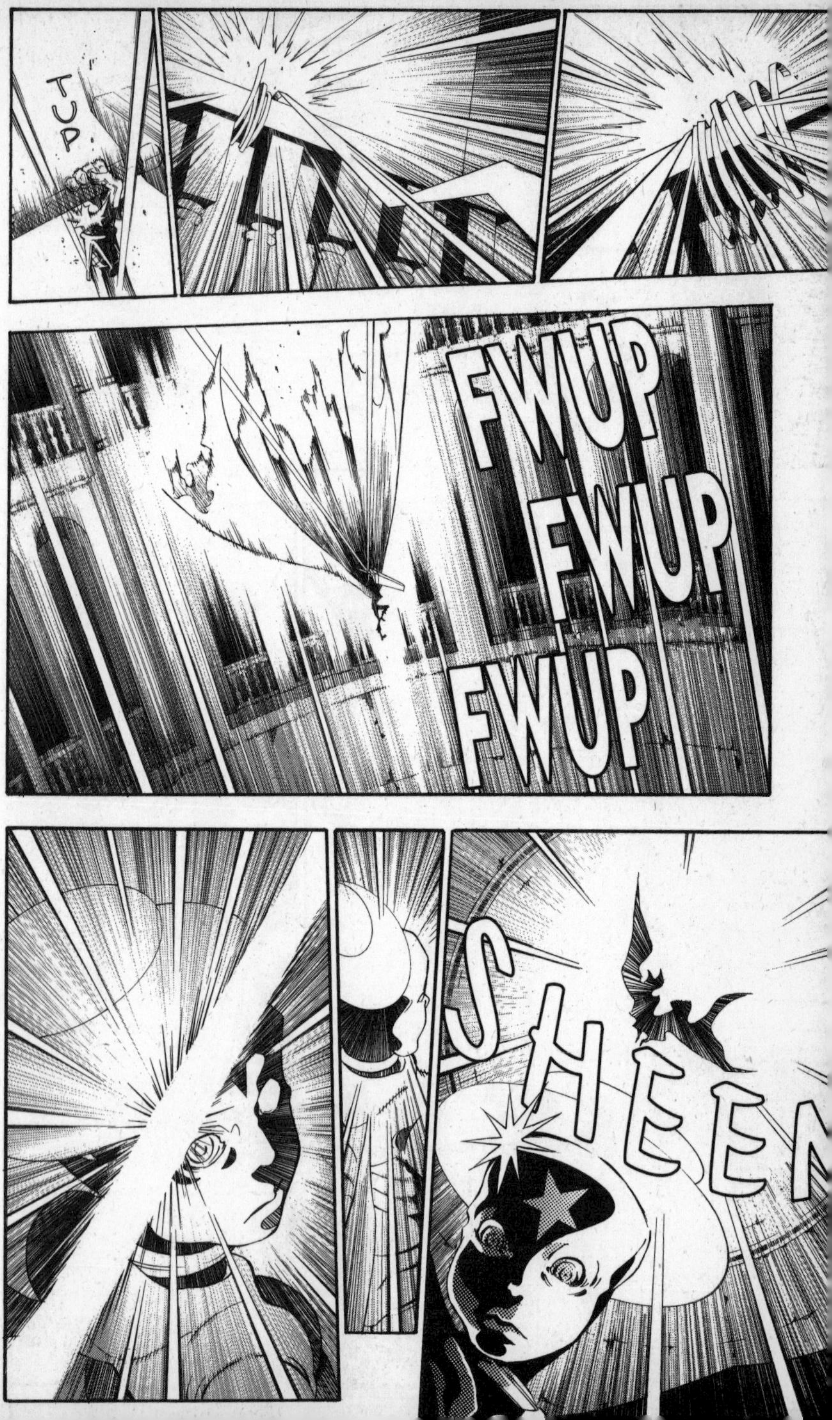
TUP
FWUP
FWUP
FWUP
SHEEN

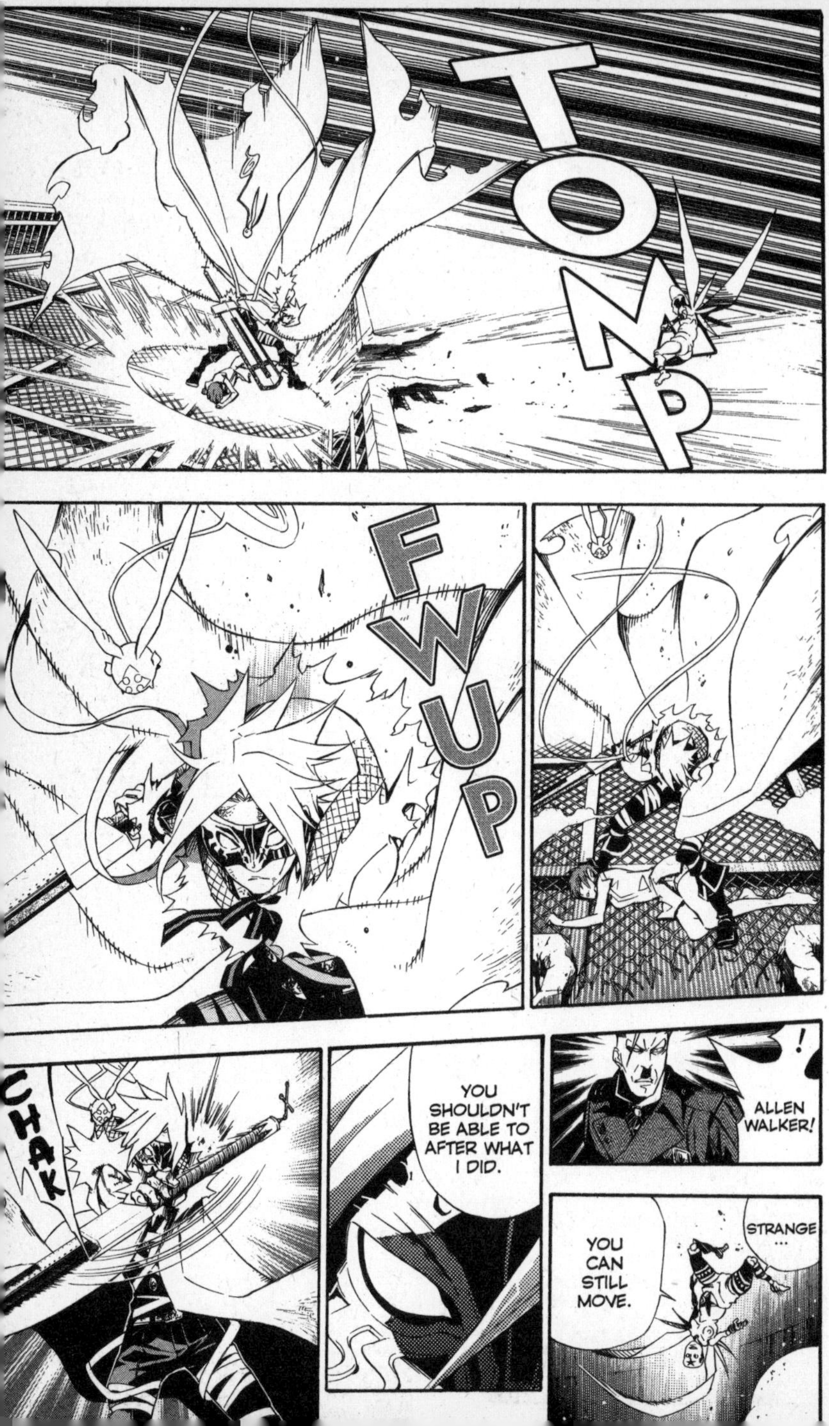
TOMP
FWUP
!
ALLEN WALKER!
STRANGE...
YOU CAN STILL MOVE.
YOU SHOULDN'T BE ABLE TO AFTER WHAT I DID.
CHAK

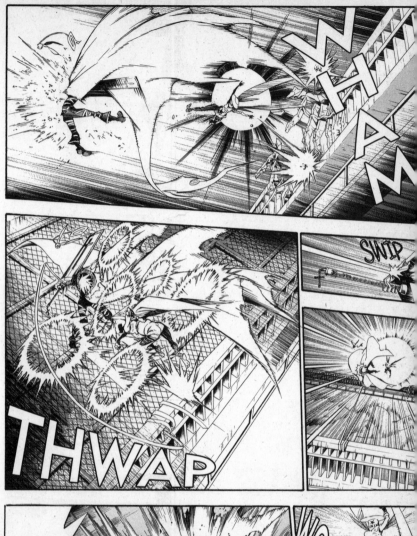

WHAM

SWIP

THWAP

ALLEN!!

THWAM

WOOO

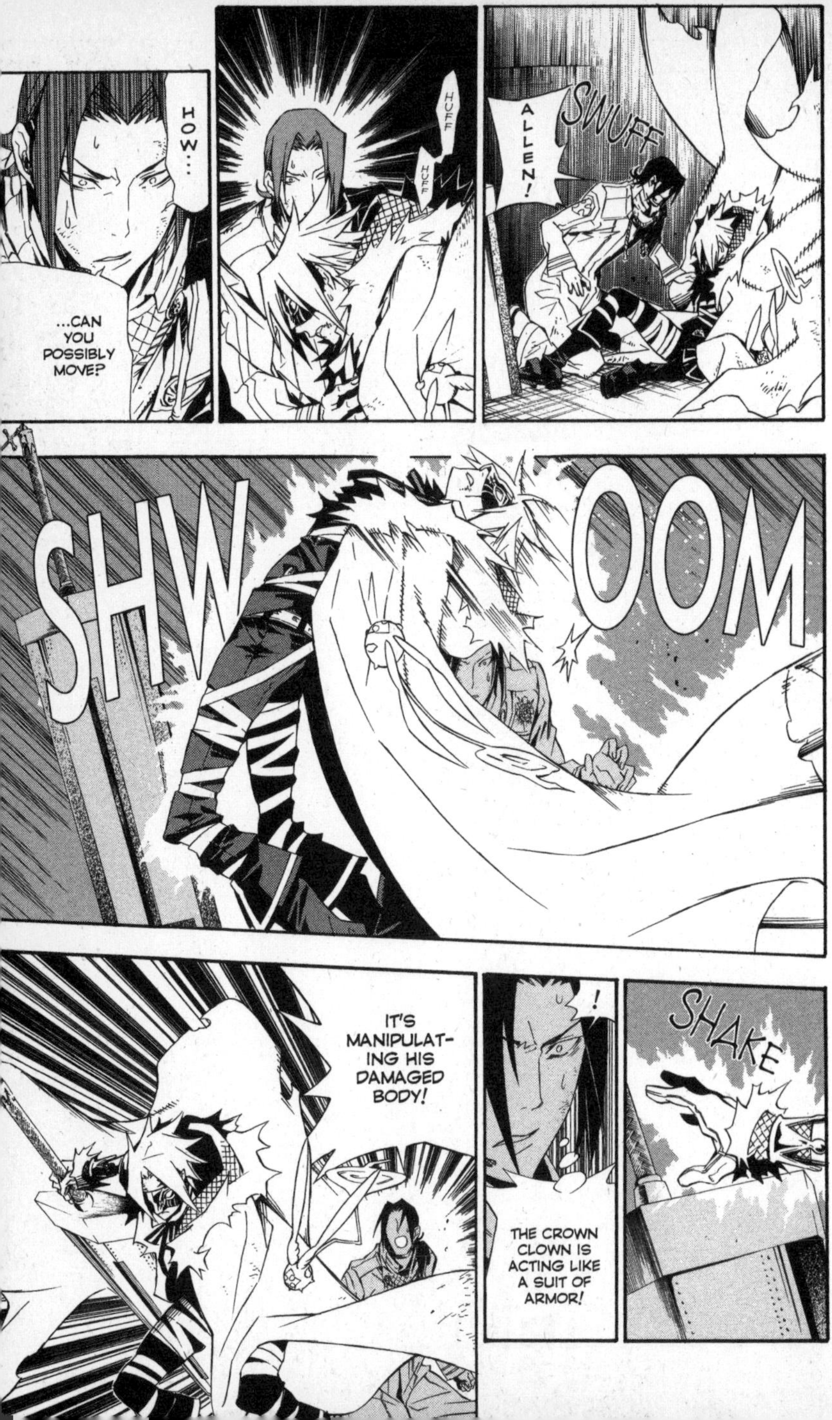
SWUFF
ALLEN!
HUFF
HUFF
HOW...
...CAN YOU POSSIBLY MOVE?
SHW
OOM
SHAKE
!
THE CROWN CLOWN IS ACTING LIKE A SUIT OF ARMOR!
IT'S MANIPULAT-ING HIS DAMAGED BODY!

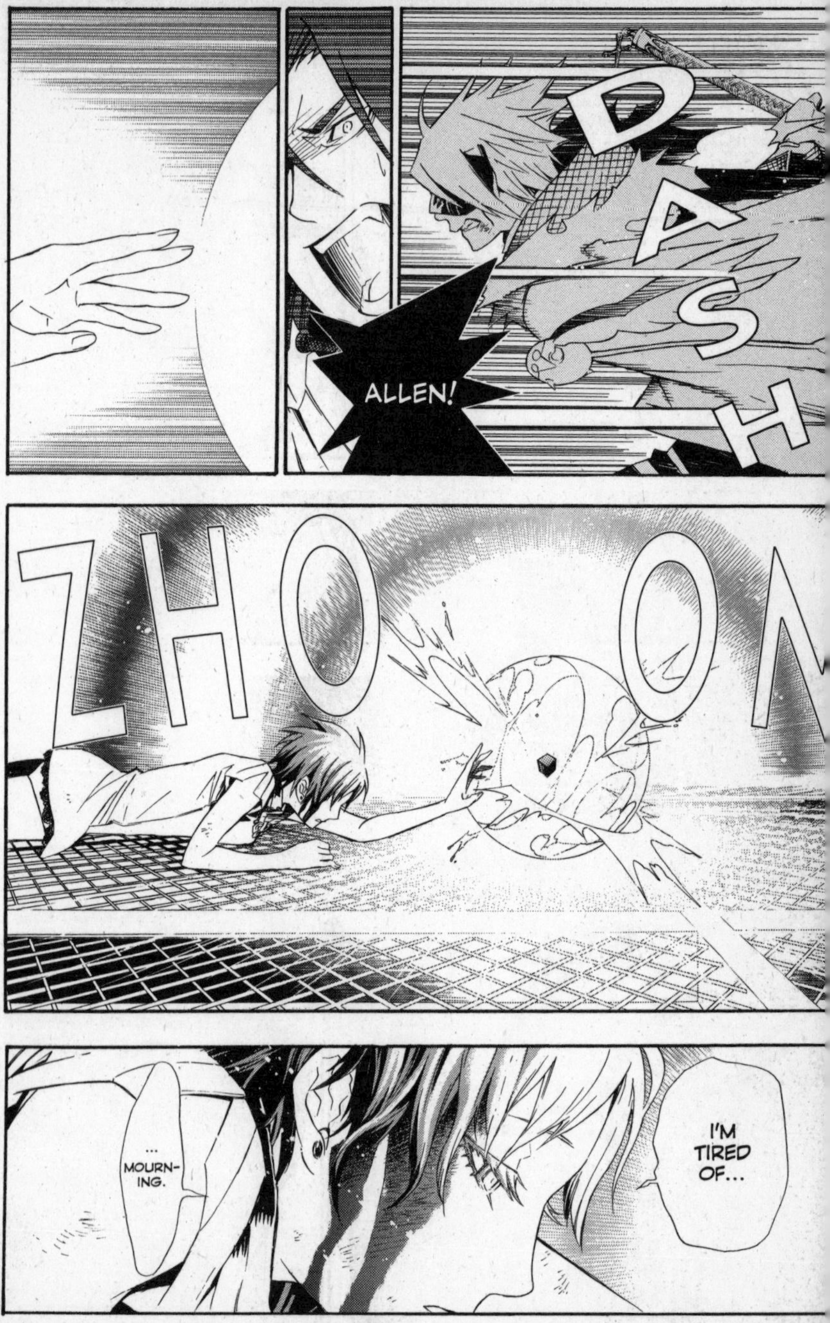
DASH
ALLEN!
ZHOON
I'M TIRED OF...
... MOURNING.

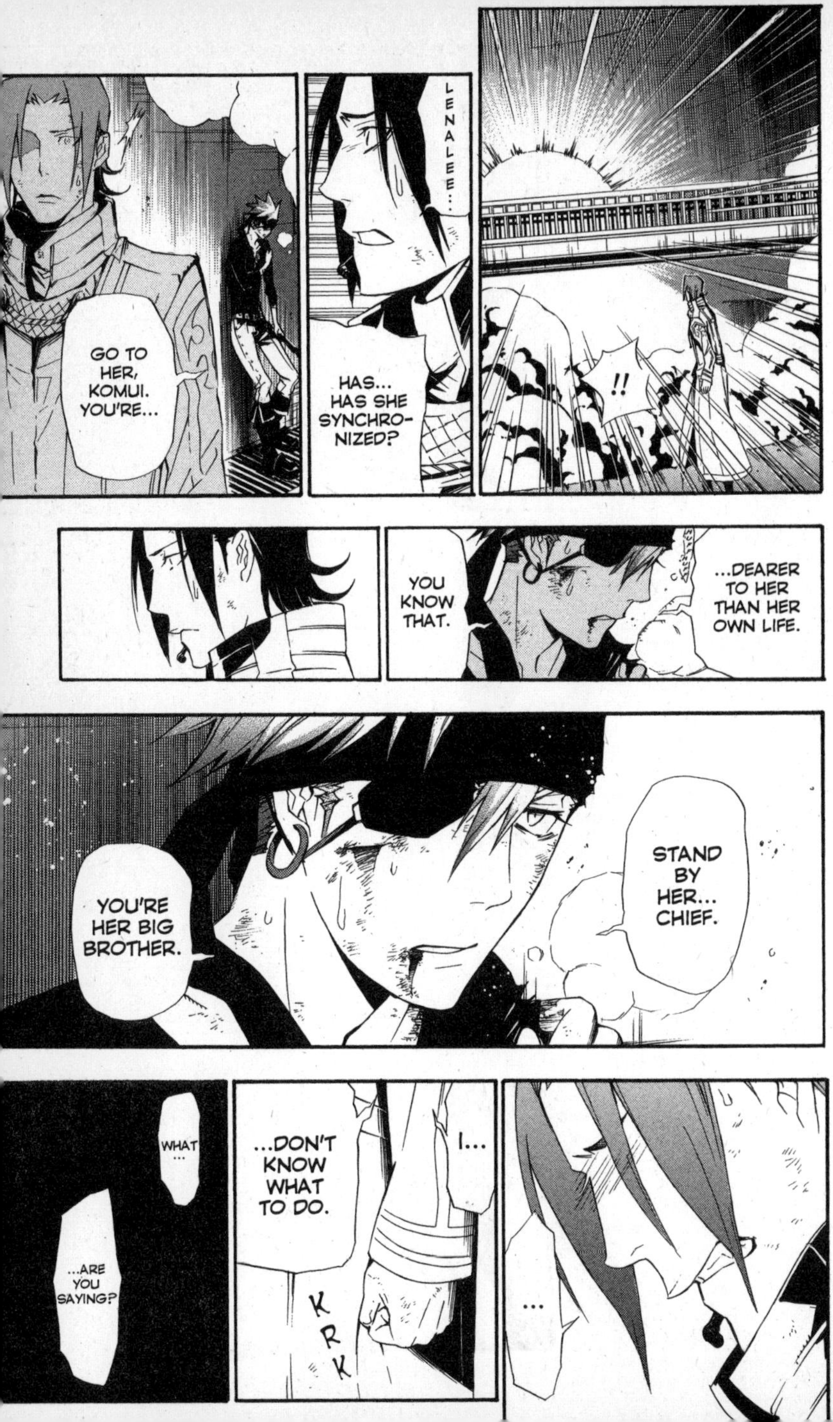
!!
LENALEE...
HAS... HAS SHE SYNCHRONIZED?
GO TO HER, KOMUI. YOU'RE...
...DEARER TO HER THAN HER OWN LIFE.
YOU KNOW THAT.
STAND BY HER... CHIEF.
YOU'RE HER BIG BROTHER.
...
I...
...DON'T KNOW WHAT TO DO.
KRK
WHAT...
...ARE YOU SAYING?

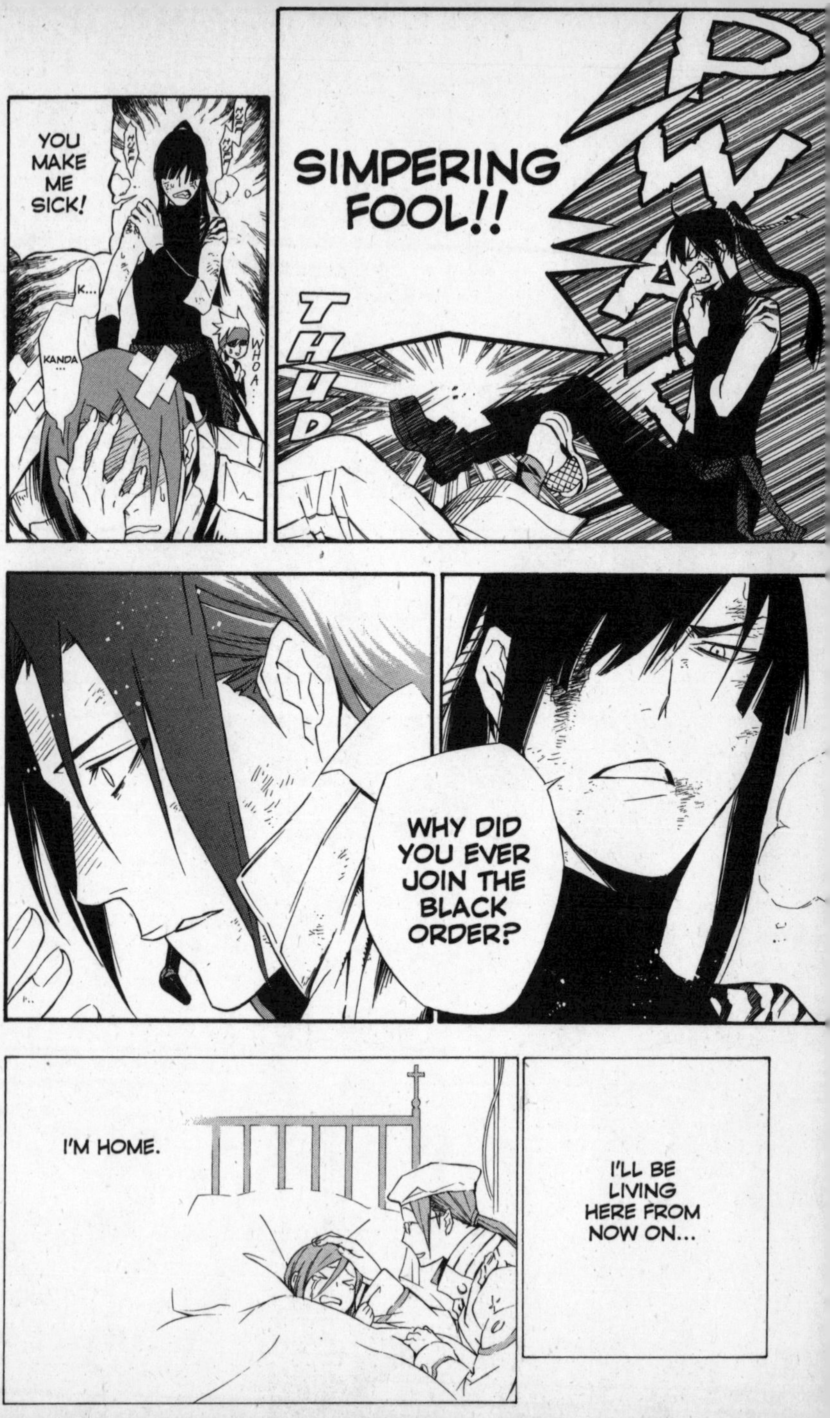
PAW
SIMPERING FOOL!!
THUD
YOU MAKE ME SICK!
K...
KANDA...
WHOA...
WHY DID YOU EVER JOIN THE BLACK ORDER?
I'LL BE LIVING HERE FROM NOW ON...
I'M HOME.

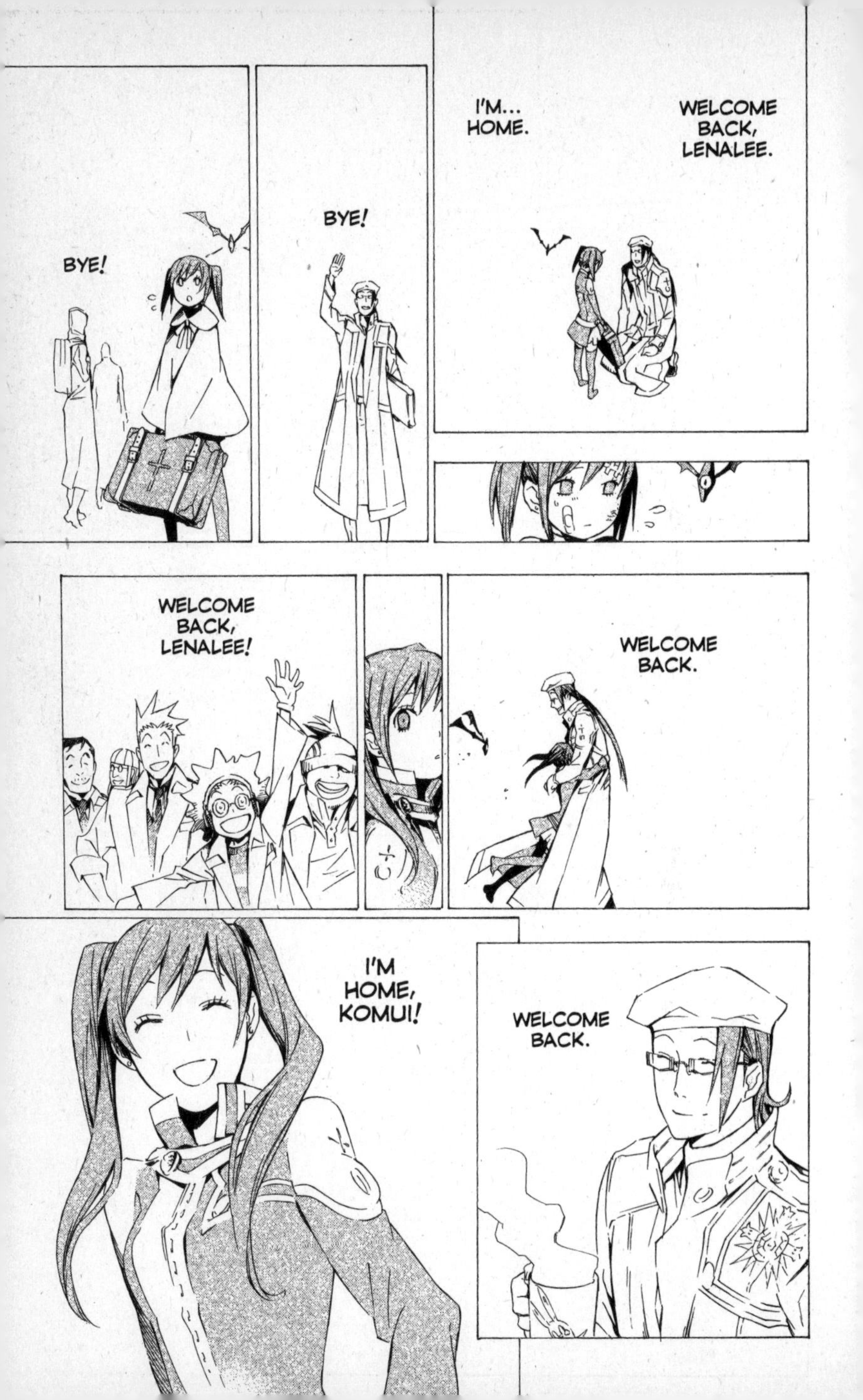
WELCOME BACK, LENALEE.
I'M... HOME.
BYE!
BYE!
WELCOME BACK.
WELCOME BACK, LENALEE!
WELCOME BACK.
I'M HOME, KOMUI!

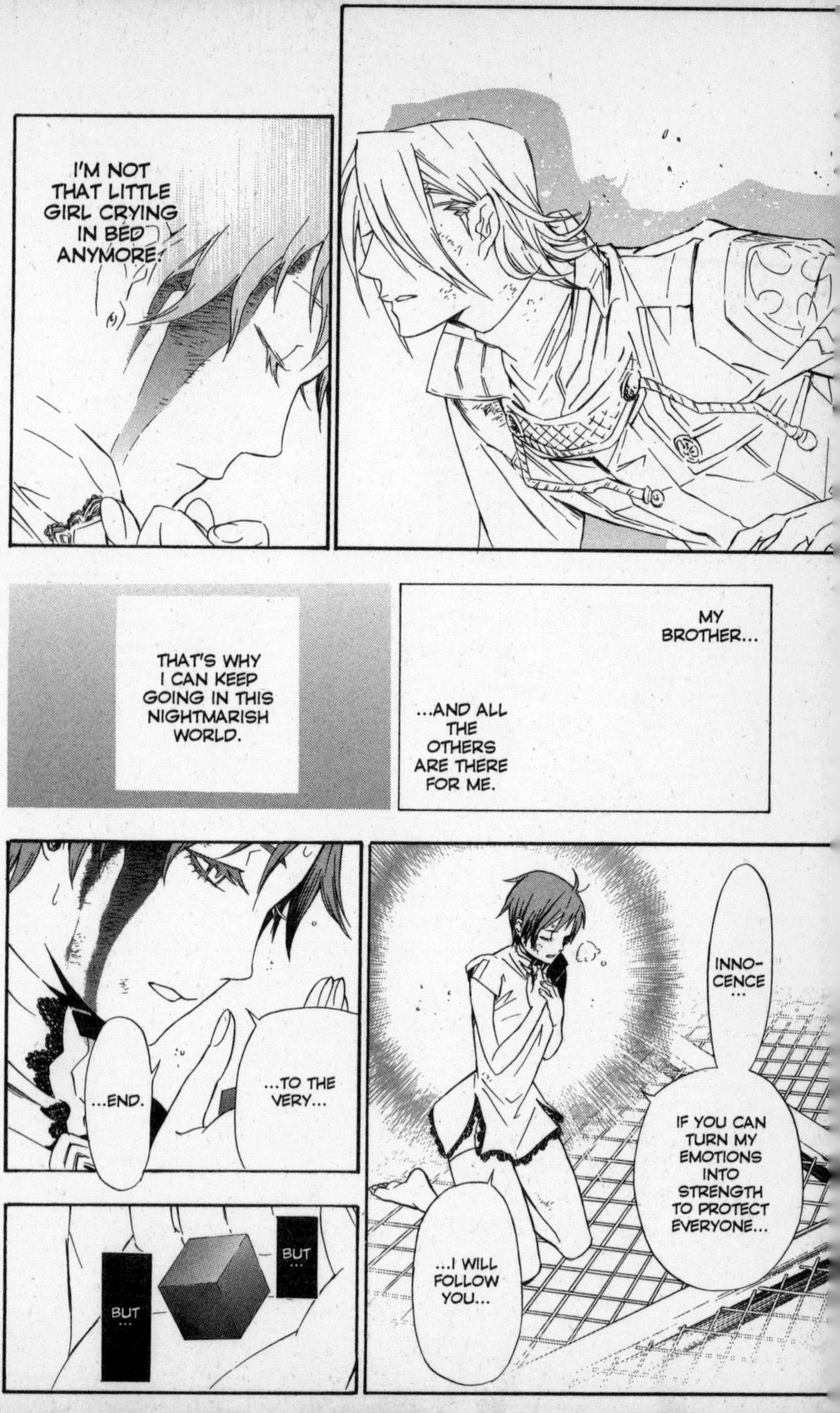
I'M NOT THAT LITTLE GIRL CRYING IN BED ANYMORE.
MY BROTHER...
...AND ALL THE OTHERS ARE THERE FOR ME.
THAT'S WHY I CAN KEEP GOING IN THIS NIGHTMARISH WORLD.
INNOCENCE...
IF YOU CAN TURN MY EMOTIONS INTO STRENGTH TO PROTECT EVERYONE...
...I WILL FOLLOW YOU...
...TO THE VERY...
...END.
BUT...
BUT...

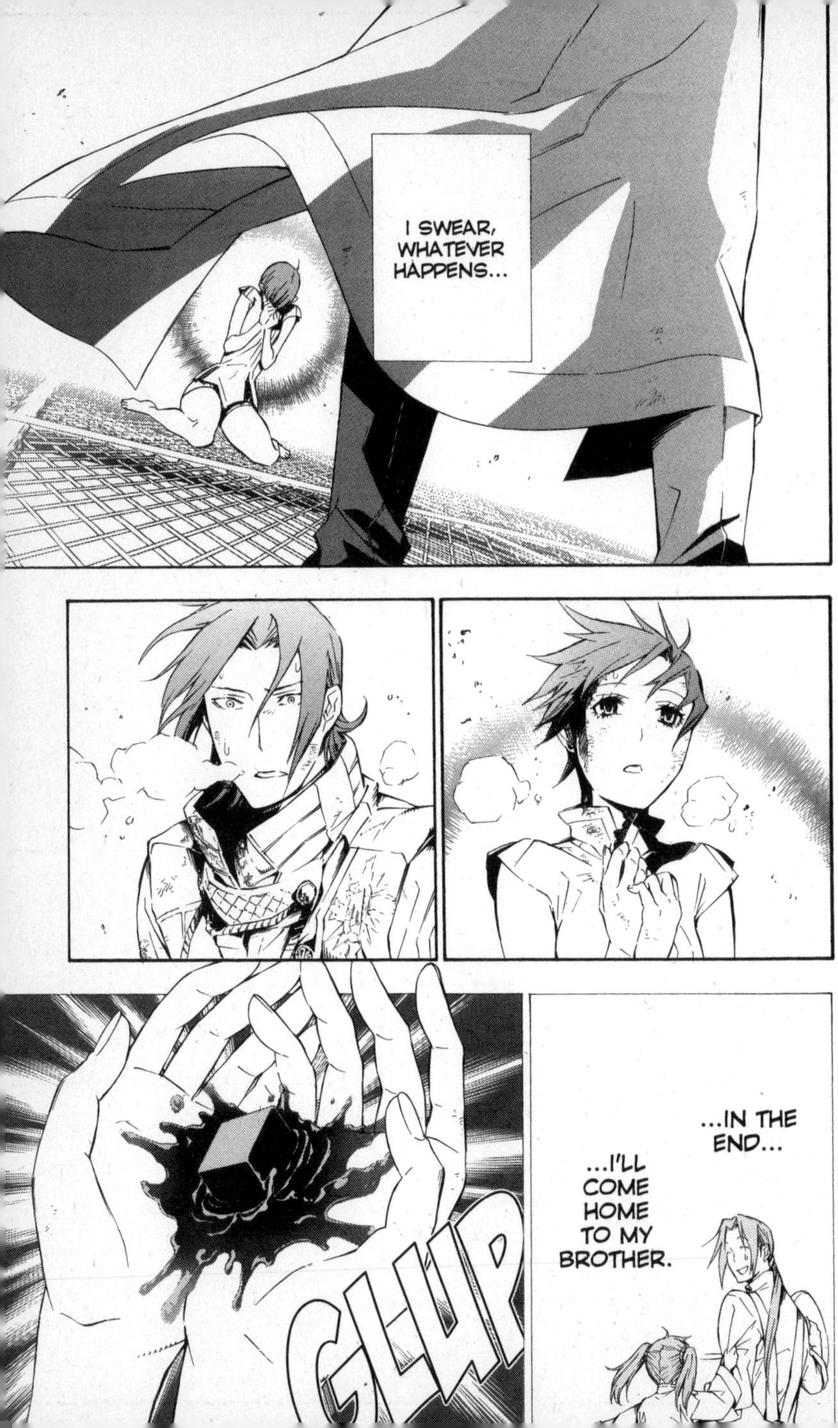
I SWEAR, WHATEVER HAPPENS...
...IN THE END...
...I'LL COME HOME TO MY BROTHER.
GLUP

SO LONG, KOMUI!

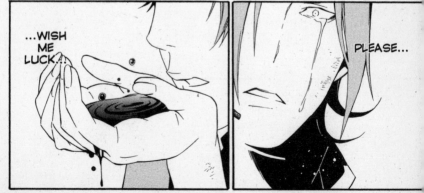

...WISH ME LUCK...

PLEASE...

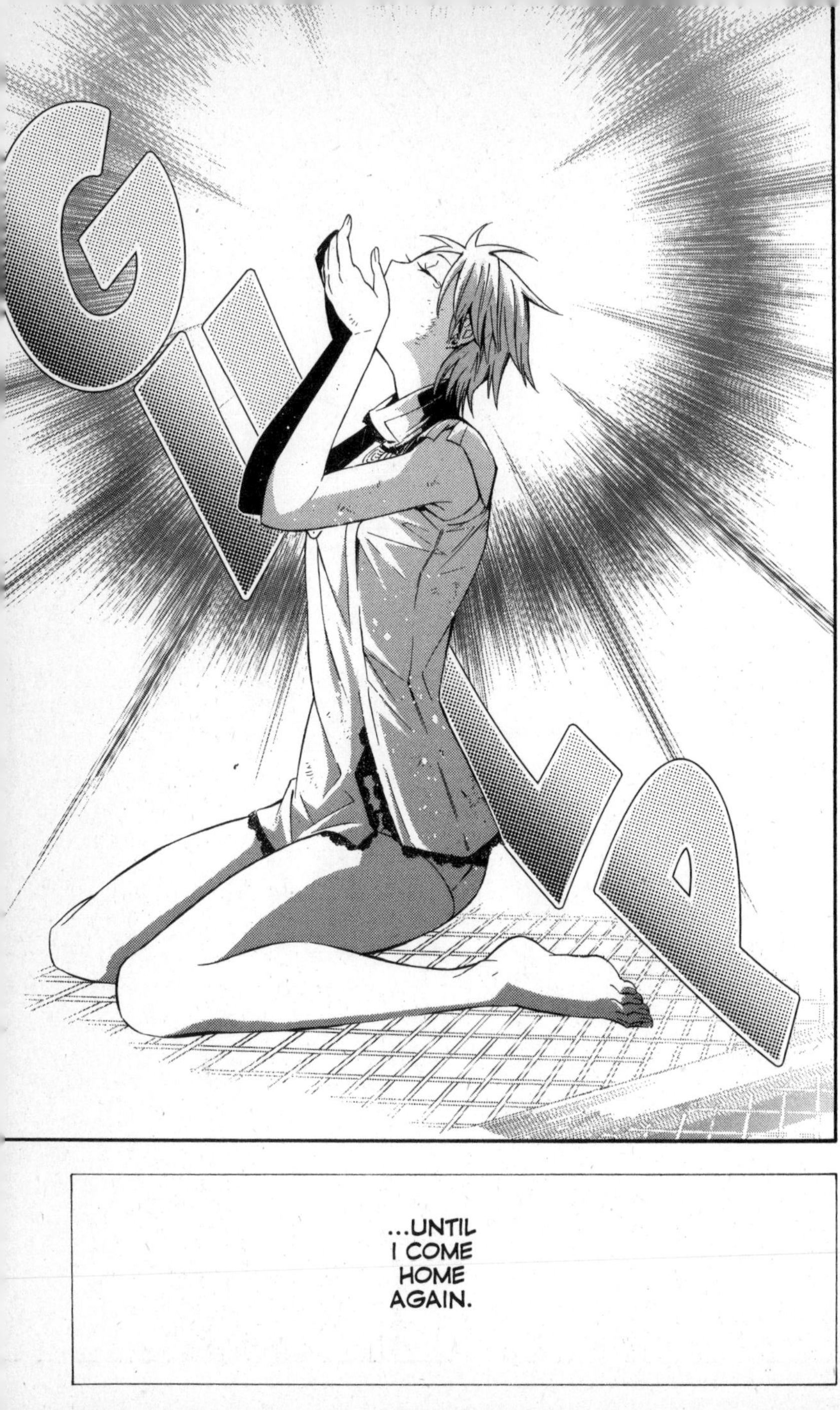
GULP
...UNTIL I COME HOME AGAIN.

THE PEOPLE OF D.GRAY HOUSE

THE LONELY FATHER II

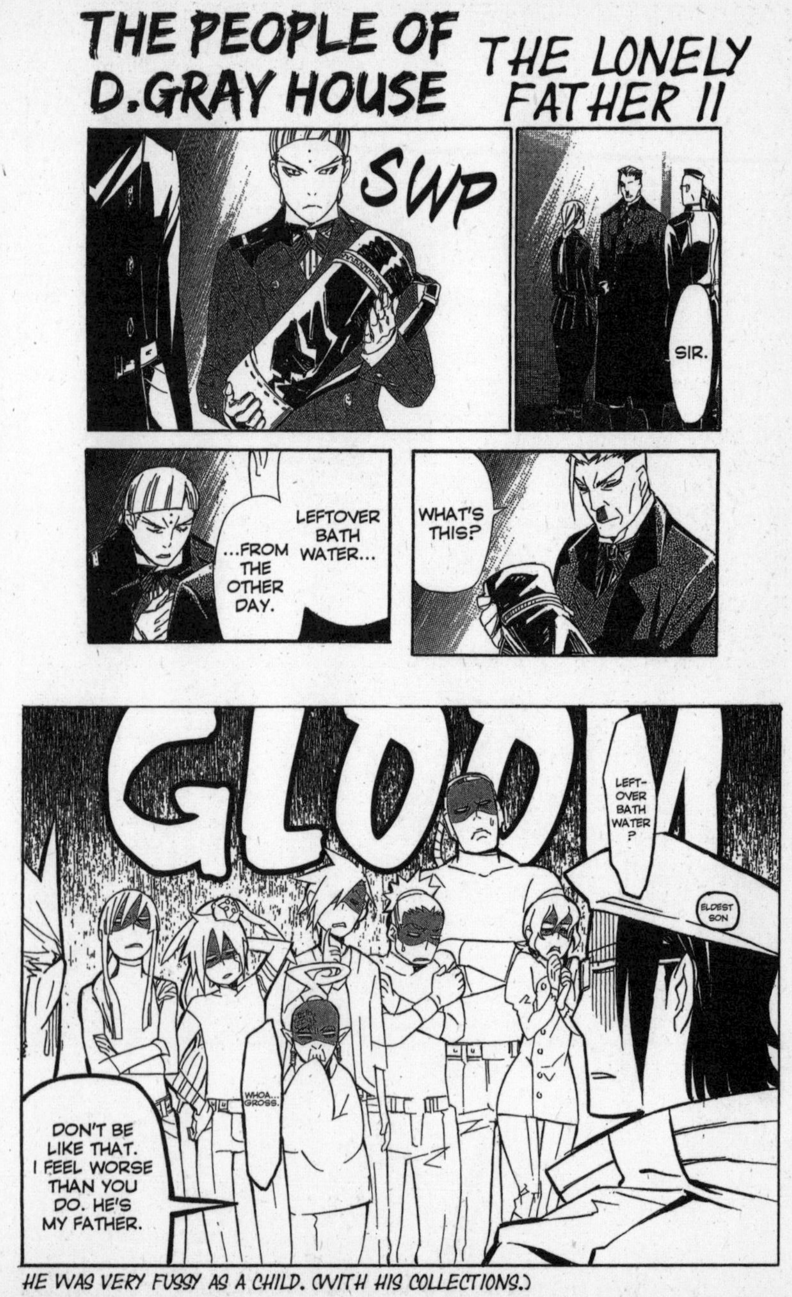
SIR.
SWP
WHAT'S THIS?
LEFTOVER BATH WATER...
...FROM THE OTHER DAY.
GLOOM
LEFT-OVER BATH WATER?
ELDEST SON
WHOA... GROSS.
DON'T BE LIKE THAT. I FEEL WORSE THAN YOU DO. HE'S MY FATHER.

HE WAS VERY FUSSY AS A CHILD. (WITH HIS COLLECTIONS.)

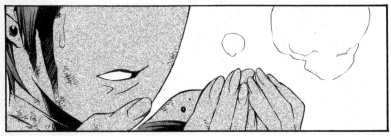

THE 153RD NIGHT: READY FOR RED

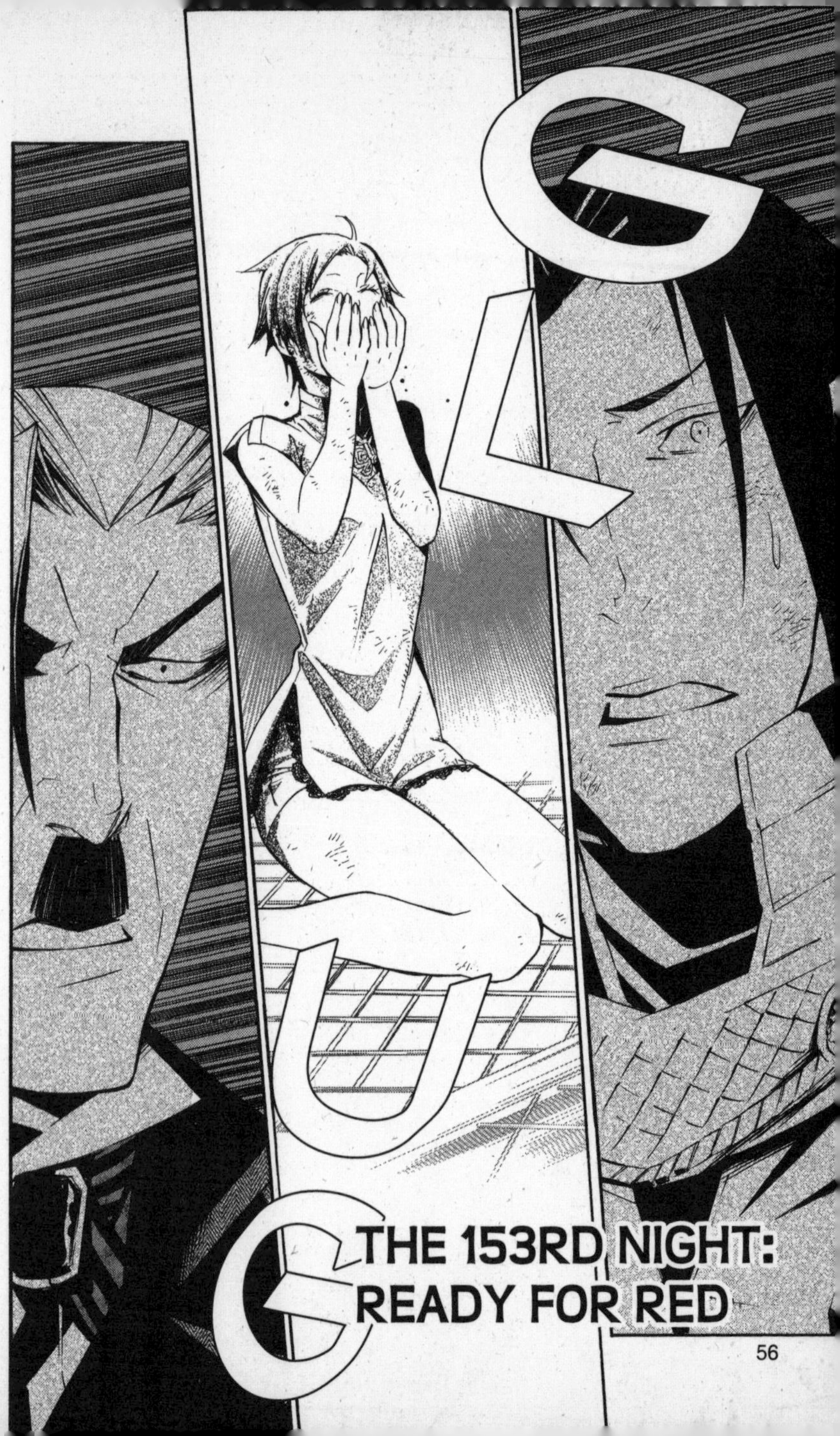
GLUG

THE 153RD NIGHT: READY FOR RED

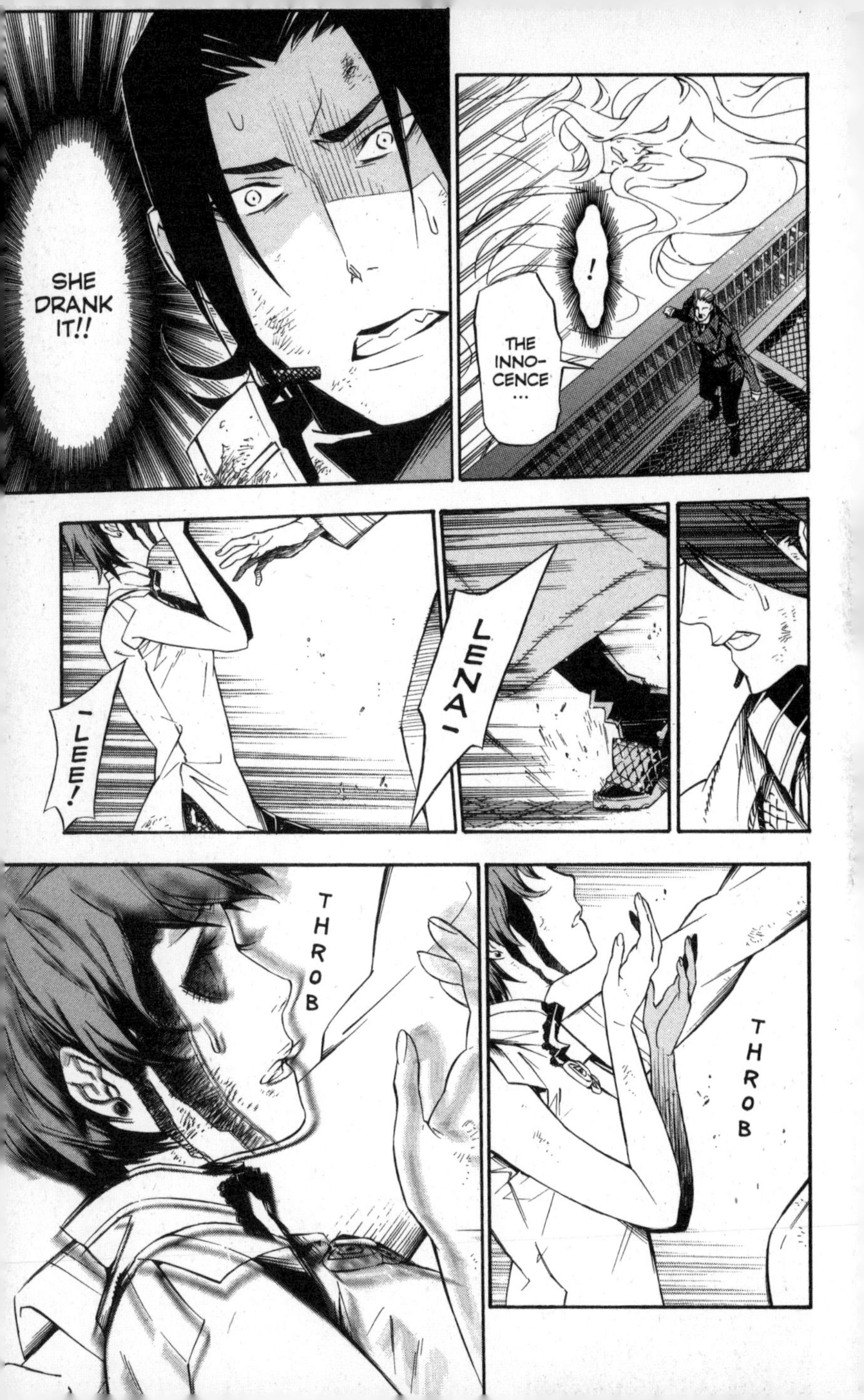
!
THE INNOCENCE...
SHE DRANK IT!!
LENA!
—LEE!
THROB
THROB

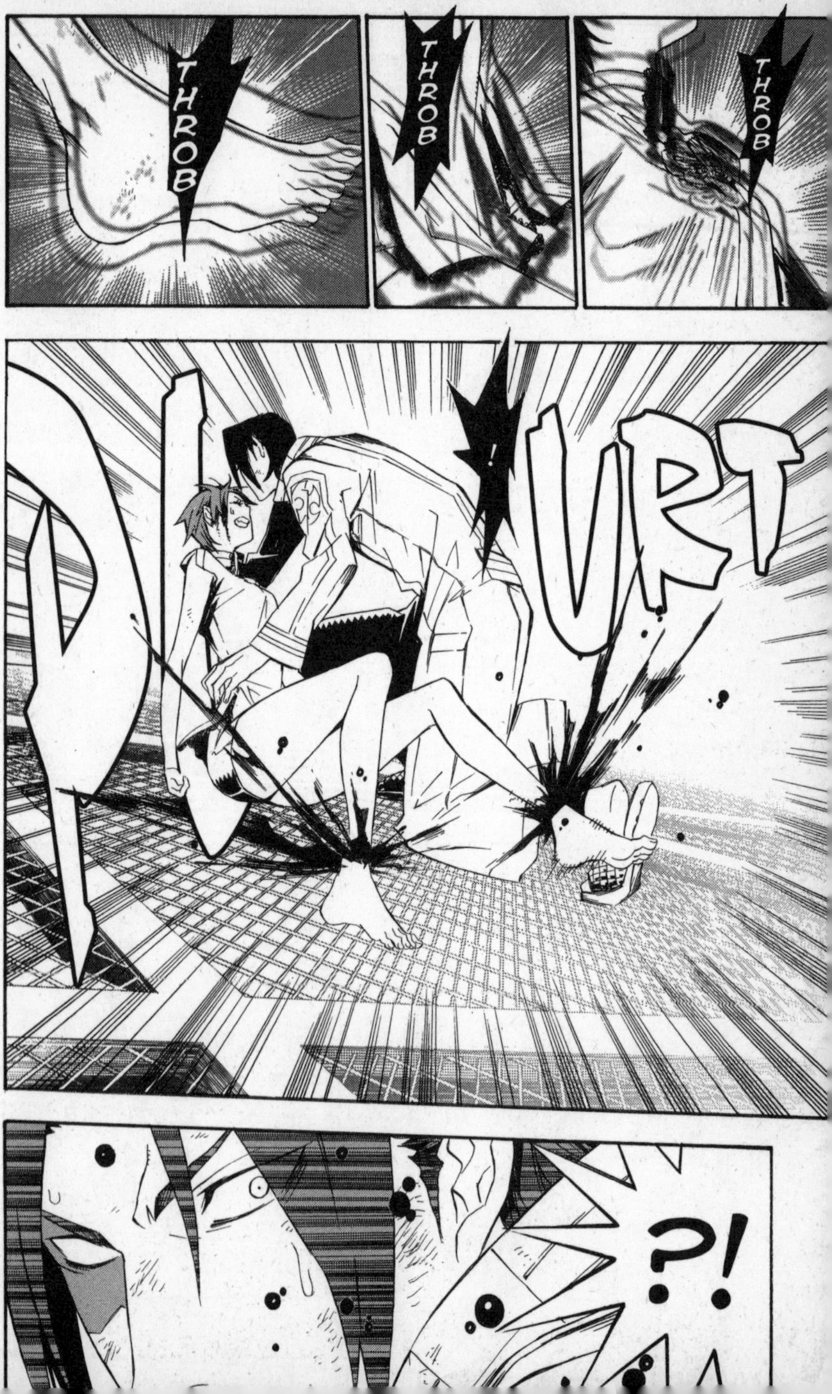

THROB
THROB
THROB
?!

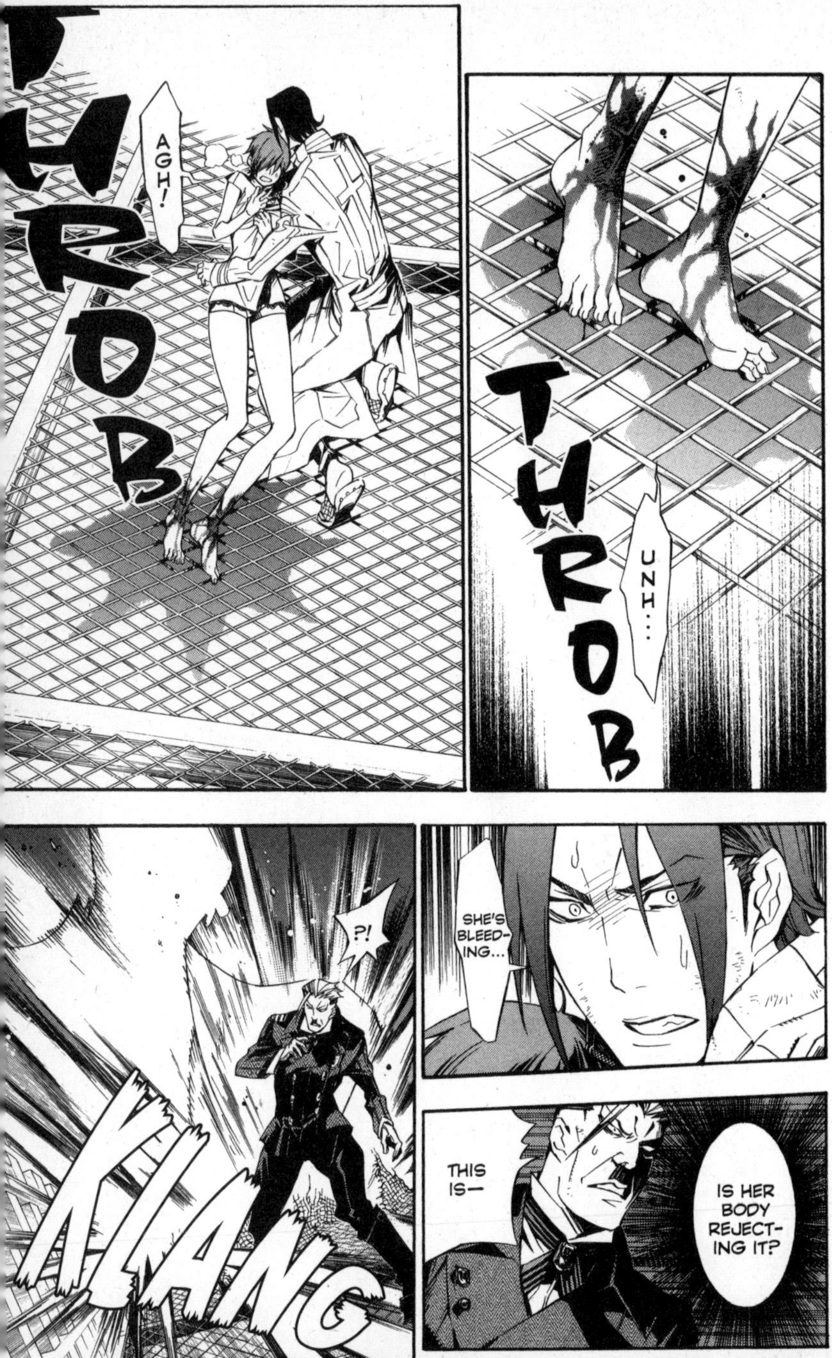
THROB
UNH...
THROB
AGH!
SHE'S BLEED-ING...
THIS IS—
IS HER BODY REJECT-ING IT?
?!
KLANG

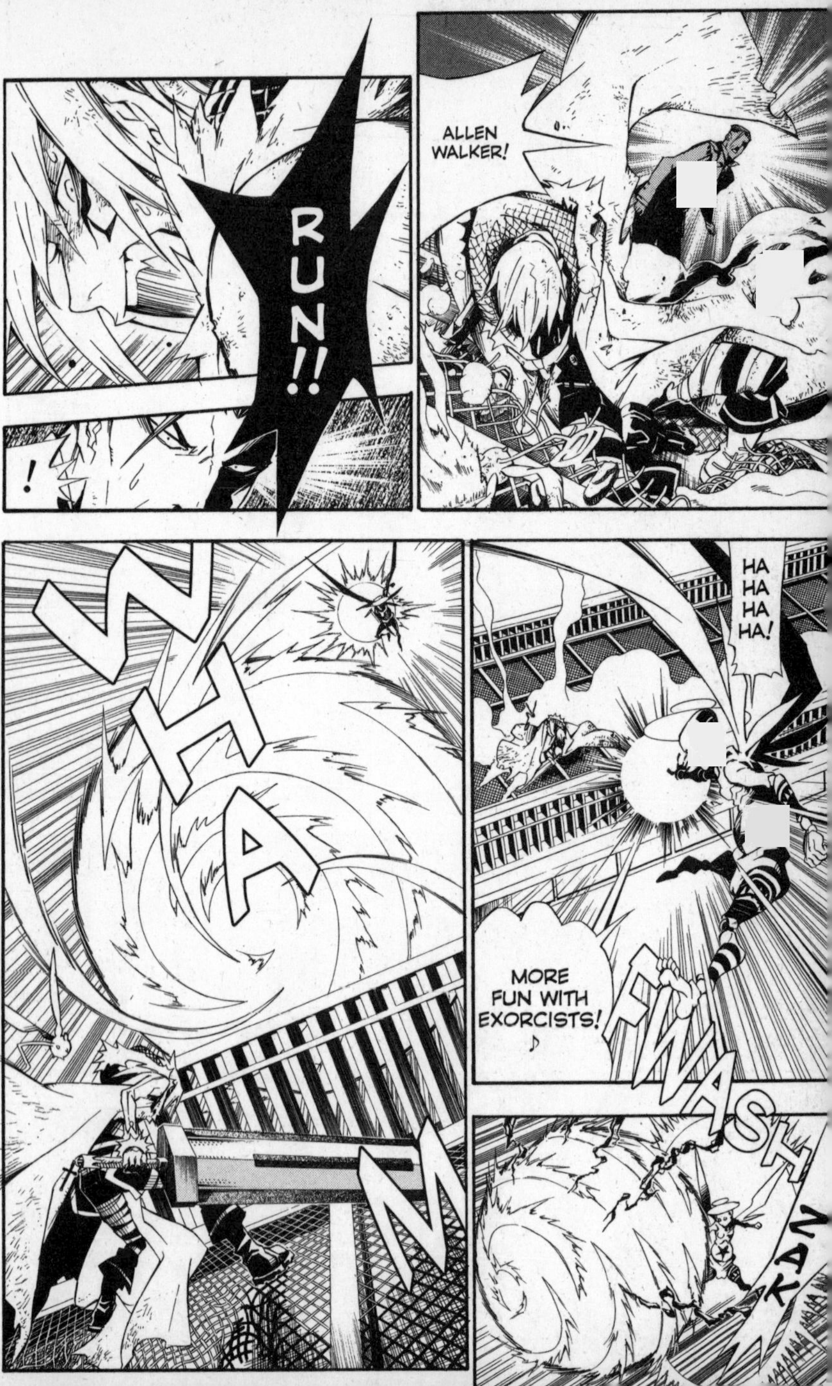
ALLEN WALKER!
RUN!!
!
HA HA HA HA!
MORE FUN WITH EXORCISTS! ♪
FWASH
ZAK
WHAM

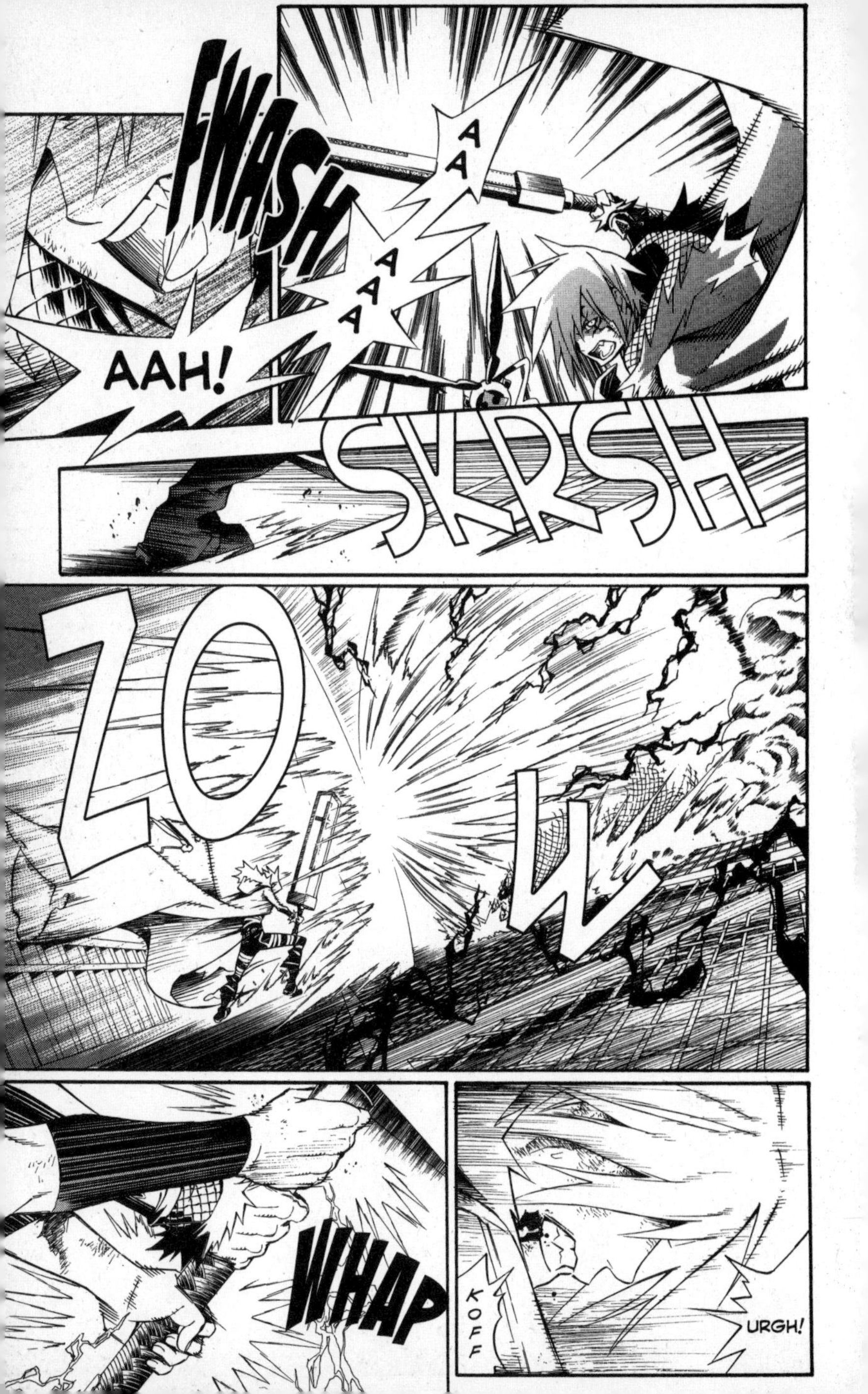
AAAAA
FWASH
AAH!
SKRSH
ZOW
URGH!
KOFF
WHAP

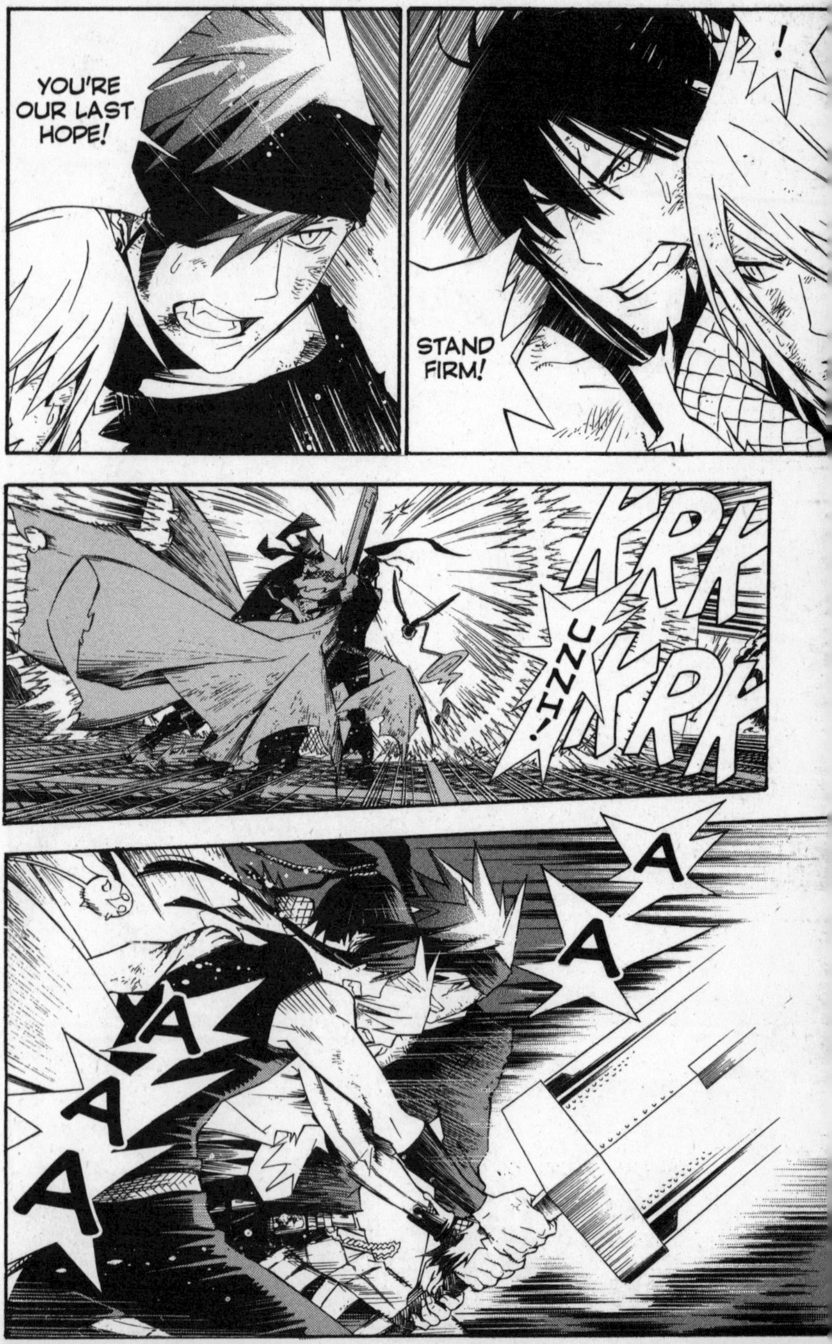
!
STAND FIRM!
YOU'RE OUR LAST HOPE!
KRK KRK
UNNH!
AA
YAAA

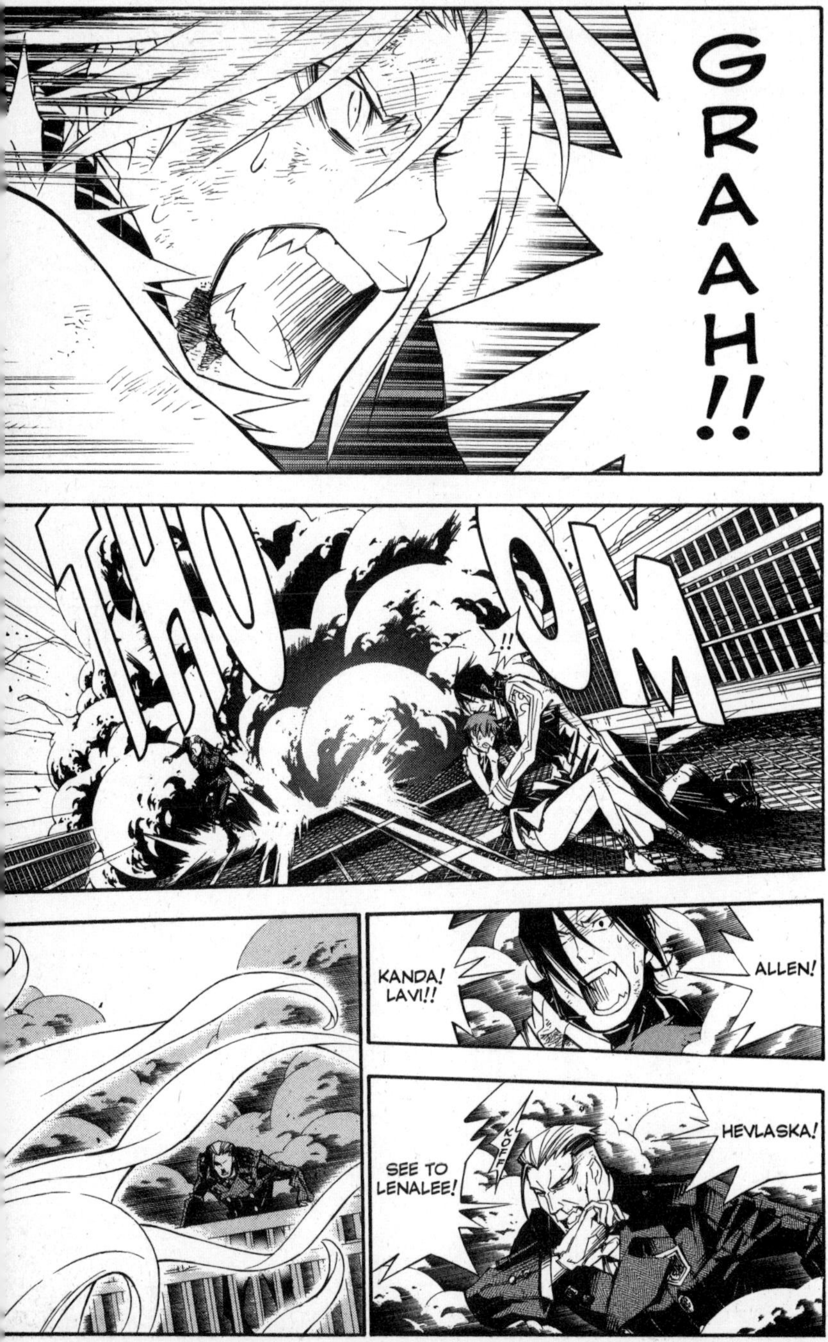
GRAAH!!
THOOM
!!
ALLEN!
KANDA! LAVI!!
HEVLASKA!
KOFF
SEE TO LENALEE!

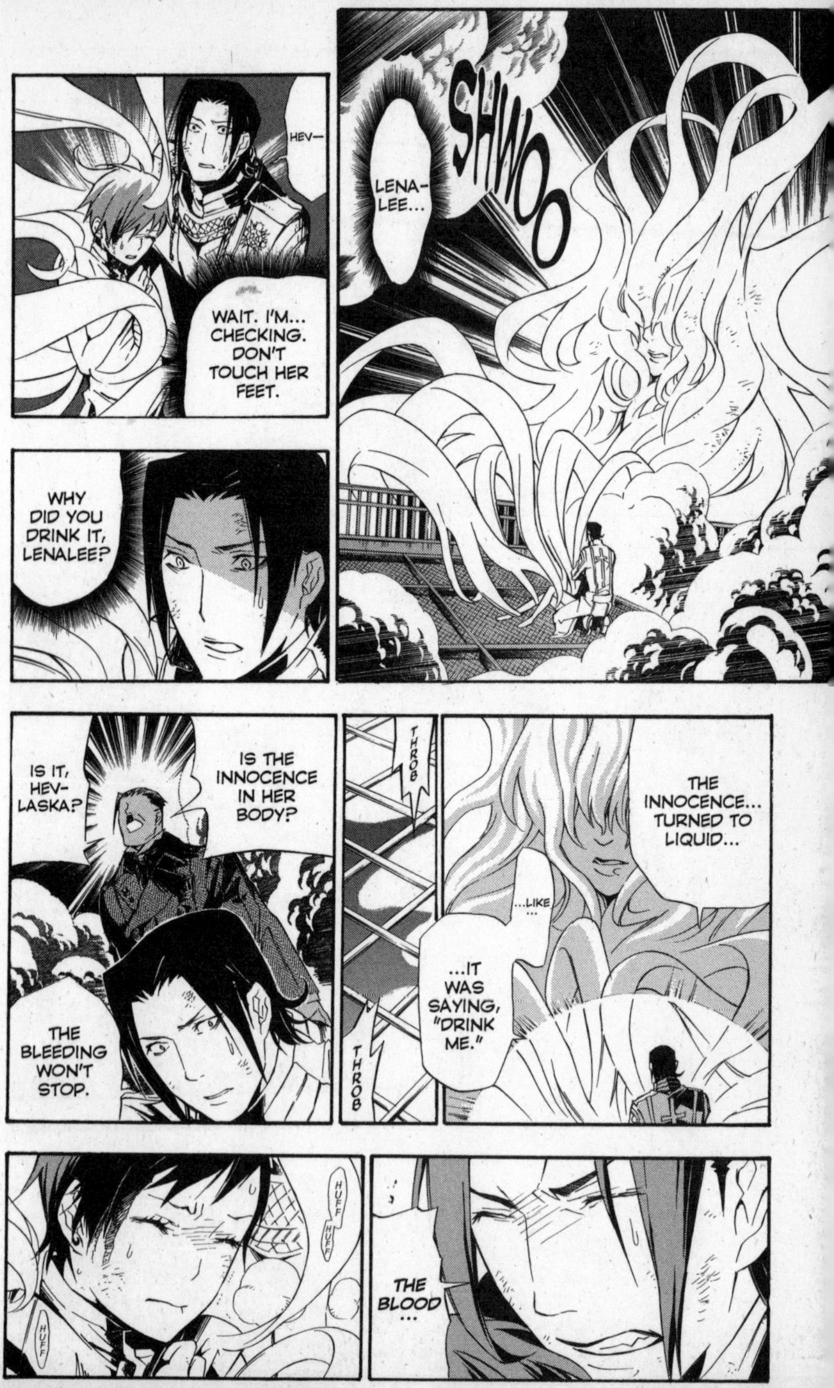
SHWOO
LENA-LEE...
HEV—
WAIT. I'M... CHECKING. DON'T TOUCH HER FEET.
WHY DID YOU DRINK IT, LENALEE?
THE INNOCENCE... TURNED TO LIQUID...
...LIKE...
...IT WAS SAYING, "DRINK ME."
THROB
THROB
IS THE INNOCENCE IN HER BODY?
IS IT, HEV-LASKA?
THE BLEEDING WON'T STOP.
THE BLOOD...
HUFF
HUFF
HUFF

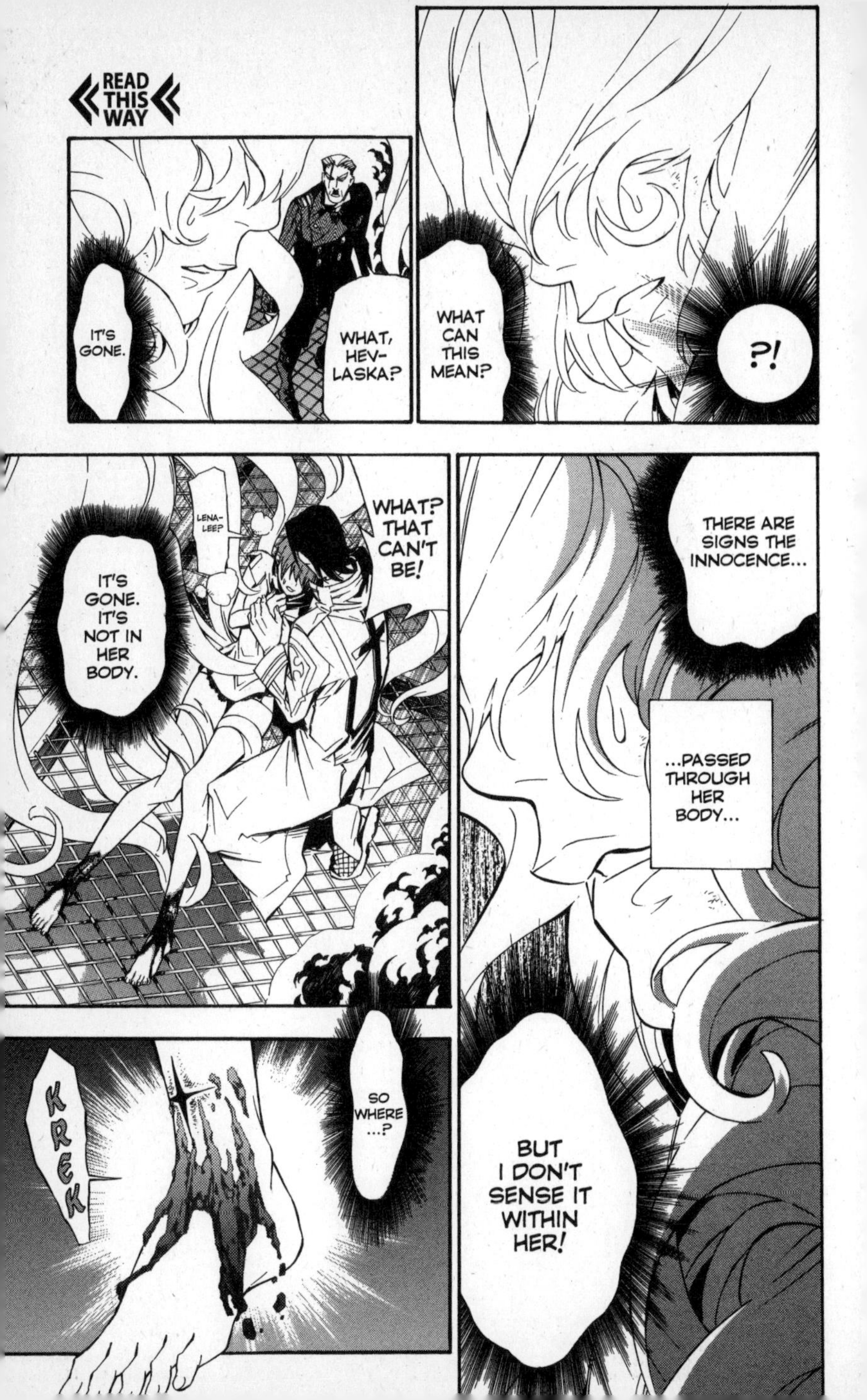
READ THIS WAY
?!
WHAT CAN THIS MEAN?
WHAT, HEV-LASKA?
IT'S GONE.
THERE ARE SIGNS THE INNOCENCE...
...PASSED THROUGH HER BODY...
BUT I DON'T SENSE IT WITHIN HER!
WHAT? THAT CAN'T BE!
LENA-LEE?
IT'S GONE. IT'S NOT IN HER BODY.
SO WHERE ...?
KREK

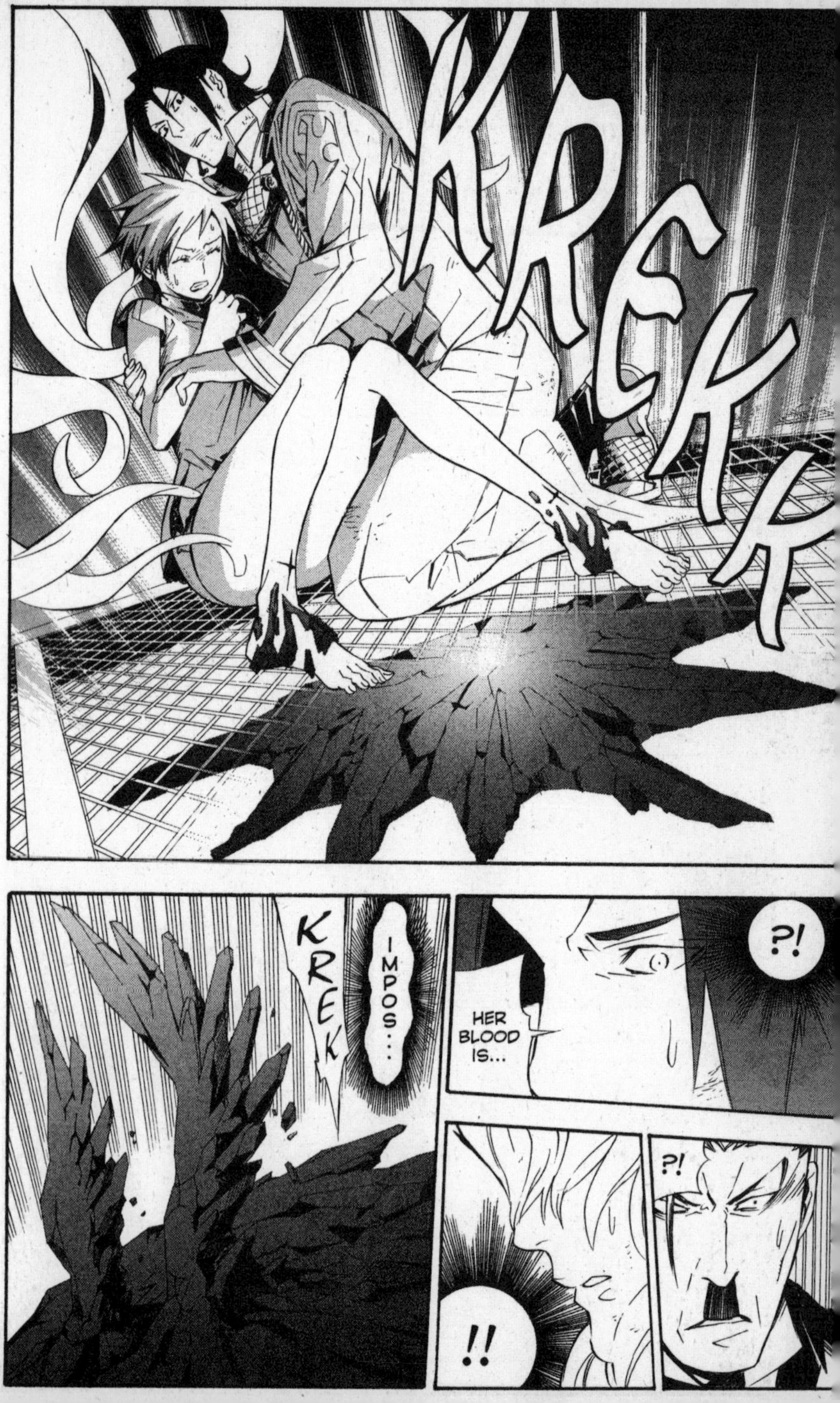
KRACKK
?!
HER BLOOD IS...
?!
!!
KREK
IMPOS...

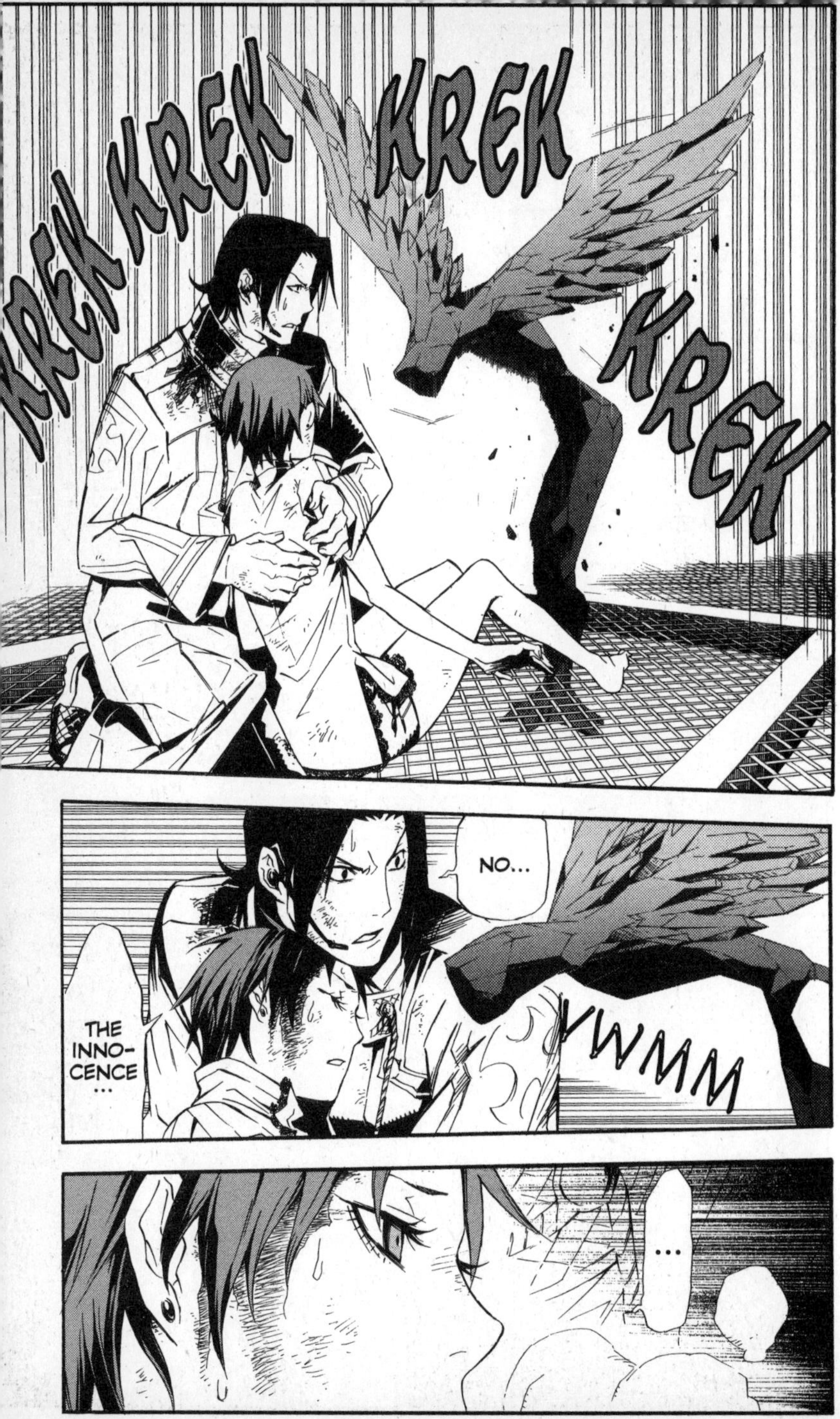
KREK
KREK
KREK KREK
NO...
VWMM
THE INNO-CENCE...
...

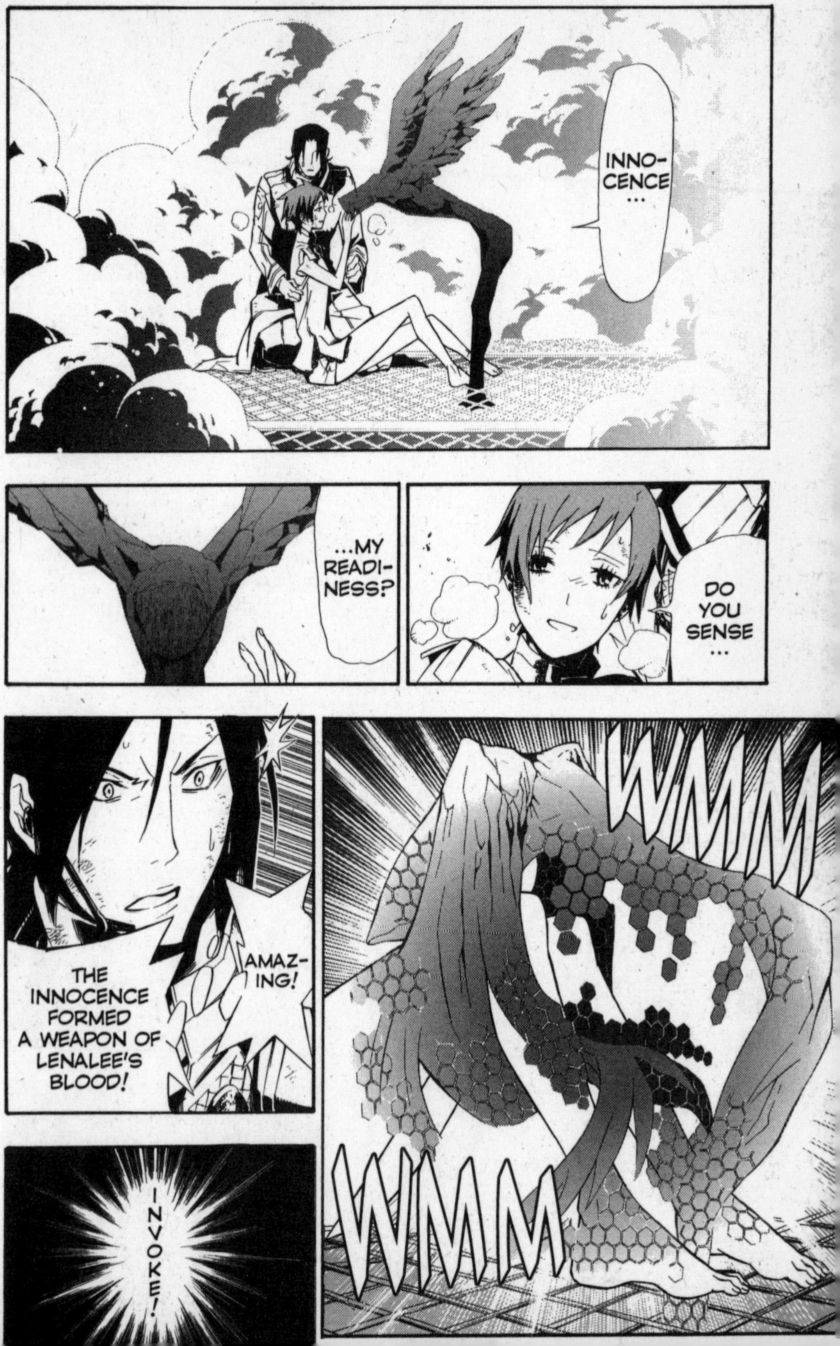
INNO-CENCE ...
DO YOU SENSE ...
...MY READINESS?
WMM
WMM
AMAZ-ING!
THE INNOCENCE FORMED A WEAPON OF LENALEE'S BLOOD!
INVOKE!

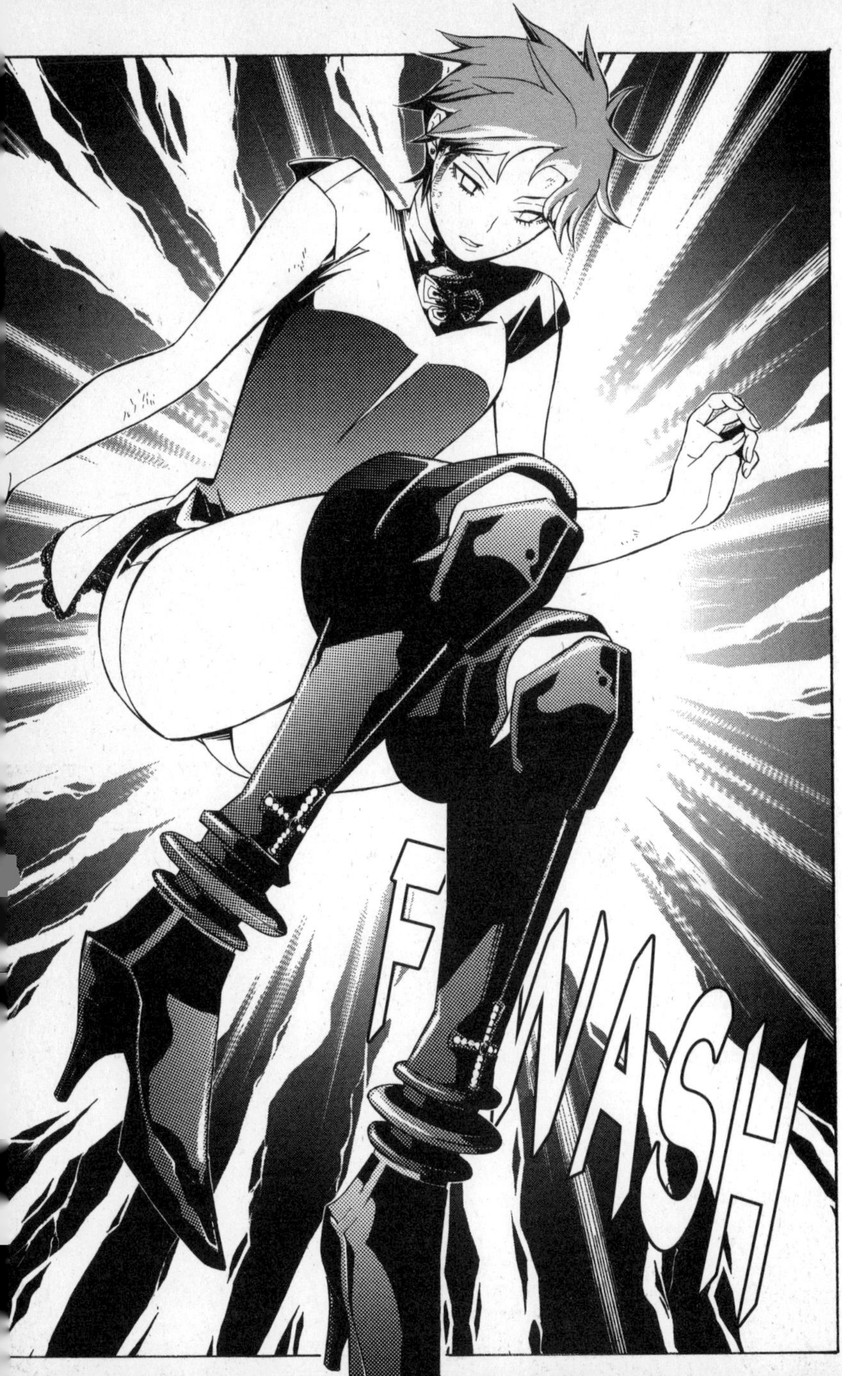
FWASH

THE PEOPLE OF D.GRAY HOUSE

LENAMI RESISTS WITH ALL HER MIGHT

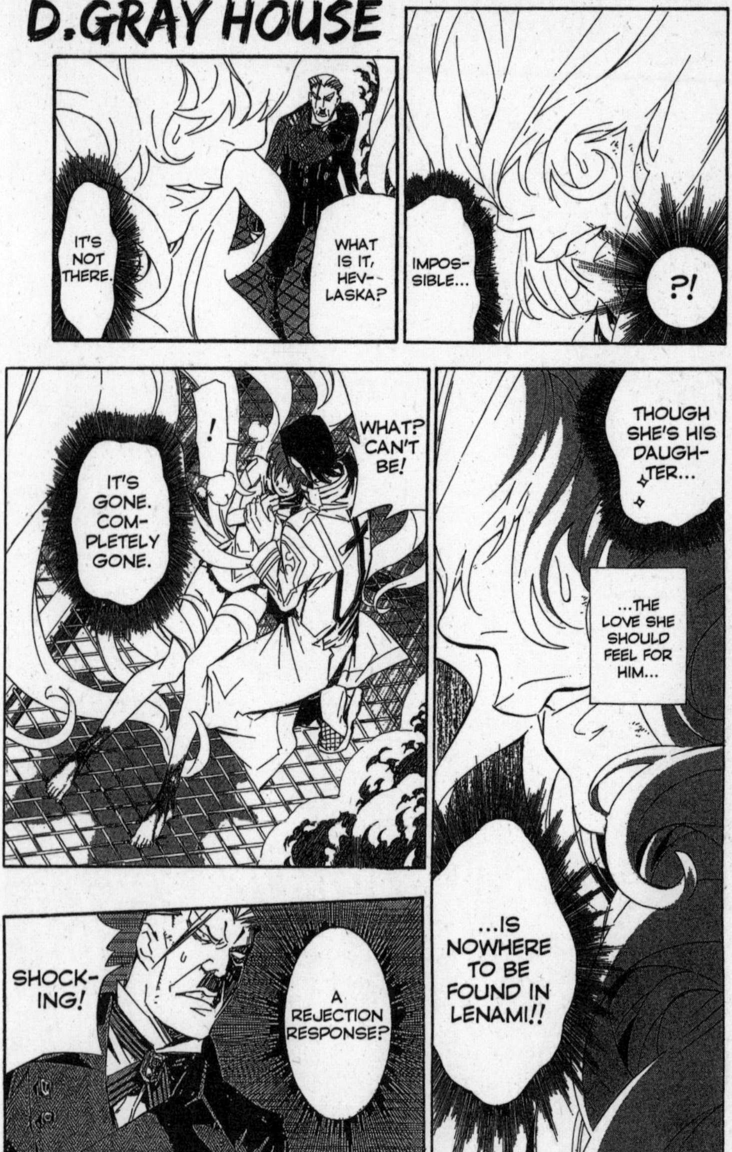
?!
IMPOSSIBLE...
WHAT IS IT, HEVLASKA?
IT'S NOT THERE.
THOUGH SHE'S HIS DAUGHTER...
...THE LOVE SHE SHOULD FEEL FOR HIM...
...IS NOWHERE TO BE FOUND IN LENAMI!!
WHAT? CAN'T BE!
!
IT'S GONE. COMPLETELY GONE.
A REJECTION RESPONSE?
SHOCKING!

EVERY FATHER EXPERIENCES THIS EVENTUALLY.

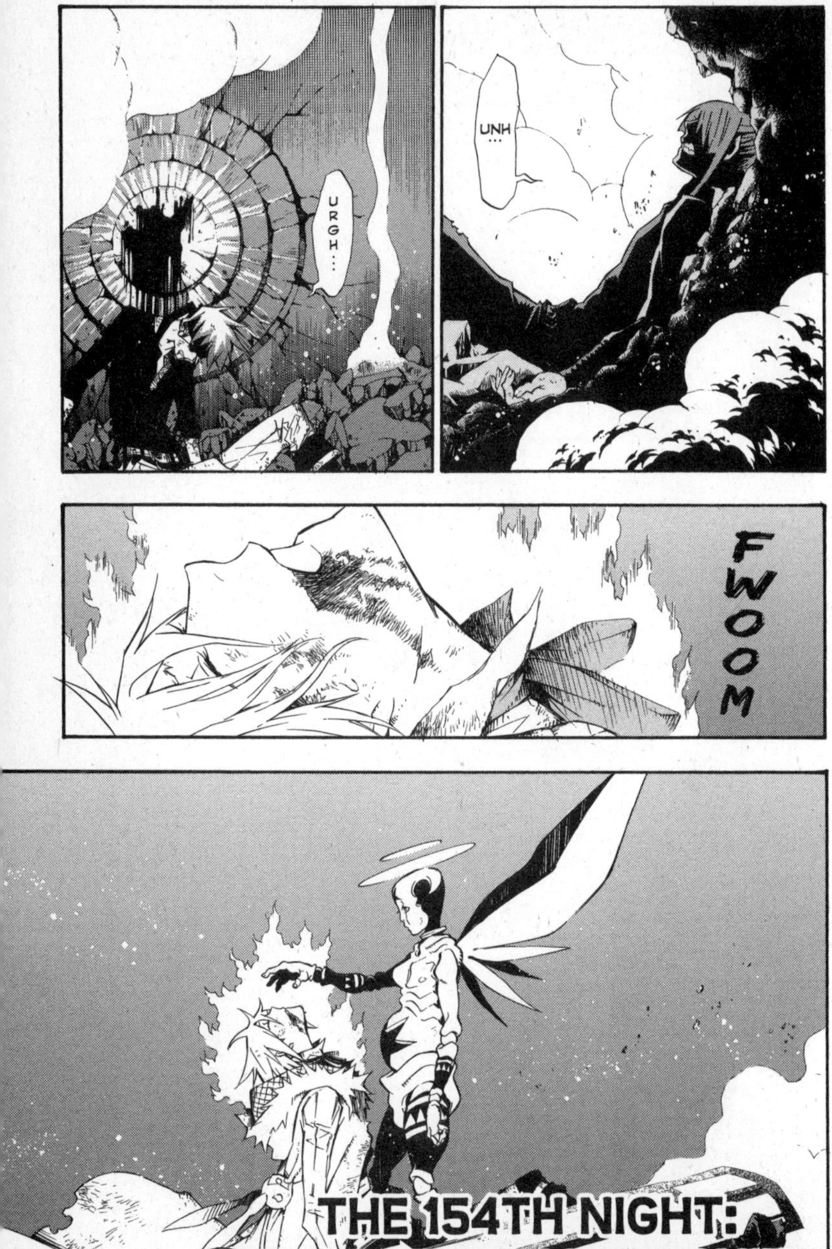
UNH...
URGH...
FWOOOM
THE 154TH NIGHT:
THE BATTLE LINES SHIFT

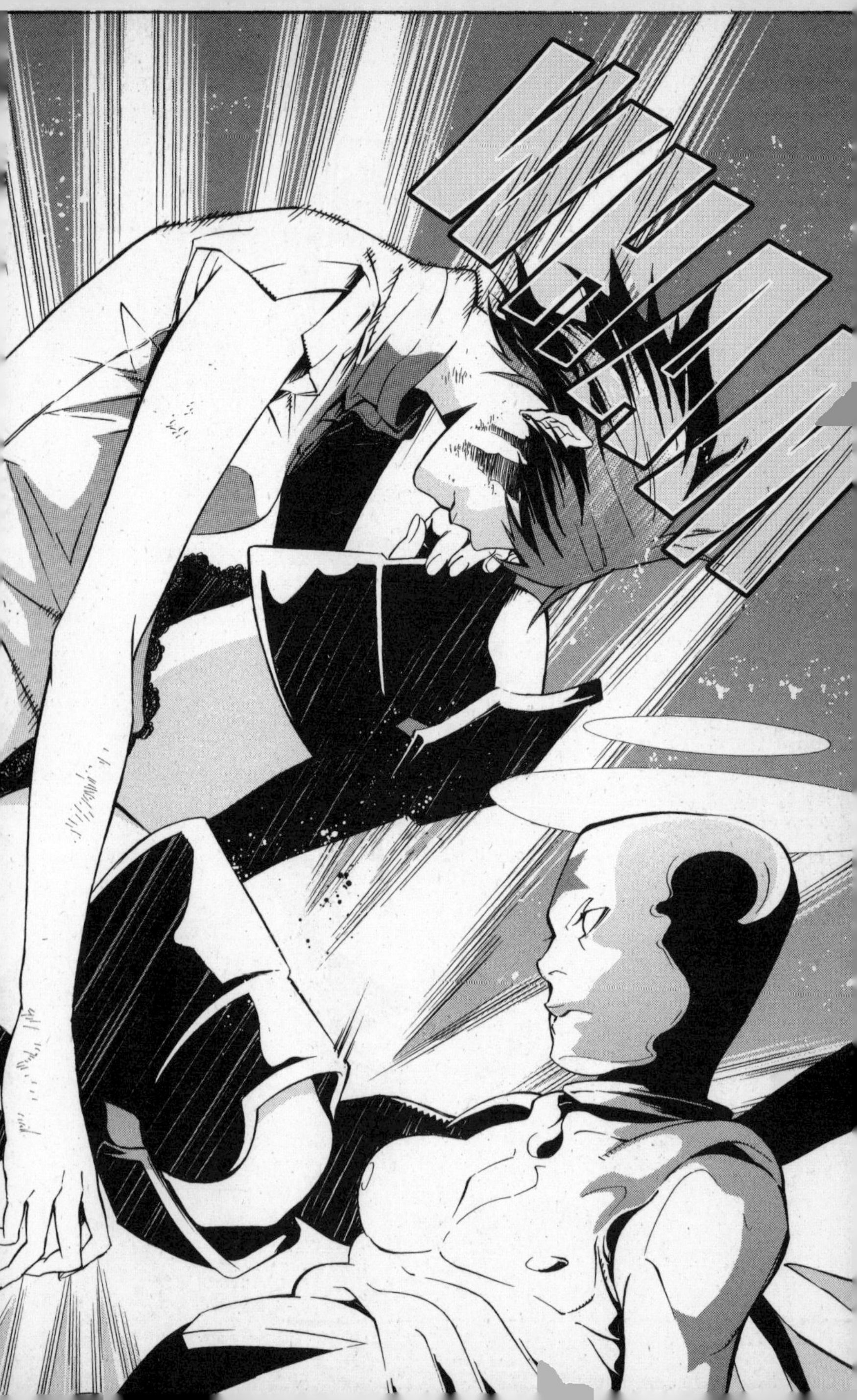

READ THIS WAY

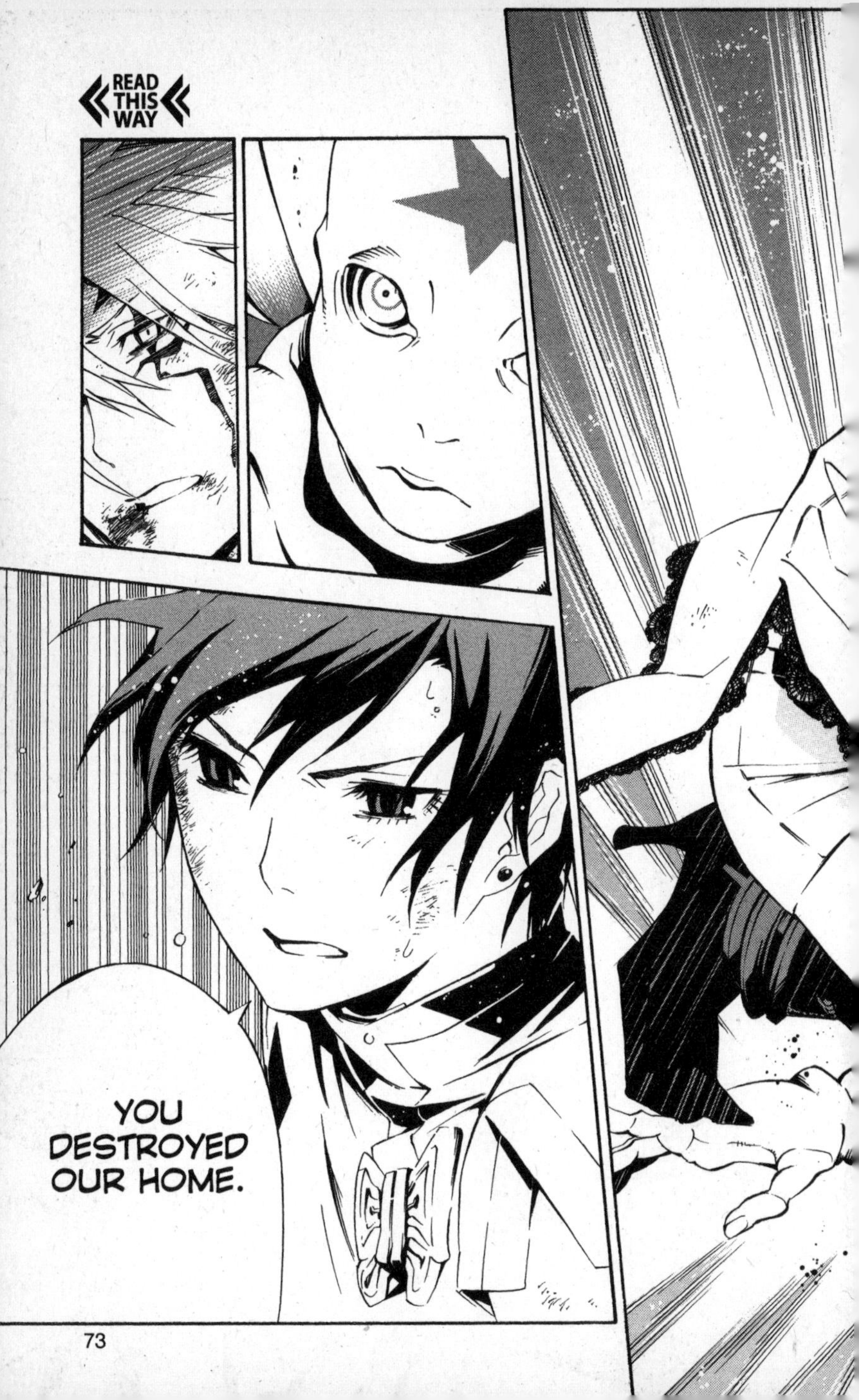
YOU DESTROYED OUR HOME.

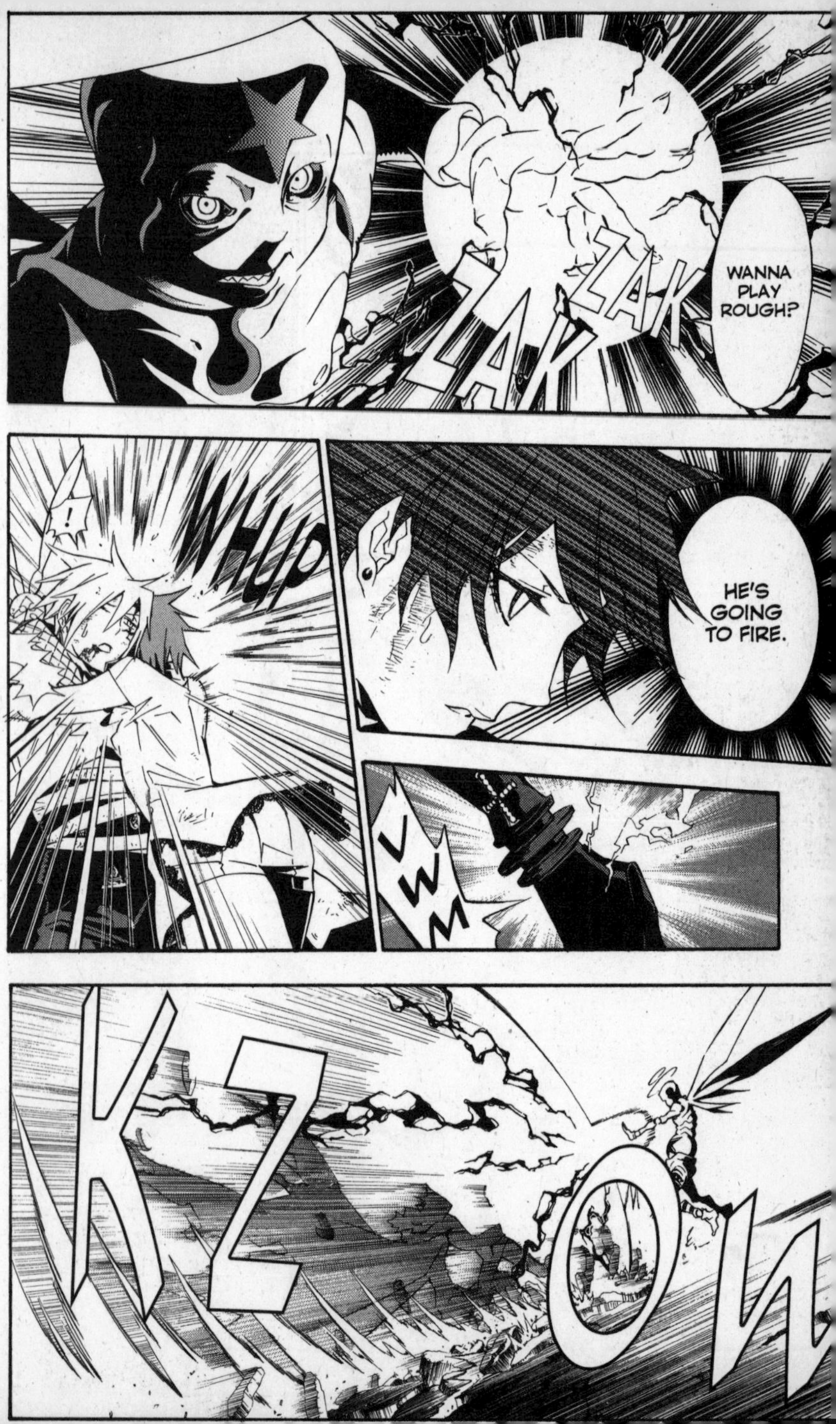
WANNA PLAY ROUGH?
ZAK ZAK
HE'S GOING TO FIRE.
VWM
!
WHUP
KZOW

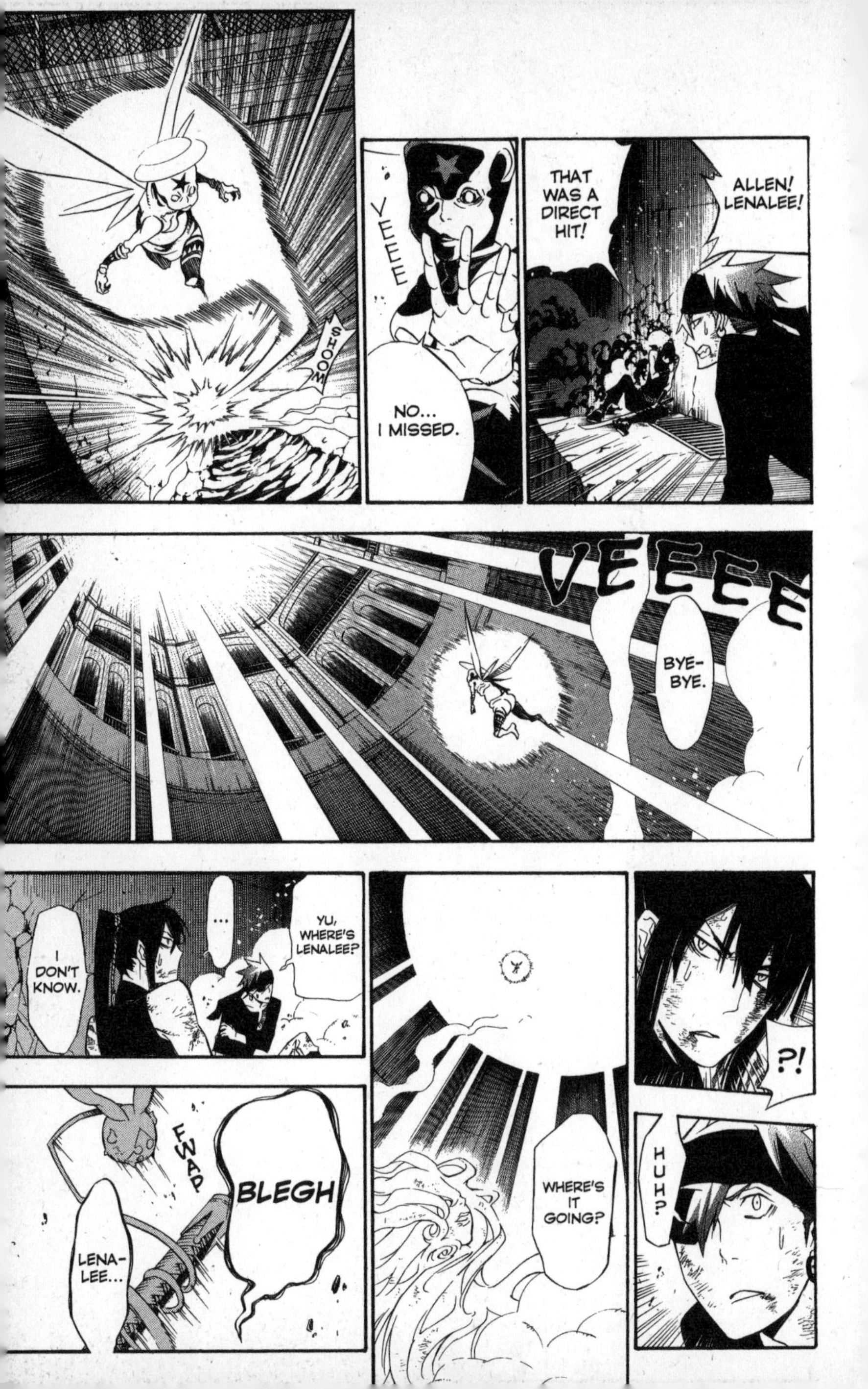
ALLEN! LENALEE!
THAT WAS A DIRECT HIT!
VEEE
NO... I MISSED.
SHOOM
VEEEE
BYE-BYE.
?!
HUH?
WHERE'S IT GOING?
YU, WHERE'S LENALEE?
...
I DON'T KNOW.
BLEGH
FWAP
LENA-LEE...

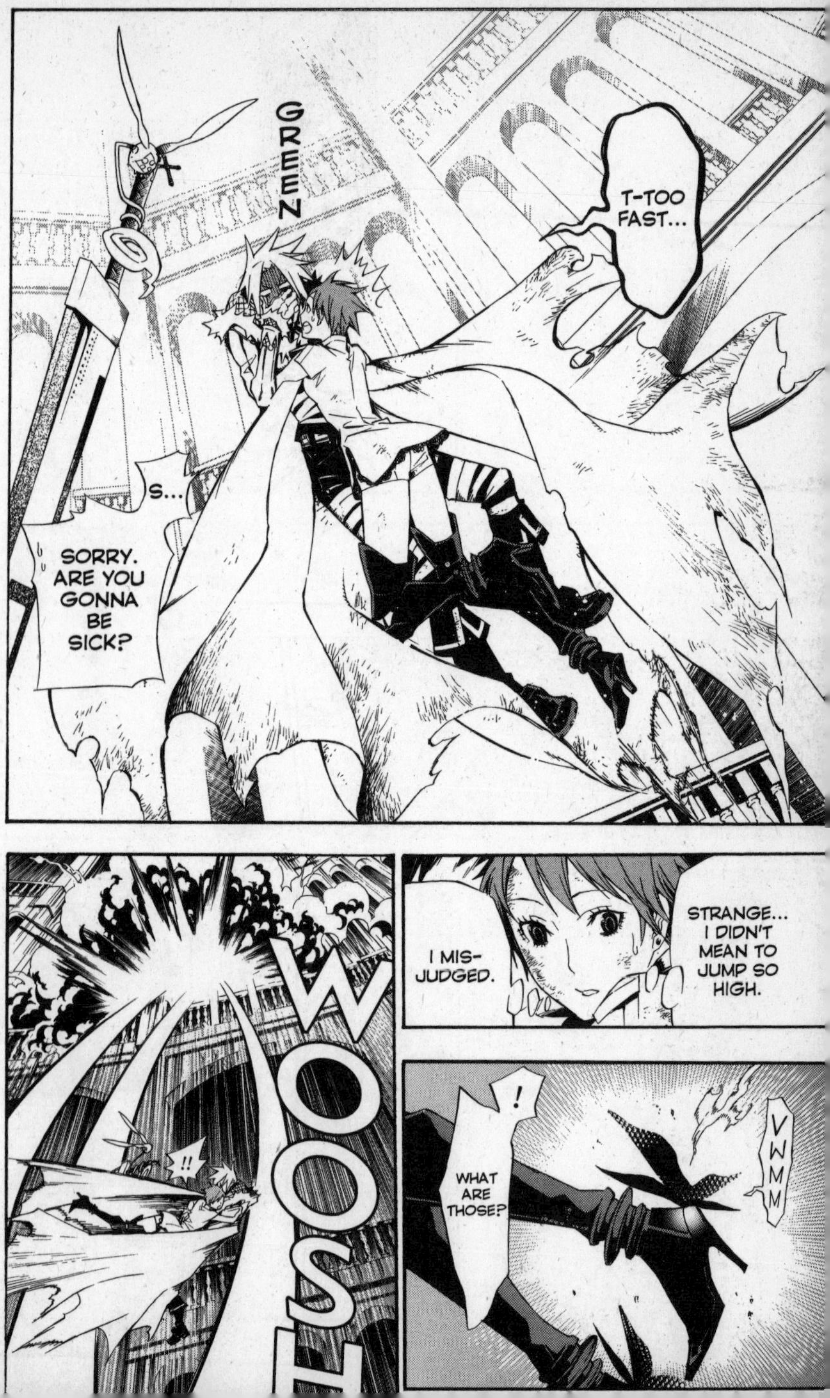

T-TOO FAST...
GREEN
S...
SORRY. ARE YOU GONNA BE SICK?
STRANGE... I DIDN'T MEAN TO JUMP SO HIGH.
I MIS-JUDGED.
VWMM
!
WHAT ARE THOSE?
WOOSH
!!

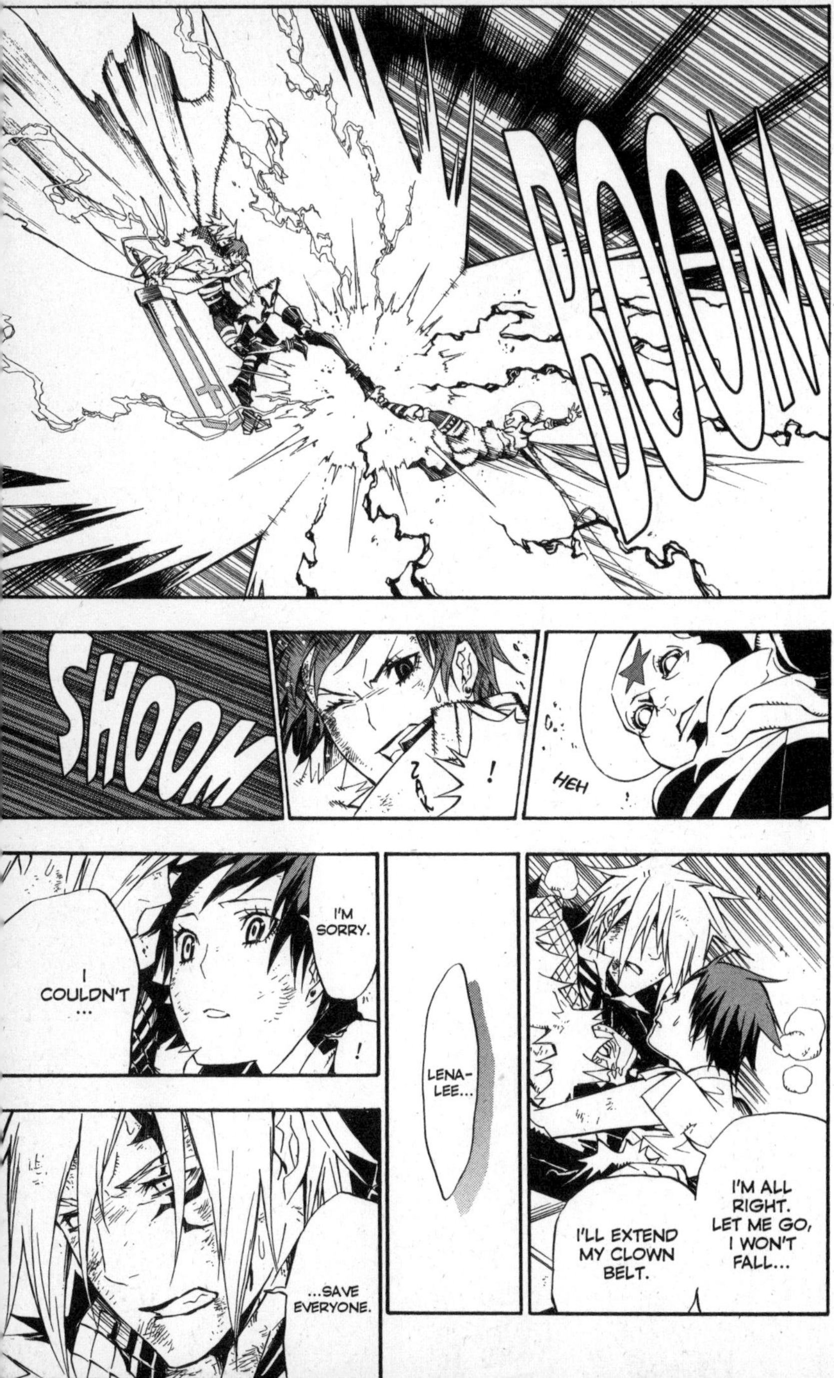
BOOM
HEH
ZAK
!
SHOOM
I'M ALL RIGHT. LET ME GO, I WON'T FALL...
I'LL EXTEND MY CLOWN BELT.
LENA-LEE...
I'M SORRY.
I COULDN'T ...
!
...SAVE EVERYONE.

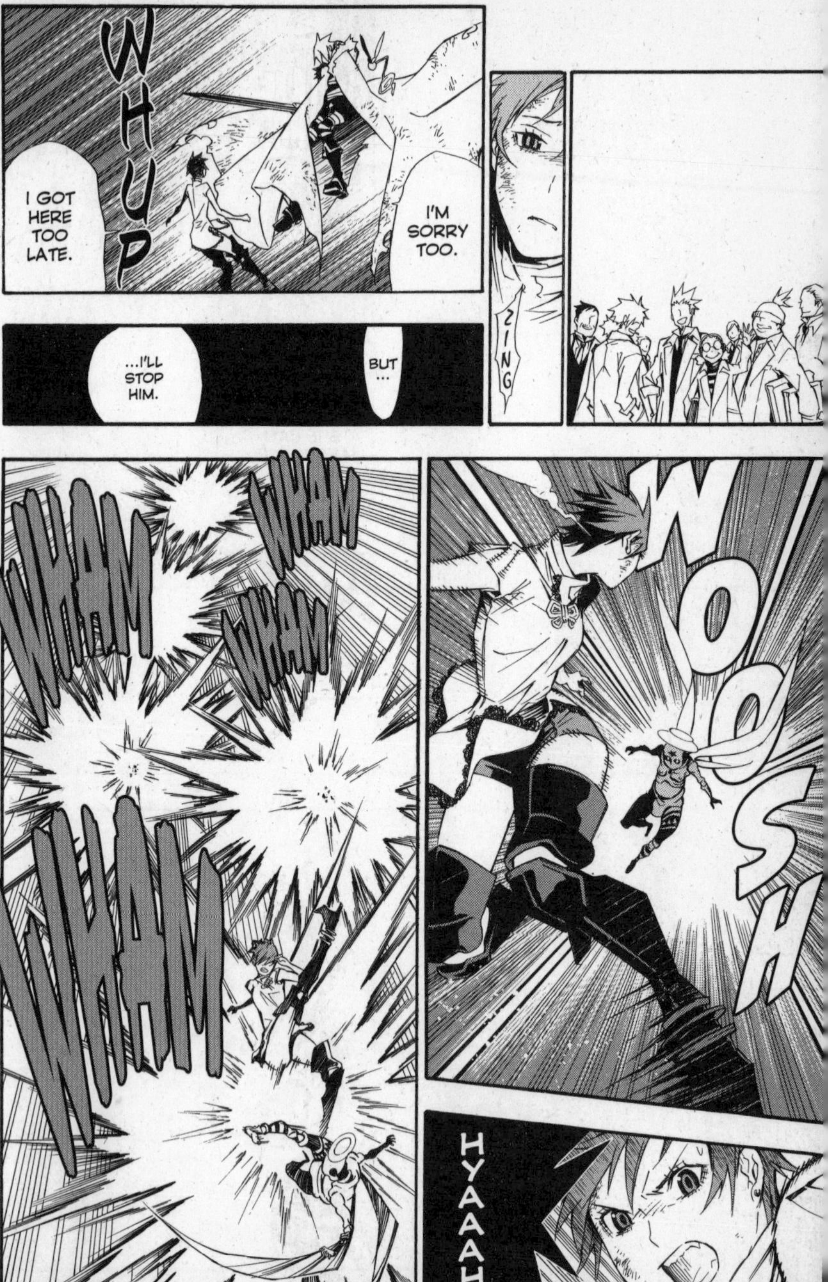
ZING
I'M SORRY TOO.
WHUP
I GOT HERE TOO LATE.
BUT ...
...I'LL STOP HIM.
WOOSH
HYAAAH!
WHAM
WHAM
WHAM
WHAM
WHAM

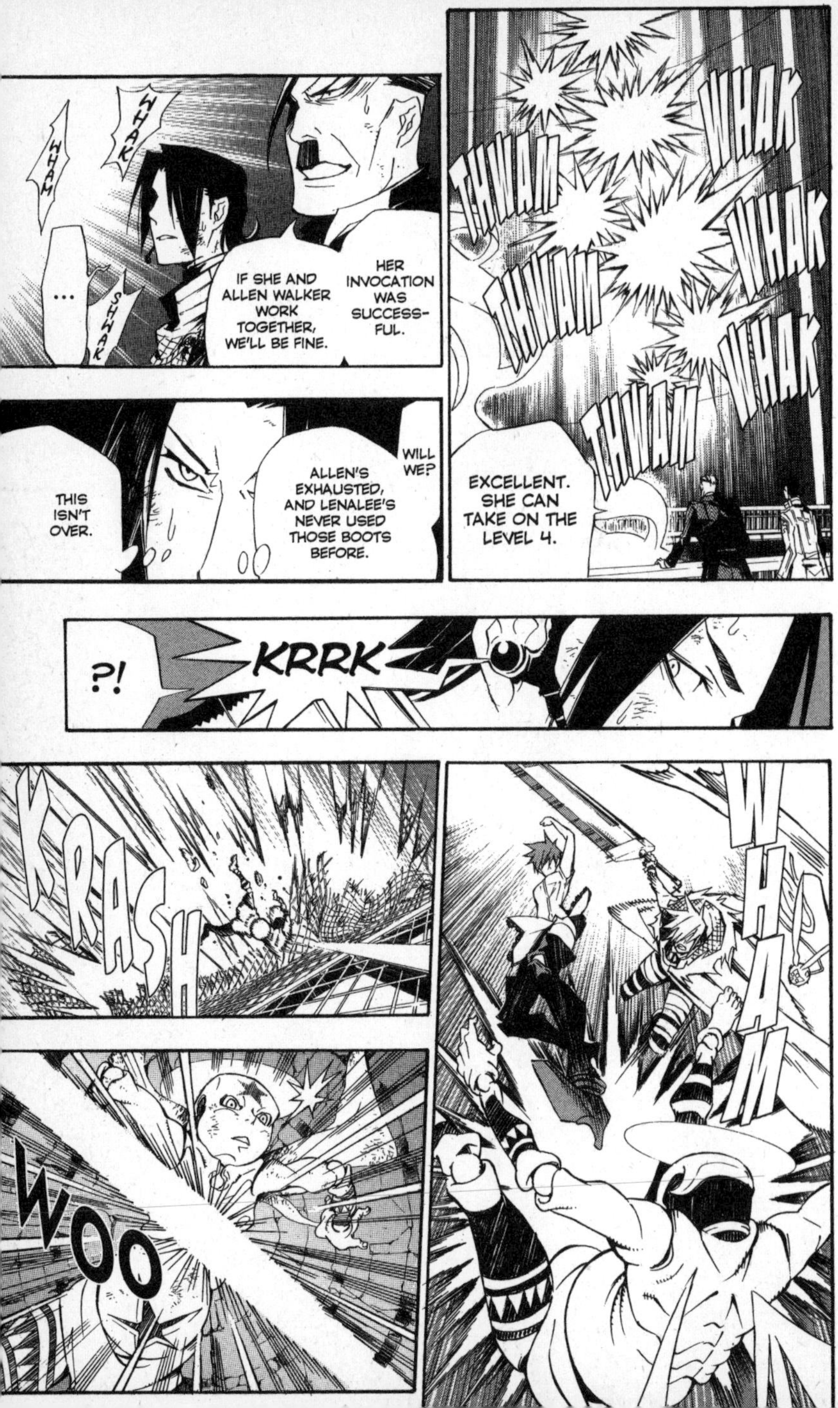

WHAK
THWAM
WHAK
THWAM
WHAK
THWAM
EXCELLENT. SHE CAN TAKE ON THE LEVEL 4.
HER INVOCATION WAS SUCCESS-FUL.
IF SHE AND ALLEN WALKER WORK TOGETHER, WE'LL BE FINE.
WHAK
WHAM
SHWAK
...
WILL WE?
ALLEN'S EXHAUSTED, AND LENALEE'S NEVER USED THOSE BOOTS BEFORE.
THIS ISN'T OVER.
KRRK
?!
WHAM
KRASH
WOO

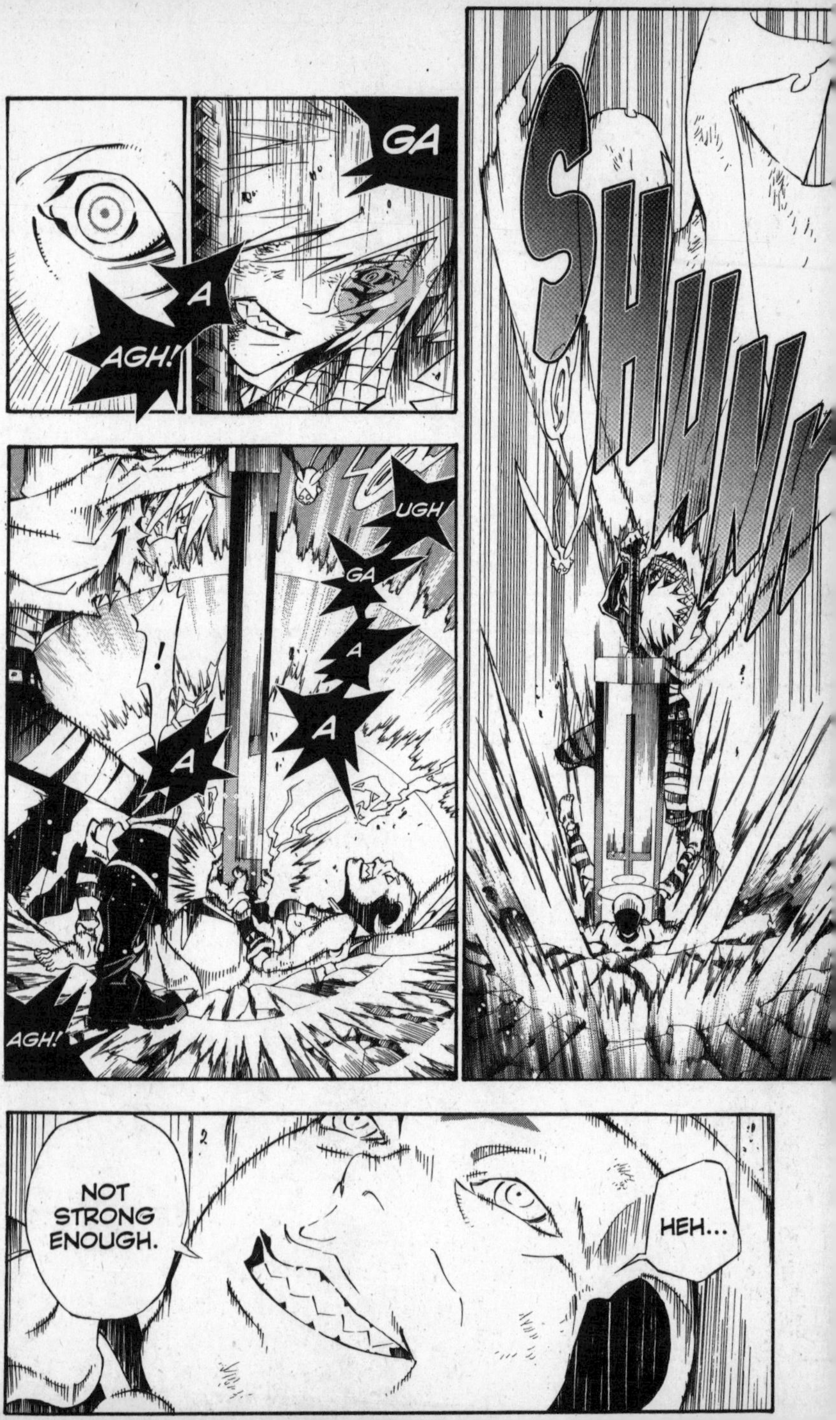
SHHUNK
GA
A
AGH!
UGH
GA
A
A
!
A
AGH!
HEH...
NOT STRONG ENOUGH.

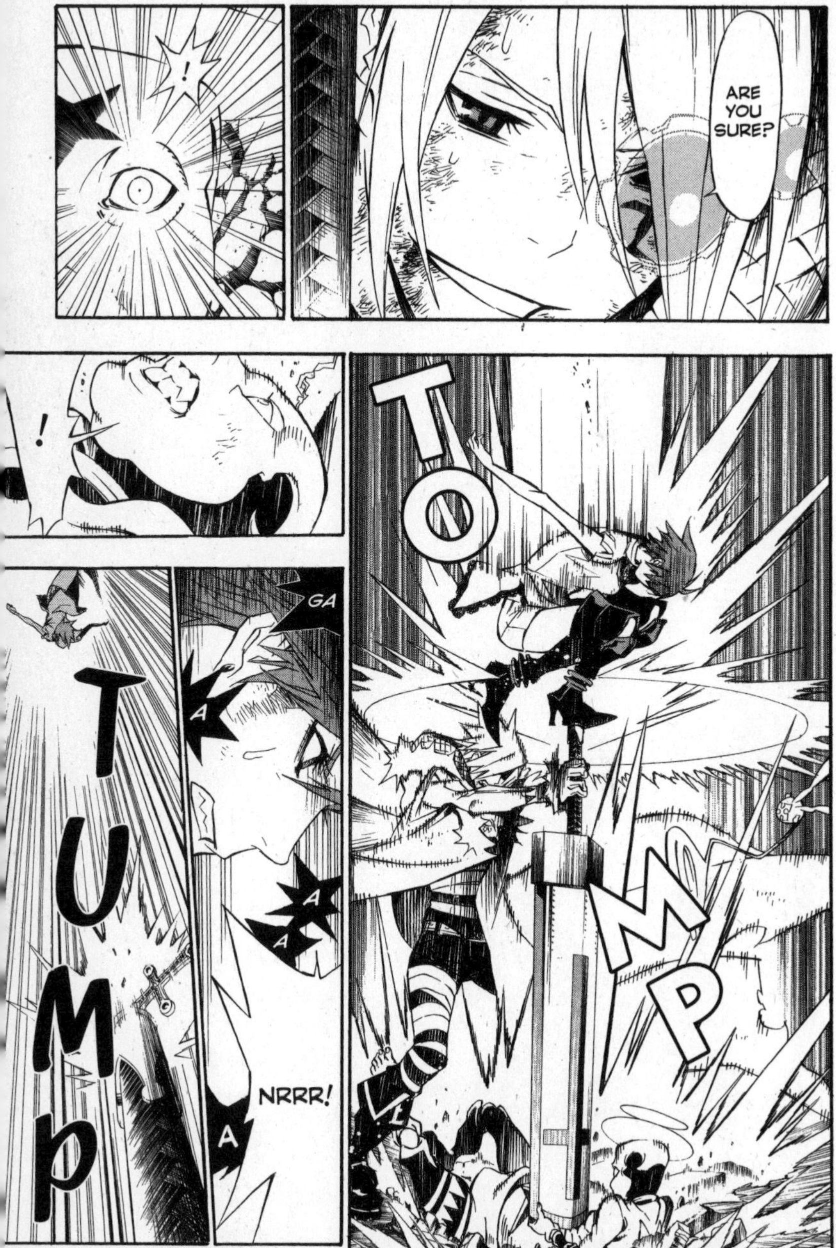
ARE YOU SURE?
!
TOMP
!
GA
A
A
A
A
NRRR!
TUMP

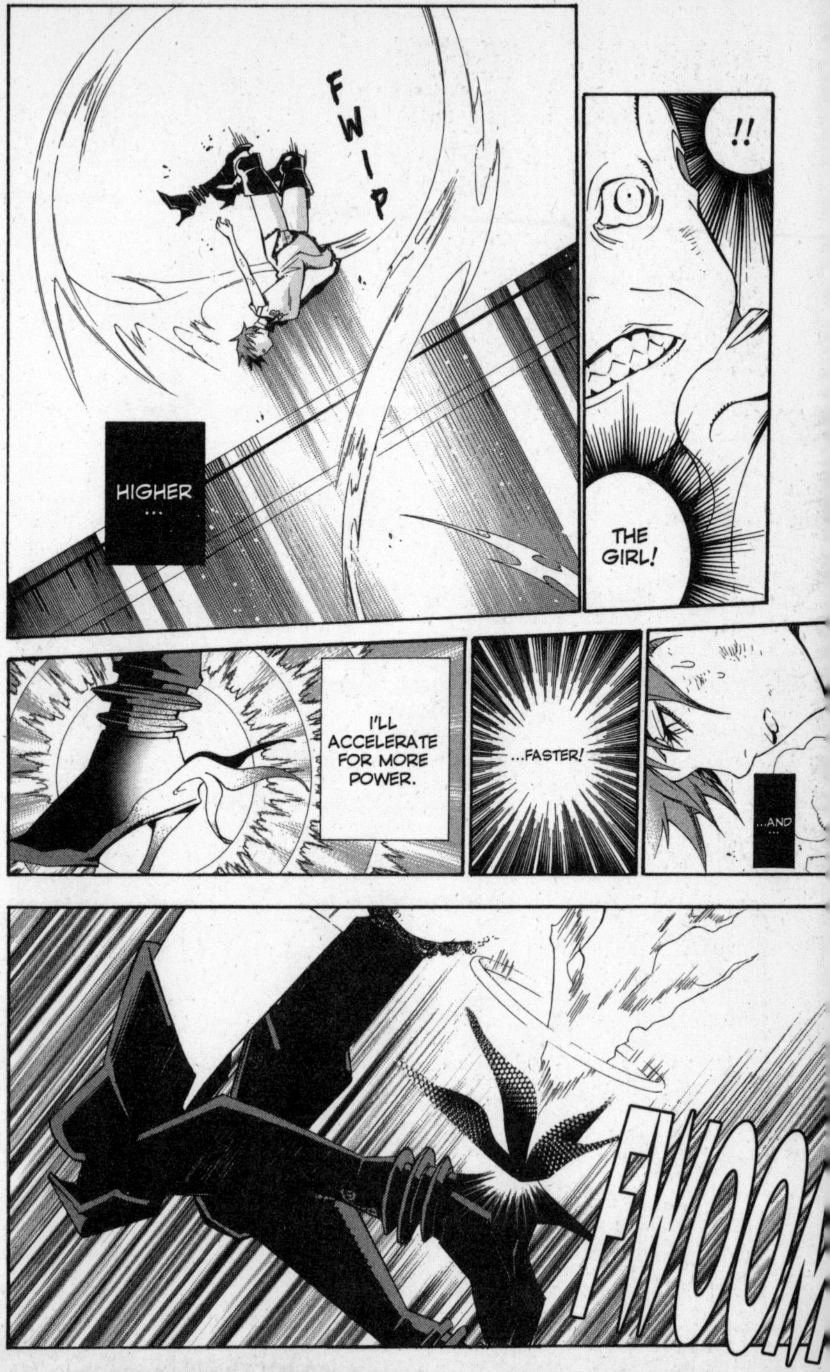
!!
THE GIRL!
FWIP
HIGHER...
...AND...
...FASTER!
I'LL ACCELERATE FOR MORE POWER.
FWOOM

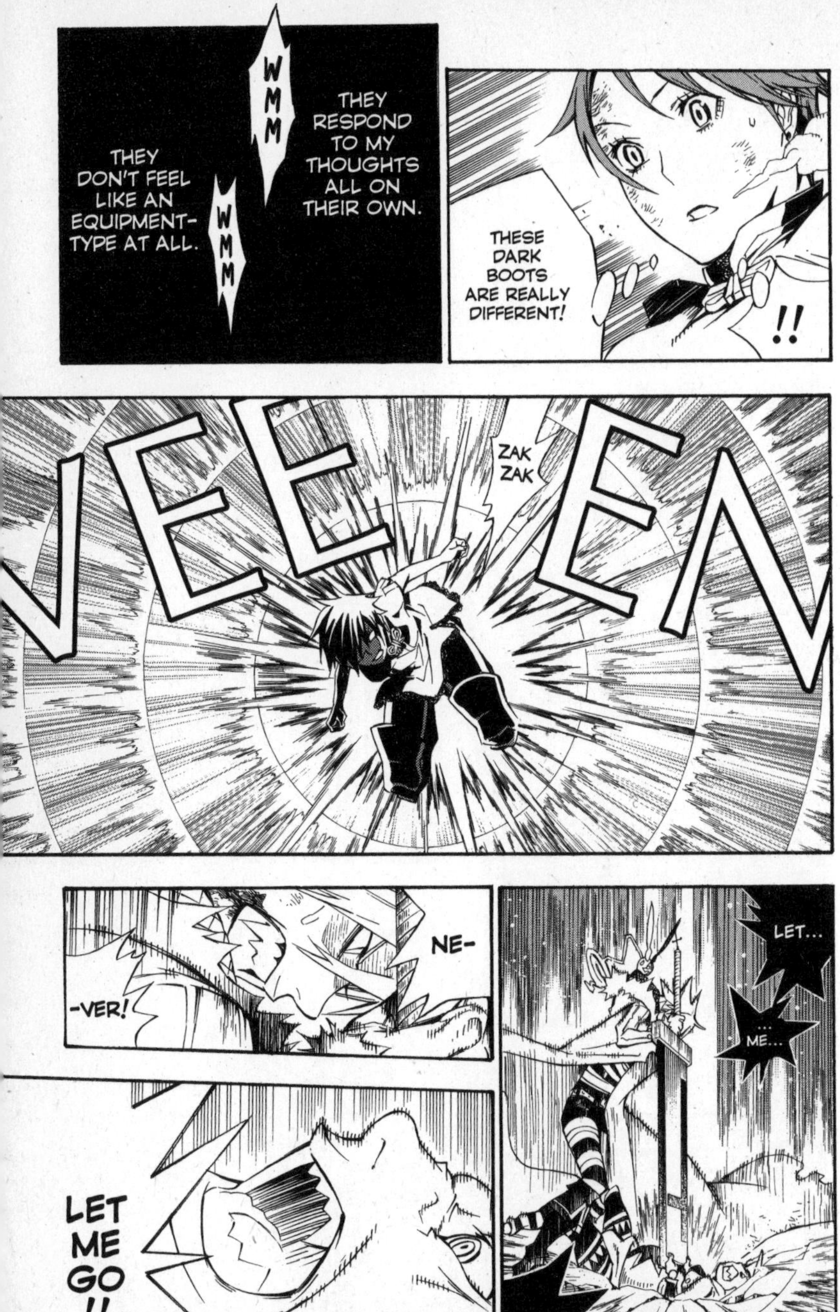
THESE DARK BOOTS ARE REALLY DIFFERENT!
!!
WMM
THEY RESPOND TO MY THOUGHTS ALL ON THEIR OWN.
WMM
THEY DON'T FEEL LIKE AN EQUIPMENT-TYPE AT ALL.
VEEEN
ZAK ZAK
LET...
... ME...
...GO!
NE-
-VER!
LET ME GO!!

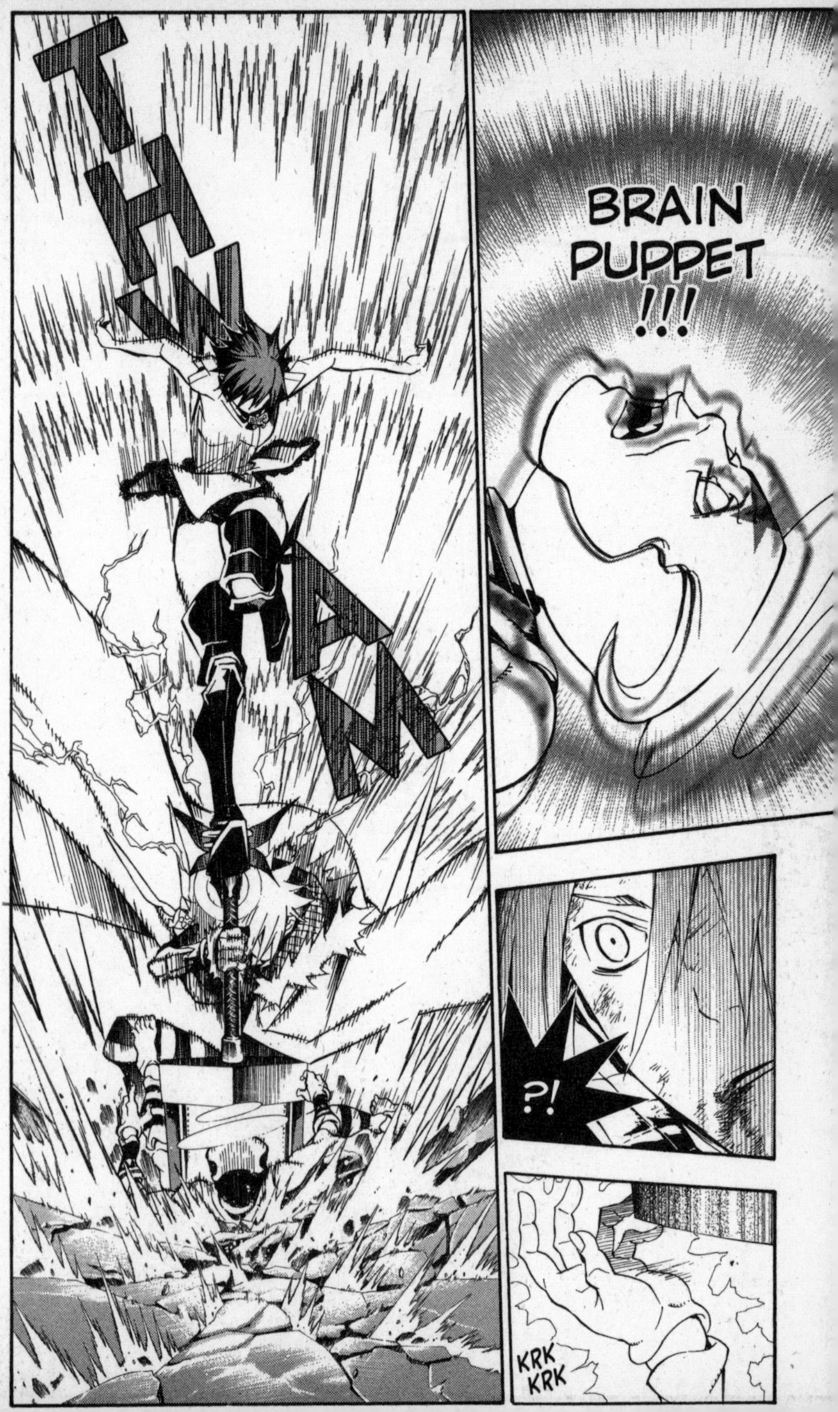
BRAIN PUPPET !!!
?!
KRK KRK
THWAM

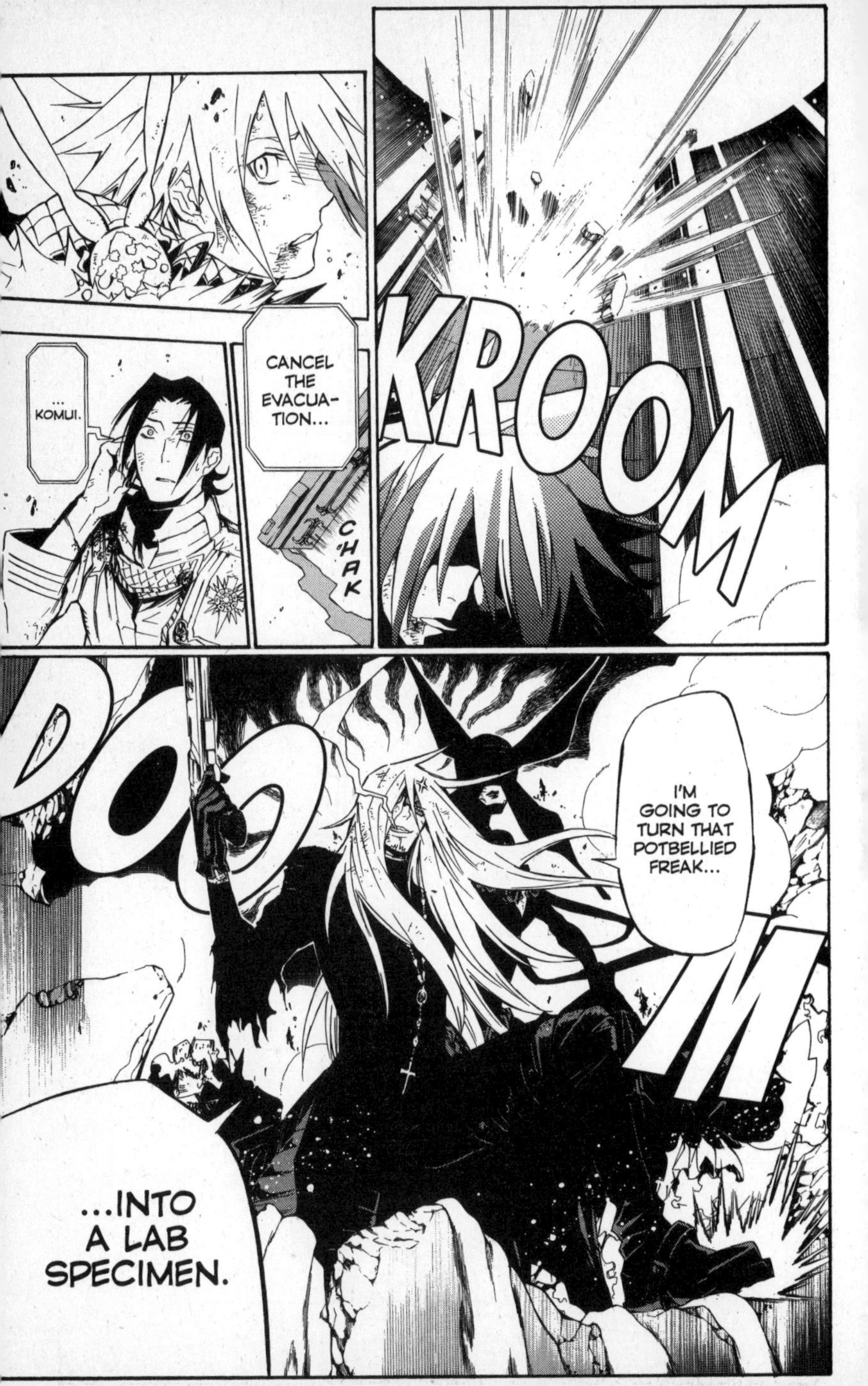
KROOM
CANCEL THE EVACUATION...
CHAK
...KOMUI.
I'M GOING TO TURN THAT POTBELLIED FREAK...
DOOM
...INTO A LAB SPECIMEN.

THE PEOPLE OF D.GRAY HOUSE

A MISUNDERSTANDING BETWEEN LOVING SIBLINGS

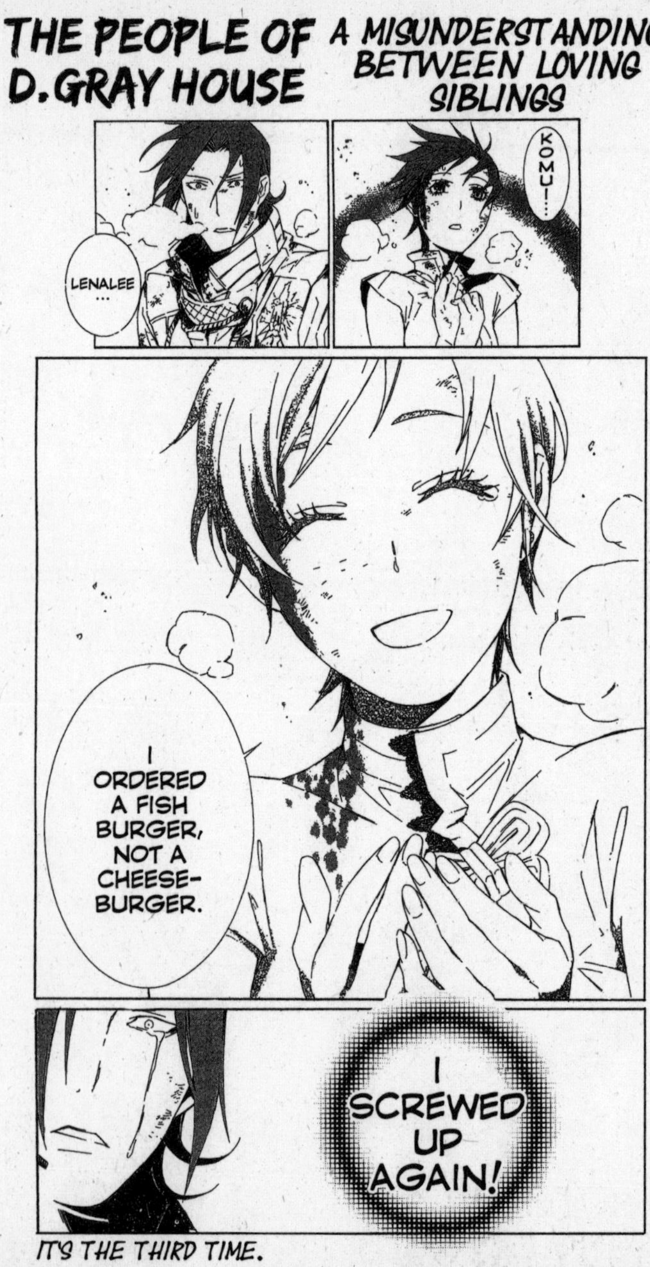
KOMUI...
LENALEE...
I ORDERED A FISH BURGER, NOT A CHEESE-BURGER.
I SCREWED UP AGAIN!

IT'S THE THIRD TIME.

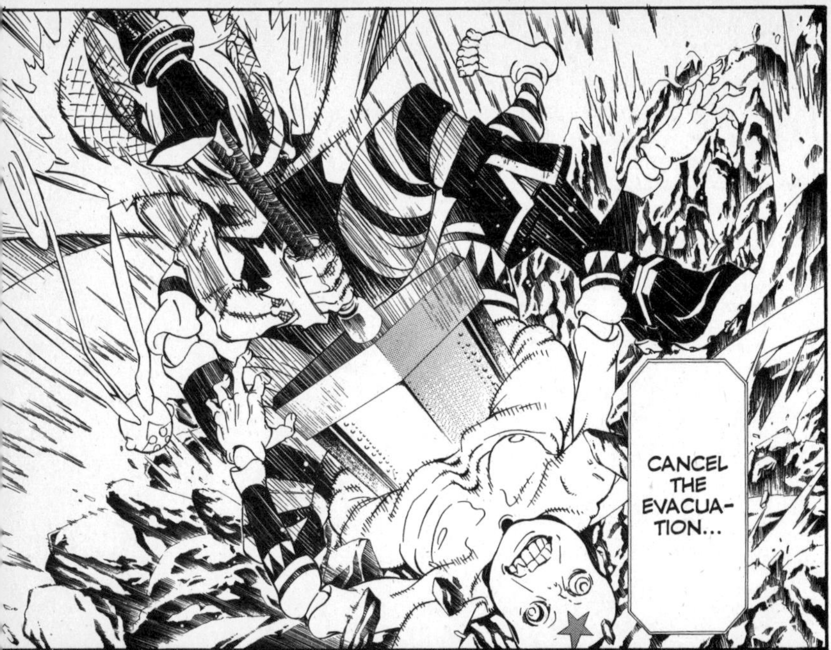
CANCEL THE EVACUA- TION...

THE 155TH NIGHT: ECHOES IN THE LONG MORNING

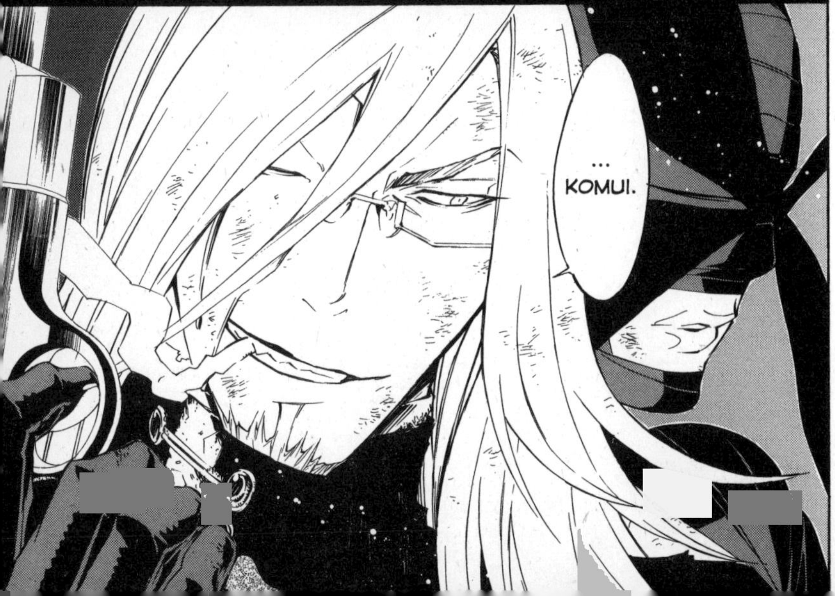
... KOMUI.

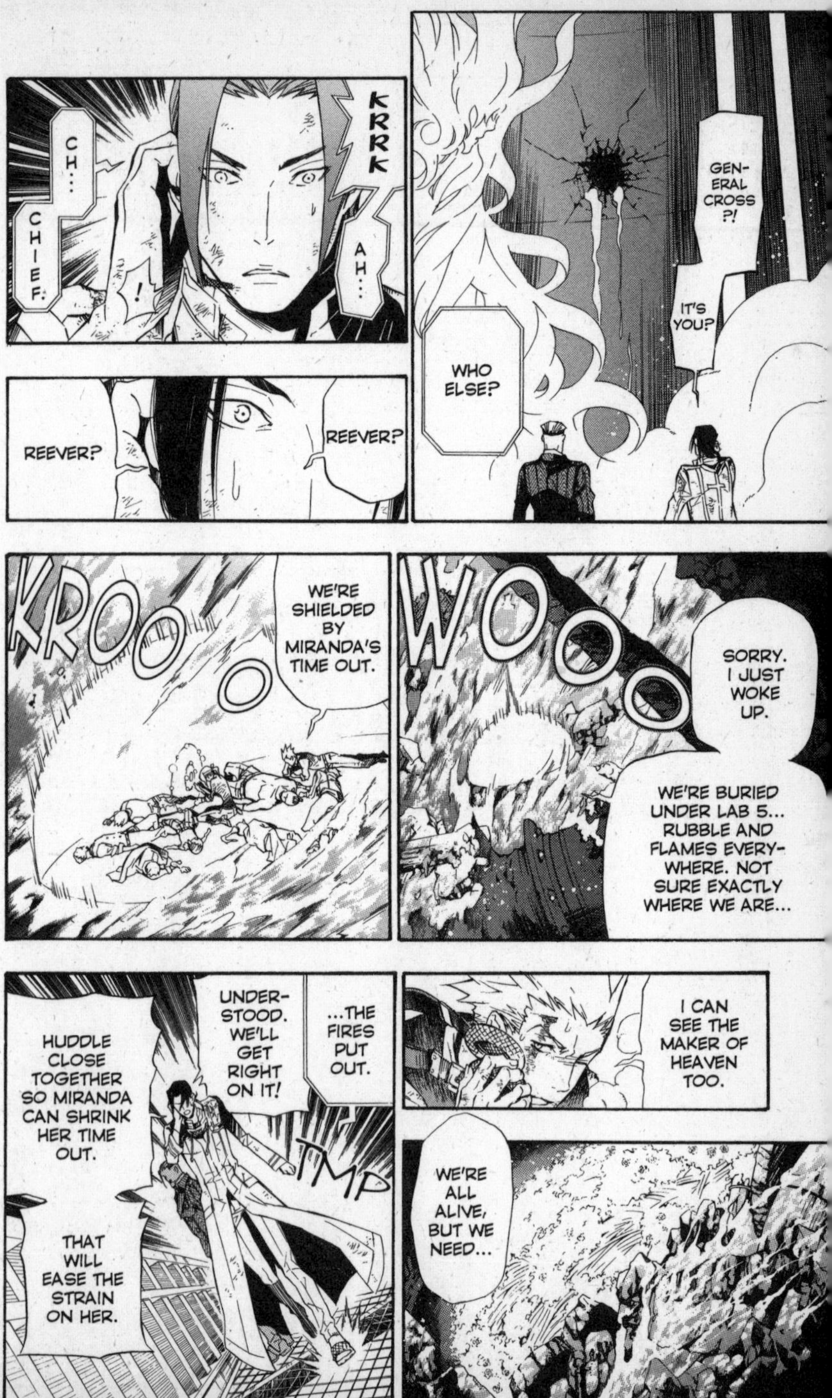
GENERAL CROSS?!
IT'S YOU?
WHO ELSE?
KRRK
AH...
!
CH...
CHIEF.
REEVER?
REEVER?
WOOOO
SORRY. I JUST WOKE UP.
WE'RE BURIED UNDER LAB 5... RUBBLE AND FLAMES EVERYWHERE. NOT SURE EXACTLY WHERE WE ARE...
WE'RE SHIELDED BY MIRANDA'S TIME OUT.
KROOOO
I CAN SEE THE MAKER OF HEAVEN TOO.
WE'RE ALL ALIVE, BUT WE NEED...
...THE FIRES PUT OUT.
UNDERSTOOD. WE'LL GET RIGHT ON IT!
HUDDLE CLOSE TOGETHER SO MIRANDA CAN SHRINK HER TIME OUT.
TMP
THAT WILL EASE THE STRAIN ON HER.

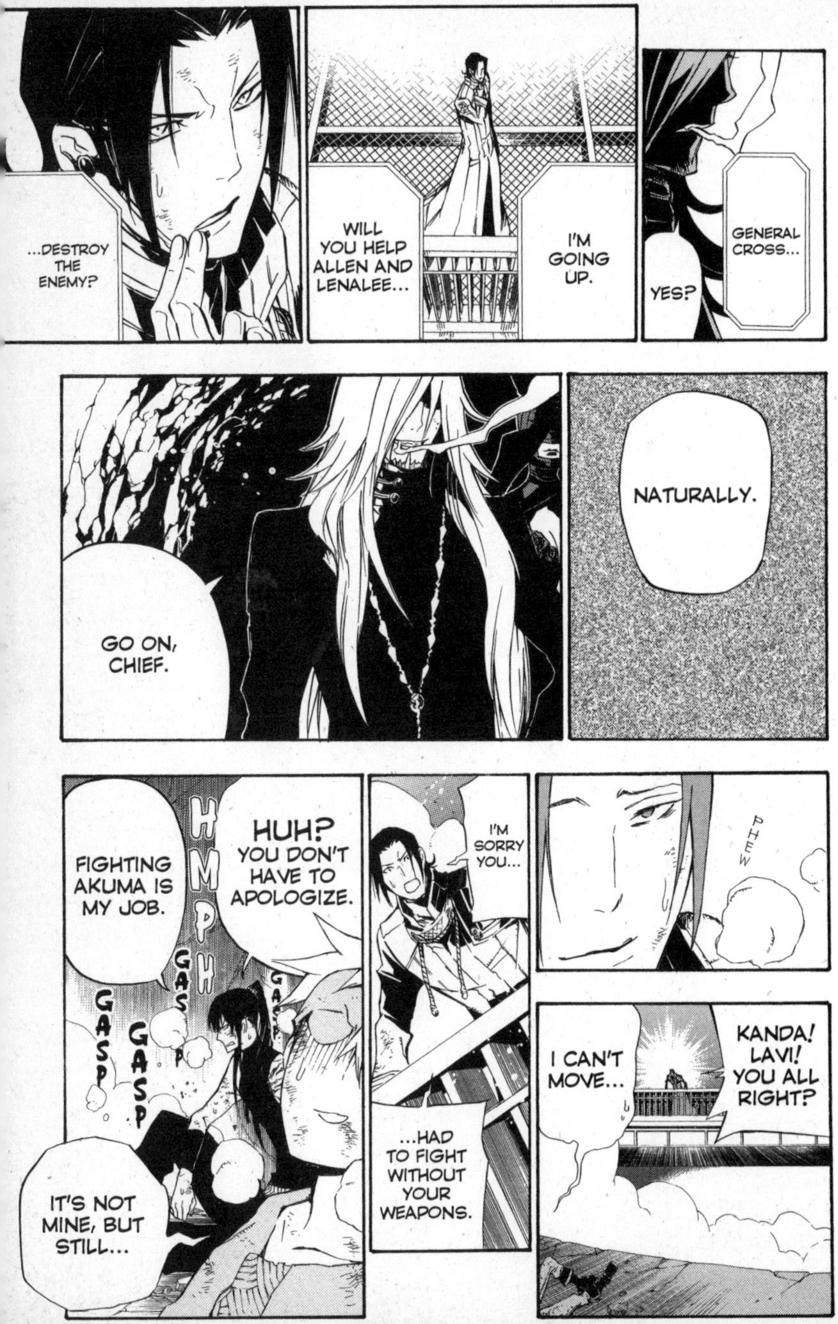
GENERAL CROSS...
YES?
I'M GOING UP.
WILL YOU HELP ALLEN AND LENALEE...
...DESTROY THE ENEMY?
NATURALLY.
GO ON, CHIEF.
PHEW
KANDA! LAVI! YOU ALL RIGHT?
I CAN'T MOVE...
I'M SORRY YOU...
...HAD TO FIGHT WITHOUT YOUR WEAPONS.
HUH? YOU DON'T HAVE TO APOLOGIZE.
HMPH
FIGHTING AKUMA IS MY JOB.
GASP GASP
GASP GASP
IT'S NOT MINE, BUT STILL...

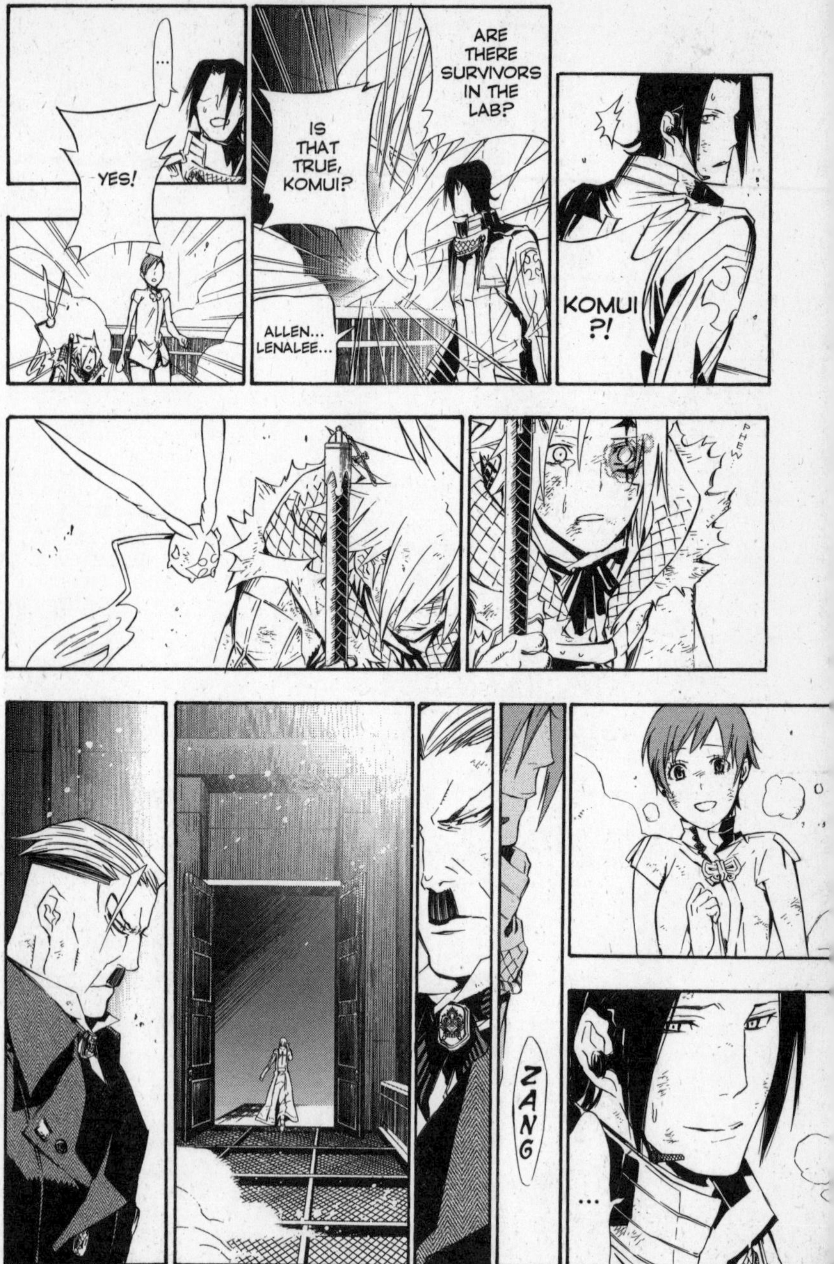
KOMUI ?!
ARE THERE SURVIVORS IN THE LAB?
IS THAT TRUE, KOMUI?
ALLEN... LENALEE...
...
YES!
PHEW
...
ZANG

READ THIS WAY

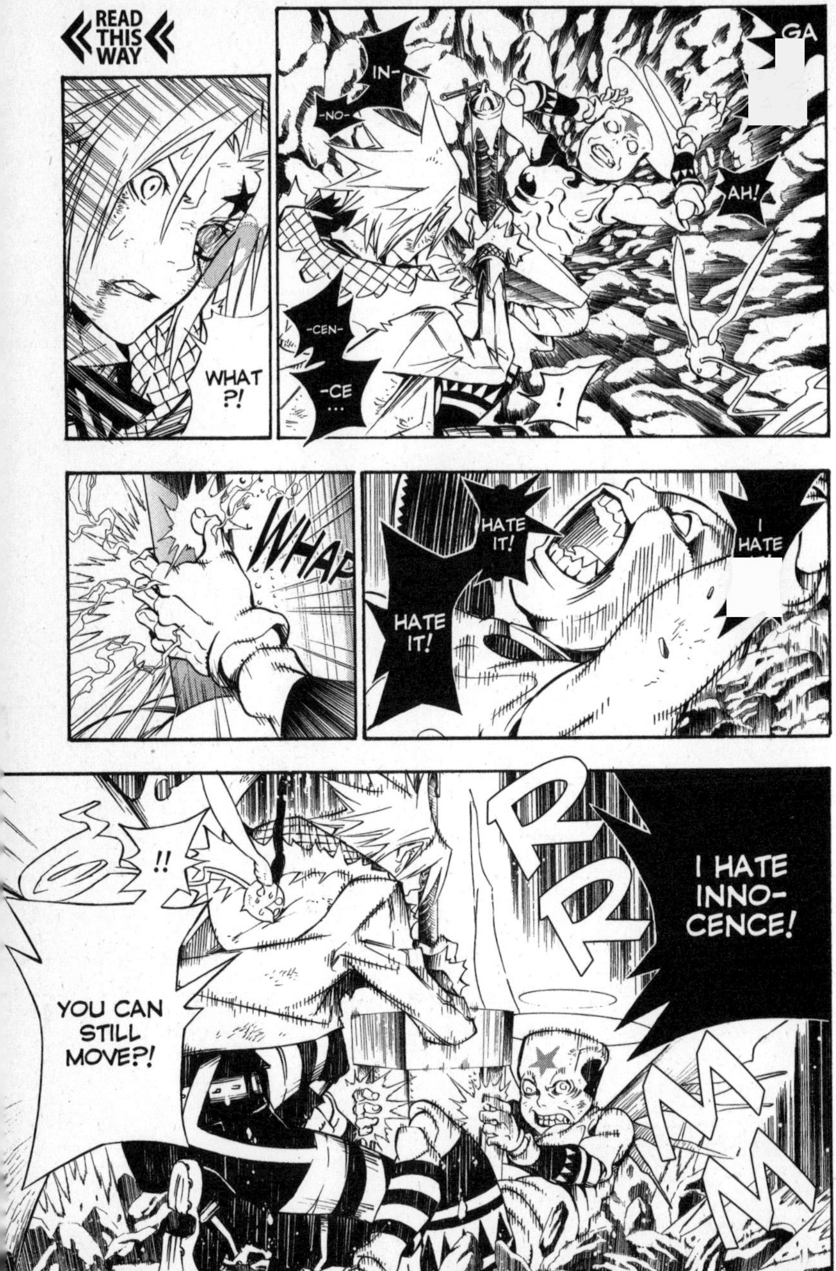
GA
AH!
IN-
-NO-
!
-CEN-
-CE ...
WHAT ?!
I HATE
HATE IT!
HATE IT!
WHAP
I HATE INNO- CENCE!
!!
YOU CAN STILL MOVE?!

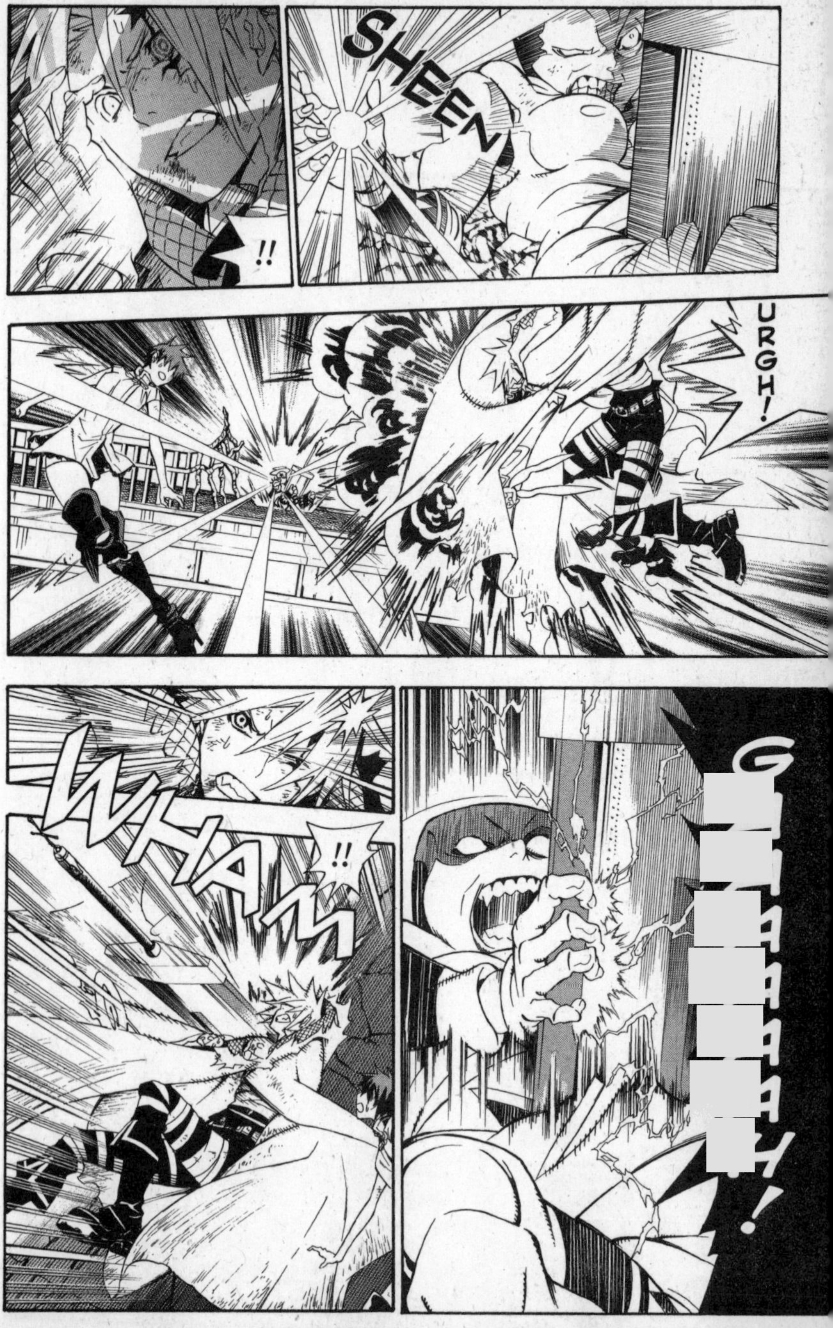
SHEEN
!!
URGH!
WHAM
!!

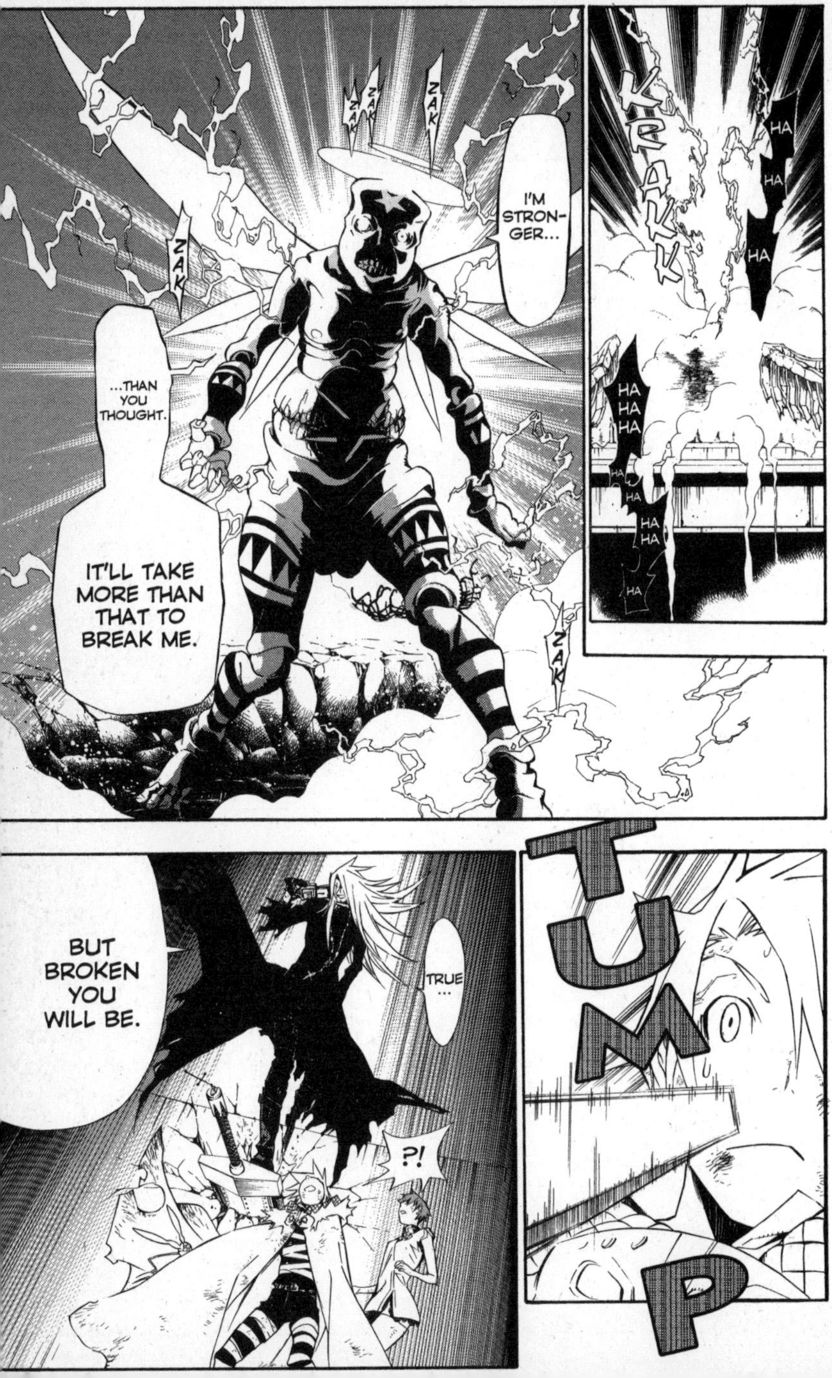
KRAKK
HA HA HA
HA HA HA
HA HA HA HA
HA
ZAK ZAK ZAK
I'M STRONGER...
ZAK
...THAN YOU THOUGHT.
IT'LL TAKE MORE THAN THAT TO BREAK ME.
ZAK
TUMP
BUT BROKEN YOU WILL BE.
TRUE...
?!

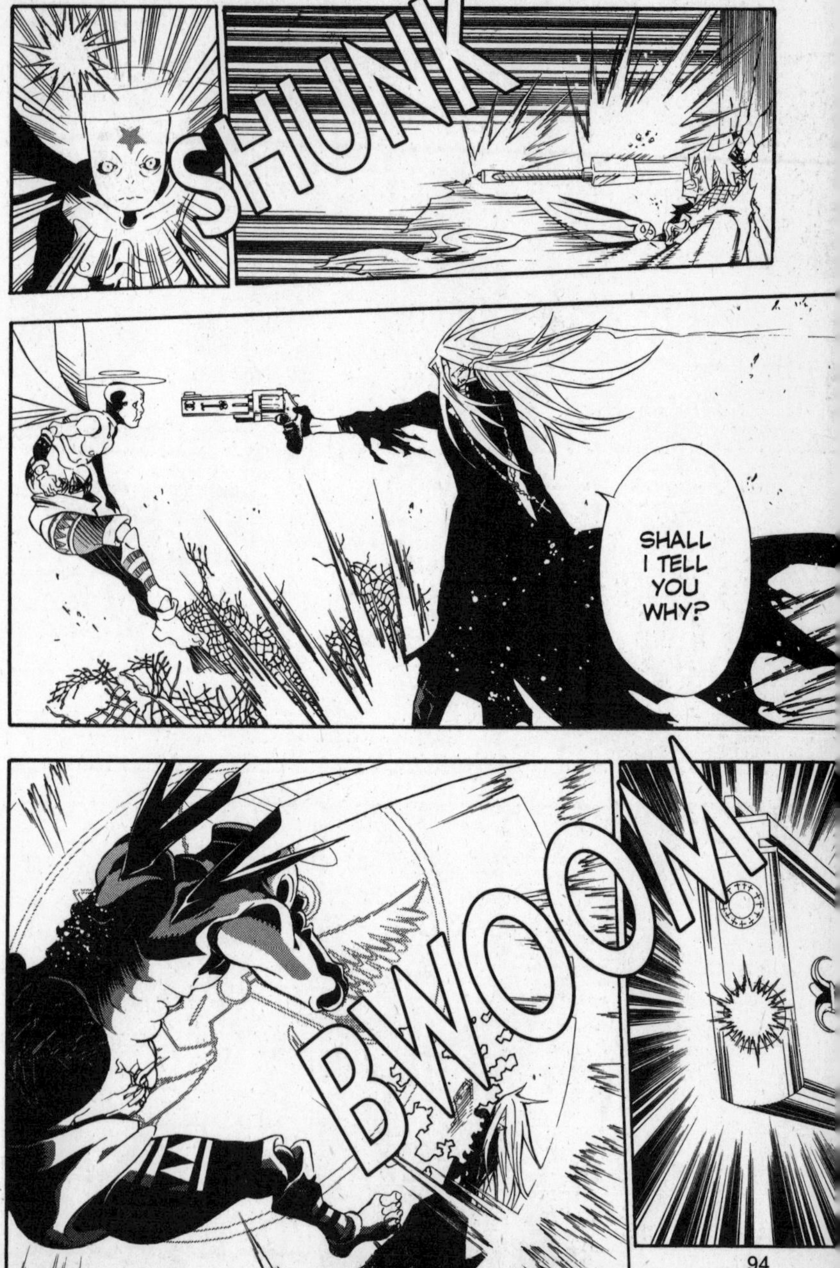
SHUNK
SHALL I TELL YOU WHY?
BWOOOM

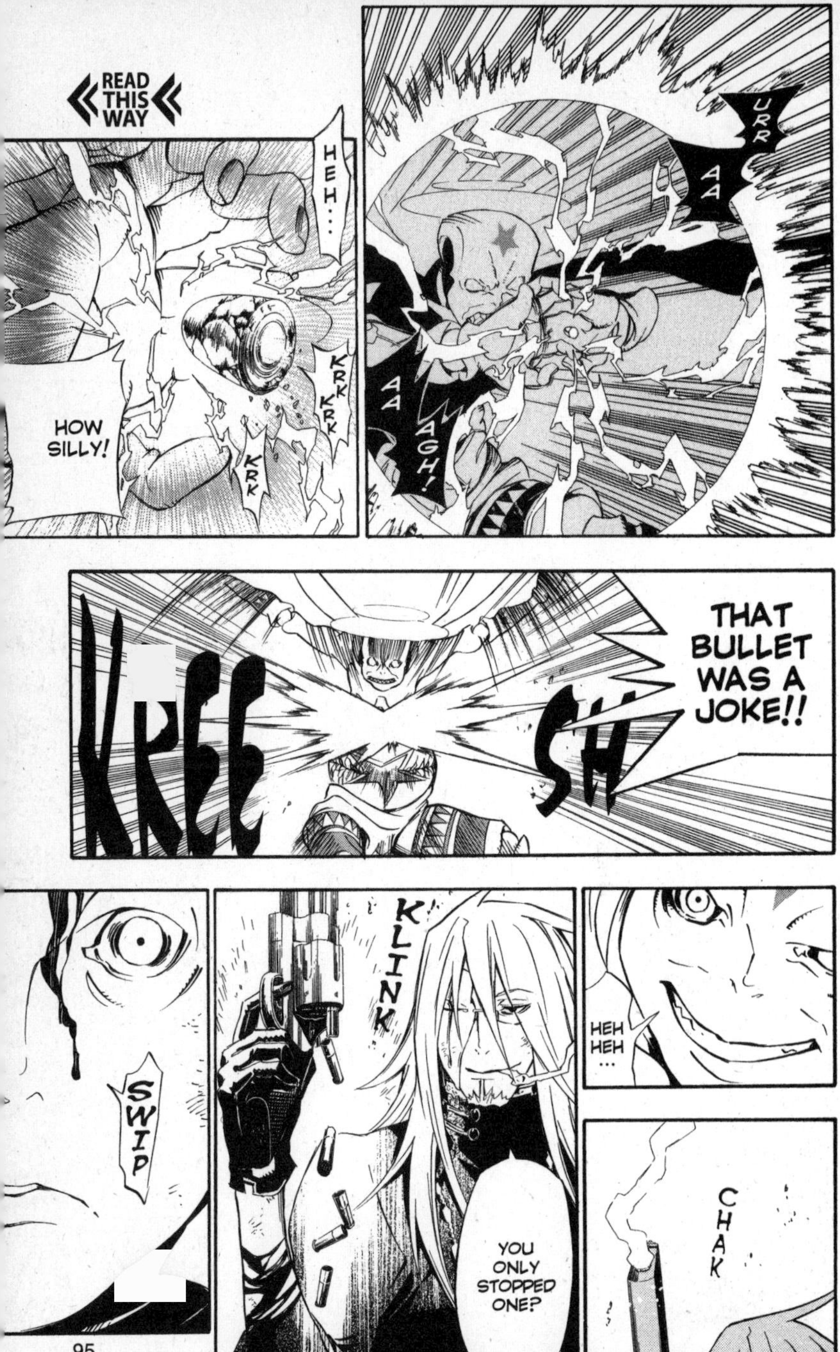
READ THIS WAY
URR AA
AA AGH!
HEH...
KRK KRK KRK
KRK
HOW SILLY!
KREE SH
THAT BULLET WAS A JOKE!!
HEH HEH...
CHAK
KLINK
YOU ONLY STOPPED ONE?
SWIP

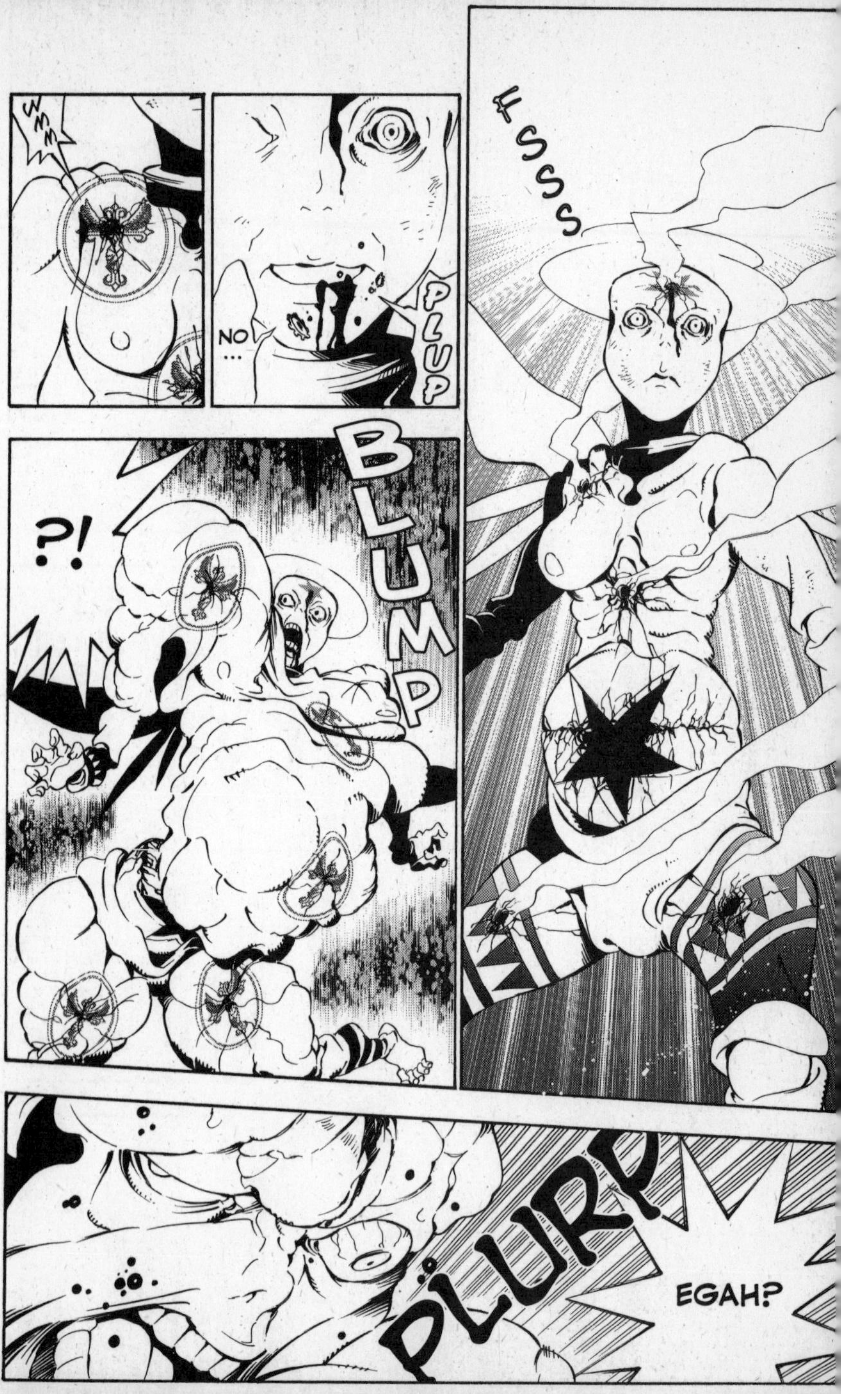
FSSSS
PLUP
NO...
WMM
BLUMP
?!
PLURP
EGAH?

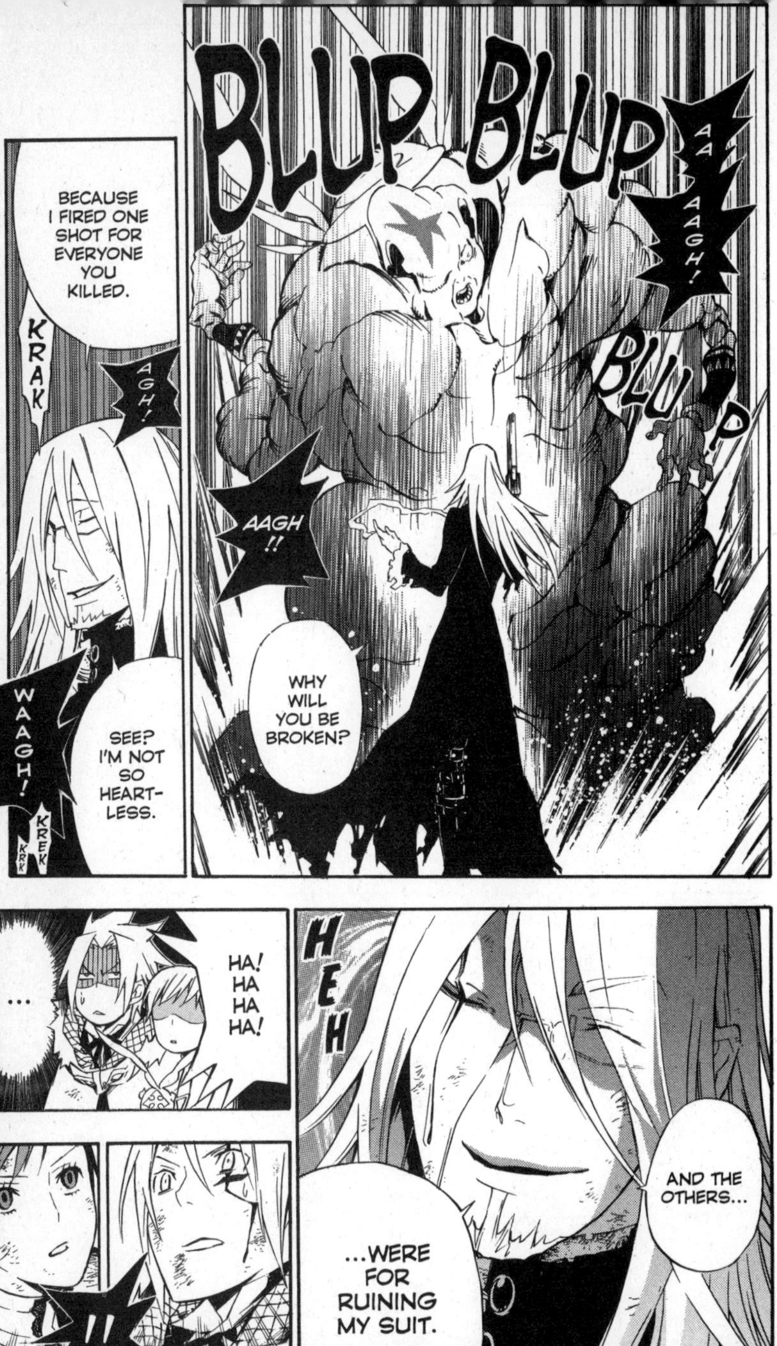

BLUP BLUP
AAAAAGH!
BLUP
AAGH!!
WHY WILL YOU BE BROKEN?
BECAUSE I FIRED ONE SHOT FOR EVERYONE YOU KILLED.
KRAK
AGH!
SEE? I'M NOT SO HEART-LESS.
WAAGH!
KREK
KRK
HEH
AND THE OTHERS...
...WERE FOR RUINING MY SUIT.
HA! HA HA HA!
...
!!

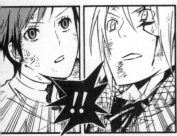

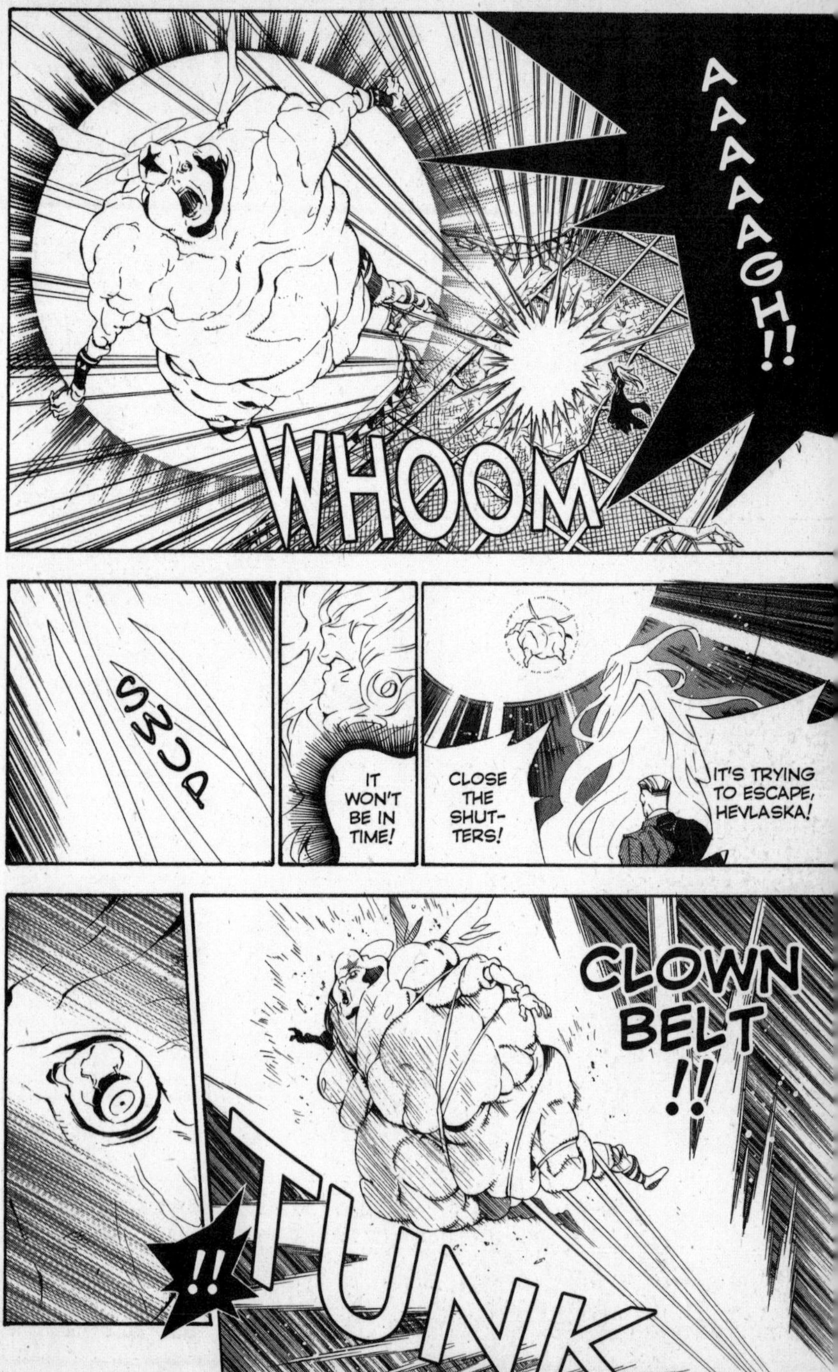
AAAAAGH!!
WHOOM
IT'S TRYING TO ESCAPE, HEVLASKA!
CLOSE THE SHUT-TERS!
IT WON'T BE IN TIME!
SWUP
CLOWN BELT!!
!!
TUNK

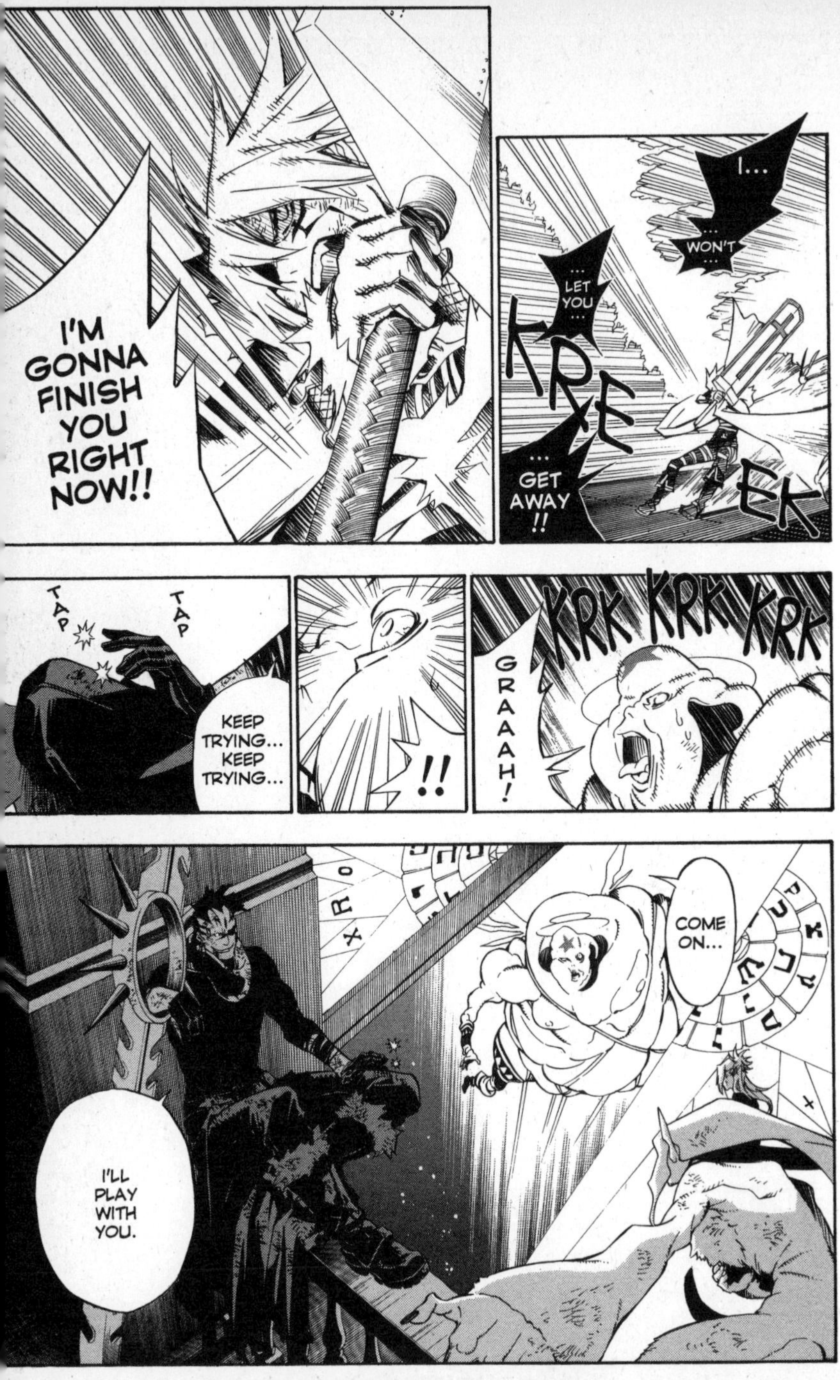
I...
...WON'T...
...LET YOU...
...GET AWAY!!
KREEEK
I'M GONNA FINISH YOU RIGHT NOW!!
KRK KRK KRK
GRAAAH!
!!
TAP TAP
KEEP TRYING... KEEP TRYING...
COME ON...
I'LL PLAY WITH YOU.

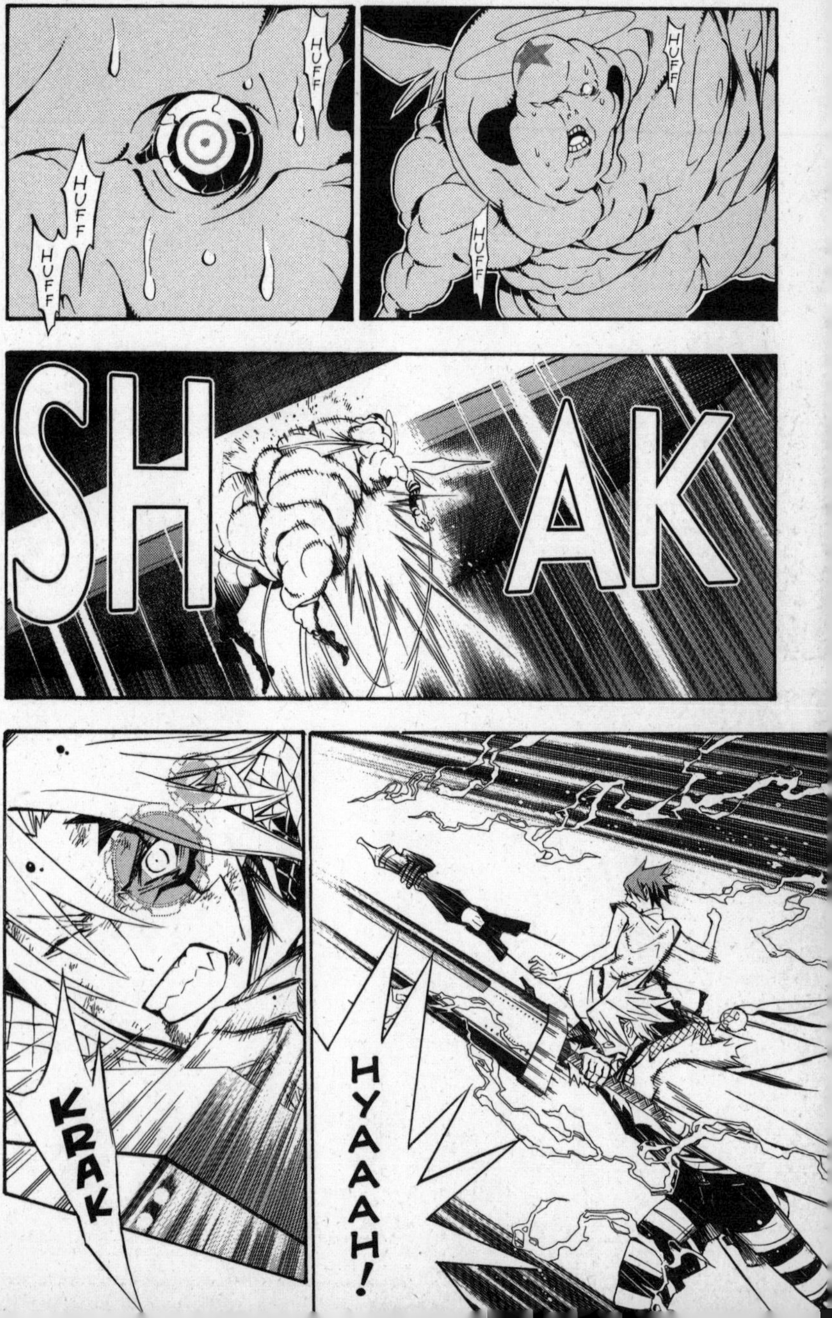
HUFF
HUFF
HUFF
HUFF
HUFF
SHAK
HYAAAH!
KRAK

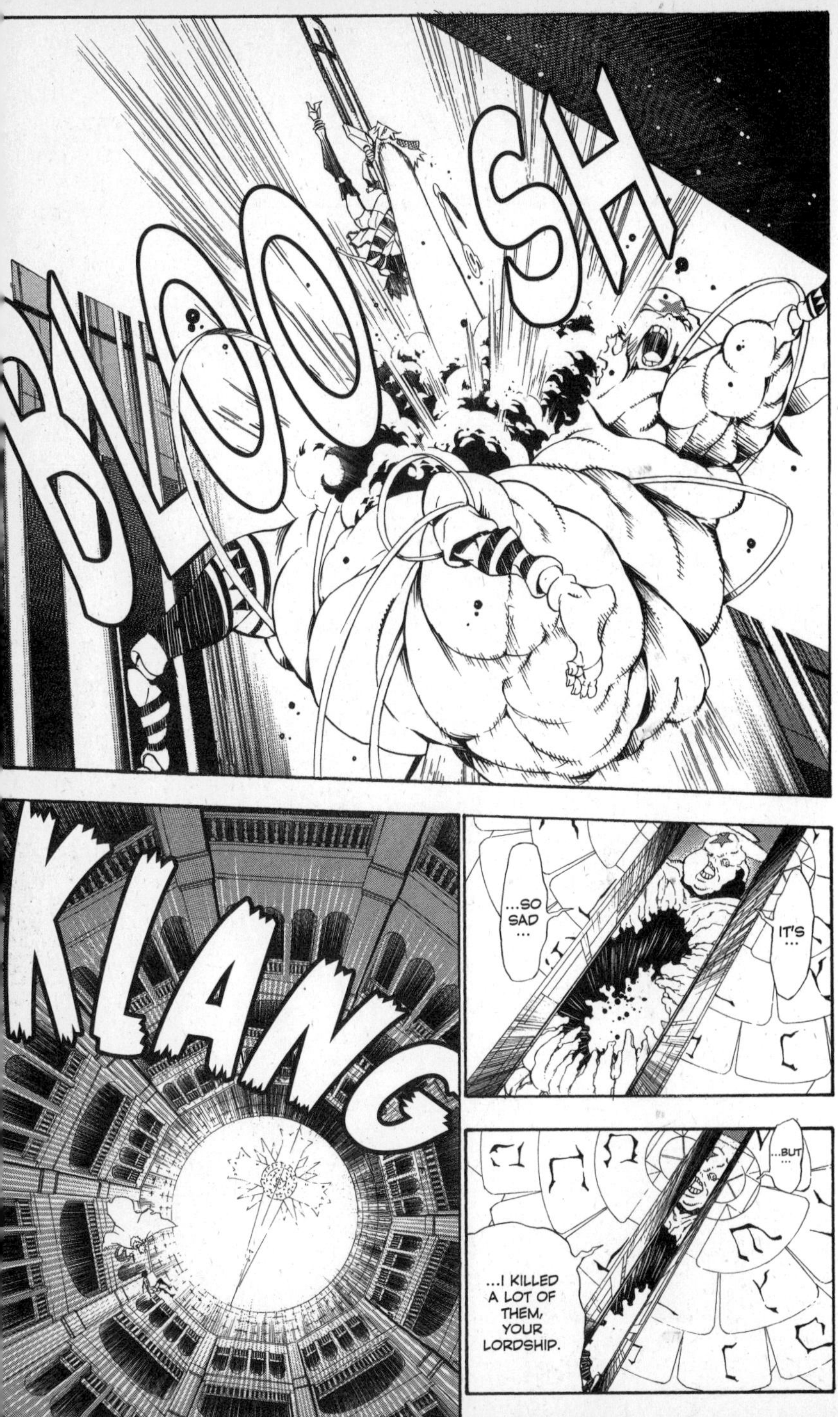
BLOOOSH
IT'S...
...SO SAD...
...BUT...
...I KILLED A LOT OF THEM, YOUR LORDSHIP.
KLANG

THE MAKERS OF D.GRAY-MAN

ROUGH LAYOUTS: FOR DETERMINING THE FLOW OF THE STORY

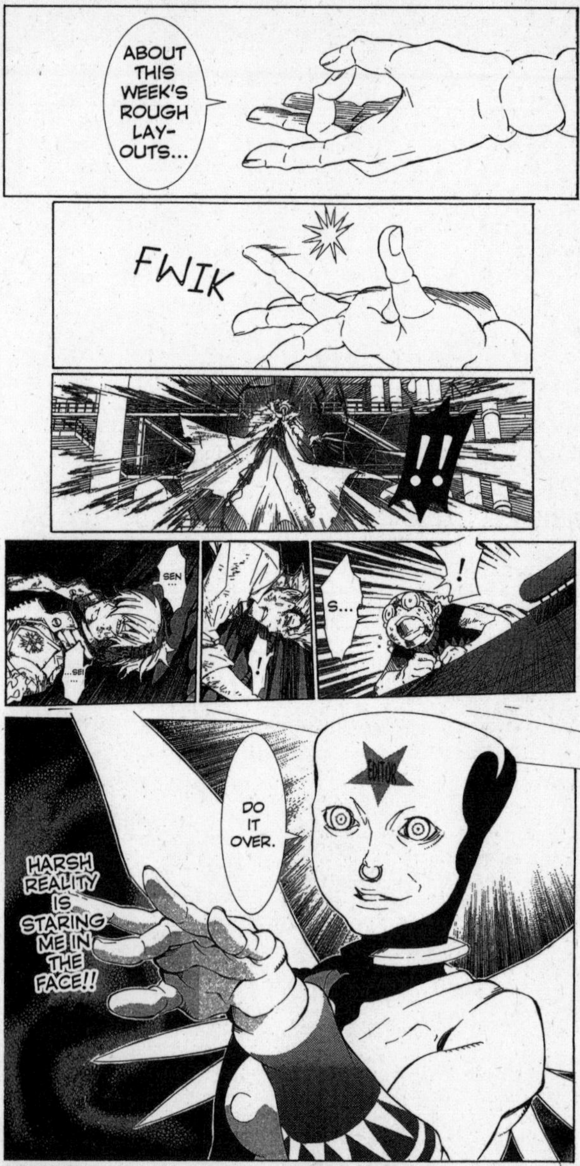
ABOUT THIS WEEK'S ROUGH LAYOUTS...
FWIK
!!
!
S...
!
SEN...
...SEI...
DO IT OVER.
EDITOR
HARSH REALITY IS STARING ME IN THE FACE!!

THREE DAYS UNTIL DEADLINE.

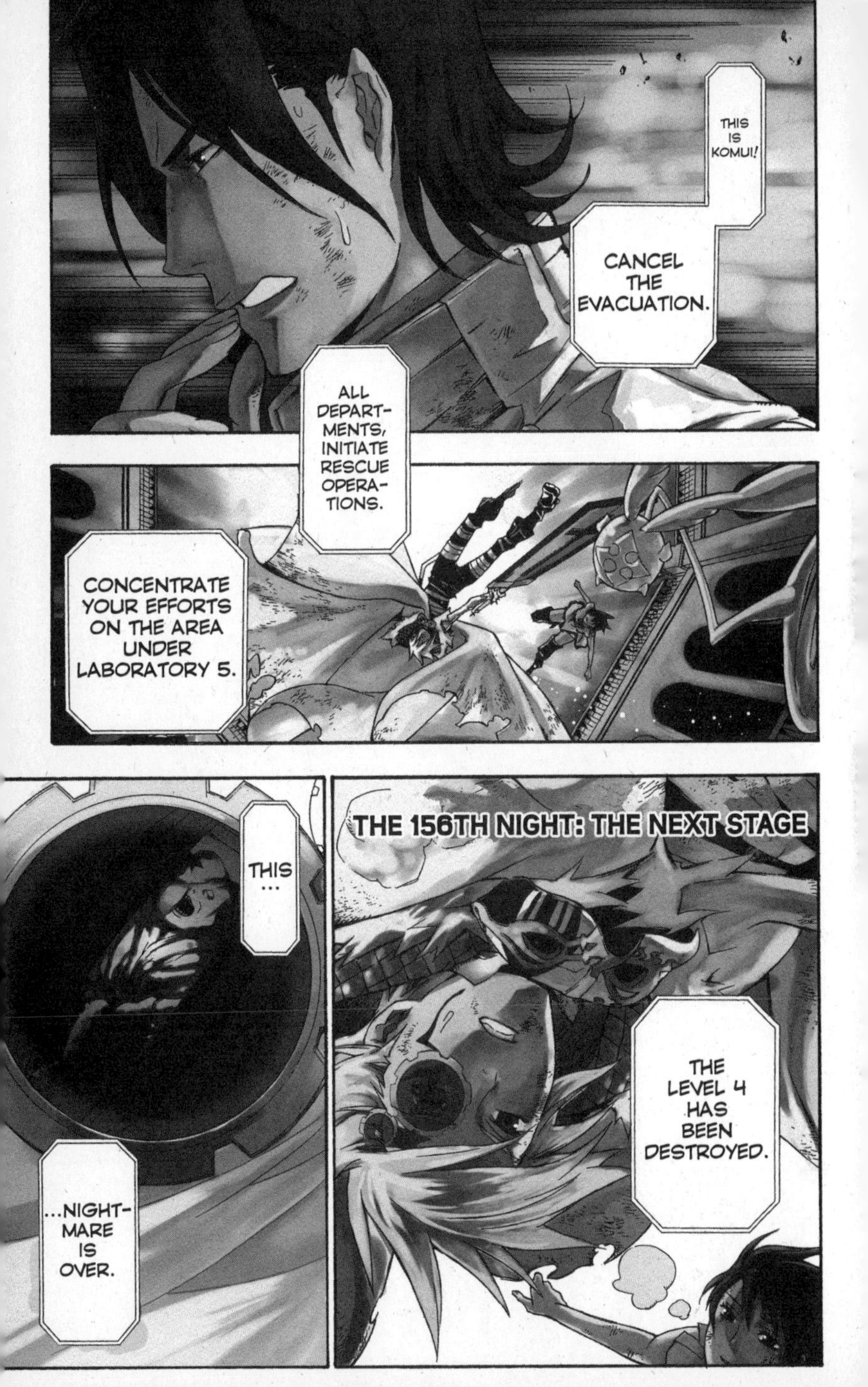
THIS IS KOMUI!
CANCEL THE EVACUATION.
ALL DEPART-MENTS, INITIATE RESCUE OPERA-TIONS.
CONCENTRATE YOUR EFFORTS ON THE AREA UNDER LABORATORY 5.
THE 156TH NIGHT: THE NEXT STAGE
THE LEVEL 4 HAS BEEN DESTROYED.
THIS ...
...NIGHT-MARE IS OVER.

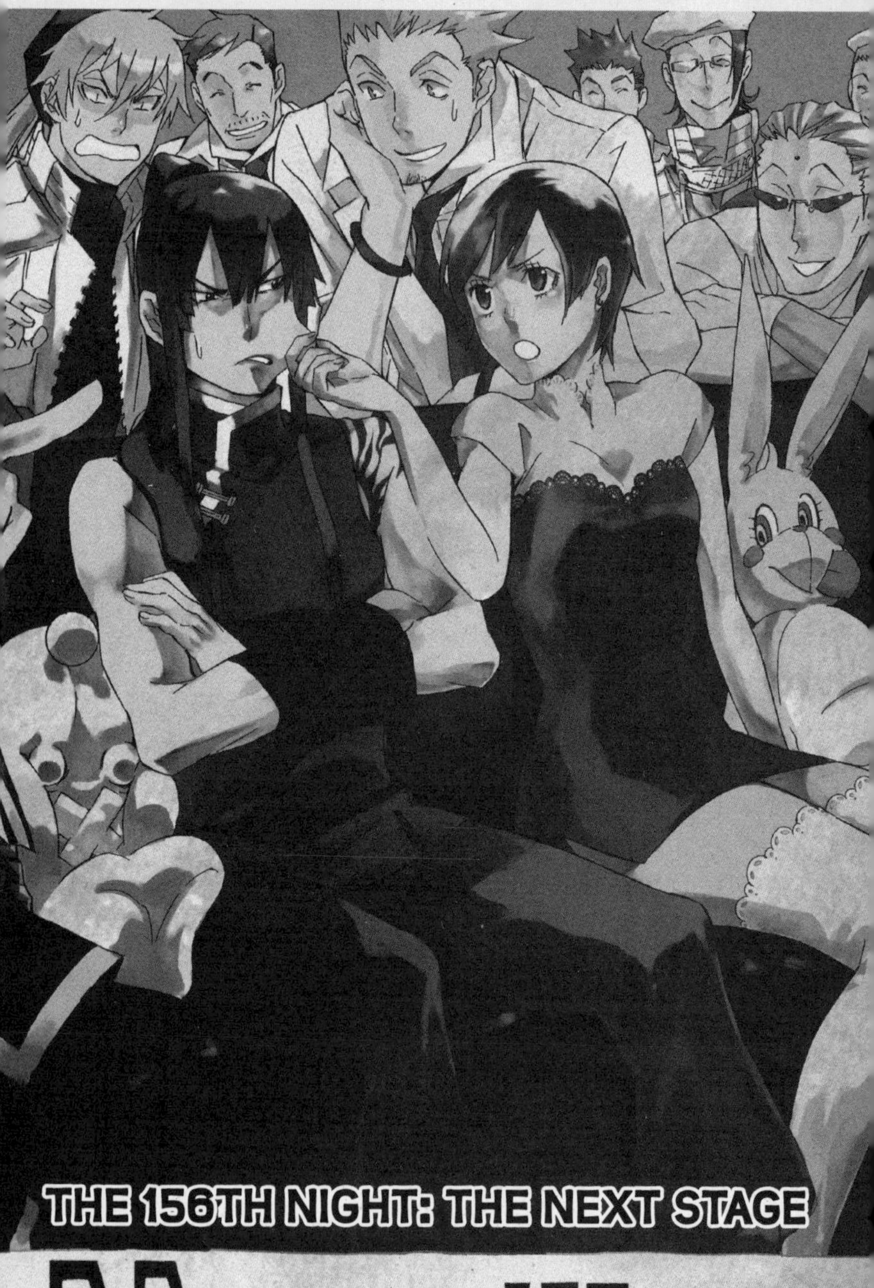
THE 156TH NIGHT: THE NEXT STAGE

D.Gray-man 156.

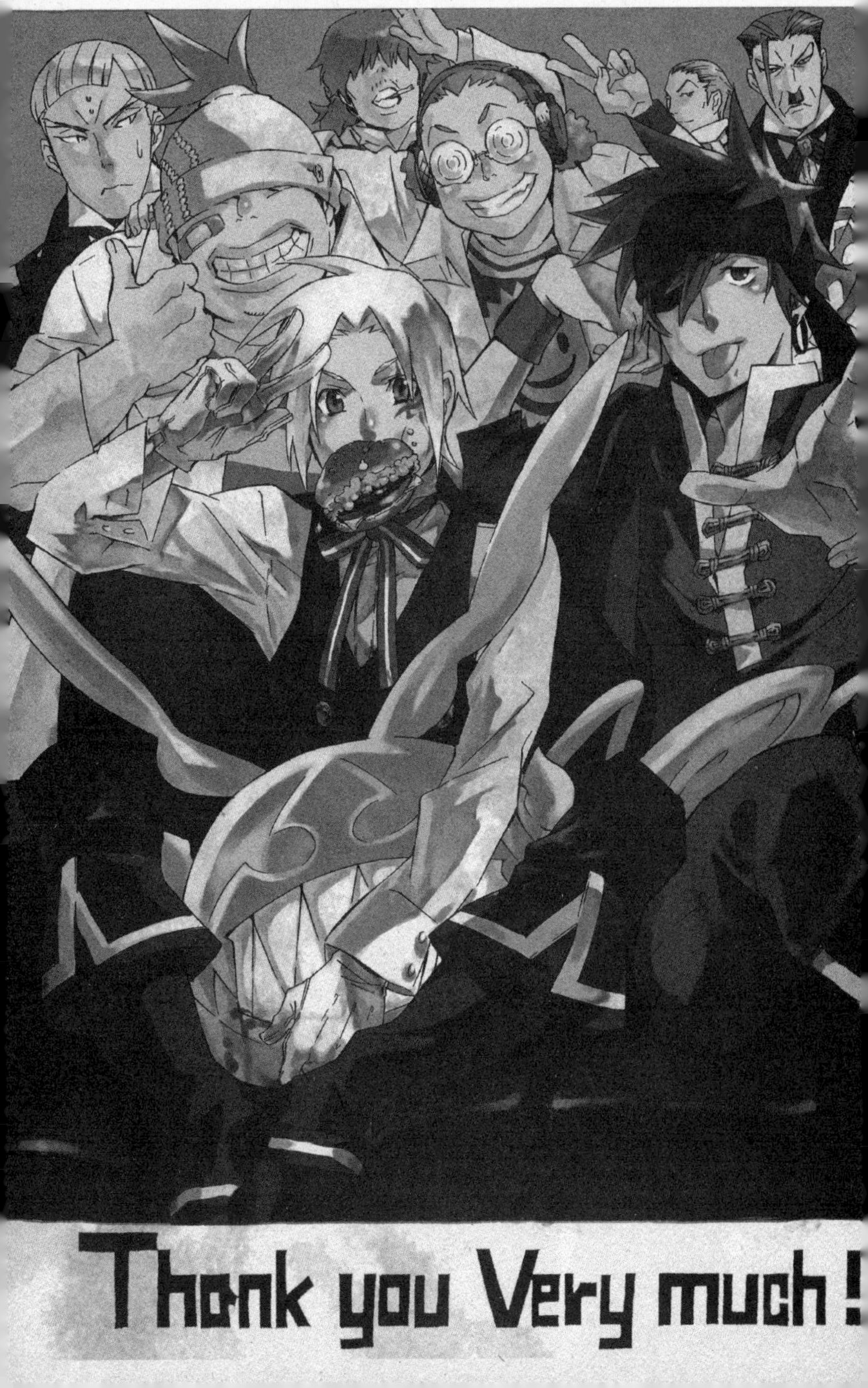
Thank you Very much!

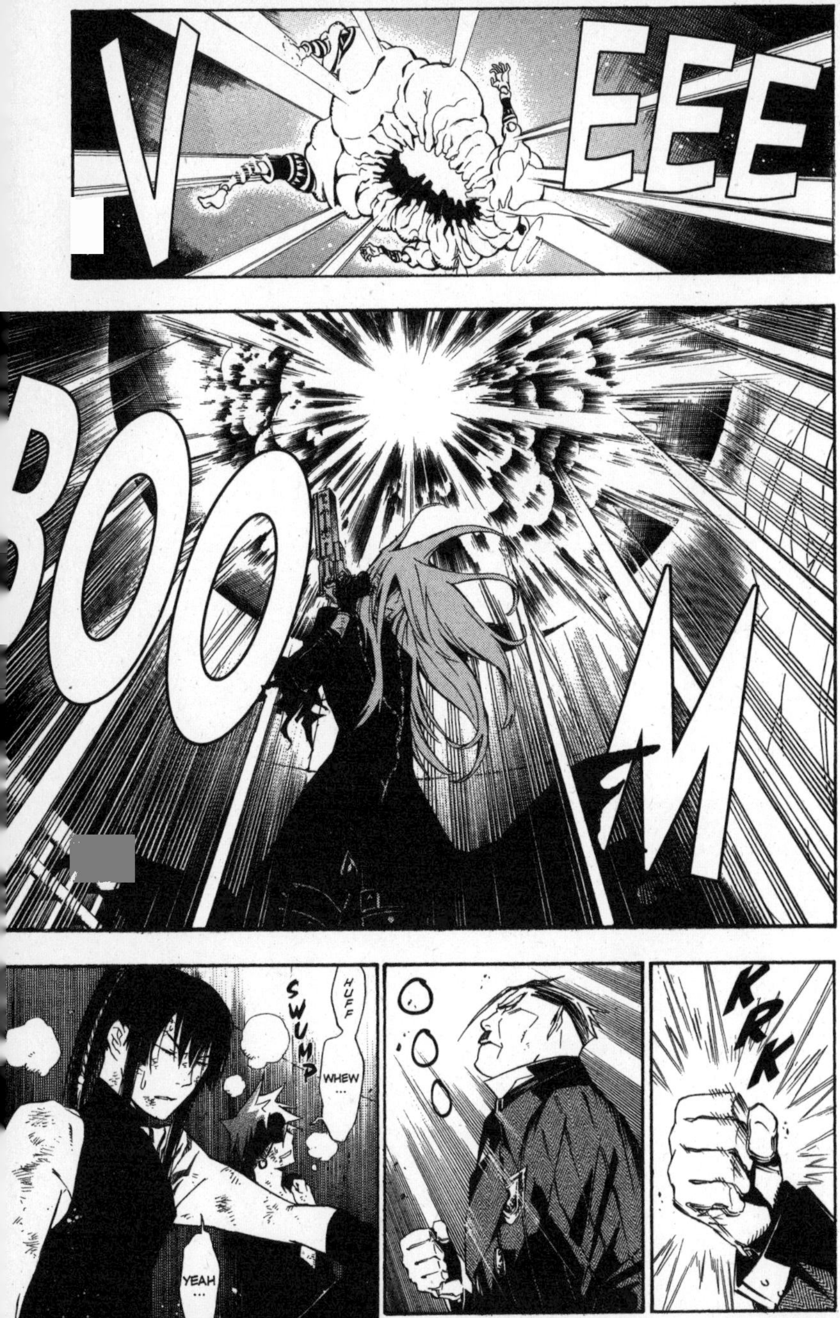
VEEE
BOOM
KRK
HUFF
SWUMP
WHEW ...
YEAH ...

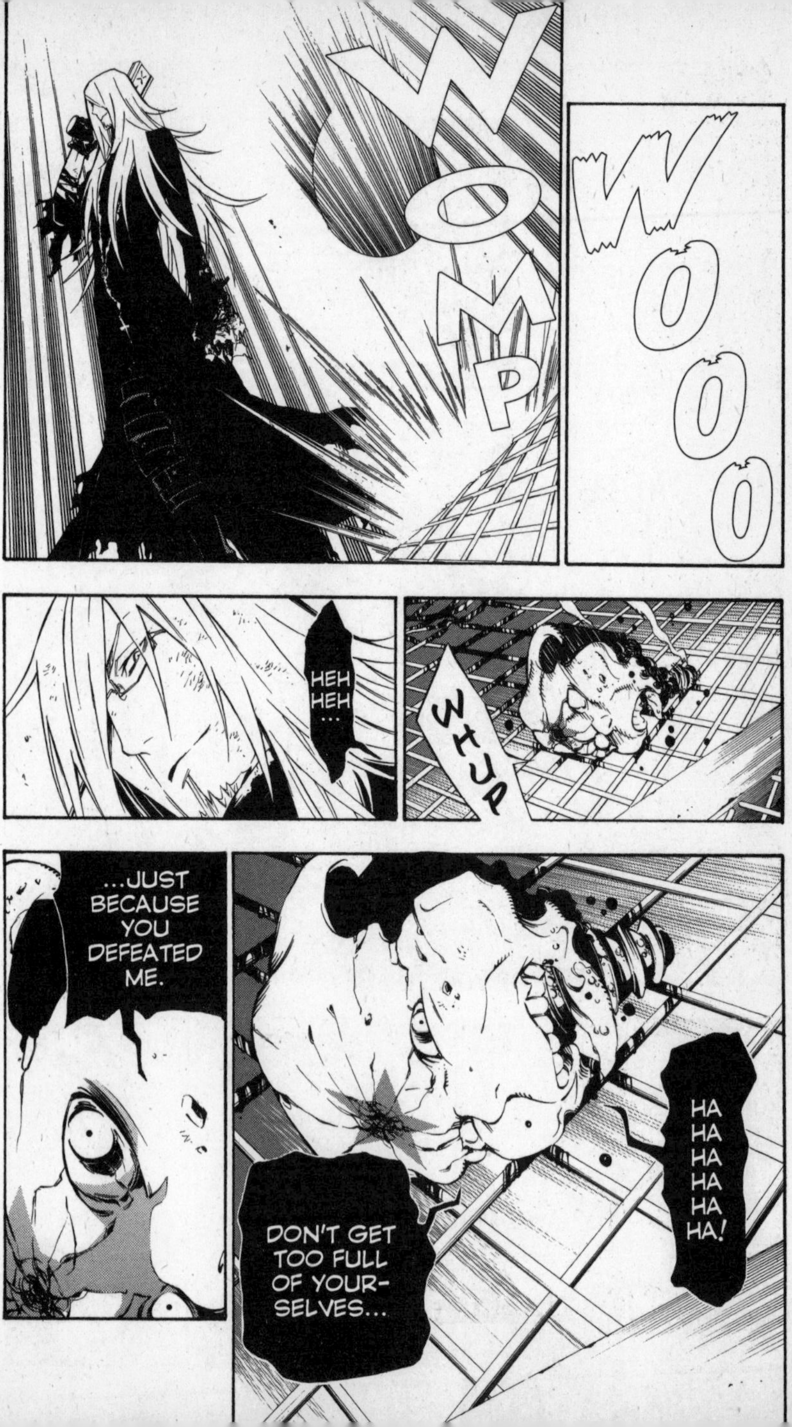
WOOOO
WOMP
WHUP
HEH HEH...
HA HA HA HA HA HA!
DON'T GET TOO FULL OF YOUR-SELVES...
...JUST BECAUSE YOU DEFEATED ME.

READ THIS WAY

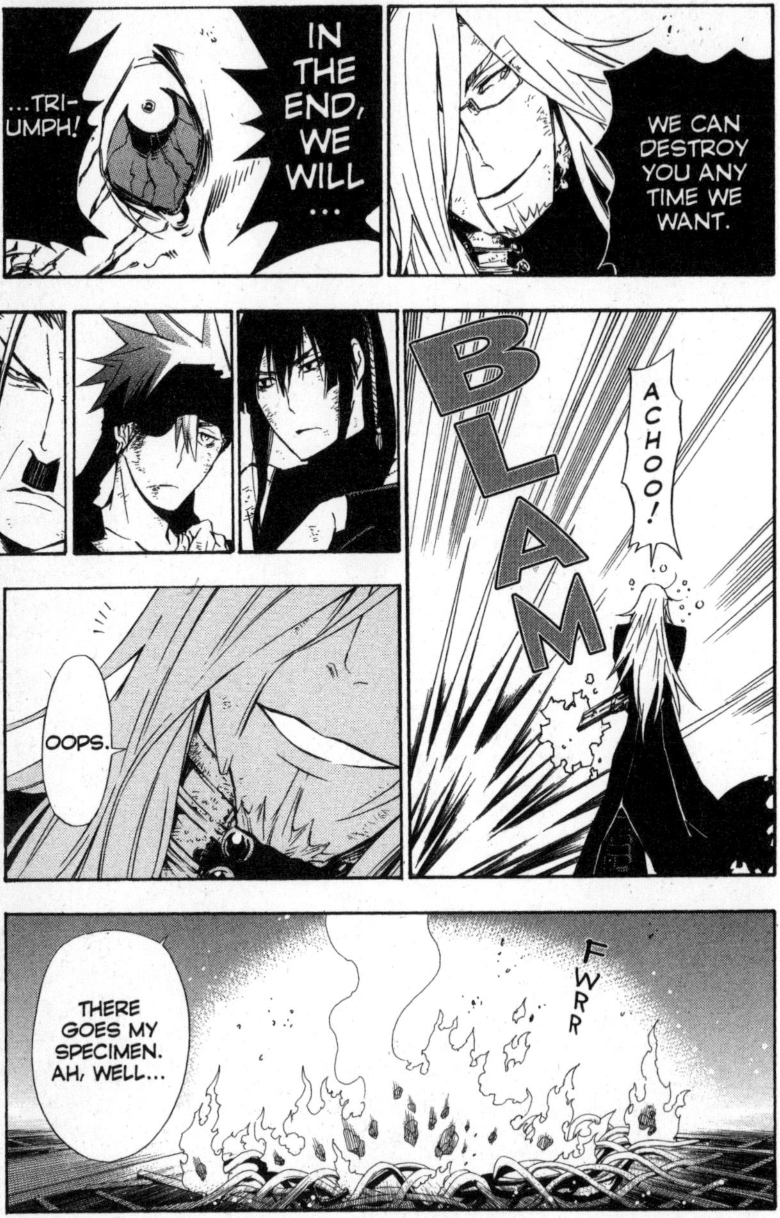
WE CAN DESTROY YOU ANY TIME WE WANT.
IN THE END, WE WILL...
...TRI-UMPH!
ACHOO!
BLAM
OOPS.
FWRR
THERE GOES MY SPECIMEN. AH, WELL...

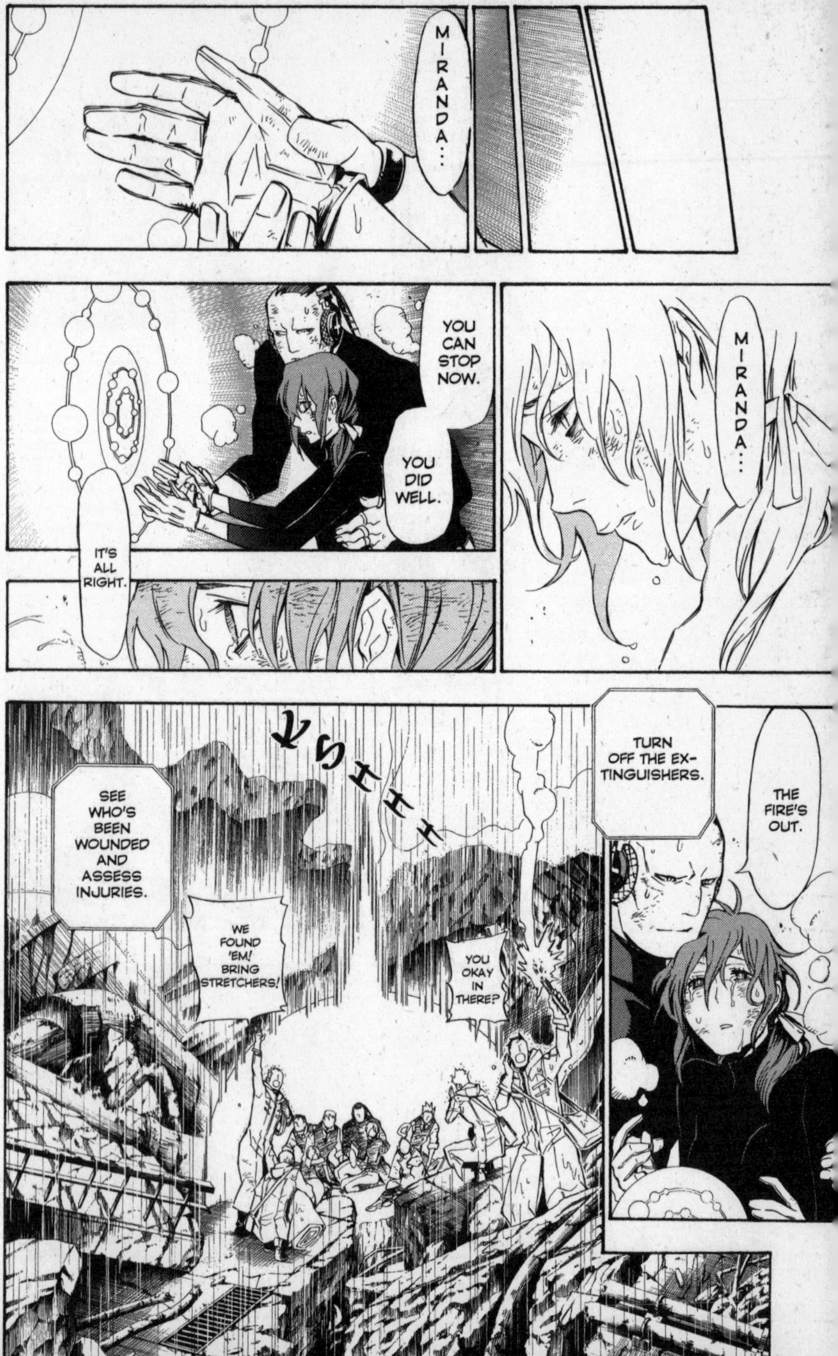
MIRANDA...
MIRANDA...
YOU CAN STOP NOW.
YOU DID WELL.
IT'S ALL RIGHT.
THE FIRE'S OUT.
TURN OFF THE EXTINGUISHERS.
SEE WHO'S BEEN WOUNDED AND ASSESS INJURIES.
YOU OKAY IN THERE?
WE FOUND 'EM! BRING STRETCHERS!

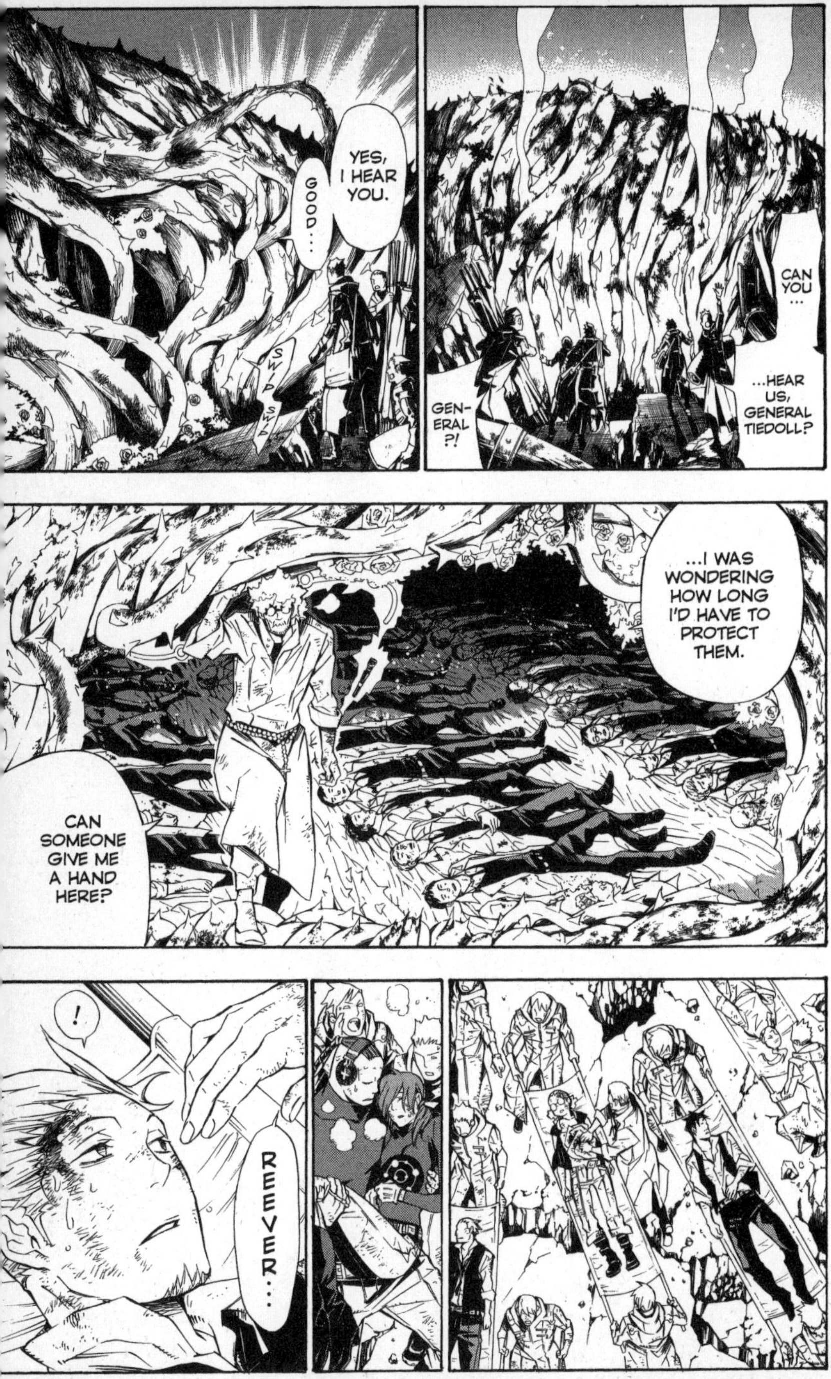
CAN YOU ...
...HEAR US, GENERAL TIEDOLL?
GENERAL ?!
YES, I HEAR YOU.
GOOD...
SWIP SWIP
...I WAS WONDERING HOW LONG I'D HAVE TO PROTECT THEM.
CAN SOMEONE GIVE ME A HAND HERE?
!
REEVER...

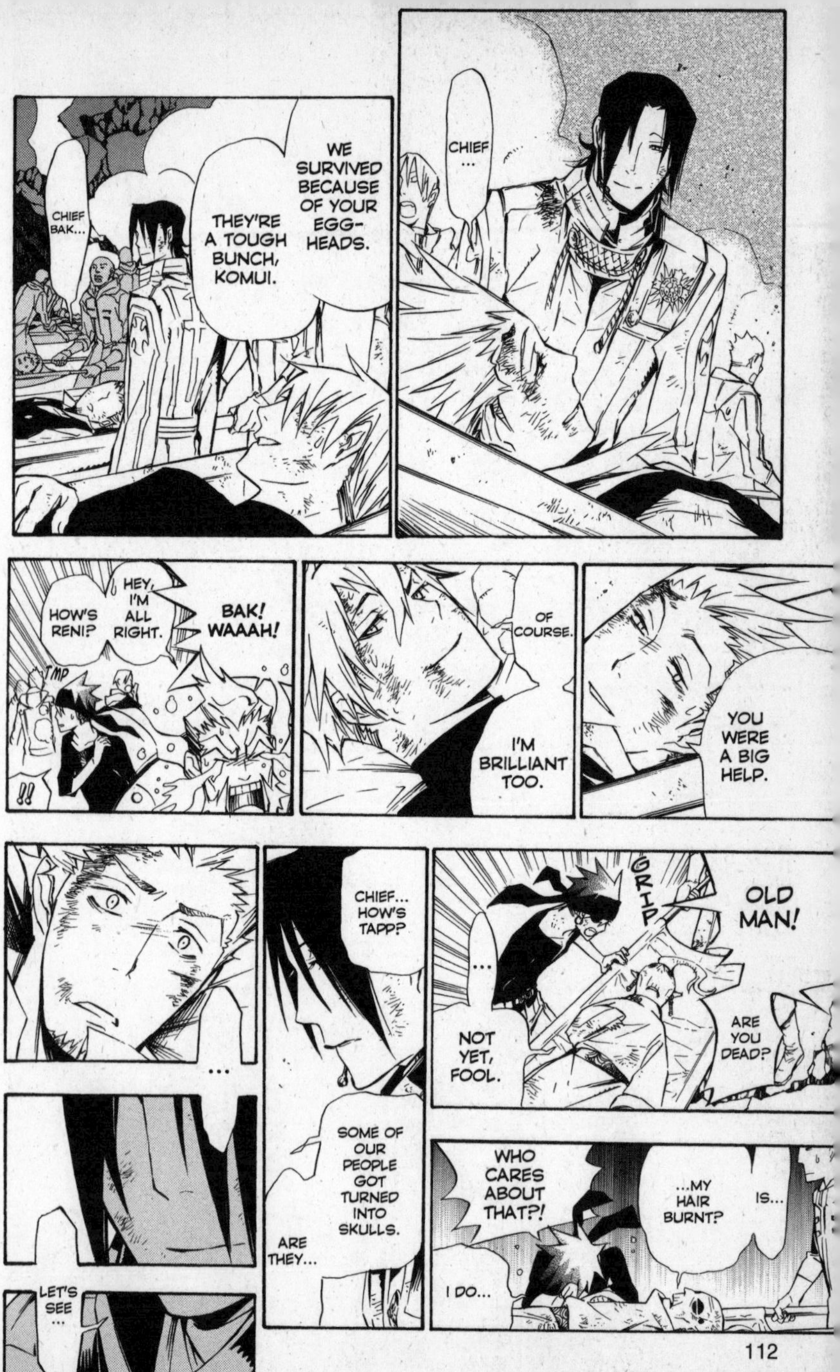
CHIEF ...
WE SURVIVED BECAUSE OF YOUR EGG-HEADS.
THEY'RE A TOUGH BUNCH, KOMUI.
CHIEF BAK...
YOU WERE A BIG HELP.
OF COURSE.
I'M BRILLIANT TOO.
BAK! WAAAH!
HEY, I'M ALL RIGHT.
HOW'S RENI?
TMP
!!
OLD MAN!
GRIP
ARE YOU DEAD?
...
NOT YET, FOOL.
IS...
...MY HAIR BURNT?
WHO CARES ABOUT THAT?!
I DO...
CHIEF... HOW'S TAPP?
SOME OF OUR PEOPLE GOT TURNED INTO SKULLS.
ARE THEY...
...
LET'S SEE ...

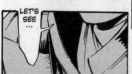

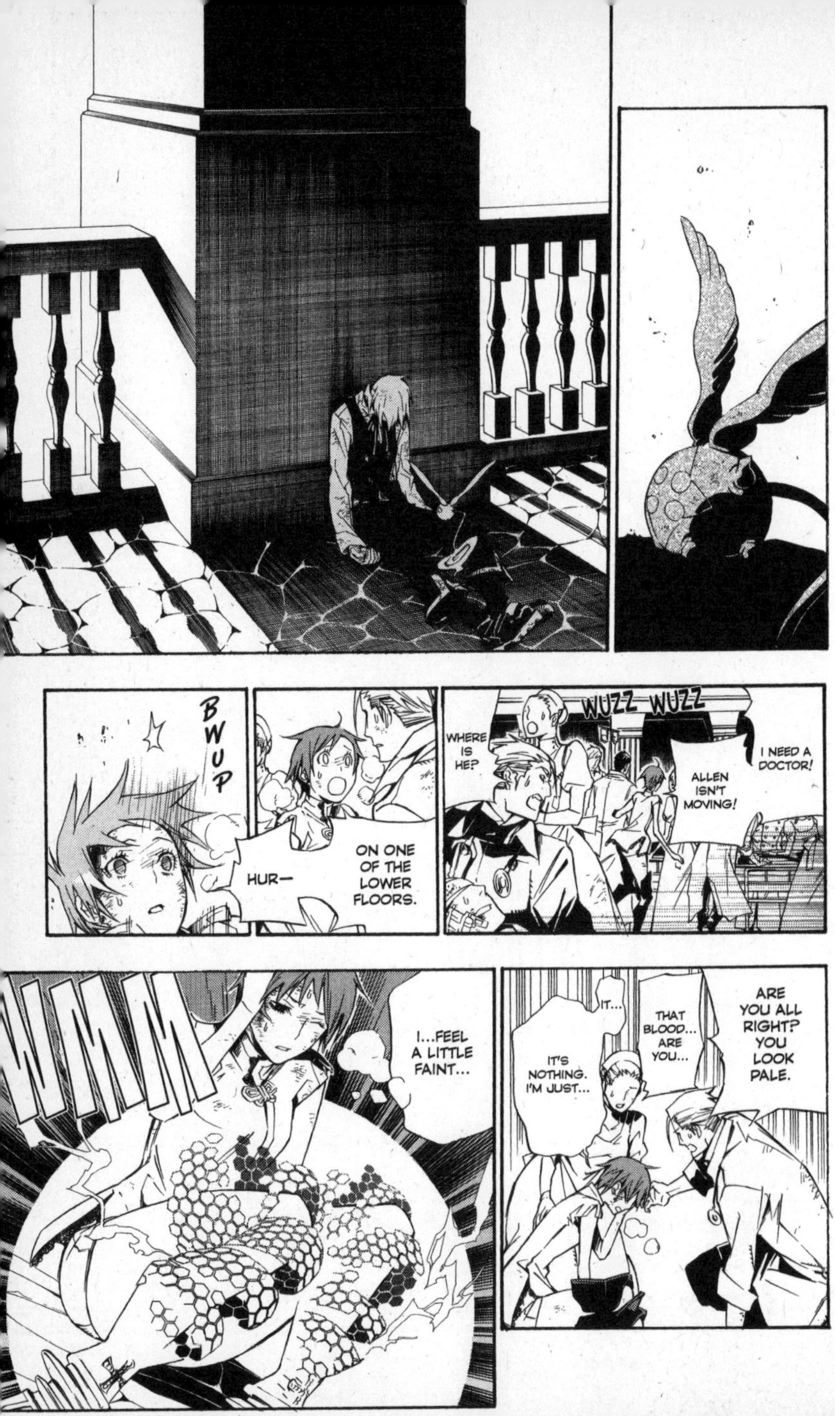
WUZZ WUZZ
I NEED A DOCTOR!
ALLEN ISN'T MOVING!
WHERE IS HE?
ON ONE OF THE LOWER FLOORS.
HUR—
BWUP
ARE YOU ALL RIGHT? YOU LOOK PALE.
THAT BLOOD... ARE YOU...
IT...
IT'S NOTHING. I'M JUST...
I...FEEL A LITTLE FAINT...

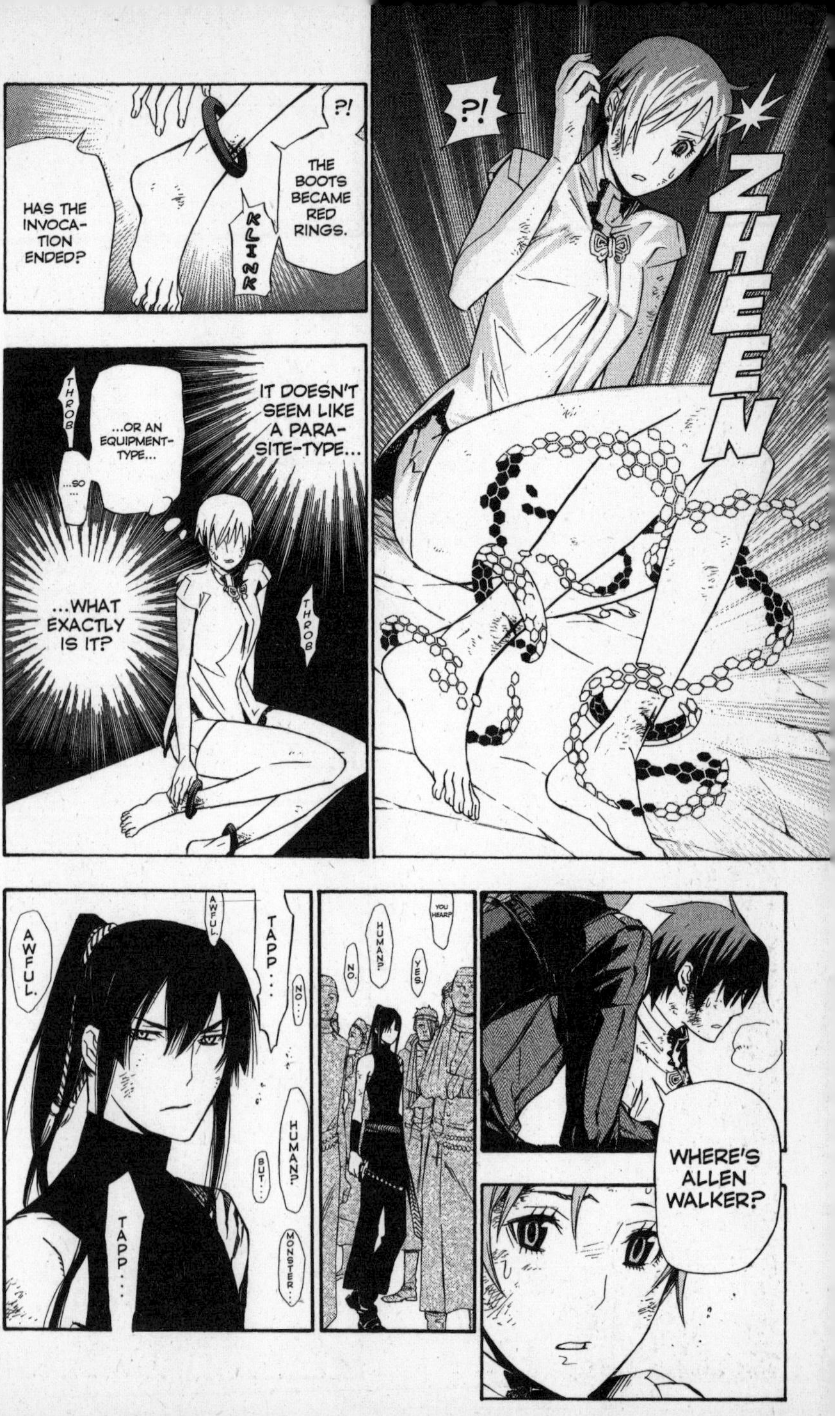
?!
ZHEEN
?!
THE BOOTS BECAME RED RINGS.
KLINK
HAS THE INVOCATION ENDED?
IT DOESN'T SEEM LIKE A PARASITE-TYPE...
THROB
...OR AN EQUIPMENT-TYPE...
...SO...
...WHAT EXACTLY IS IT?
THROB
WHERE'S ALLEN WALKER?
YOU HEAR?
YES.
HUMAN?
NO.
TAPP...
AWFUL.
NO...
HUMAN?
BUT...
MONSTER...
AWFUL.
TAPP...

READ THIS WAY

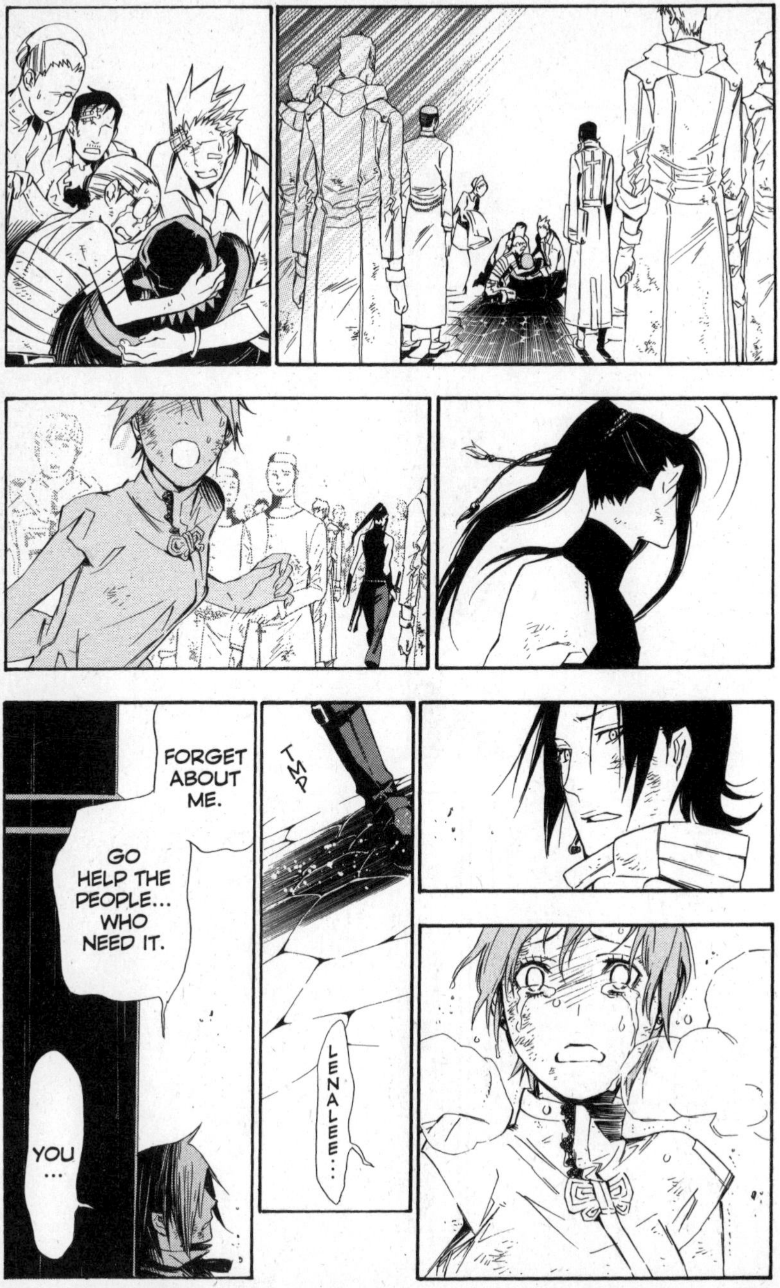
TMP
LENALEE...
FORGET ABOUT ME.
GO HELP THE PEOPLE... WHO NEED IT.
YOU...

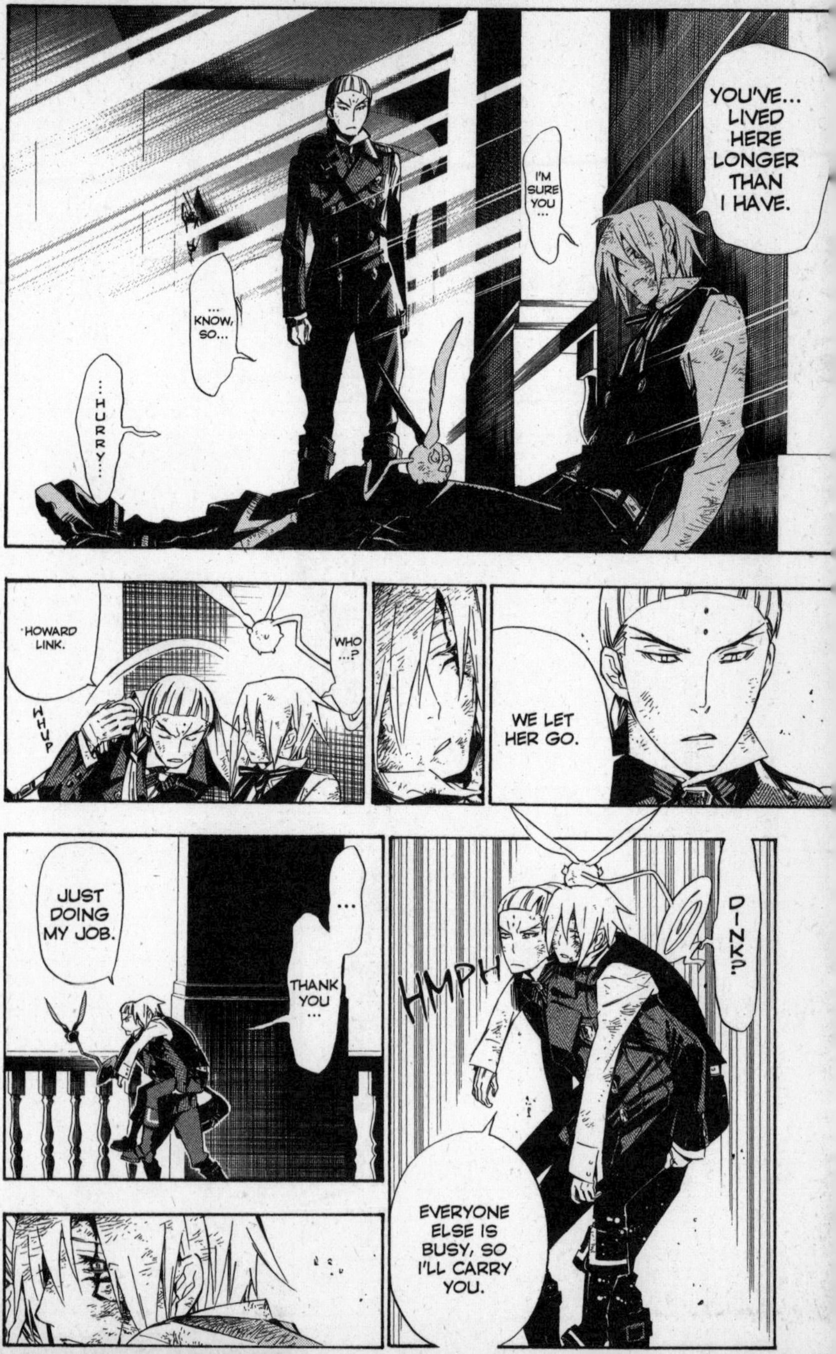
YOU'VE... LIVED HERE LONGER THAN I HAVE.
I'M SURE YOU...
...KNOW, SO...
...HURRY...
WE LET HER GO.
WHO...?
HOWARD LINK.
WHUP
DINK?
HMPH
EVERYONE ELSE IS BUSY, SO I'LL CARRY YOU.
...
THANK YOU...
JUST DOING MY JOB.

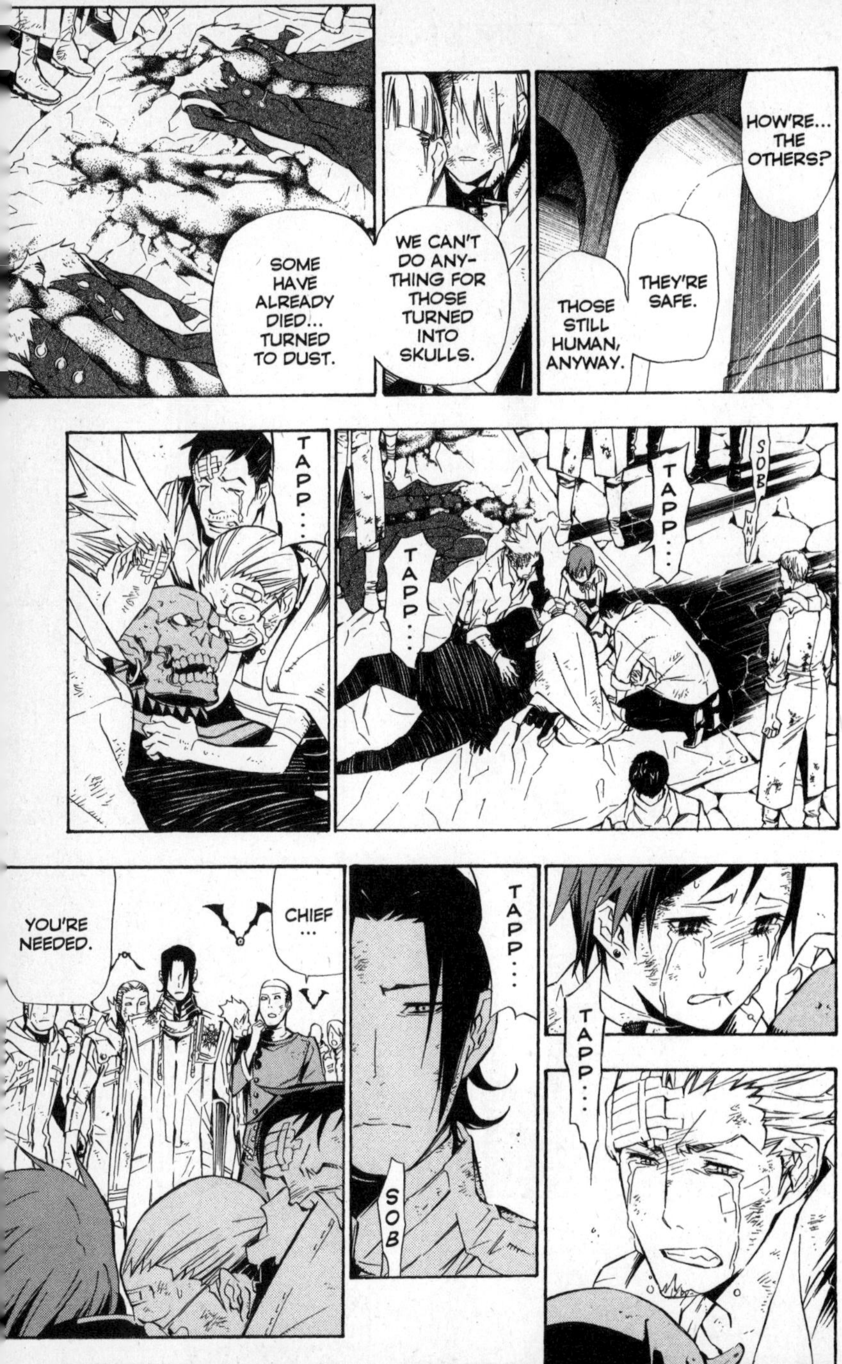
HOW'RE... THE OTHERS?
THEY'RE SAFE.
THOSE STILL HUMAN, ANYWAY.
WE CAN'T DO ANY-THING FOR THOSE TURNED INTO SKULLS.
SOME HAVE ALREADY DIED... TURNED TO DUST.
SOB
UNH
TAPP...
TAPP...
TAPP...
TAPP...
TAPP...
TAPP...
SOB
CHIEF ...
YOU'RE NEEDED.

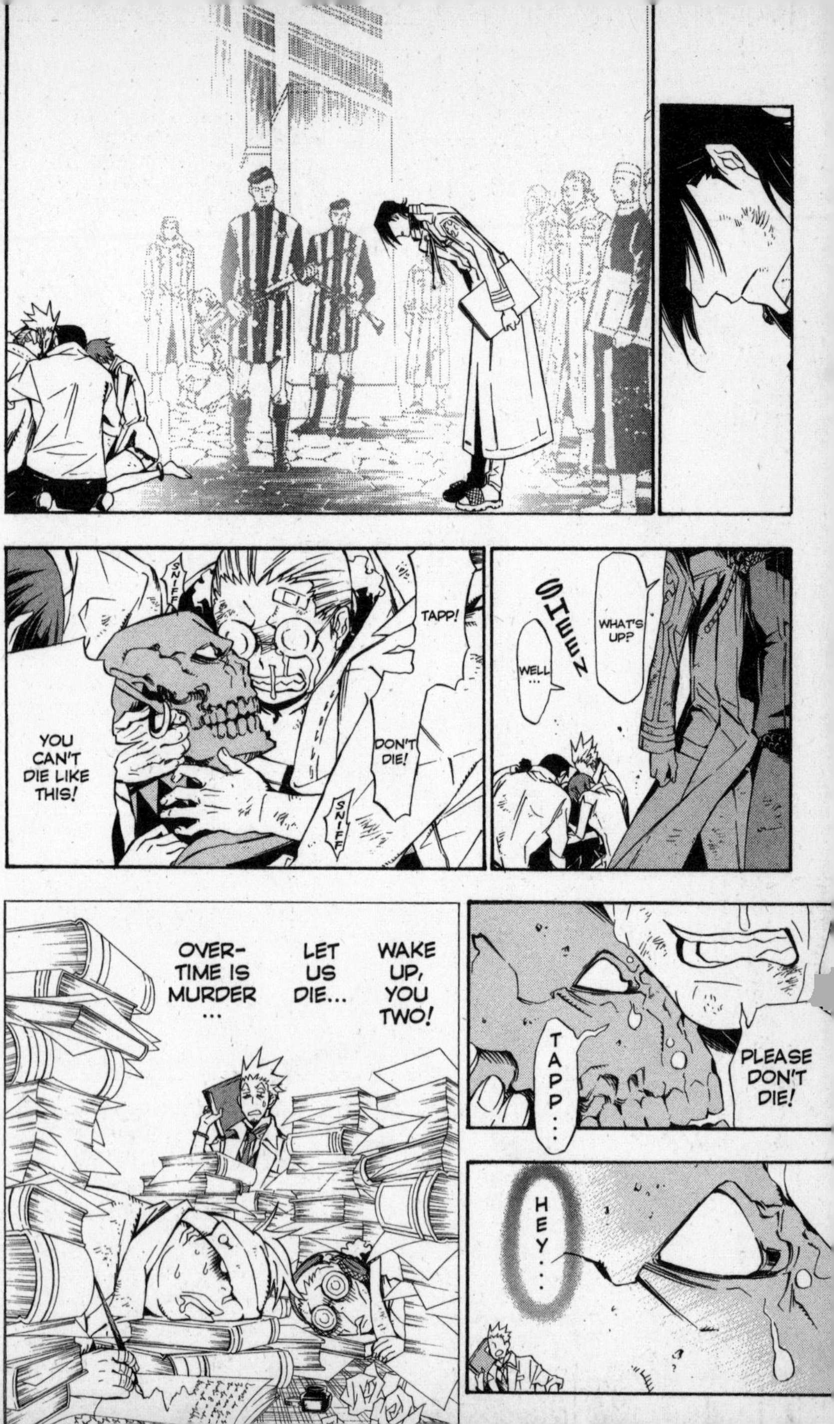
WHAT'S UP?
SHEEN
WELL...
SNIFF
TAPP!
DON'T DIE!
YOU CAN'T DIE LIKE THIS!
SNIFF
PLEASE DON'T DIE!
TAPP...
HEY...
WAKE UP, YOU TWO!
LET US DIE...
OVER-TIME IS MURDER...

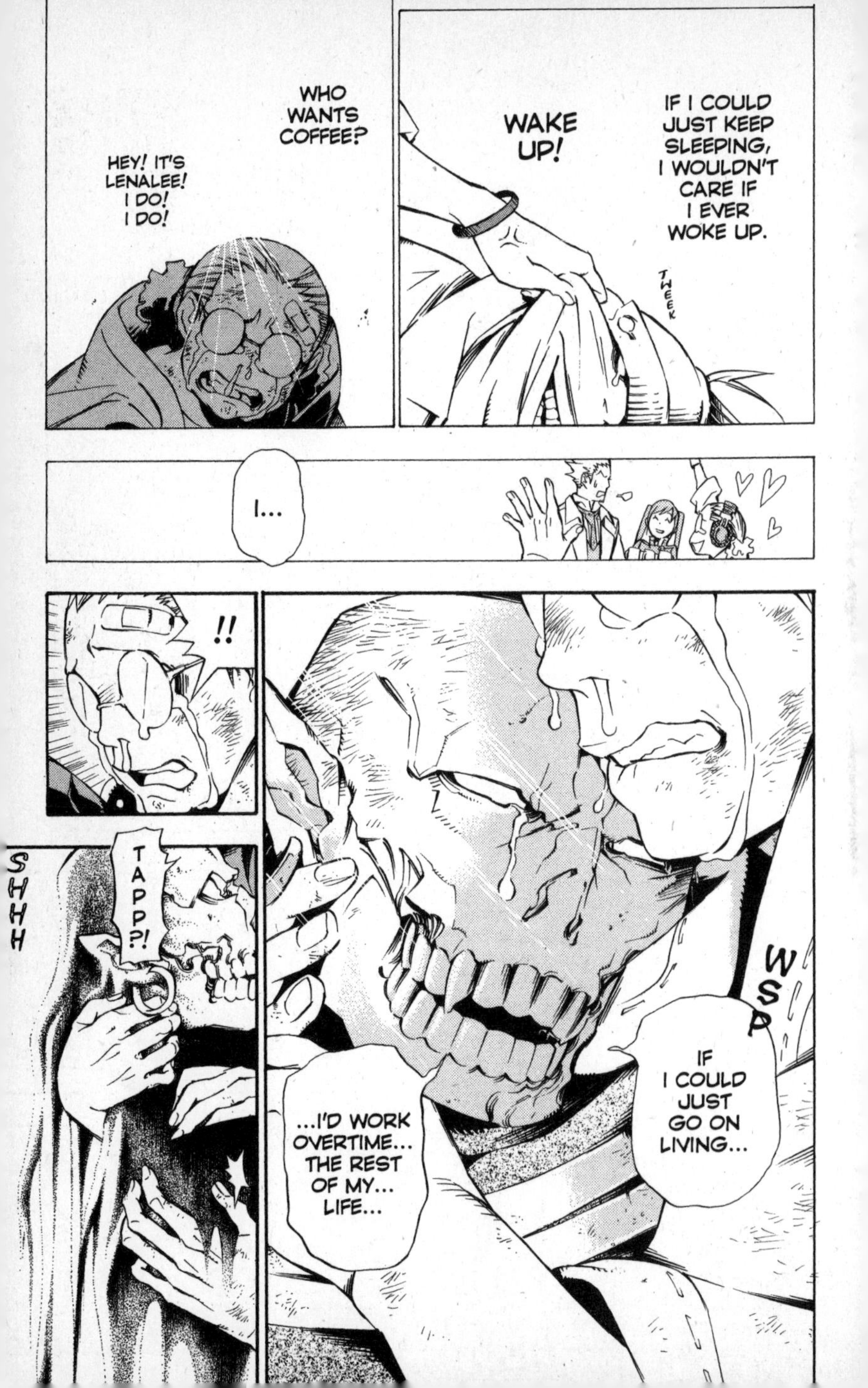
IF I COULD JUST KEEP SLEEPING, I WOULDN'T CARE IF I EVER WOKE UP.
WAKE UP!
TWEEK
WHO WANTS COFFEE?
HEY! IT'S LENALEE! I DO! I DO!
I...
WSP
IF I COULD JUST GO ON LIVING...
...I'D WORK OVERTIME... THE REST OF MY... LIFE...
!!
TAPP?!
SHHH

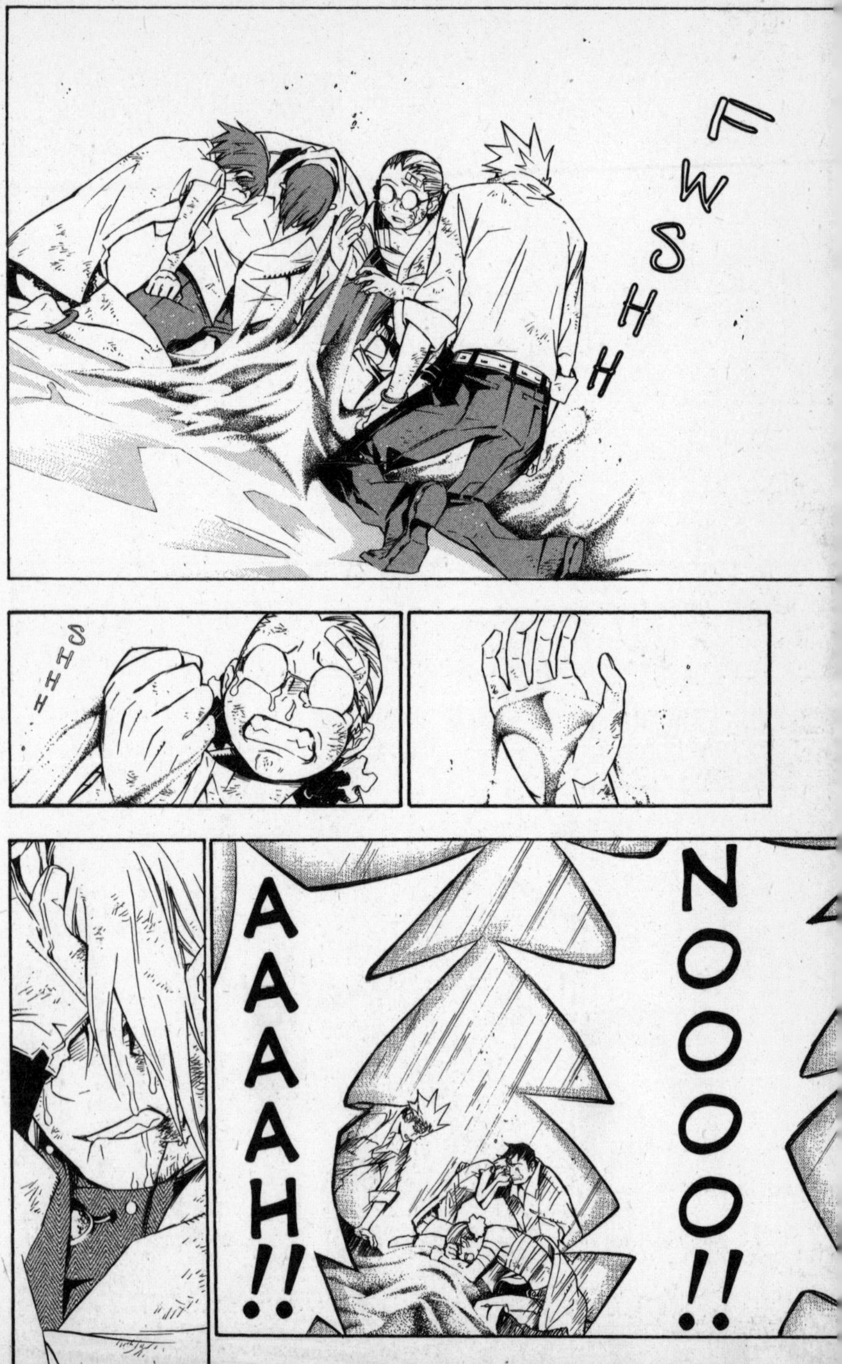
FWSHH
SHHH
NOOOO!!
AAAAH!!

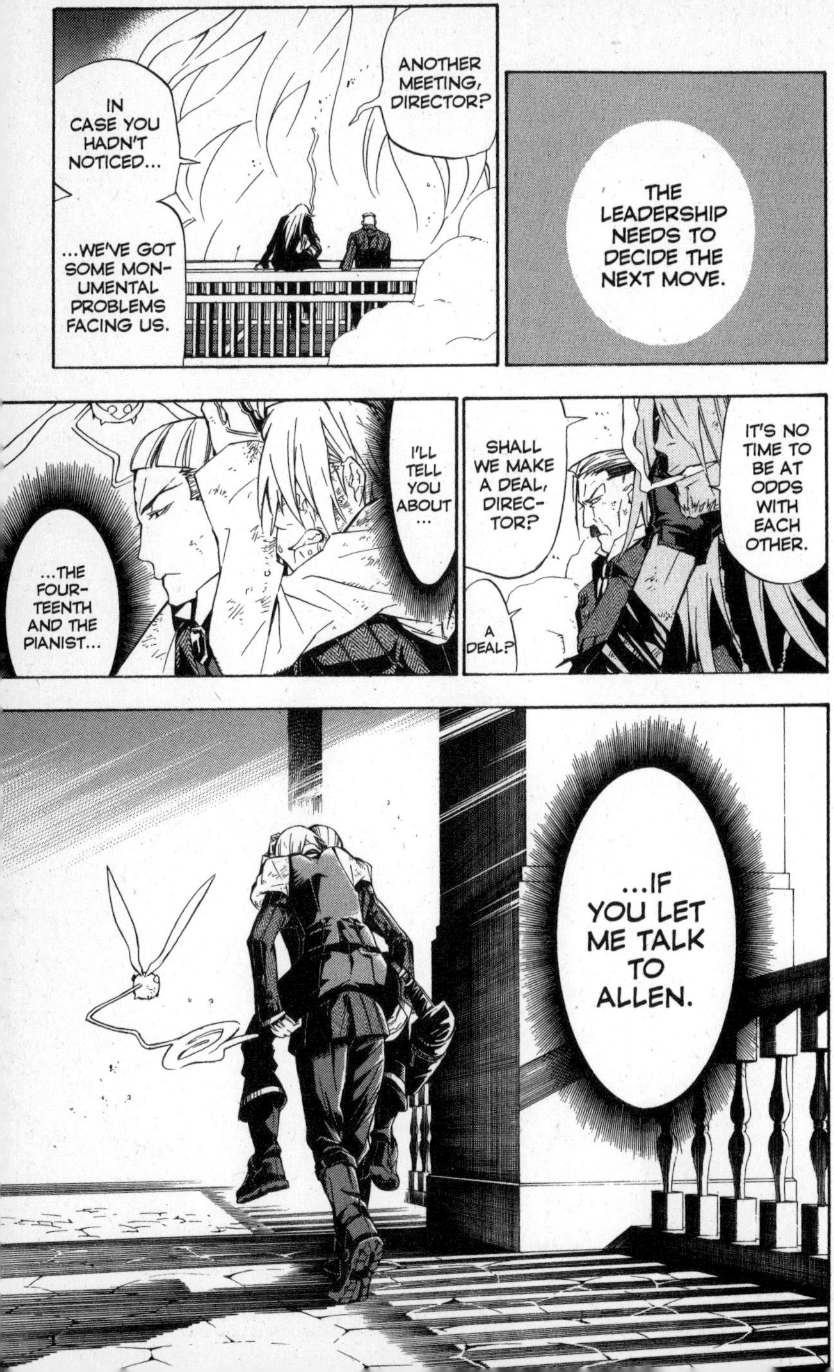
THE LEADERSHIP NEEDS TO DECIDE THE NEXT MOVE.
ANOTHER MEETING, DIRECTOR?
IN CASE YOU HADN'T NOTICED...
...WE'VE GOT SOME MON-UMENTAL PROBLEMS FACING US.
IT'S NO TIME TO BE AT ODDS WITH EACH OTHER.
SHALL WE MAKE A DEAL, DIREC-TOR?
A DEAL?
I'LL TELL YOU ABOUT...
...THE FOUR-TEENTH AND THE PIANIST...
...IF YOU LET ME TALK TO ALLEN.

THE PEOPLE OF D.GRAY HOUSE

THE OLD MAN'S SECRET ♡

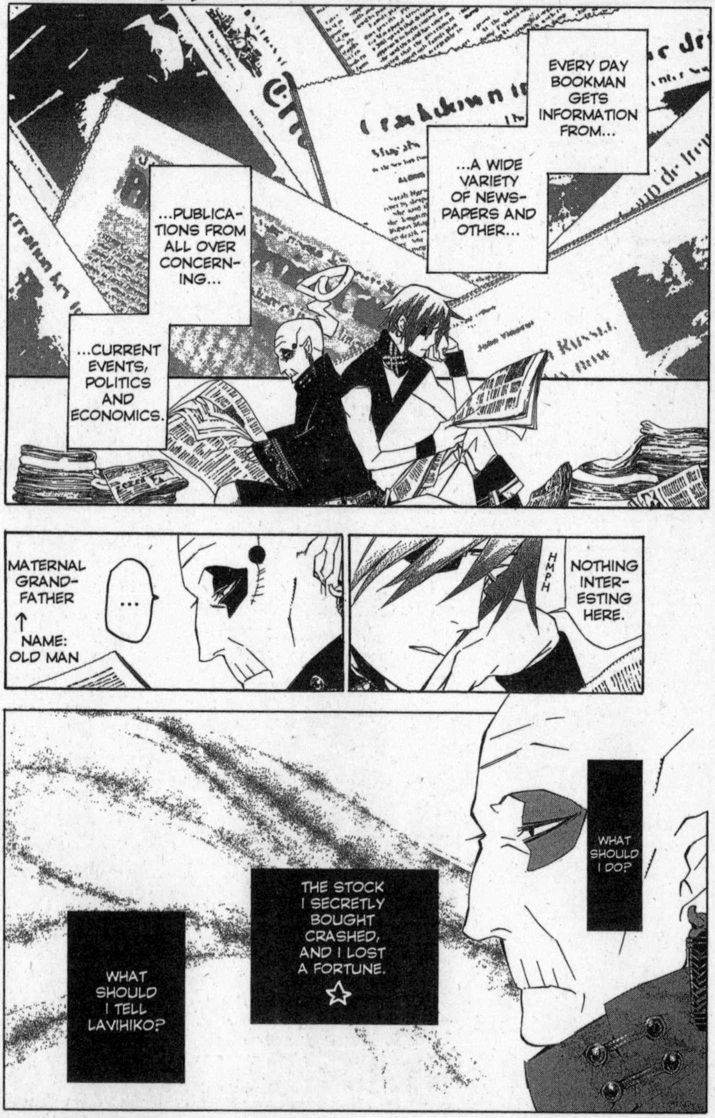

EVERY DAY BOOKMAN GETS INFORMATION FROM...
...A WIDE VARIETY OF NEWS-PAPERS AND OTHER...
...PUBLICA-TIONS FROM ALL OVER CONCERN-ING...
...CURRENT EVENTS, POLITICS AND ECONOMICS.
HMPH
NOTHING INTER-ESTING HERE.
...
MATERNAL GRAND-FATHER ↑ NAME: OLD MAN
WHAT SHOULD I DO?
THE STOCK I SECRETLY BOUGHT CRASHED, AND I LOST A FORTUNE. ☆
WHAT SHOULD I TELL LAVIHIKO?

A CRISIS APPROACHES FOR LAVIHIKO.

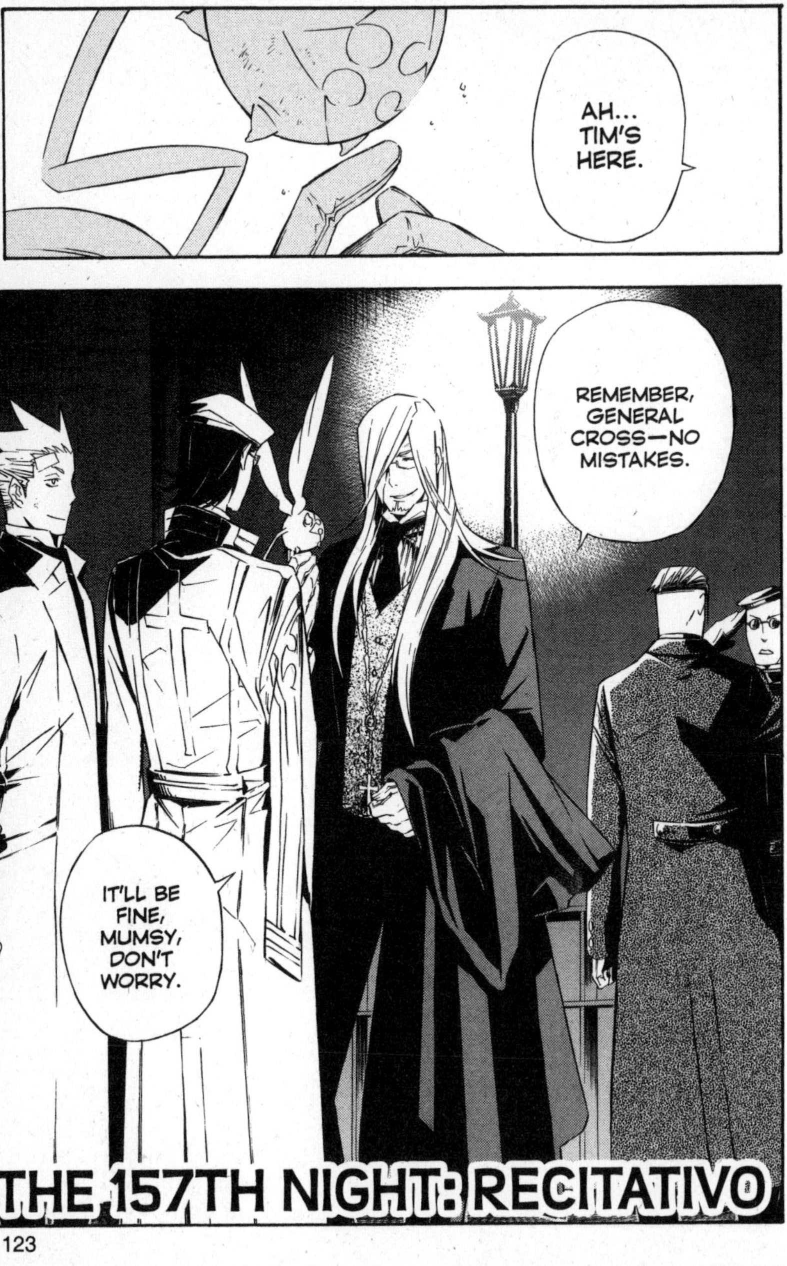
AH... TIM'S HERE.
REMEMBER, GENERAL CROSS—NO MISTAKES.
IT'LL BE FINE, MUMSY, DON'T WORRY.

THE 157TH NIGHT: RECITATIVO

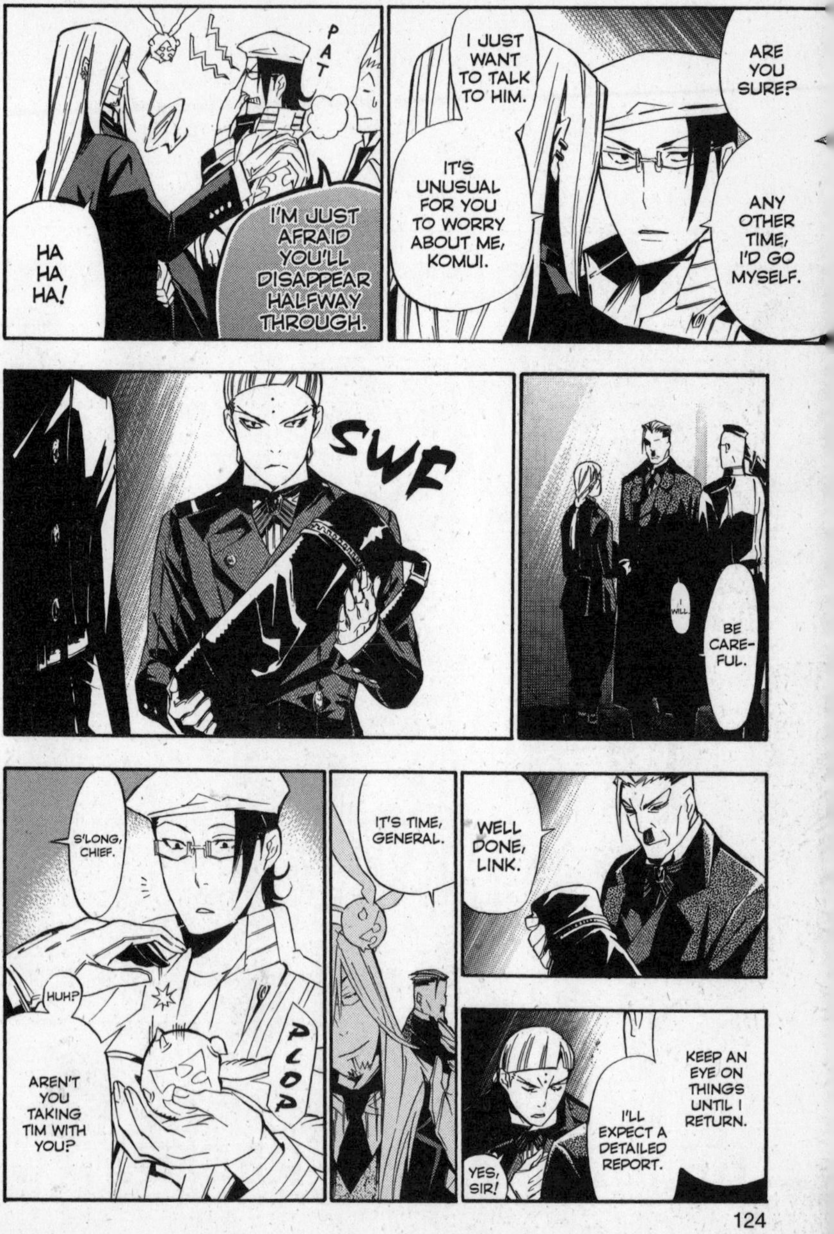
ARE YOU SURE?
I JUST WANT TO TALK TO HIM.
ANY OTHER TIME, I'D GO MYSELF.
IT'S UNUSUAL FOR YOU TO WORRY ABOUT ME, KOMUI.
PAT
I'M JUST AFRAID YOU'LL DISAPPEAR HALFWAY THROUGH.
HA HA HA!
BE CAREFUL.
I WILL...
SWF
WELL DONE, LINK.
KEEP AN EYE ON THINGS UNTIL I RETURN.
I'LL EXPECT A DETAILED REPORT.
YES, SIR!
IT'S TIME, GENERAL.
S'LONG, CHIEF.
HUH?
PLOP
AREN'T YOU TAKING TIM WITH YOU?

READ THIS WAY

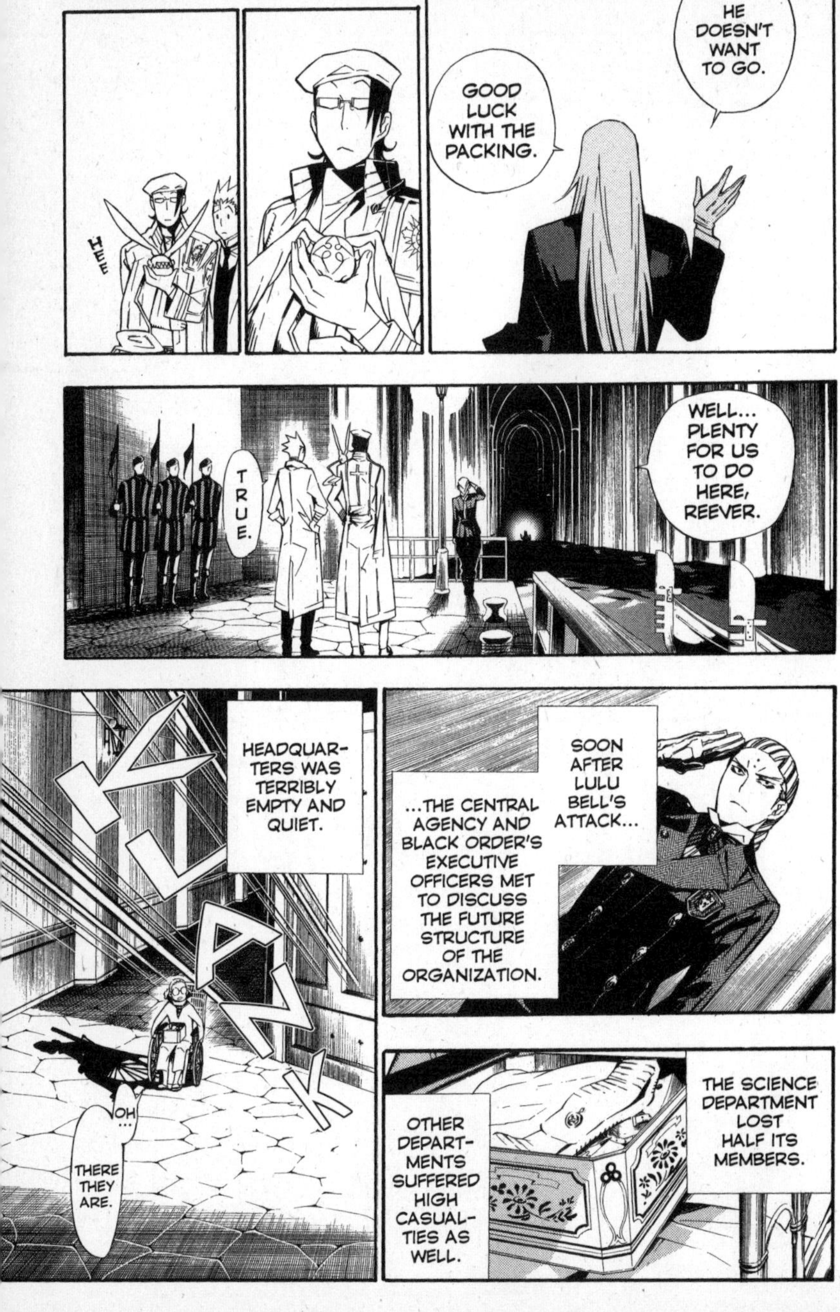
HE DOESN'T WANT TO GO.
GOOD LUCK WITH THE PACKING.
HEE
WELL... PLENTY FOR US TO DO HERE, REEVER.
TRUE.
SOON AFTER LULU BELL'S ATTACK...
...THE CENTRAL AGENCY AND BLACK ORDER'S EXECUTIVE OFFICERS MET TO DISCUSS THE FUTURE STRUCTURE OF THE ORGANIZATION.
THE SCIENCE DEPARTMENT LOST HALF ITS MEMBERS.
OTHER DEPARTMENTS SUFFERED HIGH CASUALTIES AS WELL.
HEADQUARTERS WAS TERRIBLY EMPTY AND QUIET.
OH...
THERE THEY ARE.

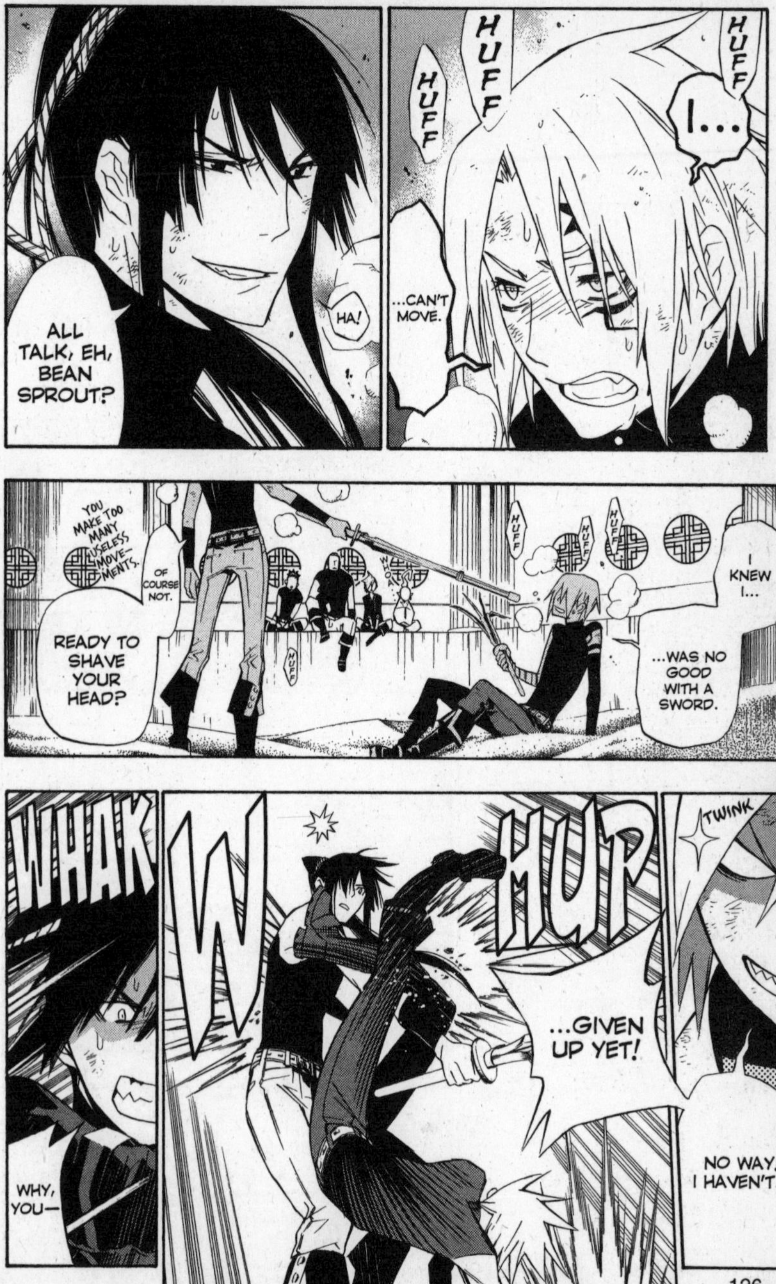
HUFF HUFF
HUFF
HUFF
I...
...CAN'T MOVE.
HA!
ALL TALK, EH, BEAN SPROUT?
HUFF
HUFF
HUFF
I KNEW I...
...WAS NO GOOD WITH A SWORD.
WHOA
OF COURSE NOT.
YOU MAKE TOO MANY USELESS MOVE-MENTS.
READY TO SHAVE YOUR HEAD?
HUFF
TWINK
NO WAY! I HAVEN'T...
HUP
...GIVEN UP YET!
W
WHAK
WHY, YOU—

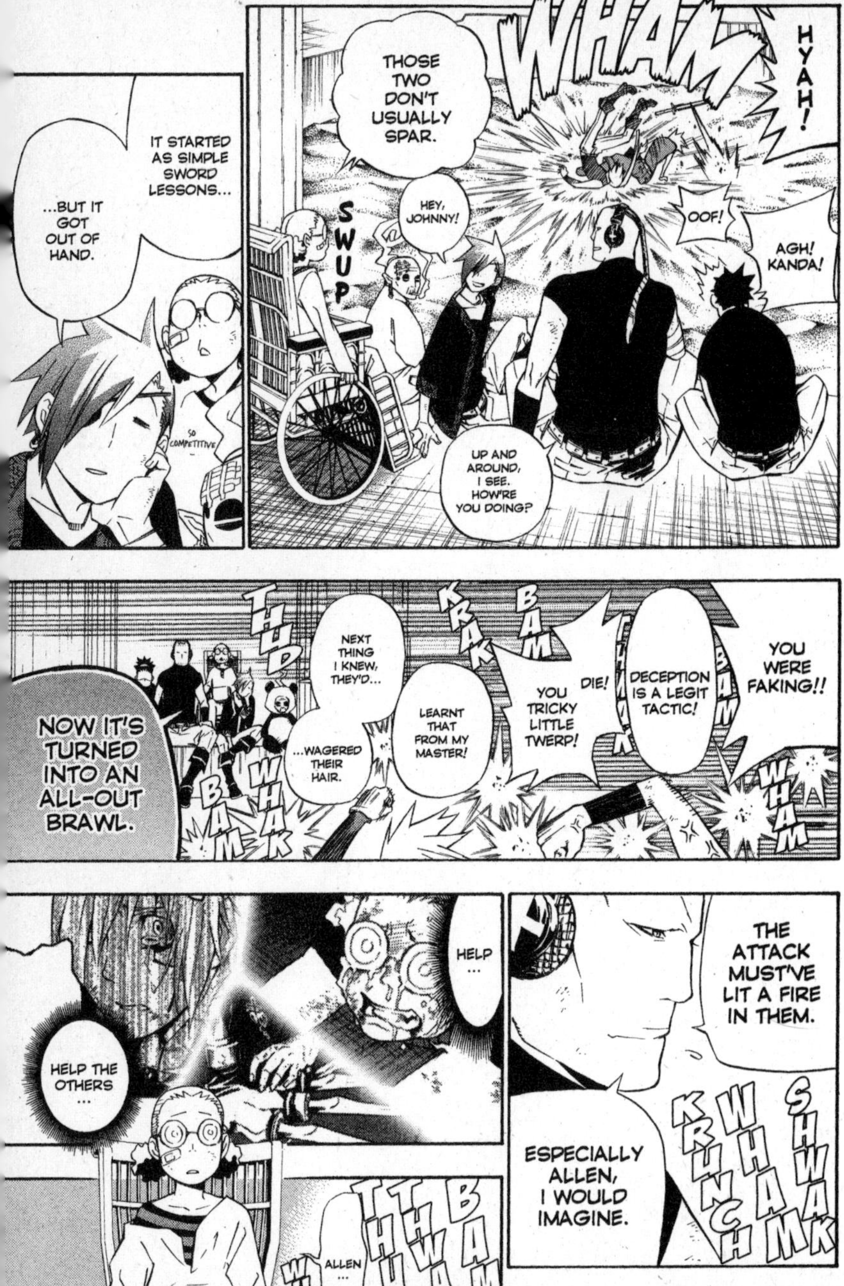
HYAH!
WHAM
THOSE TWO DON'T USUALLY SPAR.
OOF!
AGH! KANDA!
HEY, JOHNNY!
SWUP
UP AND AROUND, I SEE. HOW'RE YOU DOING?
IT STARTED AS SIMPLE SWORD LESSONS...
...BUT IT GOT OUT OF HAND.
SO COMPETITIVE
YOU WERE FAKING!!
BAM
WHAM
DECEPTION IS A LEGIT TACTIC!
BAM
DIE!
YOU TRICKY LITTLE TWERP!
KRAK
LEARNT THAT FROM MY MASTER!
NEXT THING I KNEW, THEY'D...
...WAGERED THEIR HAIR.
THUD
WHAK
BAM
NOW IT'S TURNED INTO AN ALL-OUT BRAWL.
THE ATTACK MUST'VE LIT A FIRE IN THEM.
SHWAK
WHAM
KRUNCH
ESPECIALLY ALLEN, I WOULD IMAGINE.
HELP ...
HELP THE OTHERS ...
BAM
THWAM
THUD
ALLEN ...
WHAK

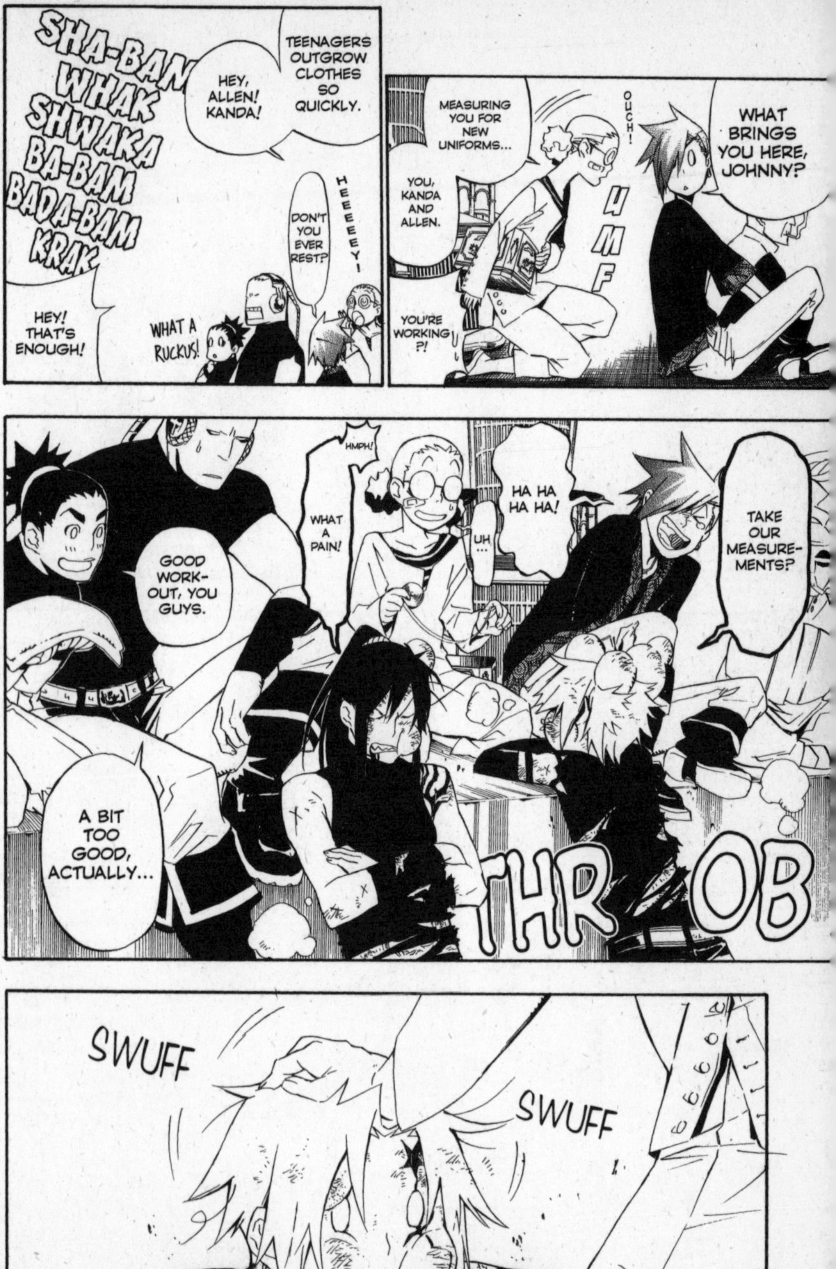

WHAT BRINGS YOU HERE, JOHNNY?
OUCH!
UMF
MEASURING YOU FOR NEW UNIFORMS...
YOU, KANDA AND ALLEN.
YOU'RE WORKING?!
TEENAGERS OUTGROW CLOTHES SO QUICKLY.
HEY, ALLEN! KANDA!
SHA-BAN WHAK SHWAKA BA-BAM BADA-BAM KRAK
HEEEEEY!
DON'T YOU EVER REST?
WHAT A RUCKUS!
HEY! THAT'S ENOUGH!
TAKE OUR MEASUREMENTS?
HA HA HA HA!
UH...
HMPH!
WHAT A PAIN!
GOOD WORK-OUT, YOU GUYS.
A BIT TOO GOOD, ACTUALLY...
THR OB
SWUFF
SWUFF

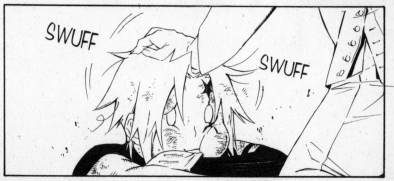

READ THIS WAY

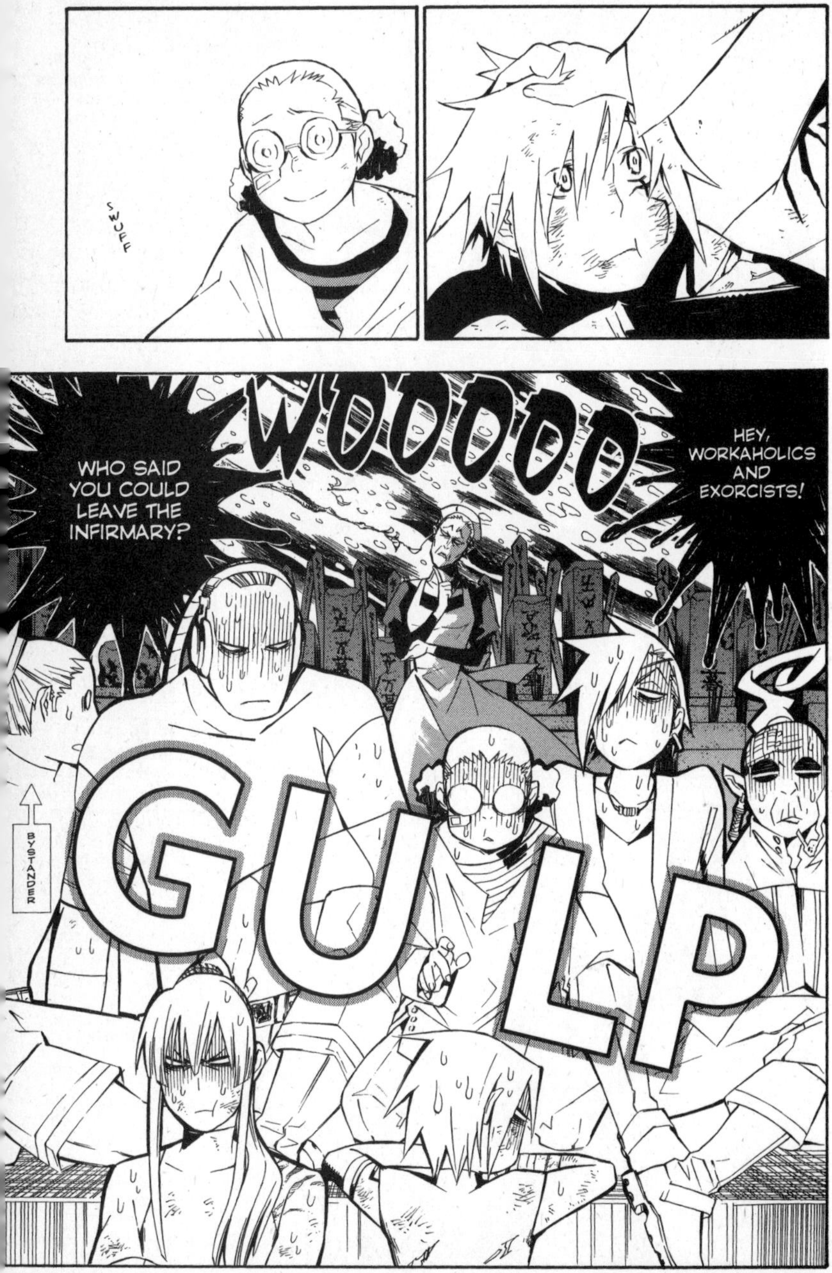
SWUFF
HEY, WORKAHOLICS AND EXORCISTS!
WOOOOOO
WHO SAID YOU COULD LEAVE THE INFIRMARY?
GULP
BYSTANDER

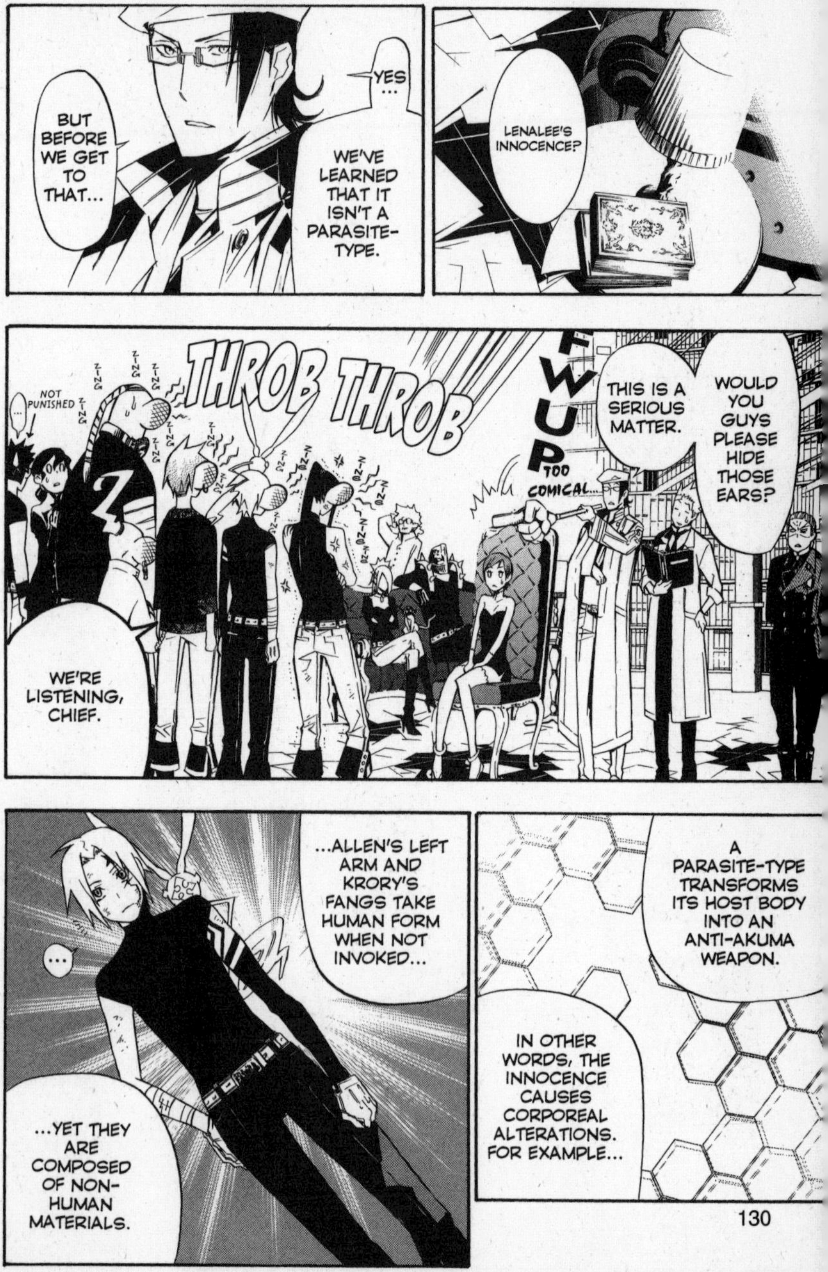
LENALEE'S INNOCENCE?
YES...
WE'VE LEARNED THAT IT ISN'T A PARASITE-TYPE.
BUT BEFORE WE GET TO THAT...
WOULD YOU GUYS PLEASE HIDE THOSE EARS?
THIS IS A SERIOUS MATTER.
FWUP
TOO COMICAL...
THROB THROB
ZING ZING ZING ZING
NOT PUNISHED
...
WE'RE LISTENING, CHIEF.
A PARASITE-TYPE TRANSFORMS ITS HOST BODY INTO AN ANTI-AKUMA WEAPON.
IN OTHER WORDS, THE INNOCENCE CAUSES CORPOREAL ALTERATIONS. FOR EXAMPLE...
...ALLEN'S LEFT ARM AND KRORY'S FANGS TAKE HUMAN FORM WHEN NOT INVOKED...
...
...YET THEY ARE COMPOSED OF NON-HUMAN MATERIALS.

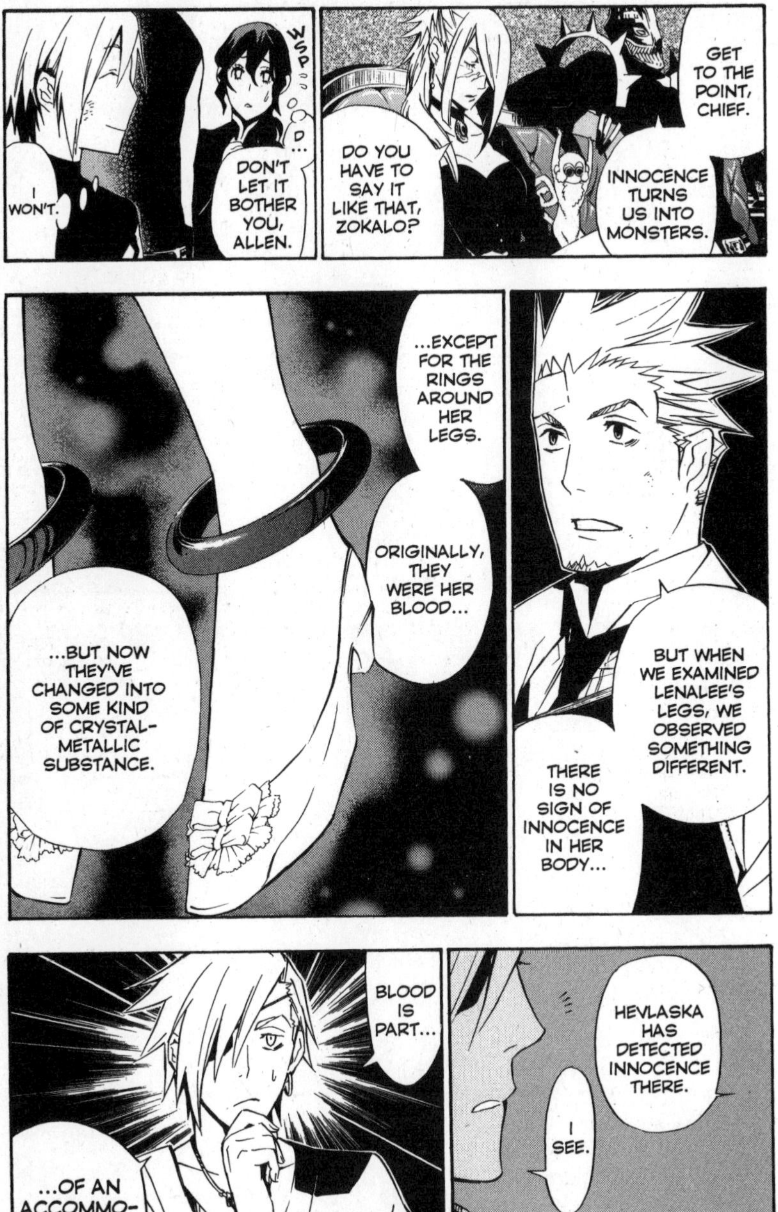
GET TO THE POINT, CHIEF.
INNOCENCE TURNS US INTO MONSTERS.
DO YOU HAVE TO SAY IT LIKE THAT, ZOKALO?
WSP
D...
DON'T LET IT BOTHER YOU, ALLEN.
I WON'T.
BUT WHEN WE EXAMINED LENALEE'S LEGS, WE OBSERVED SOMETHING DIFFERENT.
THERE IS NO SIGN OF INNOCENCE IN HER BODY...
...EXCEPT FOR THE RINGS AROUND HER LEGS.
ORIGINALLY, THEY WERE HER BLOOD...
...BUT NOW THEY'VE CHANGED INTO SOME KIND OF CRYSTAL-METALLIC SUBSTANCE.
HEVLASKA HAS DETECTED INNOCENCE THERE.
I SEE.
BLOOD IS PART...
...OF AN ACCOMMODATOR'S BODY.

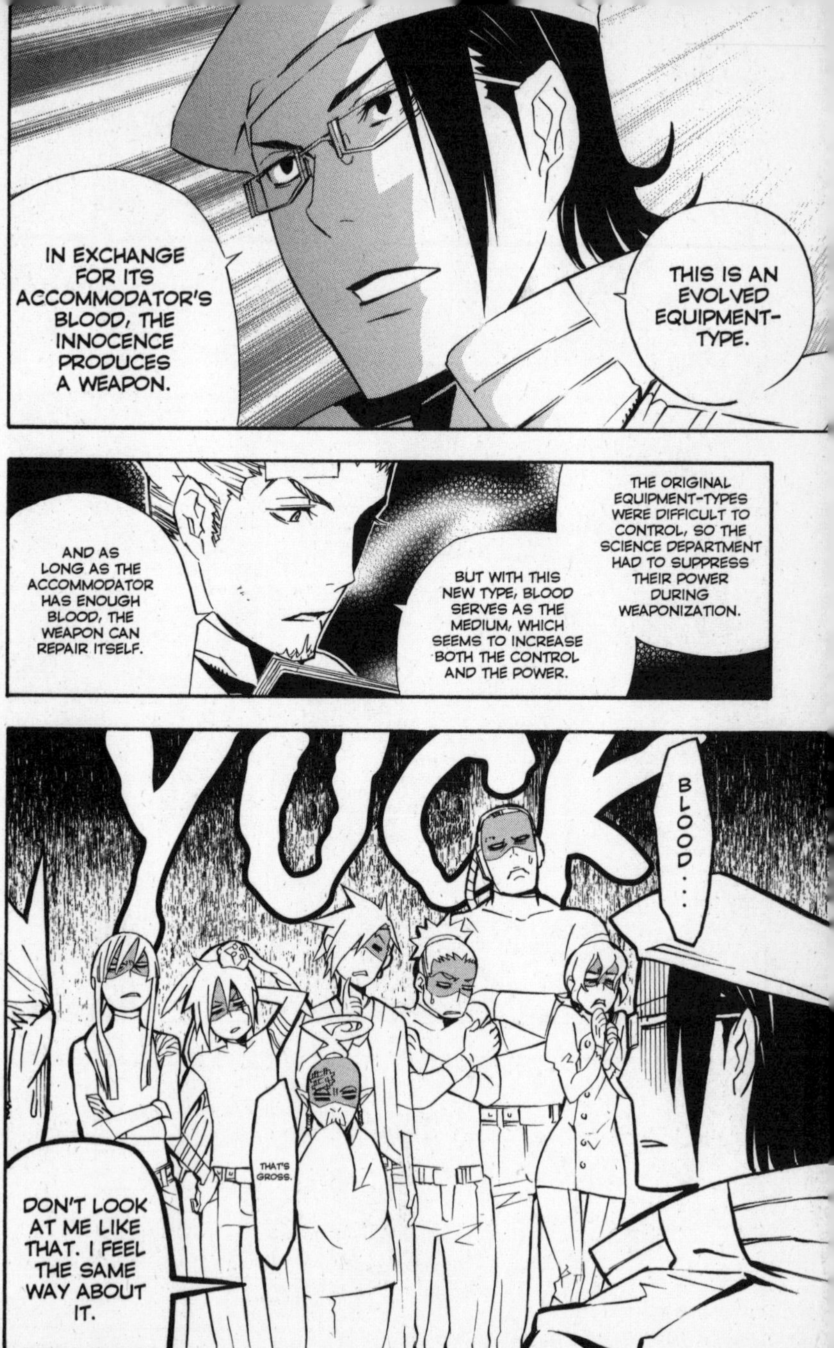
THIS IS AN EVOLVED EQUIPMENT-TYPE.
IN EXCHANGE FOR ITS ACCOMMODATOR'S BLOOD, THE INNOCENCE PRODUCES A WEAPON.
THE ORIGINAL EQUIPMENT-TYPES WERE DIFFICULT TO CONTROL, SO THE SCIENCE DEPARTMENT HAD TO SUPPRESS THEIR POWER DURING WEAPONIZATION.
BUT WITH THIS NEW TYPE, BLOOD SERVES AS THE MEDIUM, WHICH SEEMS TO INCREASE BOTH THE CONTROL AND THE POWER.
AND AS LONG AS THE ACCOMMODATOR HAS ENOUGH BLOOD, THE WEAPON CAN REPAIR ITSELF.
YUCK
BLOOD...
THAT'S GROSS.
DON'T LOOK AT ME LIKE THAT. I FEEL THE SAME WAY ABOUT IT.

READ THIS WAY

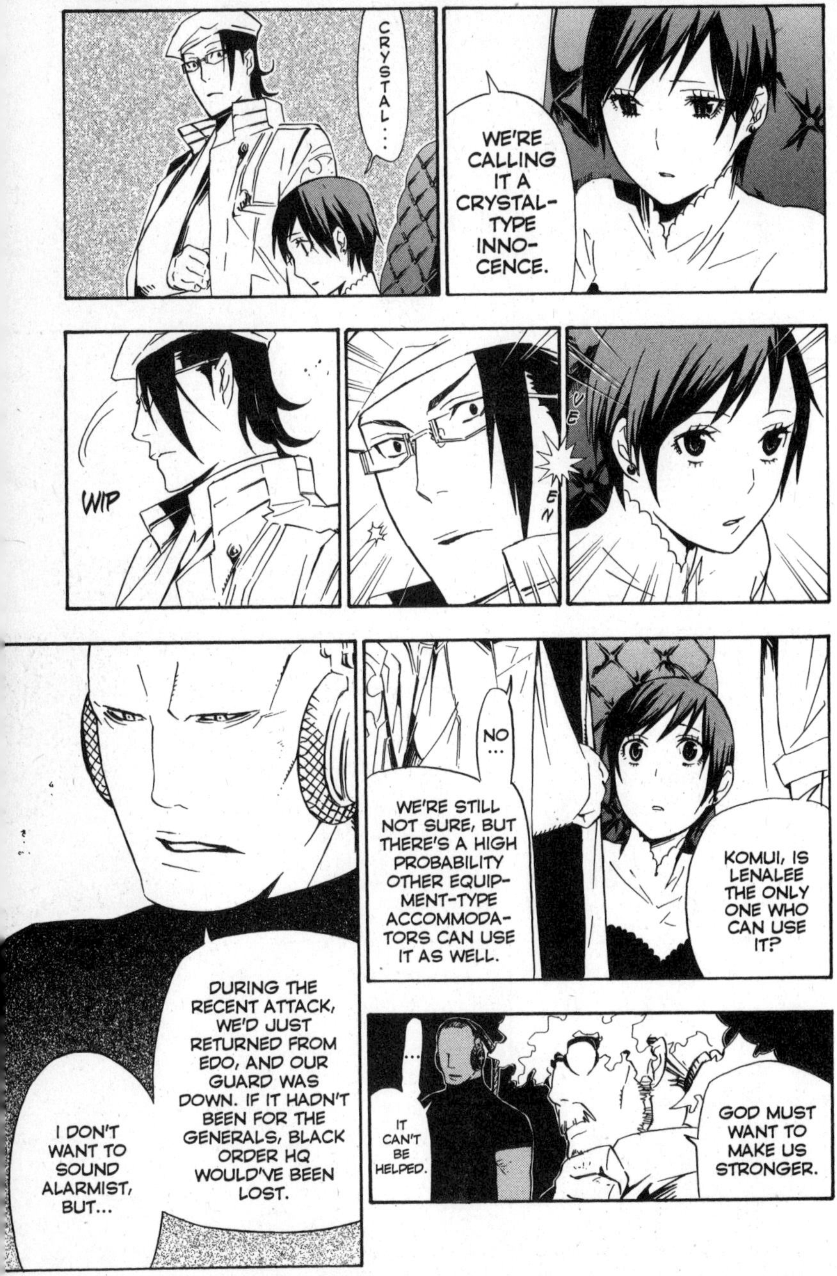

WE'RE CALLING IT A CRYSTAL-TYPE INNOCENCE.
CRYSTAL...
VE
EN
WIP
KOMUI, IS LENALEE THE ONLY ONE WHO CAN USE IT?
NO...
WE'RE STILL NOT SURE, BUT THERE'S A HIGH PROBABILITY OTHER EQUIPMENT-TYPE ACCOMMODATORS CAN USE IT AS WELL.
GOD MUST WANT TO MAKE US STRONGER.
IT CAN'T BE HELPED.
...
DURING THE RECENT ATTACK, WE'D JUST RETURNED FROM EDO, AND OUR GUARD WAS DOWN. IF IT HADN'T BEEN FOR THE GENERALS, BLACK ORDER HQ WOULD'VE BEEN LOST.
I DON'T WANT TO SOUND ALARMIST, BUT...

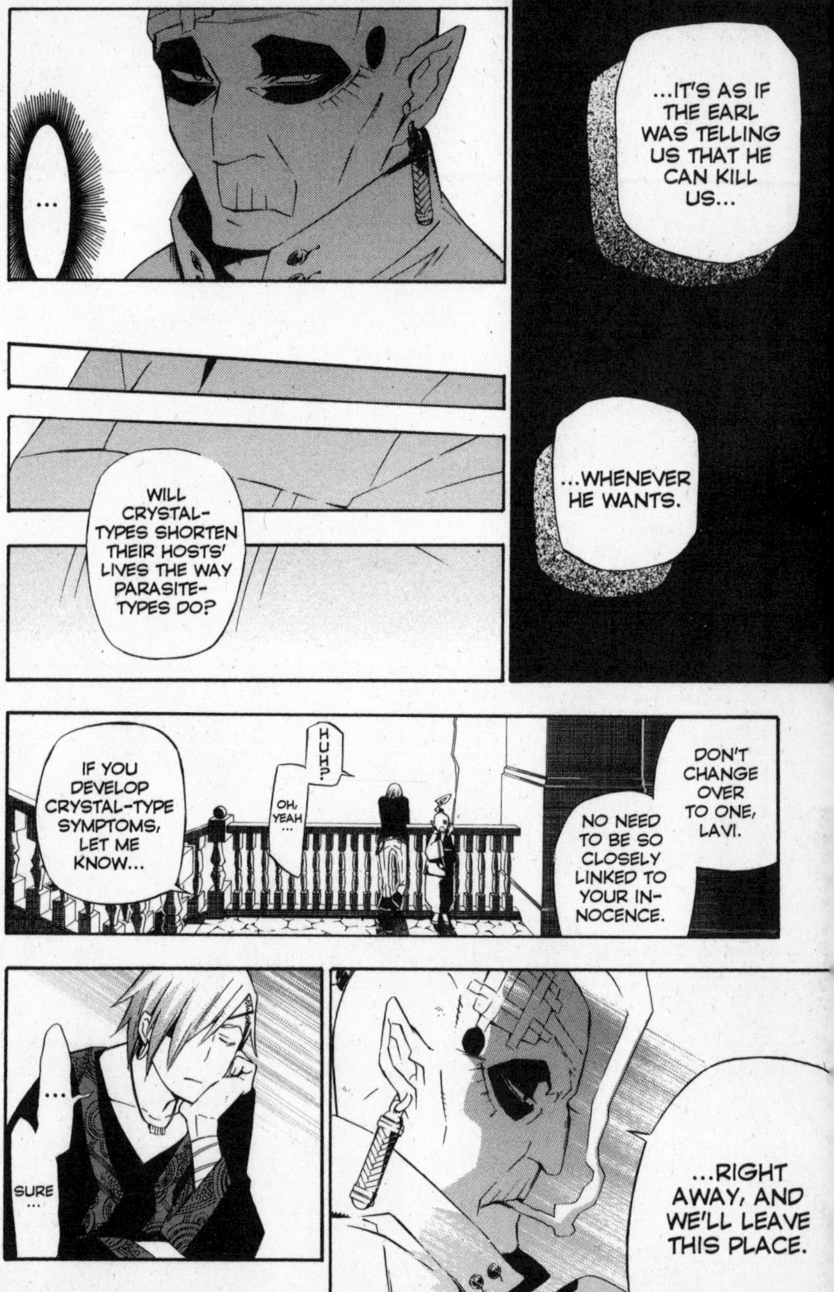
...IT'S AS IF THE EARL WAS TELLING US THAT HE CAN KILL US...
...WHENEVER HE WANTS.
...
WILL CRYSTAL-TYPES SHORTEN THEIR HOSTS' LIVES THE WAY PARASITE-TYPES DO?
DON'T CHANGE OVER TO ONE, LAVI.
NO NEED TO BE SO CLOSELY LINKED TO YOUR IN-NOCENCE.
HUH?
OH, YEAH...
IF YOU DEVELOP CRYSTAL-TYPE SYMPTOMS, LET ME KNOW...
...RIGHT AWAY, AND WE'LL LEAVE THIS PLACE.
...
SURE...

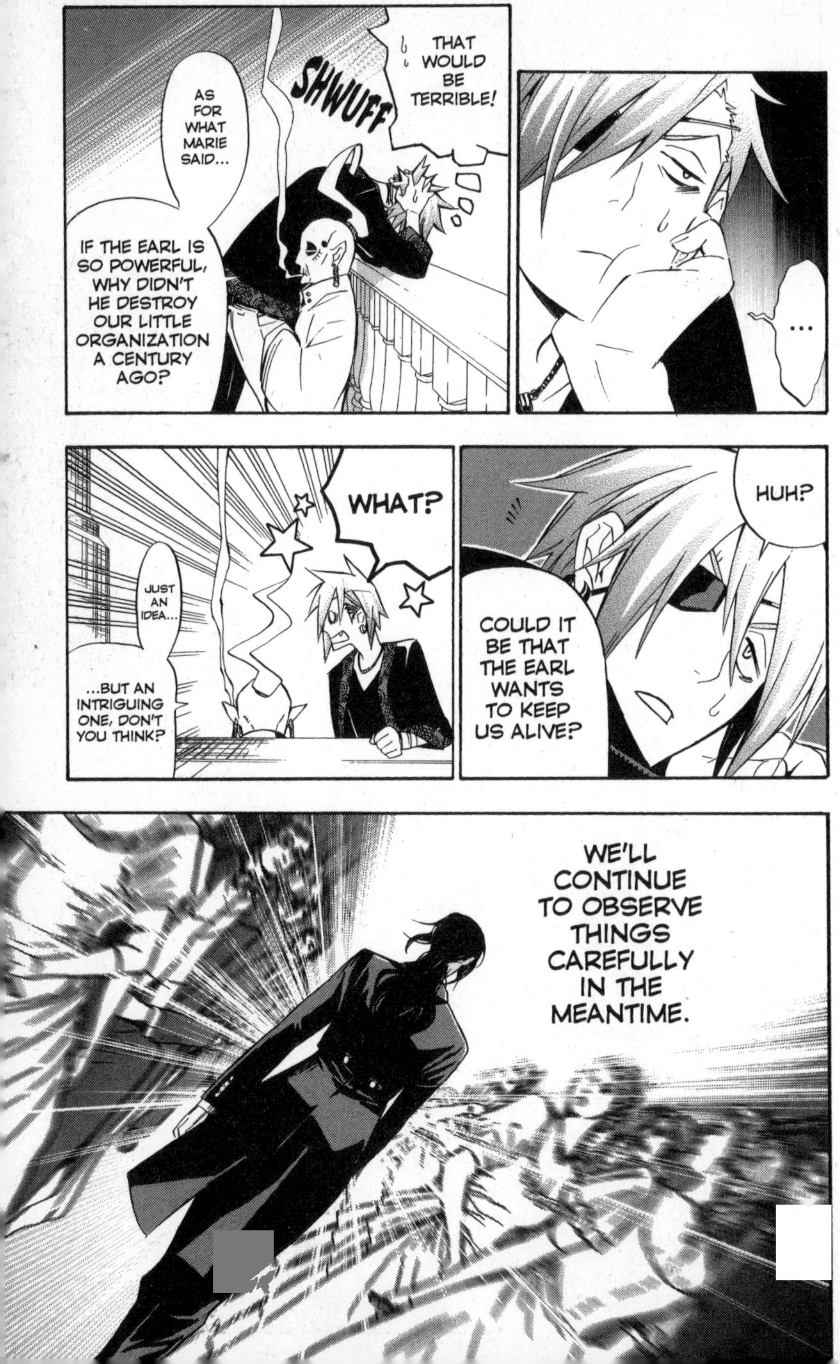
...
THAT WOULD BE TERRIBLE!
SHWUFF
AS FOR WHAT MARIE SAID...
IF THE EARL IS SO POWERFUL, WHY DIDN'T HE DESTROY OUR LITTLE ORGANIZATION A CENTURY AGO?
HUH?
COULD IT BE THAT THE EARL WANTS TO KEEP US ALIVE?
WHAT?
JUST AN IDEA...
...BUT AN INTRIGUING ONE, DON'T YOU THINK?
WE'LL CONTINUE TO OBSERVE THINGS CAREFULLY IN THE MEANTIME.

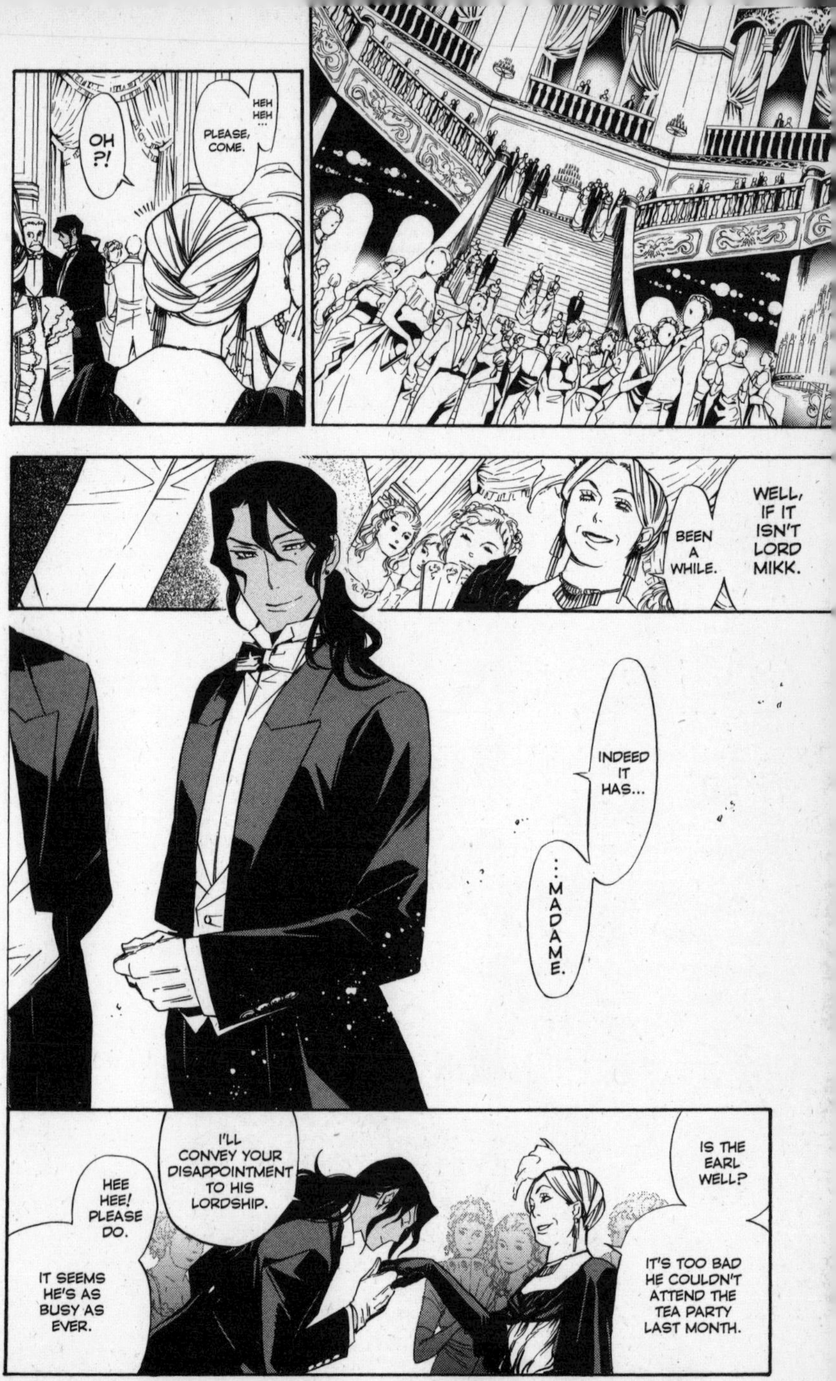
HEH HEH... PLEASE, COME.
OH ?!
WELL, IF IT ISN'T LORD MIKK.
BEEN A WHILE.
INDEED IT HAS...
...MADAME.
IS THE EARL WELL?
IT'S TOO BAD HE COULDN'T ATTEND THE TEA PARTY LAST MONTH.
I'LL CONVEY YOUR DISAPPOINTMENT TO HIS LORDSHIP.
HEE HEE! PLEASE DO.
IT SEEMS HE'S AS BUSY AS EVER.

READ THIS WAY

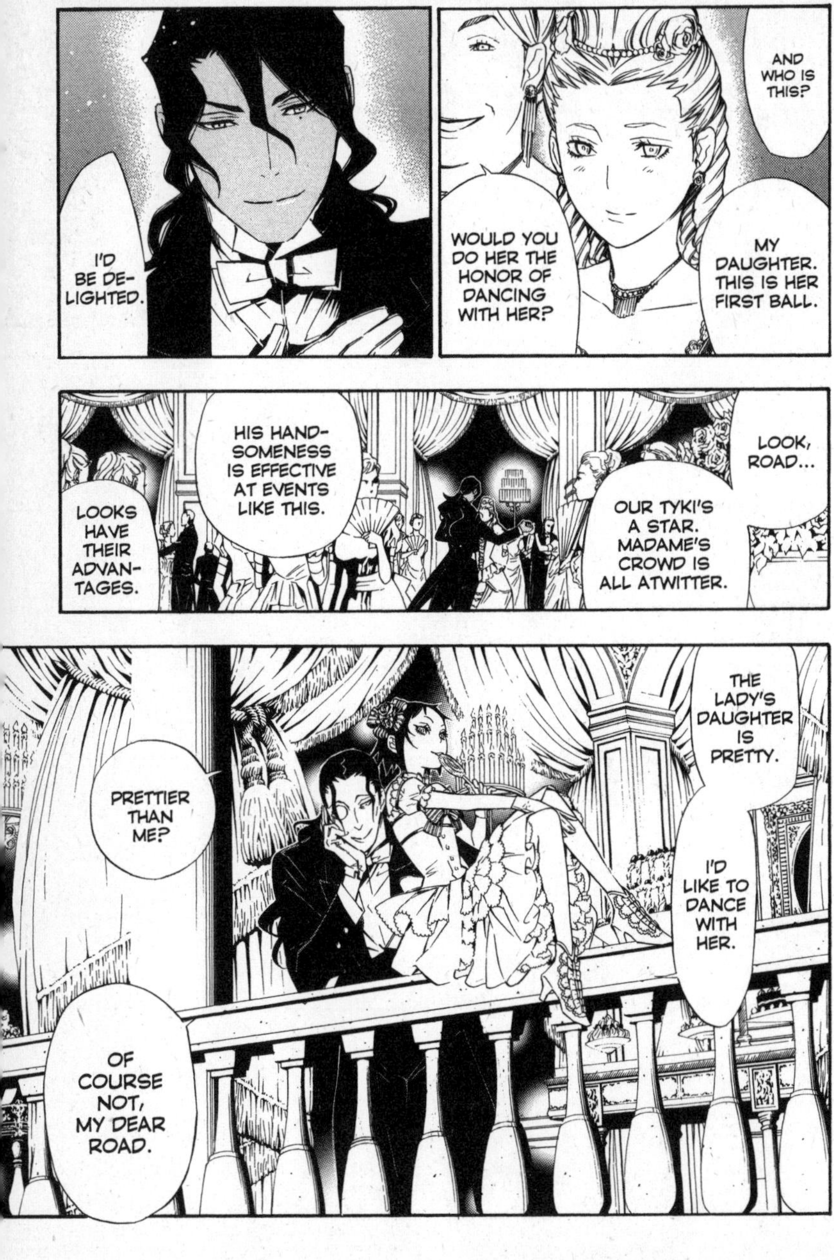

AND WHO IS THIS?
MY DAUGHTER. THIS IS HER FIRST BALL.
WOULD YOU DO HER THE HONOR OF DANCING WITH HER?
I'D BE DELIGHTED.
LOOK, ROAD...
OUR TYKI'S A STAR. MADAME'S CROWD IS ALL ATWITTER.
HIS HANDSOMENESS IS EFFECTIVE AT EVENTS LIKE THIS.
LOOKS HAVE THEIR ADVANTAGES.
THE LADY'S DAUGHTER IS PRETTY.
I'D LIKE TO DANCE WITH HER.
PRETTIER THAN ME?
OF COURSE NOT, MY DEAR ROAD.

THE PEOPLE OF D.GRAY HOUSE

LAVIHIKO'S ☆ THRILLING NOTICE OF IMPOVERISHMENT

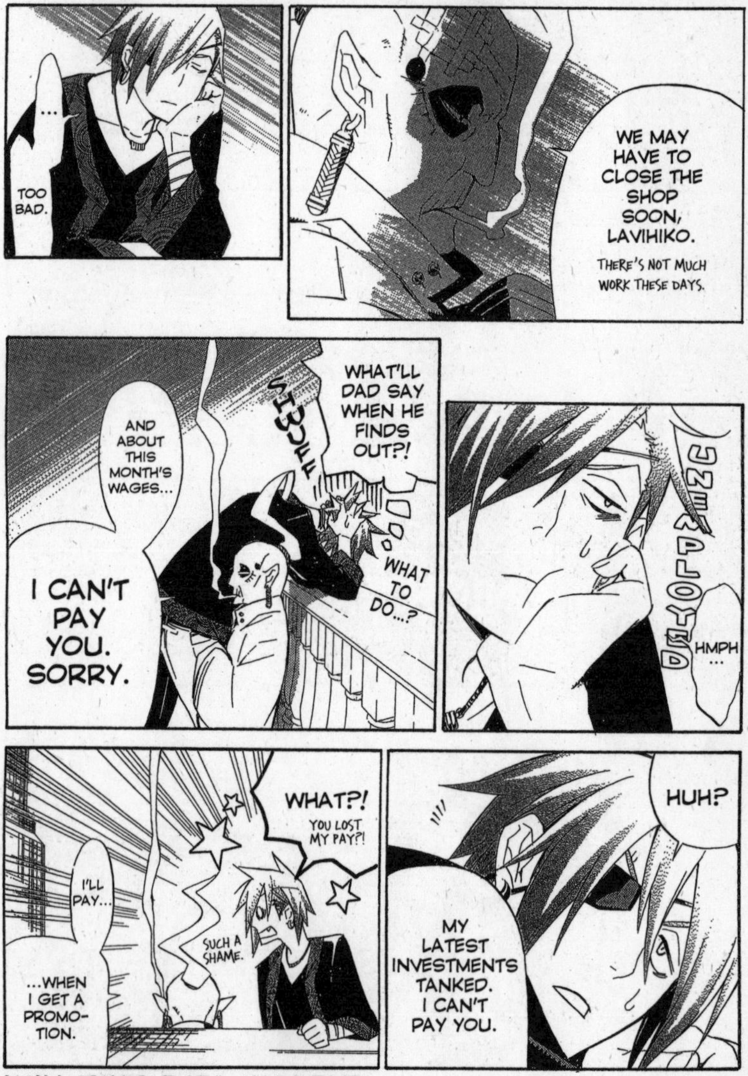
WE MAY HAVE TO CLOSE THE SHOP SOON, LAVIHIKO.
THERE'S NOT MUCH WORK THESE DAYS.
...
TOO BAD.
UNEMPLOYED
HMPH...
WHAT'LL DAD SAY WHEN HE FINDS OUT?!
SHUFF
AND ABOUT THIS MONTH'S WAGES...
WHAT TO DO...?
I CAN'T PAY YOU. SORRY.
HUH?
MY LATEST INVESTMENTS TANKED. I CAN'T PAY YOU.
WHAT?!
YOU LOST MY PAY?!
SUCH A SHAME.
I'LL PAY...
...WHEN I GET A PROMOTION.

WILL THAT EVER HAPPEN?

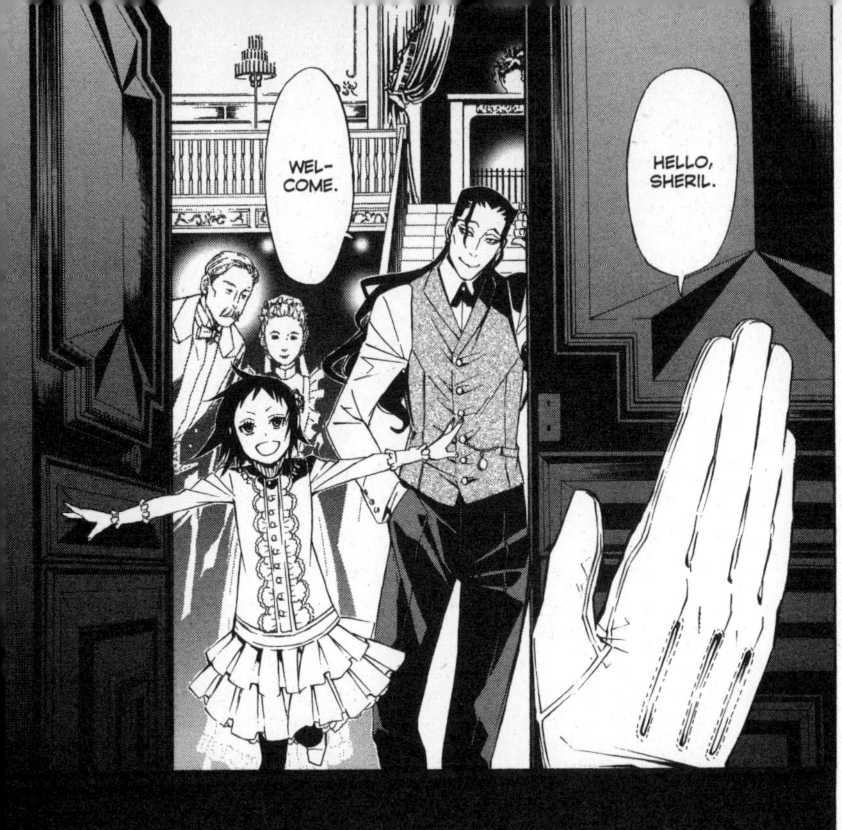
HELLO, SHERIL.
WEL- COME.

THE 158TH NIGHT: EVIL FLOWER

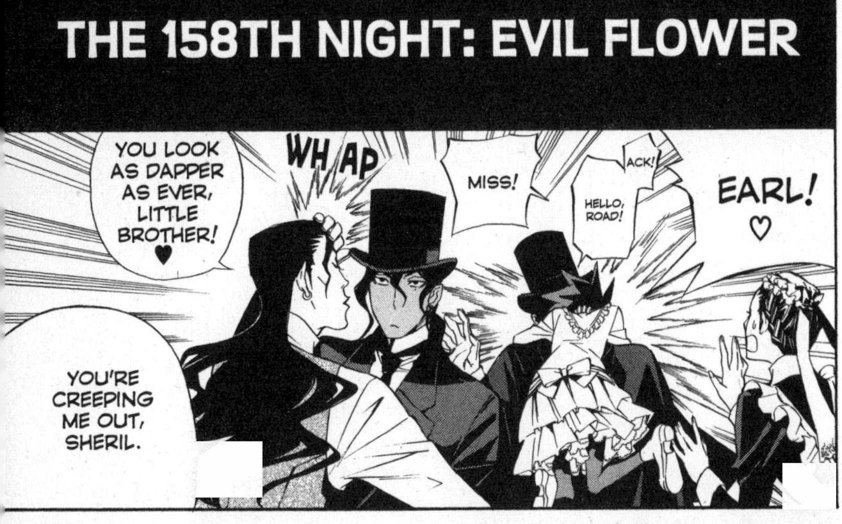
EARL! ♡
ACK!
HELLO, ROAD!
MISS!
WHAP
YOU LOOK AS DAPPER AS EVER, LITTLE BROTHER! ♥
YOU'RE CREEPING ME OUT, SHERIL.

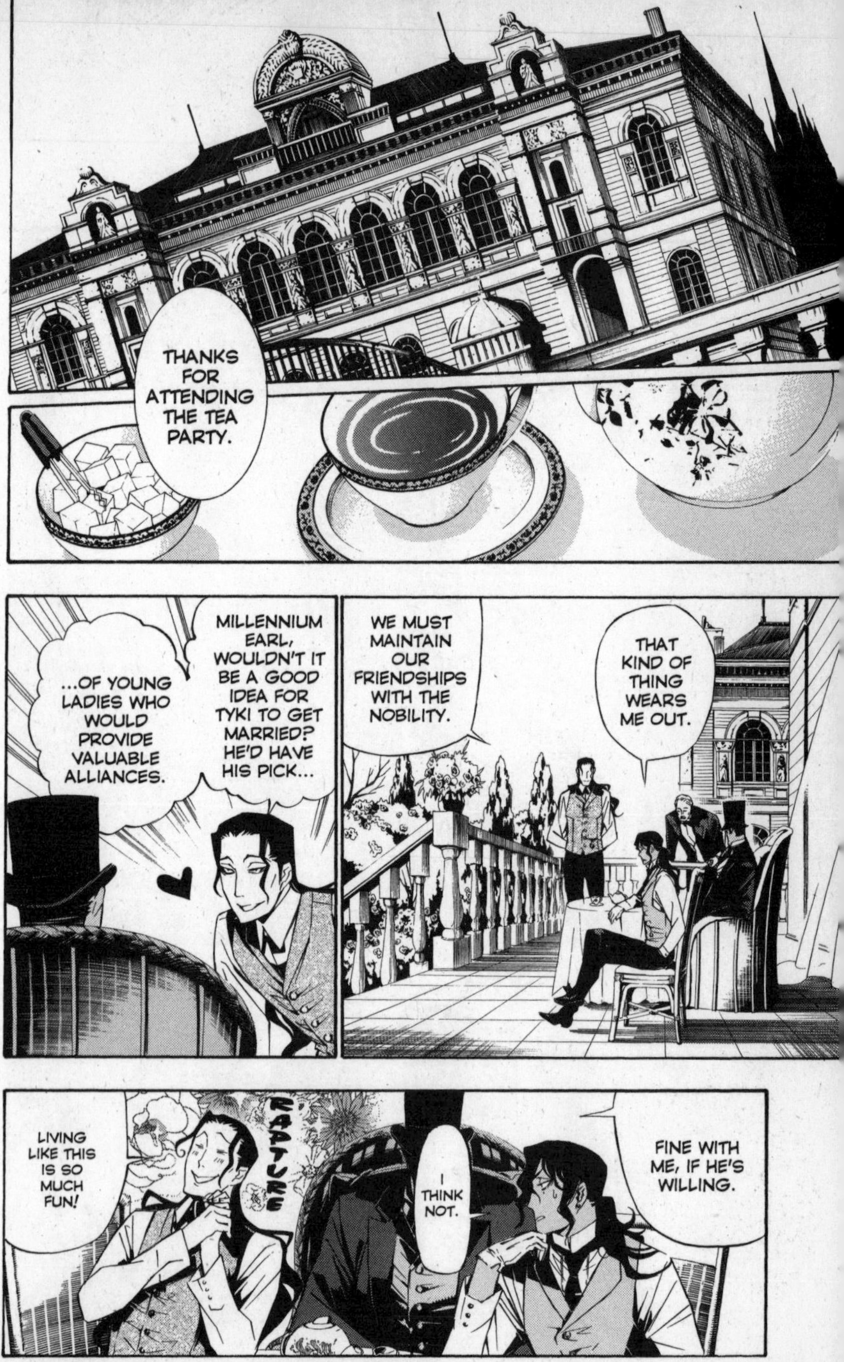
THANKS FOR ATTENDING THE TEA PARTY.
WE MUST MAINTAIN OUR FRIENDSHIPS WITH THE NOBILITY.
THAT KIND OF THING WEARS ME OUT.
MILLENNIUM EARL, WOULDN'T IT BE A GOOD IDEA FOR TYKI TO GET MARRIED? HE'D HAVE HIS PICK...
...OF YOUNG LADIES WHO WOULD PROVIDE VALUABLE ALLIANCES.
LIVING LIKE THIS IS SO MUCH FUN!
RAPTURE
I THINK NOT.
FINE WITH ME, IF HE'S WILLING.

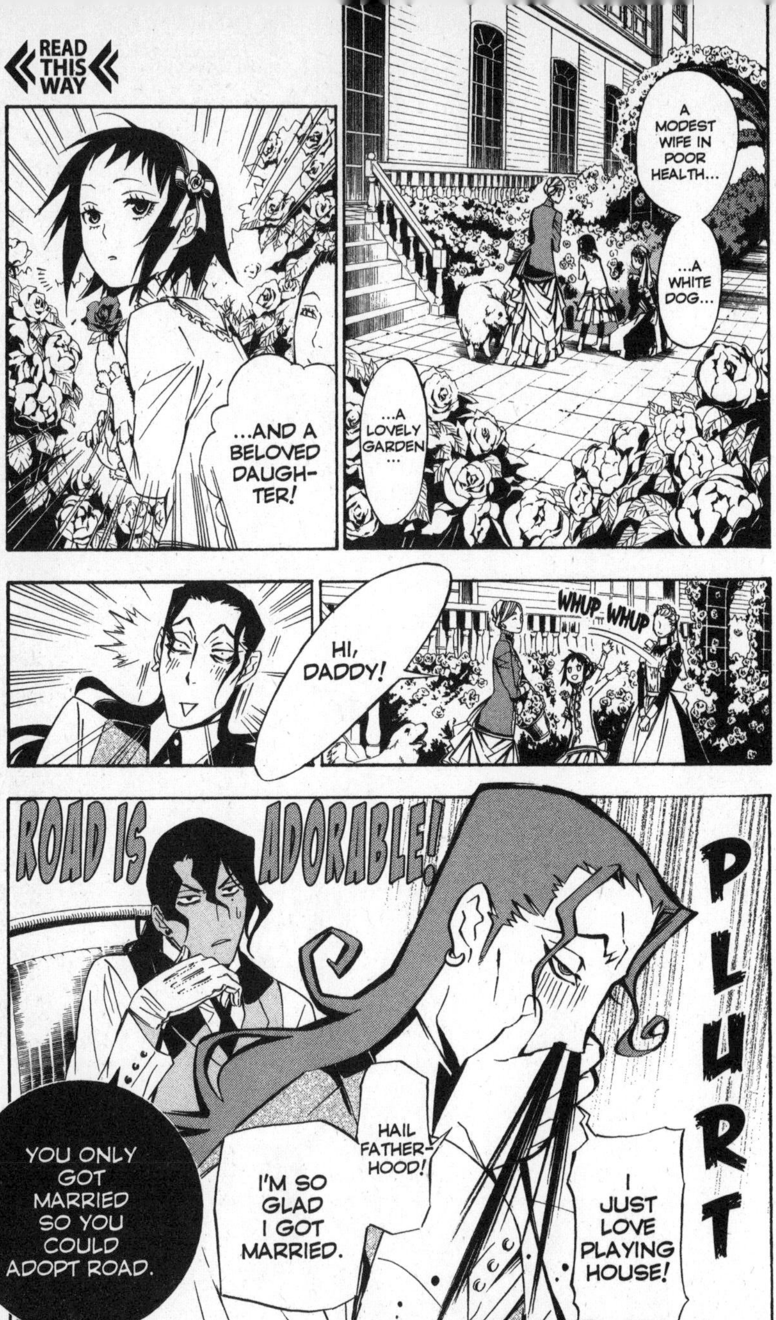
READ THIS WAY
A MODEST WIFE IN POOR HEALTH...
...A WHITE DOG...
...A LOVELY GARDEN...
...AND A BELOVED DAUGHTER!
WHUP WHUP
HI, DADDY!
PLURT
I JUST LOVE PLAYING HOUSE!
HAIL FATHERHOOD!
I'M SO GLAD I GOT MARRIED.
ROAD IS ADORABLE!
YOU ONLY GOT MARRIED SO YOU COULD ADOPT ROAD.

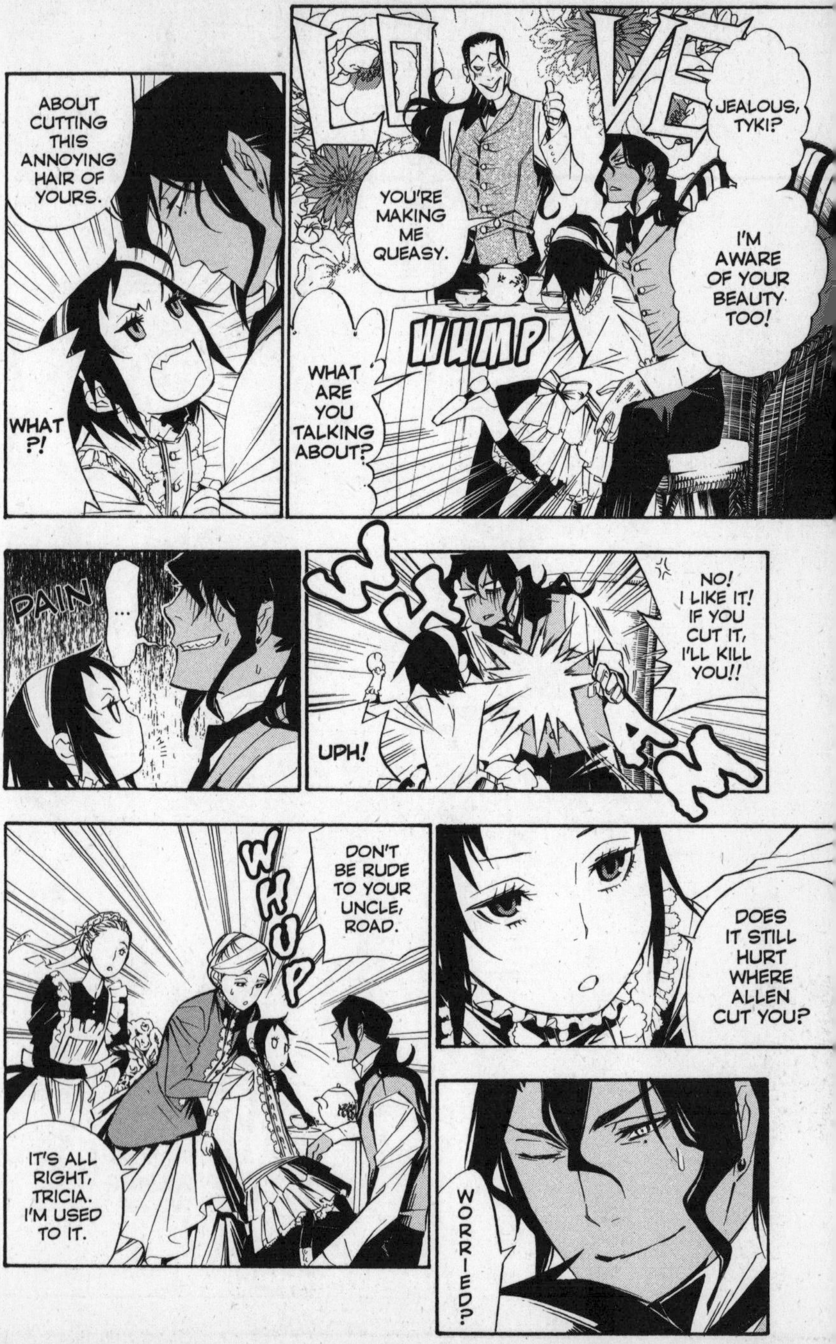
LOVE
JEALOUS, TYKI?
I'M AWARE OF YOUR BEAUTY TOO!
YOU'RE MAKING ME QUEASY.
WUMP
WHAT ARE YOU TALKING ABOUT?
ABOUT CUTTING THIS ANNOYING HAIR OF YOURS.
WHAT?!
NO! I LIKE IT! IF YOU CUT IT, I'LL KILL YOU!!
UPH!
PAIN
...
DOES IT STILL HURT WHERE ALLEN CUT YOU?
WORRIED?
DON'T BE RUDE TO YOUR UNCLE, ROAD.
WHUP
IT'S ALL RIGHT, TRICIA. I'M USED TO IT.

READ THIS WAY

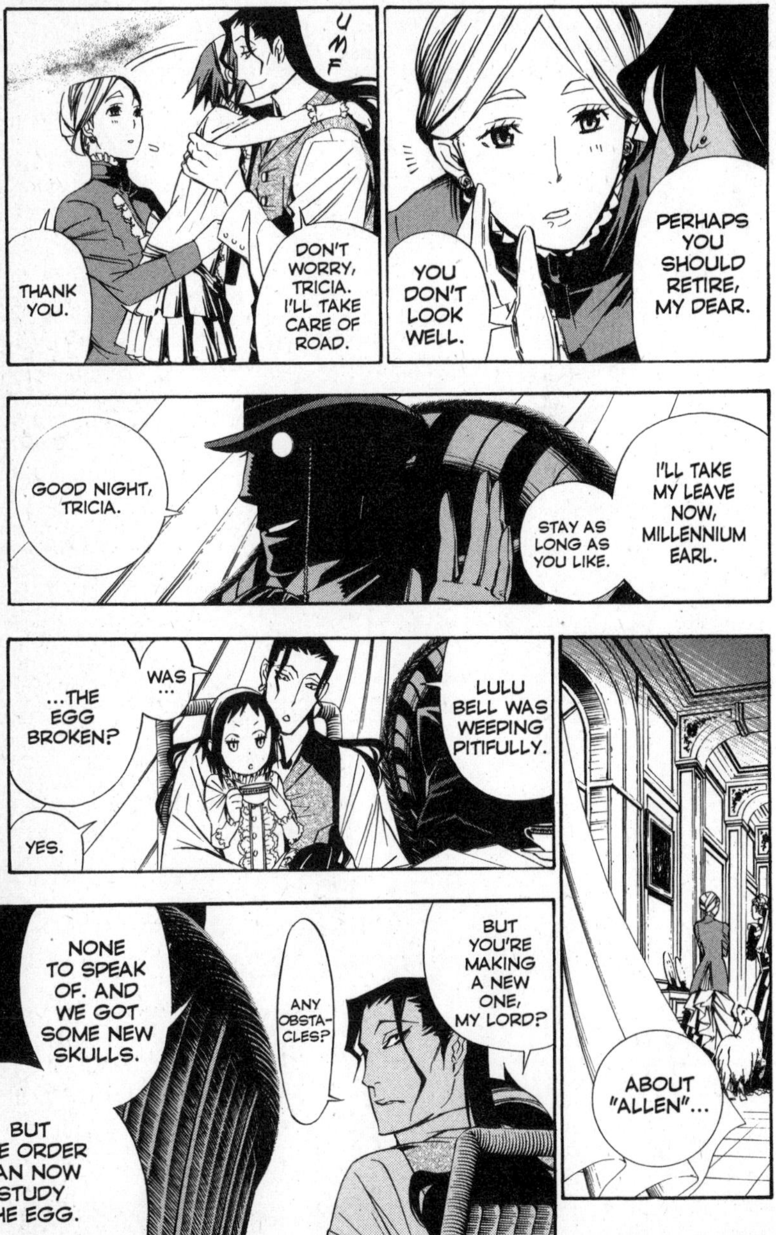
PERHAPS YOU SHOULD RETIRE, MY DEAR.
YOU DON'T LOOK WELL.
UMF
DON'T WORRY, TRICIA. I'LL TAKE CARE OF ROAD.
THANK YOU.
I'LL TAKE MY LEAVE NOW, MILLENNIUM EARL.
STAY AS LONG AS YOU LIKE.
GOOD NIGHT, TRICIA.
ABOUT "ALLEN"...
LULU BELL WAS WEEPING PITIFULLY.
WAS...
...THE EGG BROKEN?
YES.
BUT YOU'RE MAKING A NEW ONE, MY LORD?
ANY OBSTACLES?
NONE TO SPEAK OF. AND WE GOT SOME NEW SKULLS.
BUT THE ORDER CAN NOW STUDY THE EGG.

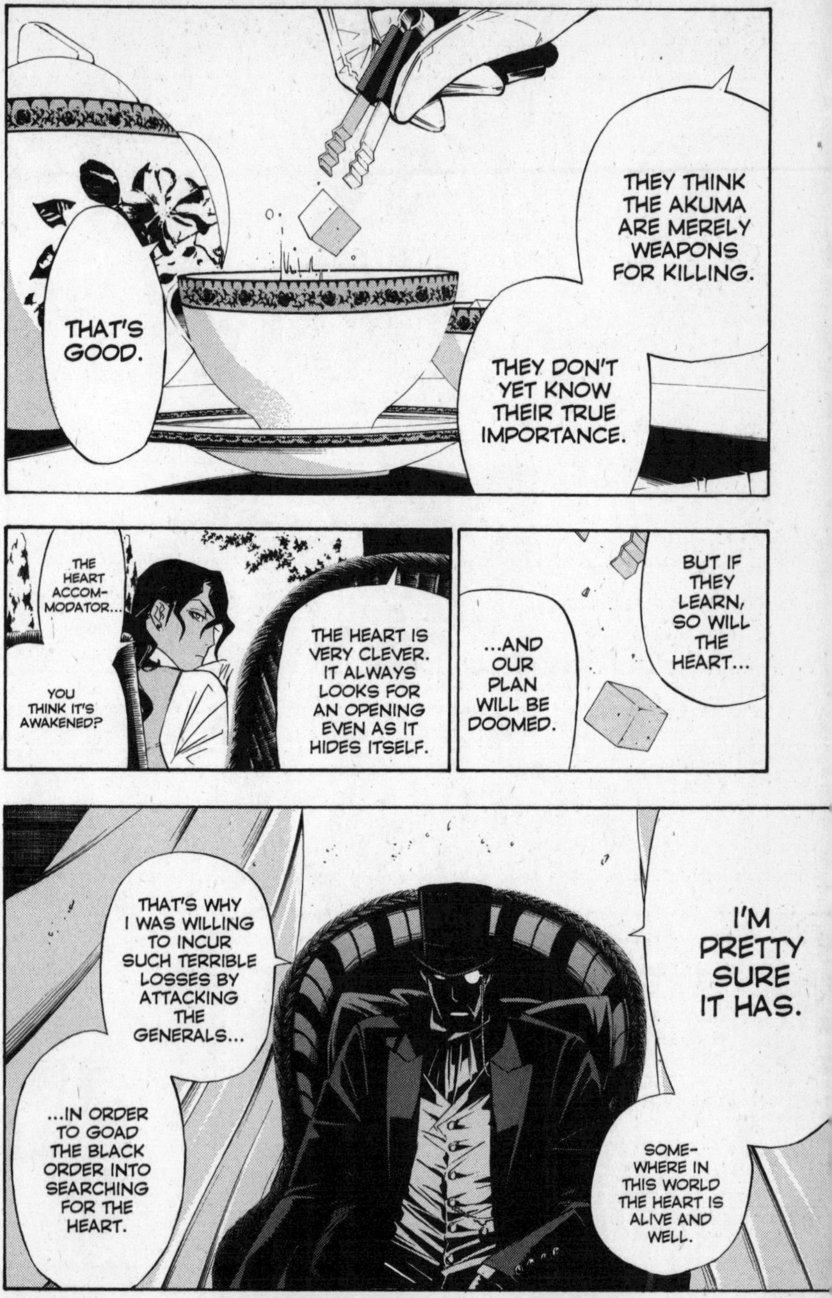
THEY THINK THE AKUMA ARE MERELY WEAPONS FOR KILLING.
THEY DON'T YET KNOW THEIR TRUE IMPORTANCE.
THAT'S GOOD.
BUT IF THEY LEARN, SO WILL THE HEART...
...AND OUR PLAN WILL BE DOOMED.
THE HEART IS VERY CLEVER. IT ALWAYS LOOKS FOR AN OPENING EVEN AS IT HIDES ITSELF.
THE HEART ACCOM-MODATOR...
YOU THINK IT'S AWAKENED?
I'M PRETTY SURE IT HAS.
SOME-WHERE IN THIS WORLD THE HEART IS ALIVE AND WELL.
THAT'S WHY I WAS WILLING TO INCUR SUCH TERRIBLE LOSSES BY ATTACKING THE GENERALS...
...IN ORDER TO GOAD THE BLACK ORDER INTO SEARCHING FOR THE HEART.

READ THIS WAY

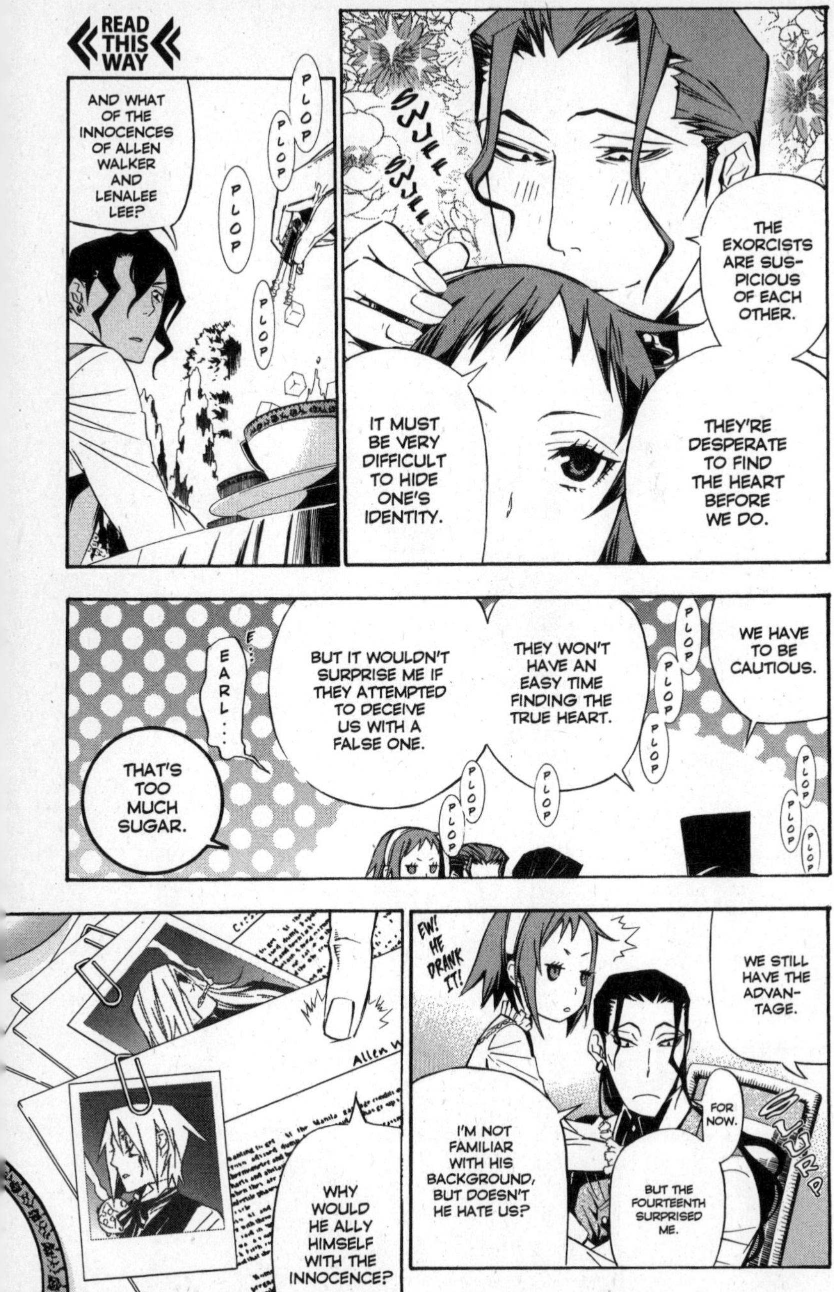
THE EXORCISTS ARE SUSPICIOUS OF EACH OTHER.
THEY'RE DESPERATE TO FIND THE HEART BEFORE WE DO.
IT MUST BE VERY DIFFICULT TO HIDE ONE'S IDENTITY.
PLOP PLOP PLOP PLOP
AND WHAT OF THE INNOCENCES OF ALLEN WALKER AND LENALEE LEE?
WE HAVE TO BE CAUTIOUS.
PLOP PLOP PLOP PLOP
THEY WON'T HAVE AN EASY TIME FINDING THE TRUE HEART.
BUT IT WOULDN'T SURPRISE ME IF THEY ATTEMPTED TO DECEIVE US WITH A FALSE ONE.
PLOP PLOP PLOP
E... EARL...
THAT'S TOO MUCH SUGAR.
WE STILL HAVE THE ADVANTAGE.
EW! HE DRANK IT!
FOR NOW.
BUT THE FOURTEENTH SURPRISED ME.
I'M NOT FAMILIAR WITH HIS BACKGROUND, BUT DOESN'T HE HATE US?
Allen W
WHY WOULD HE ALLY HIMSELF WITH THE INNOCENCE?

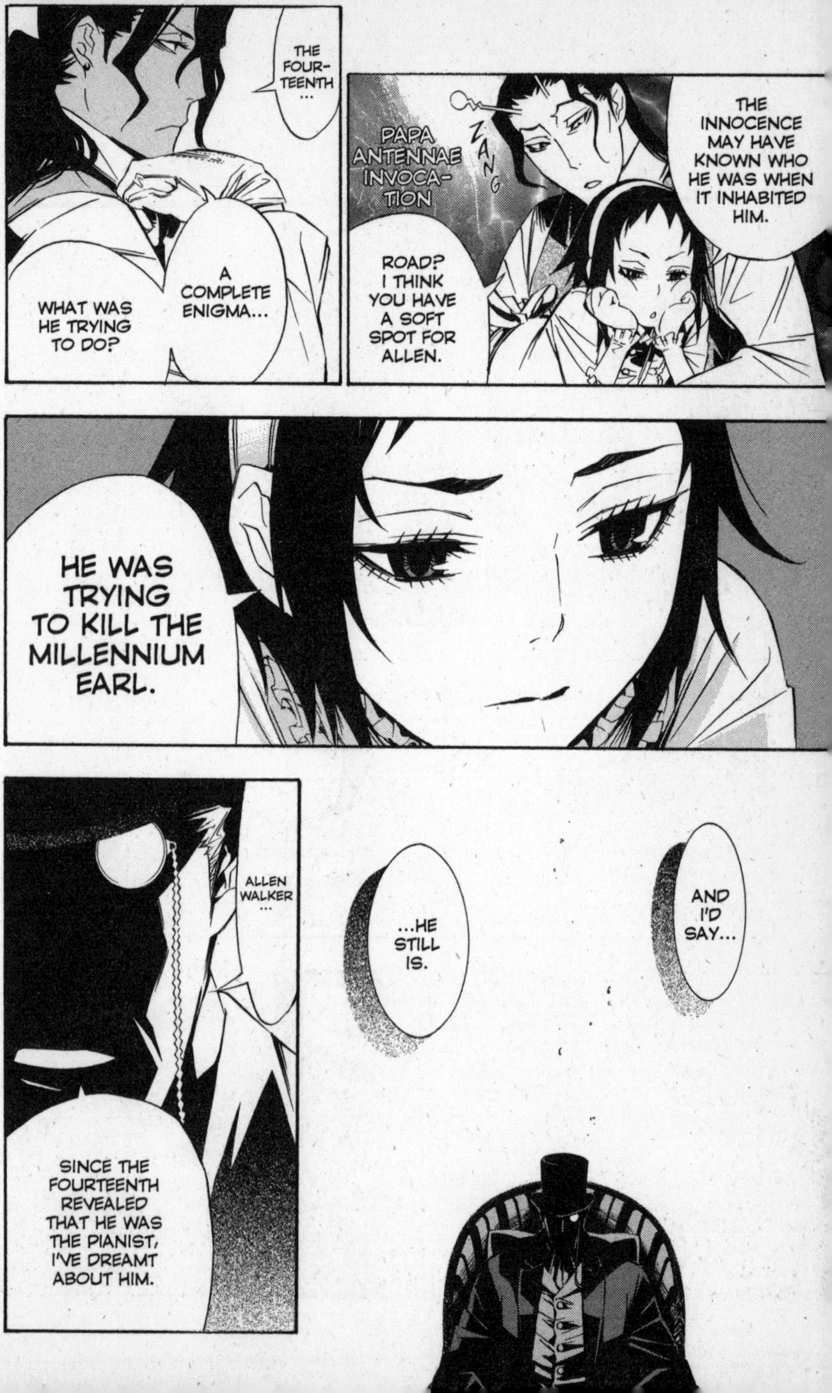
THE INNOCENCE MAY HAVE KNOWN WHO HE WAS WHEN IT INHABITED HIM.
ZANG
PAPA ANTENNAE INVOCATION
ROAD? I THINK YOU HAVE A SOFT SPOT FOR ALLEN.
THE FOURTEENTH...
A COMPLETE ENIGMA...
WHAT WAS HE TRYING TO DO?
HE WAS TRYING TO KILL THE MILLENNIUM EARL.
AND I'D SAY...
...HE STILL IS.
ALLEN WALKER...
SINCE THE FOURTEENTH REVEALED THAT HE WAS THE PIANIST, I'VE DREAMT ABOUT HIM.

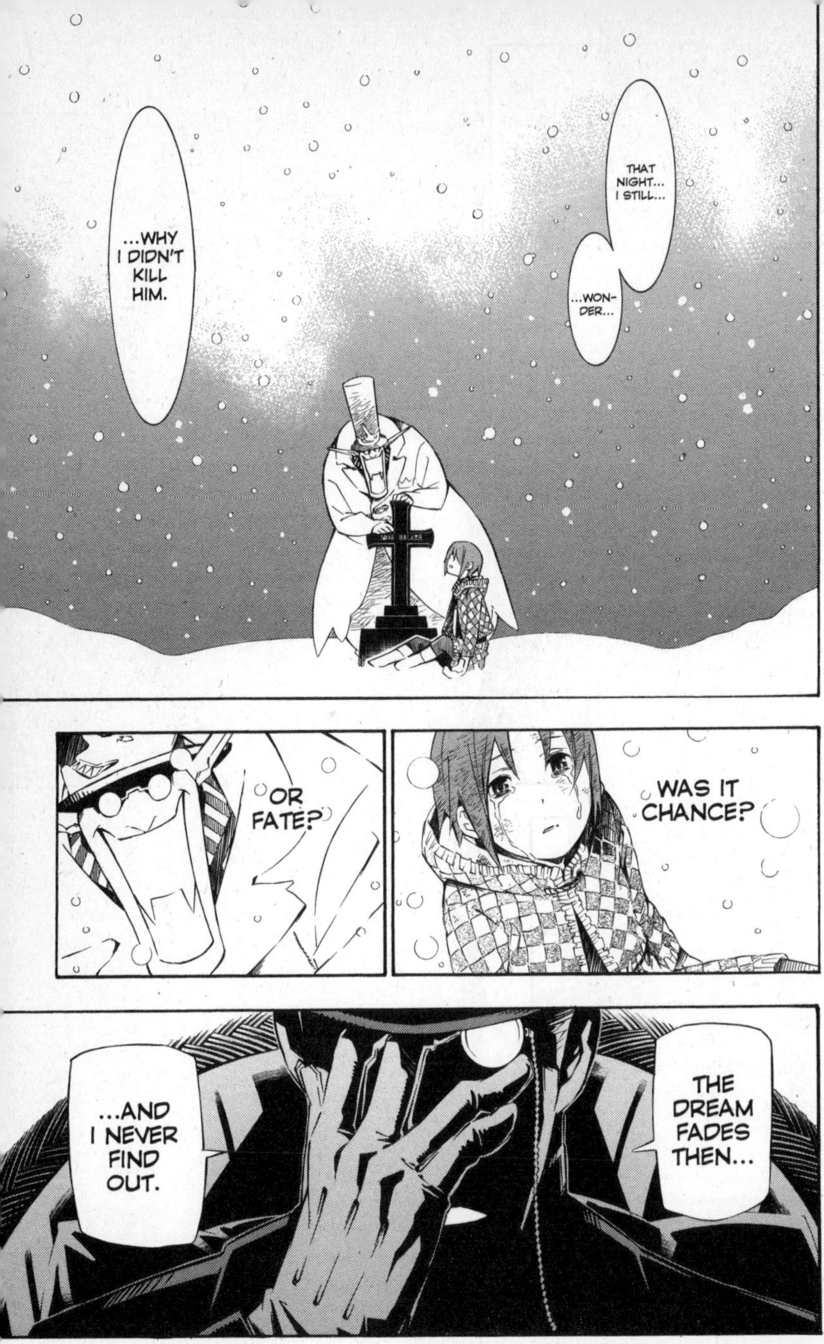
THAT NIGHT... I STILL...
...WONDER...
...WHY I DIDN'T KILL HIM.
WAS IT CHANCE?
OR FATE?
THE DREAM FADES THEN...
...AND I NEVER FIND OUT.

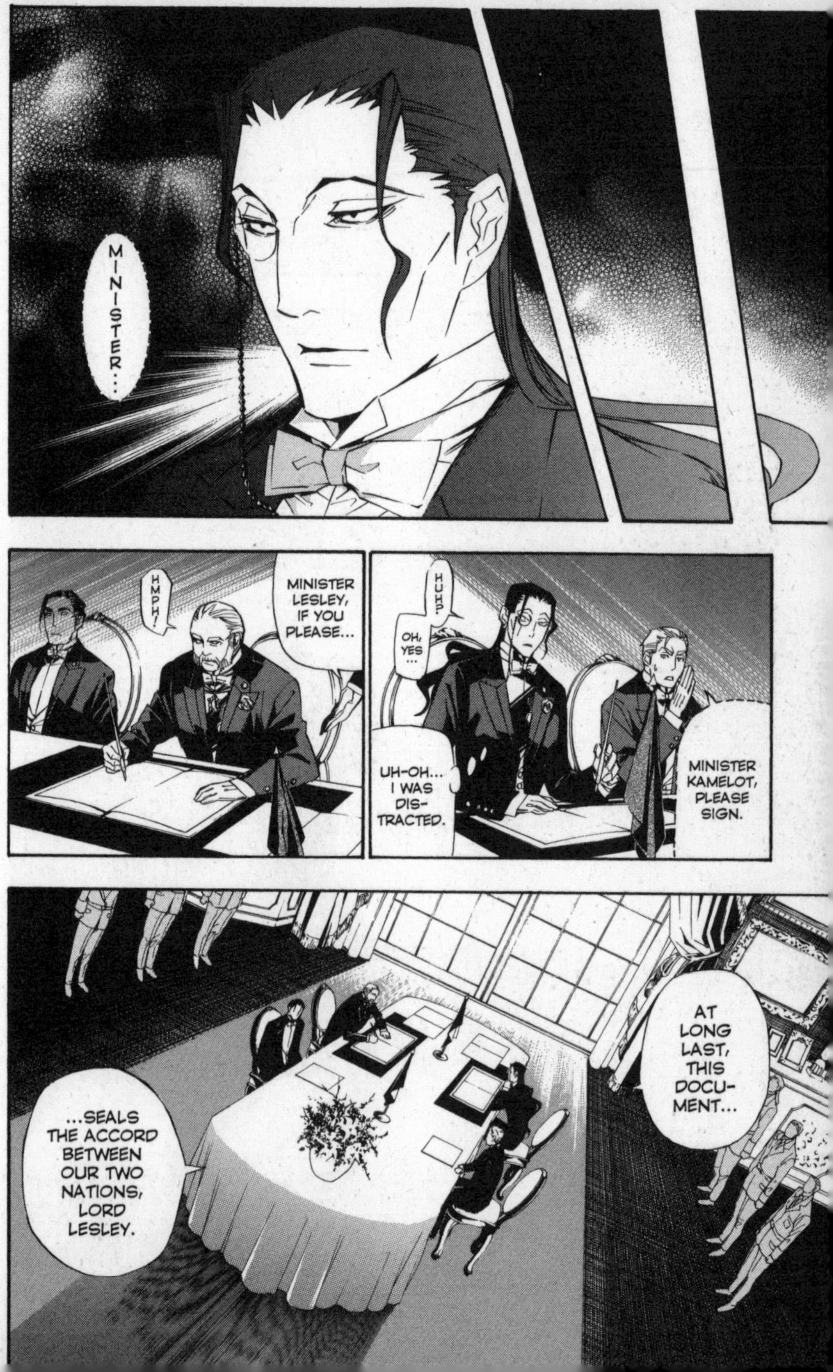
MINISTER...
MINISTER KAMELOT, PLEASE SIGN.
HUH?
OH, YES...
UH-OH... I WAS DISTRACTED.
MINISTER LESLEY, IF YOU PLEASE...
HMPH!
AT LONG LAST, THIS DOCUMENT...
...SEALS THE ACCORD BETWEEN OUR TWO NATIONS, LORD LESLEY.

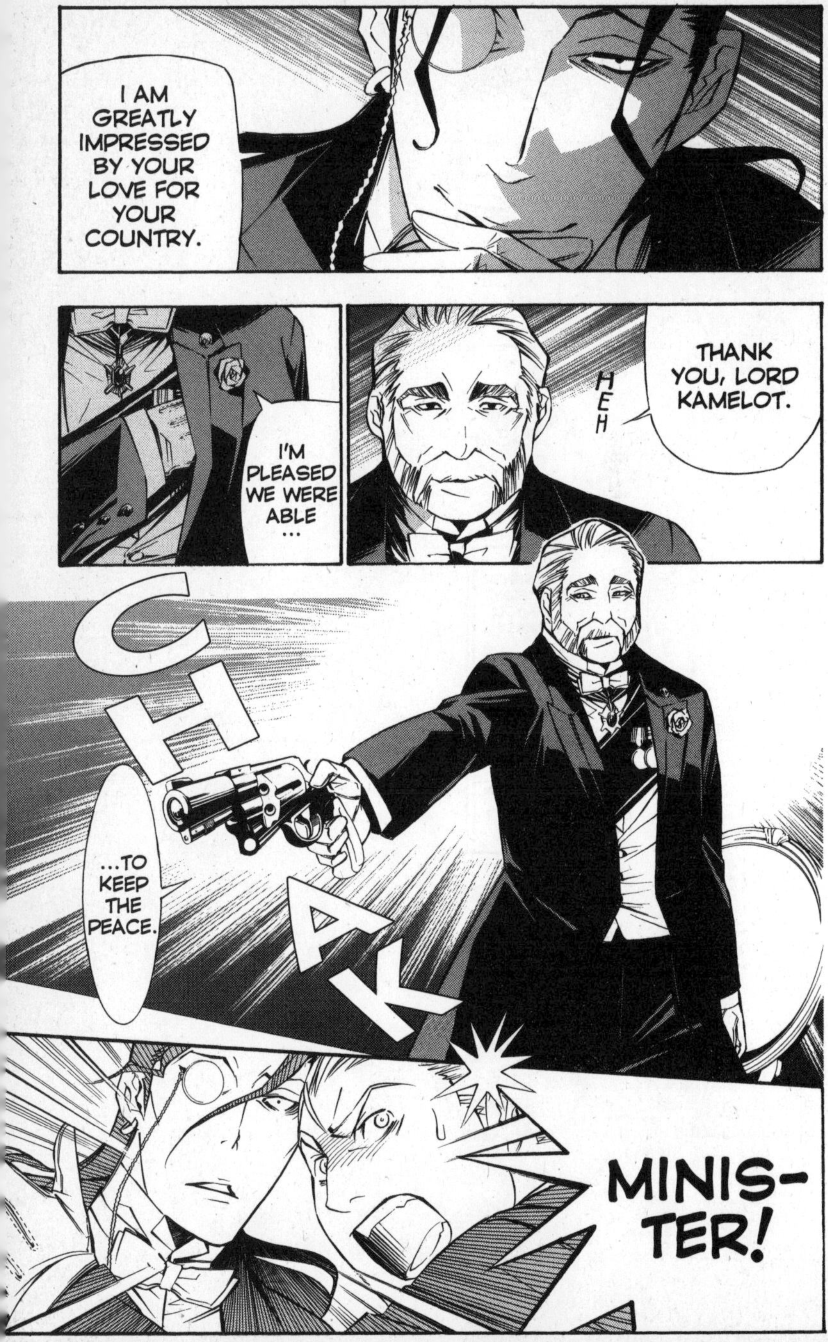
I AM GREATLY IMPRESSED BY YOUR LOVE FOR YOUR COUNTRY.
THANK YOU, LORD KAMELOT.
HEH
I'M PLEASED WE WERE ABLE ...
...TO KEEP THE PEACE.
CHAK
MINIS-TER!

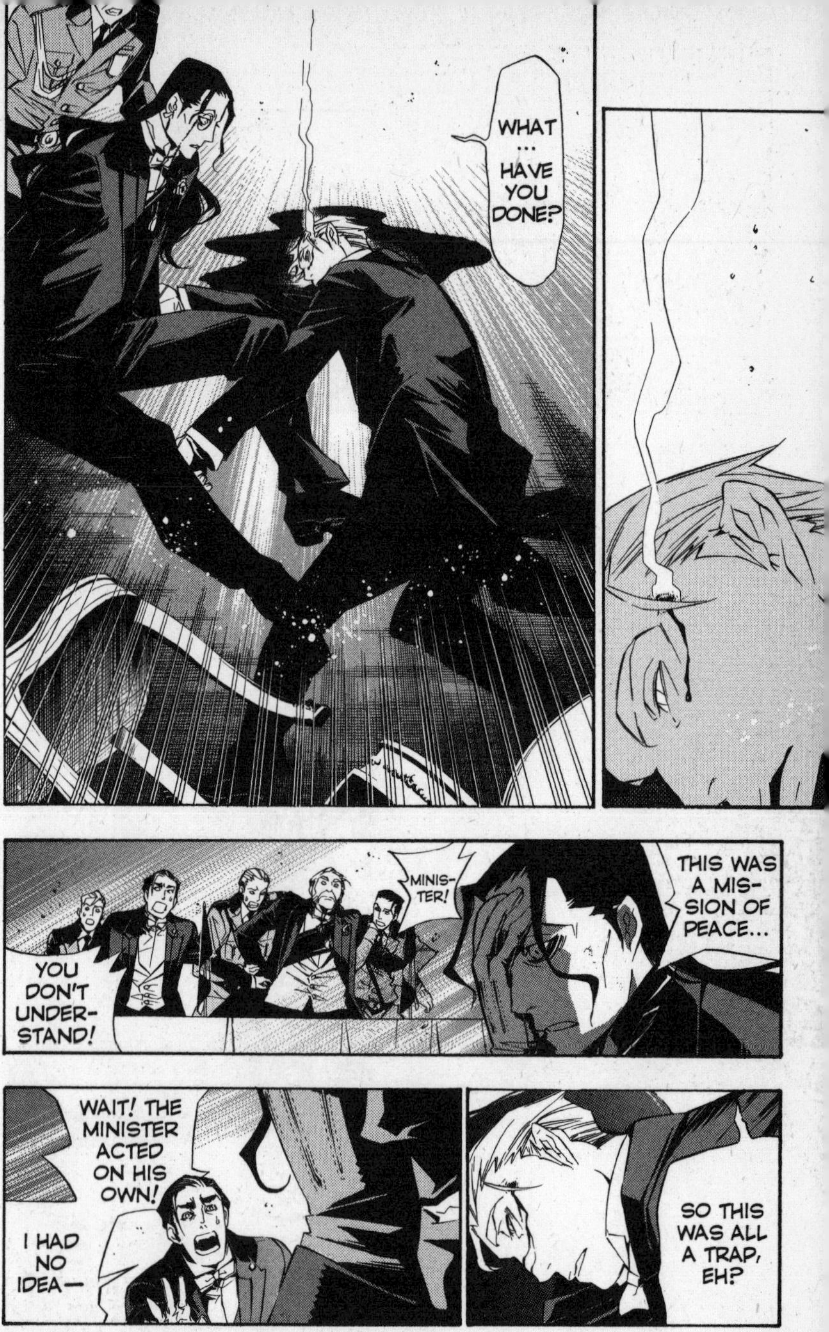
WHAT ... HAVE YOU DONE?
THIS WAS A MISSION OF PEACE...
MINISTER!
YOU DON'T UNDERSTAND!
SO THIS WAS ALL A TRAP, EH?
WAIT! THE MINISTER ACTED ON HIS OWN!
I HAD NO IDEA—

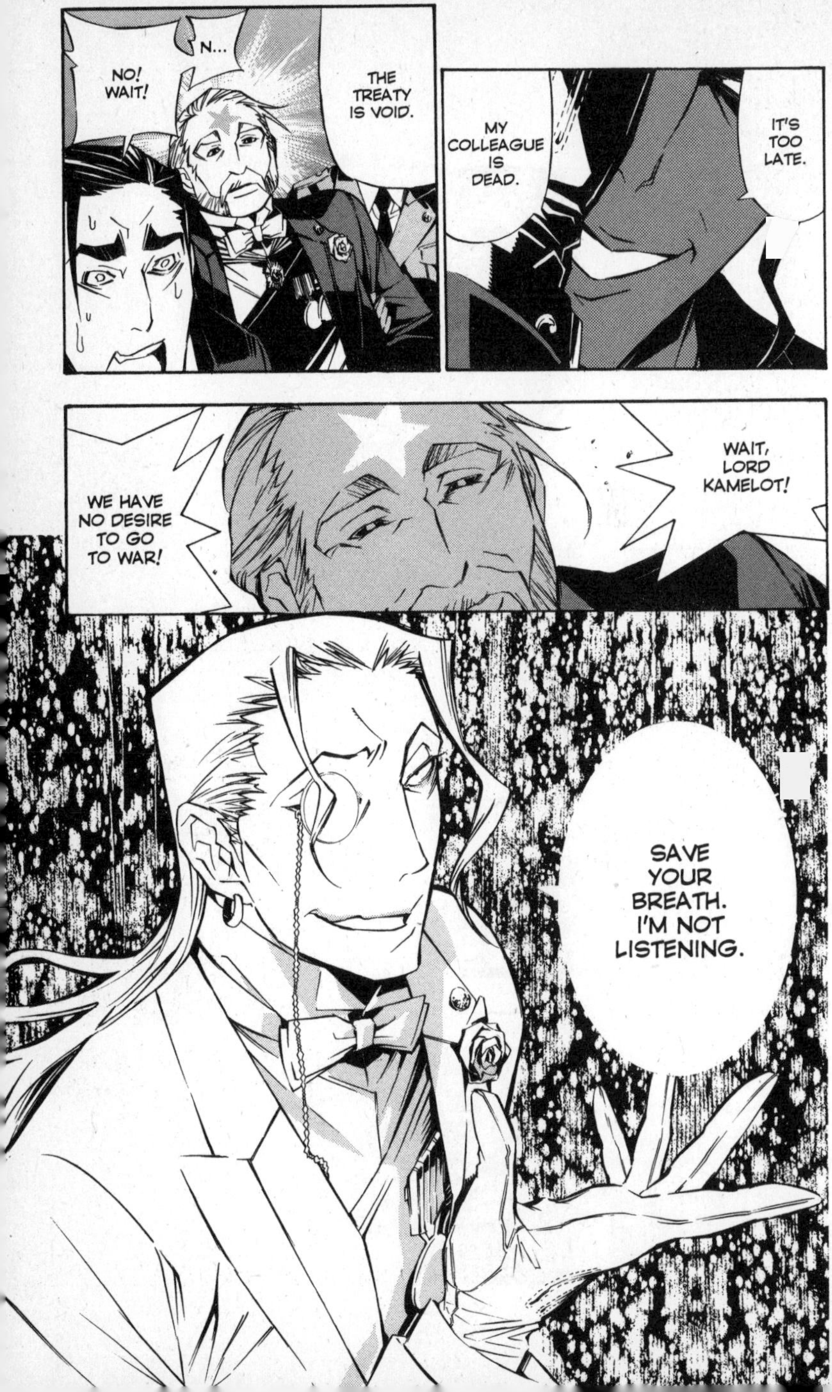
IT'S TOO LATE.
MY COLLEAGUE IS DEAD.
THE TREATY IS VOID.
N...
NO! WAIT!
WAIT, LORD KAMELOT!
WE HAVE NO DESIRE TO GO TO WAR!
SAVE YOUR BREATH. I'M NOT LISTENING.

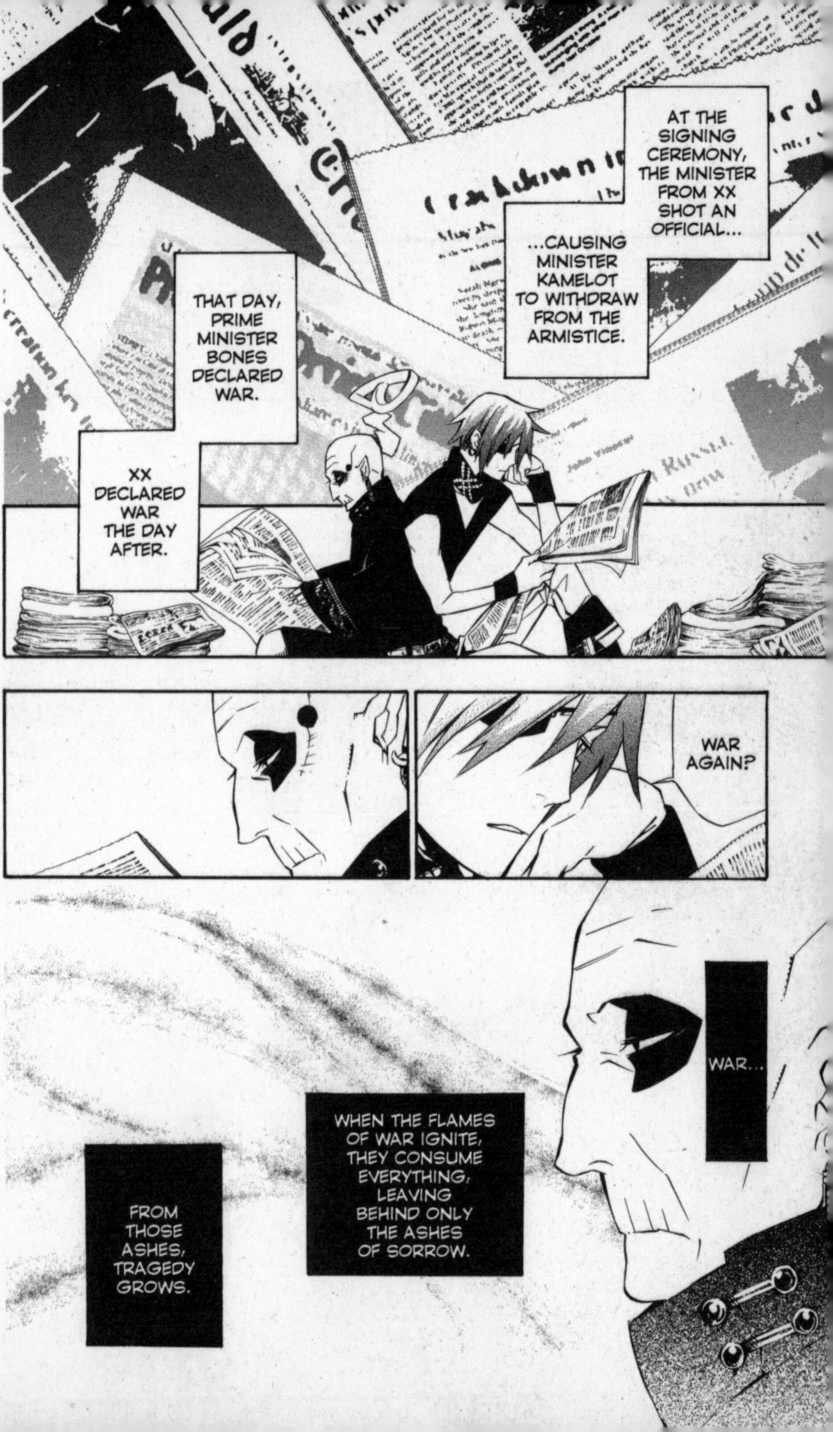
AT THE SIGNING CEREMONY, THE MINISTER FROM XX SHOT AN OFFICIAL...
...CAUSING MINISTER KAMELOT TO WITHDRAW FROM THE ARMISTICE.
THAT DAY, PRIME MINISTER BONES DECLARED WAR.
XX DECLARED WAR THE DAY AFTER.
WAR AGAIN?
WAR...
WHEN THE FLAMES OF WAR IGNITE, THEY CONSUME EVERYTHING, LEAVING BEHIND ONLY THE ASHES OF SORROW.
FROM THOSE ASHES, TRAGEDY GROWS.

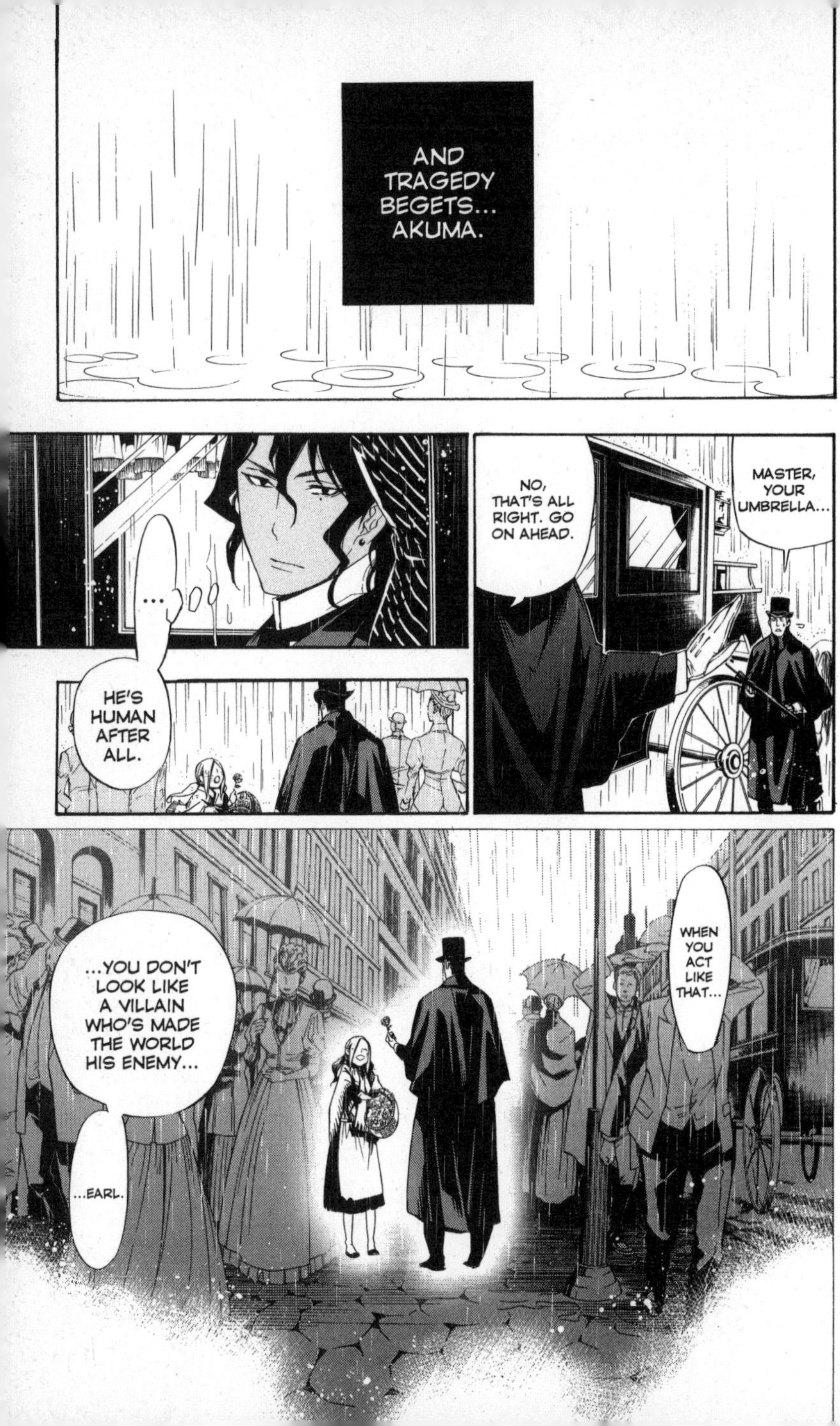
AND TRAGEDY BEGETS... AKUMA.
MASTER, YOUR UMBRELLA...
NO, THAT'S ALL RIGHT. GO ON AHEAD.
...
HE'S HUMAN AFTER ALL.
WHEN YOU ACT LIKE THAT...
...YOU DON'T LOOK LIKE A VILLAIN WHO'S MADE THE WORLD HIS ENEMY...
...EARL.

THE PEOPLE OF D.GRAY HOUSE

GRANDFATHER IS SENSITIVE ABOUT HIS ☆ SWEET TOOTH

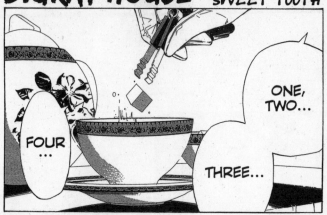

ONE, TWO...
THREE...
FOUR ...
FIVE, SIX...
SEVEN ...
EIGHT, NINE...
...
...
TEN.
RAISE YOUR HANDS IF YOU THINK...
...I'M CHUBBY.
YOU WILL ALL...
...BE PUT TO DEATH.

IF YOU QUIT EATING CANDY, CAKE AND OTHER SWEETS, YOU'LL NEVER GET FAT. (TOO MANY SYLLABLES.)

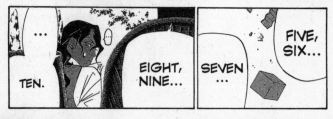

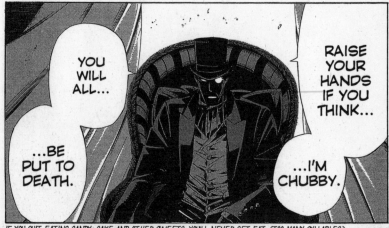

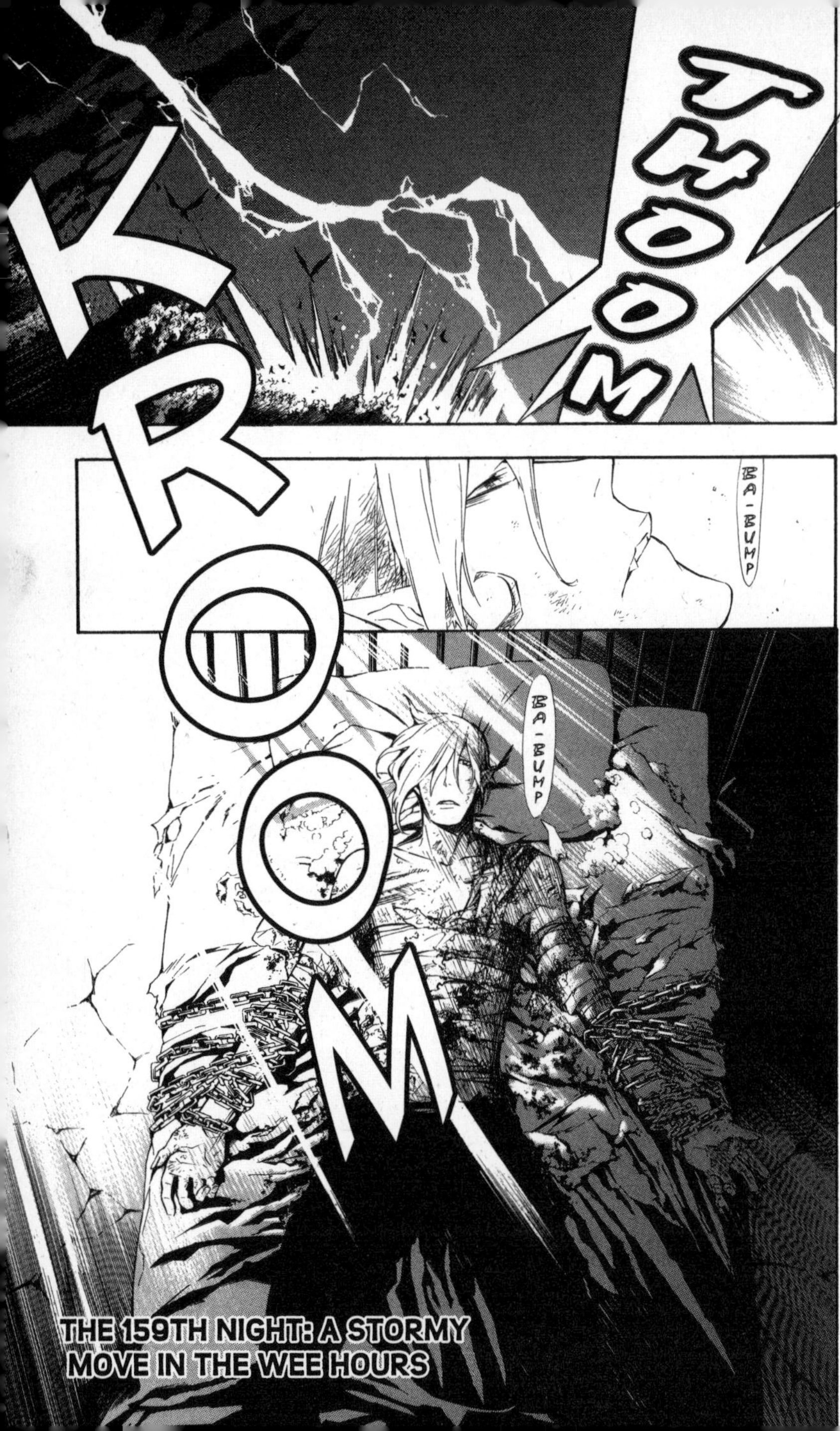
THOOM
KROOOM
BA-BUMP
BA-BUMP
THE 159TH NIGHT: A STORMY MOVE IN THE WEE HOURS

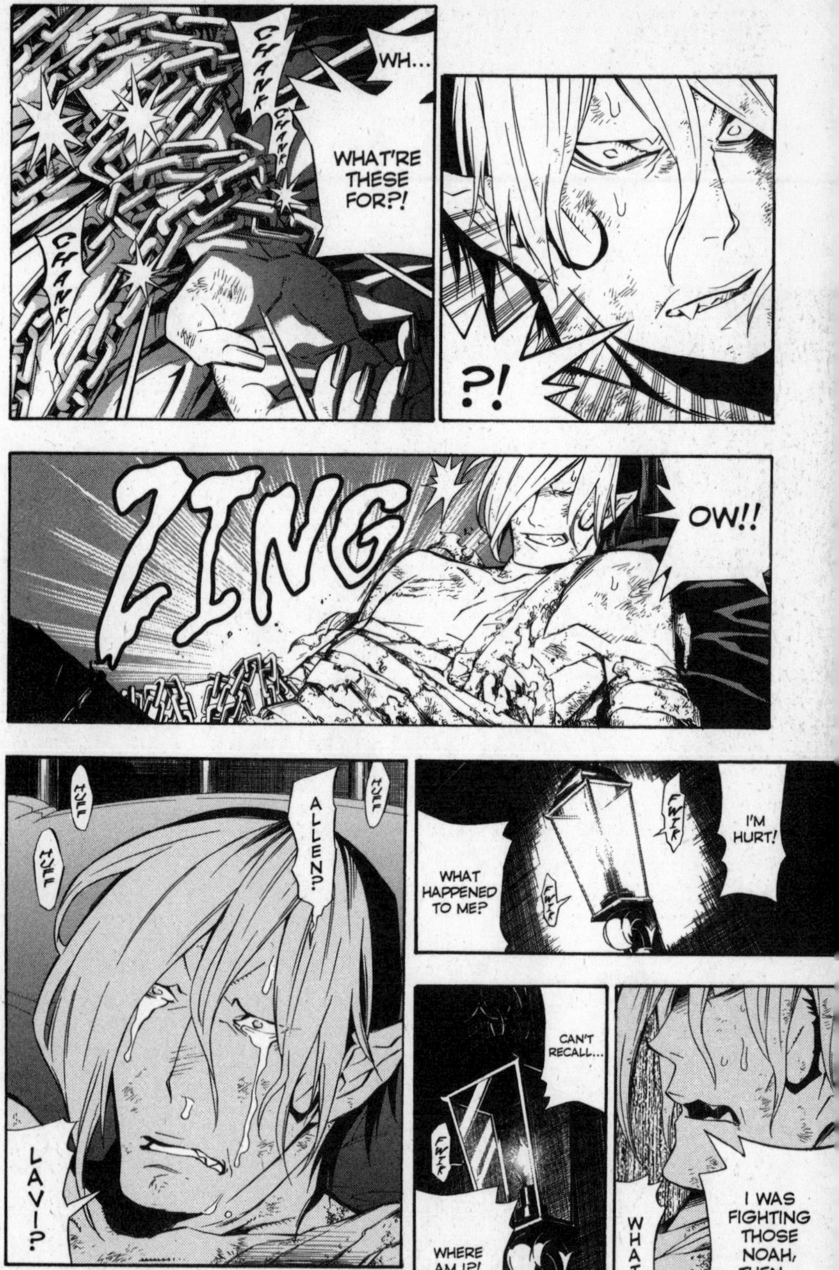
?!
WH...
WHAT'RE THESE FOR?!
CHANK
CHANK
CHANK
OW!!
ZING
I'M HURT!
FWIK
WHAT HAPPENED TO ME?
FWIK
I WAS FIGHTING THOSE NOAH, THEN...
WHAT?
CAN'T RECALL...
FWIK
WHERE AM I?!
HUFF
ALLEN?
HUFF
HUFF
LAVI?

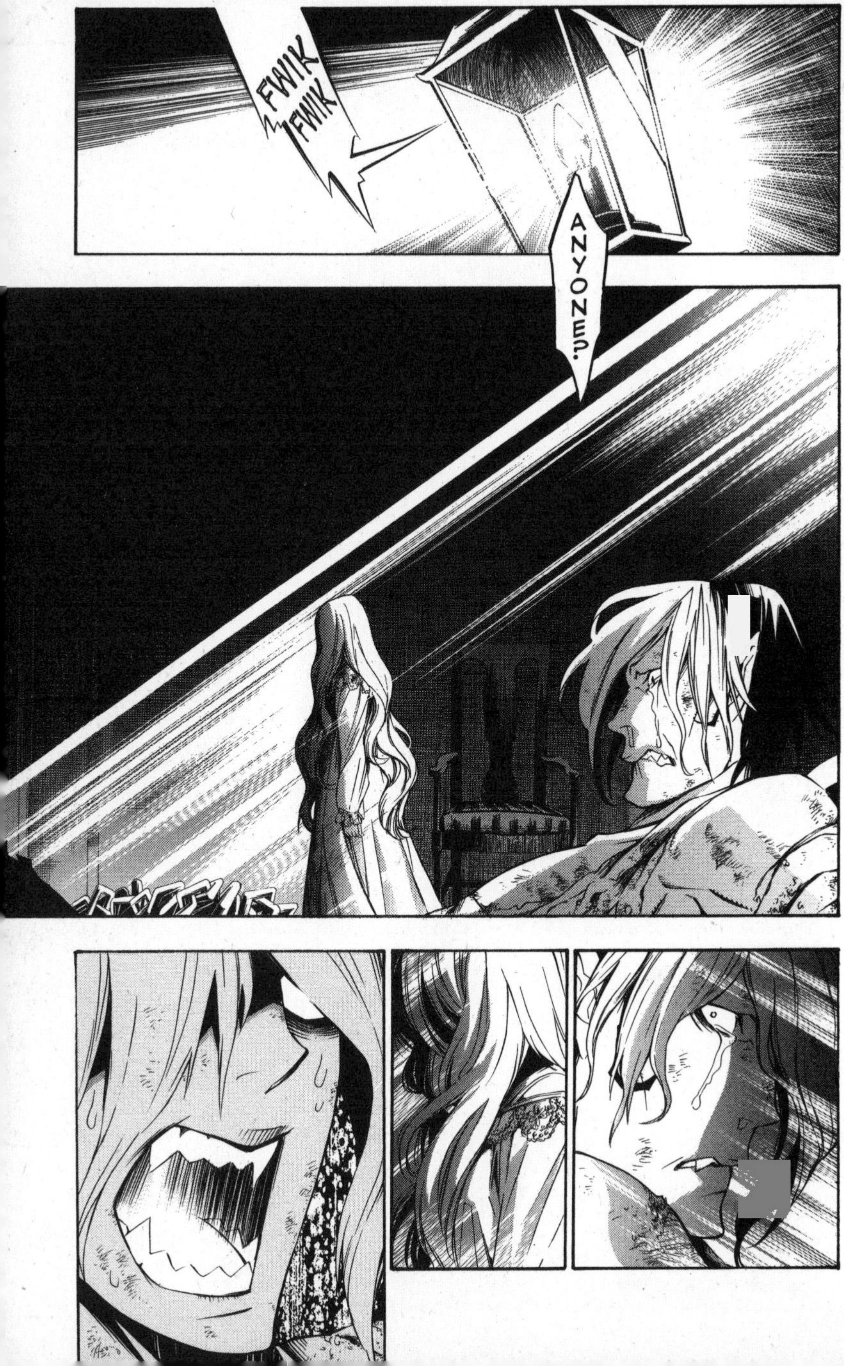
FWIK FWIK
ANYONE?

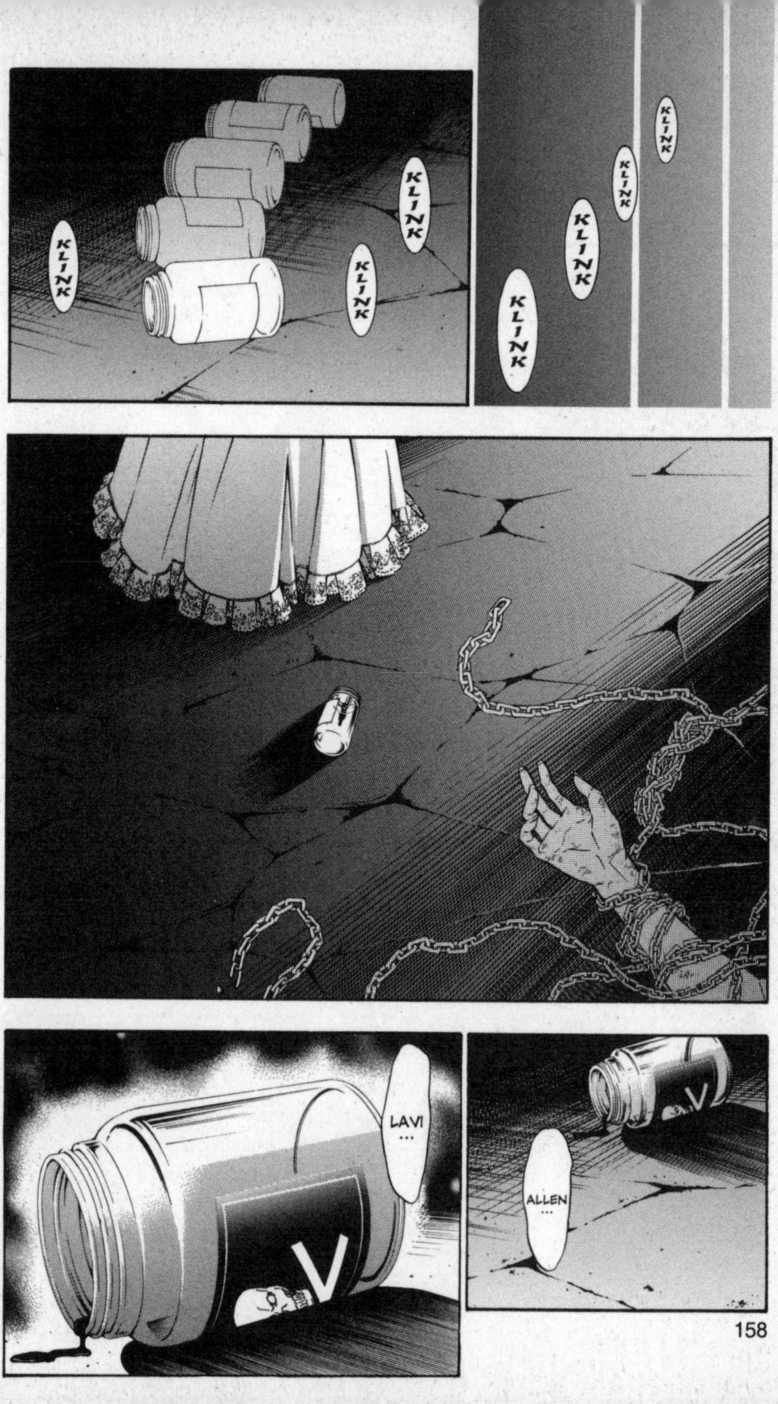
KLINK
KLINK
KLINK
KLINK
KLINK
KLINK
KLINK
ALLEN...
LAVI...

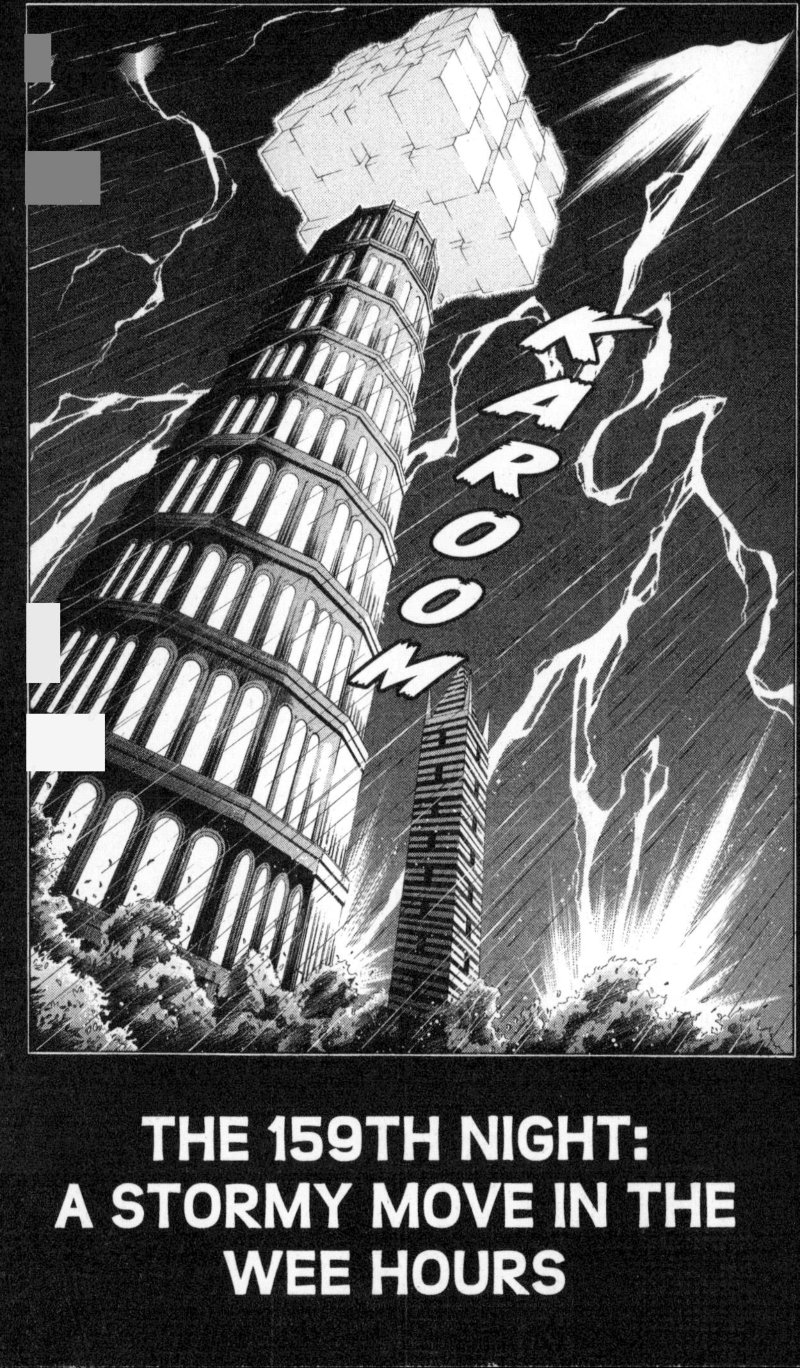
KA-ROOOM

THE 159TH NIGHT: A STORMY MOVE IN THE WEE HOURS

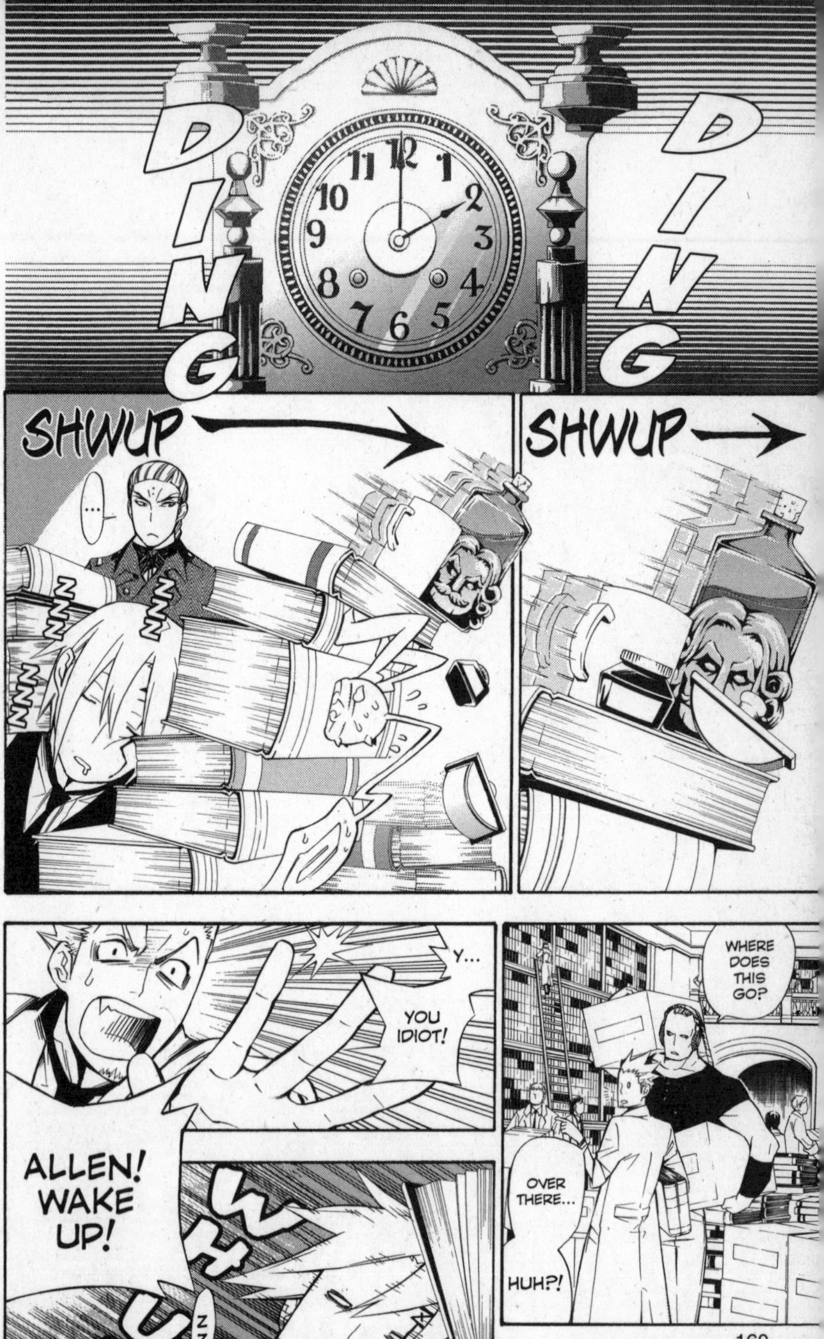

DING
DING
SHWUP
SHWUP
...
ZZZ
ZZZ
ZZZ
WHERE DOES THIS GO?
OVER THERE...
HUH?!
Y...
YOU IDIOT!
ALLEN! WAKE UP!
WHUP
ZZZ

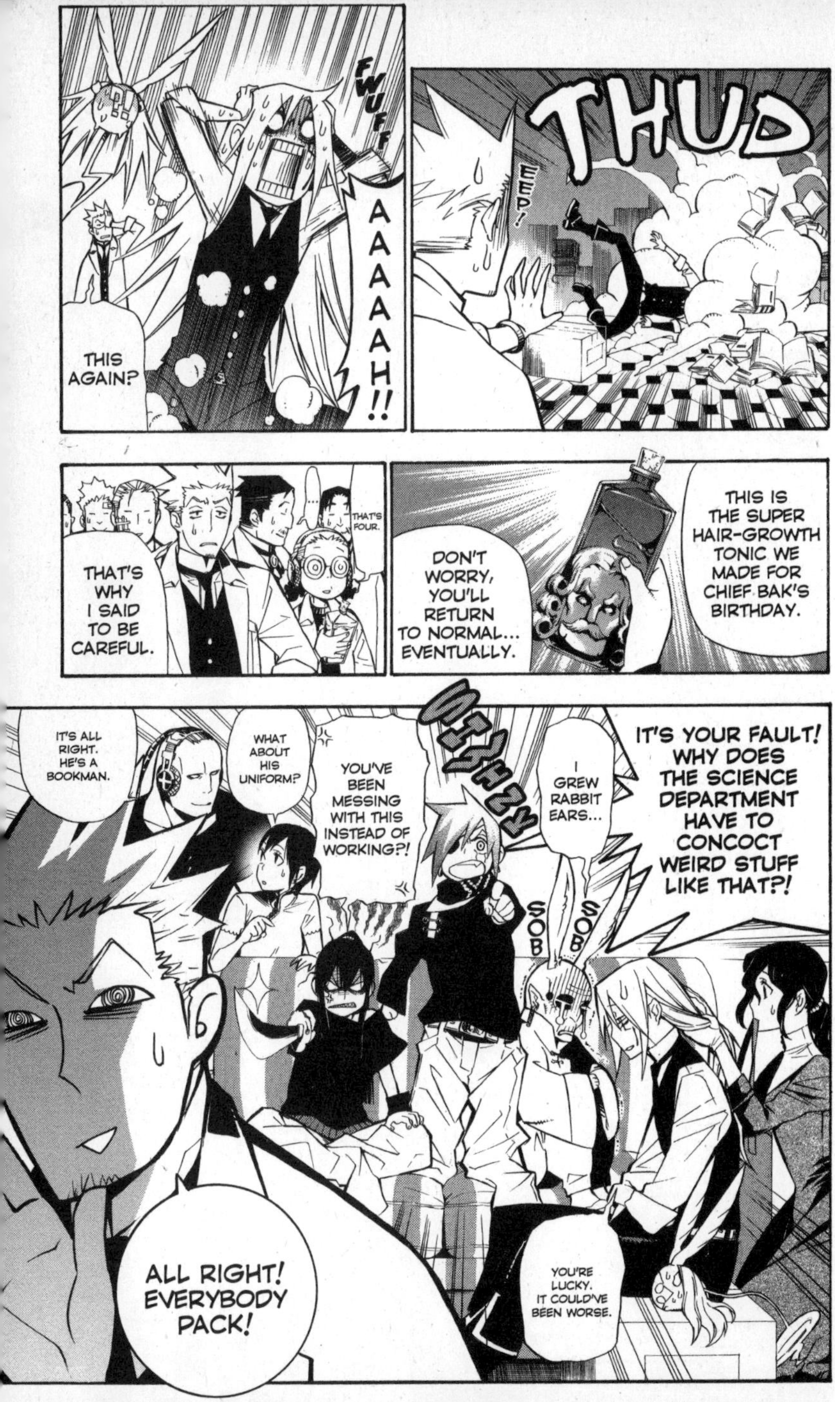
THUD
EEP!
FWUFF
AAAAAAH!!
THIS AGAIN?
THIS IS THE SUPER HAIR-GROWTH TONIC WE MADE FOR CHIEF BAK'S BIRTHDAY.
DON'T WORRY, YOU'LL RETURN TO NORMAL... EVENTUALLY.
...
THAT'S FOUR.
THAT'S WHY I SAID TO BE CAREFUL.
IT'S YOUR FAULT! WHY DOES THE SCIENCE DEPARTMENT HAVE TO CONCOCT WEIRD STUFF LIKE THAT?!
I GREW RABBIT EARS...
SOB SOB
YOU'VE BEEN MESSING WITH THIS INSTEAD OF WORKING?!
WHAT ABOUT HIS UNIFORM?
IT'S ALL RIGHT. HE'S A BOOKMAN.
YOU'RE LUCKY. IT COULD'VE BEEN WORSE.
ALL RIGHT! EVERYBODY PACK!

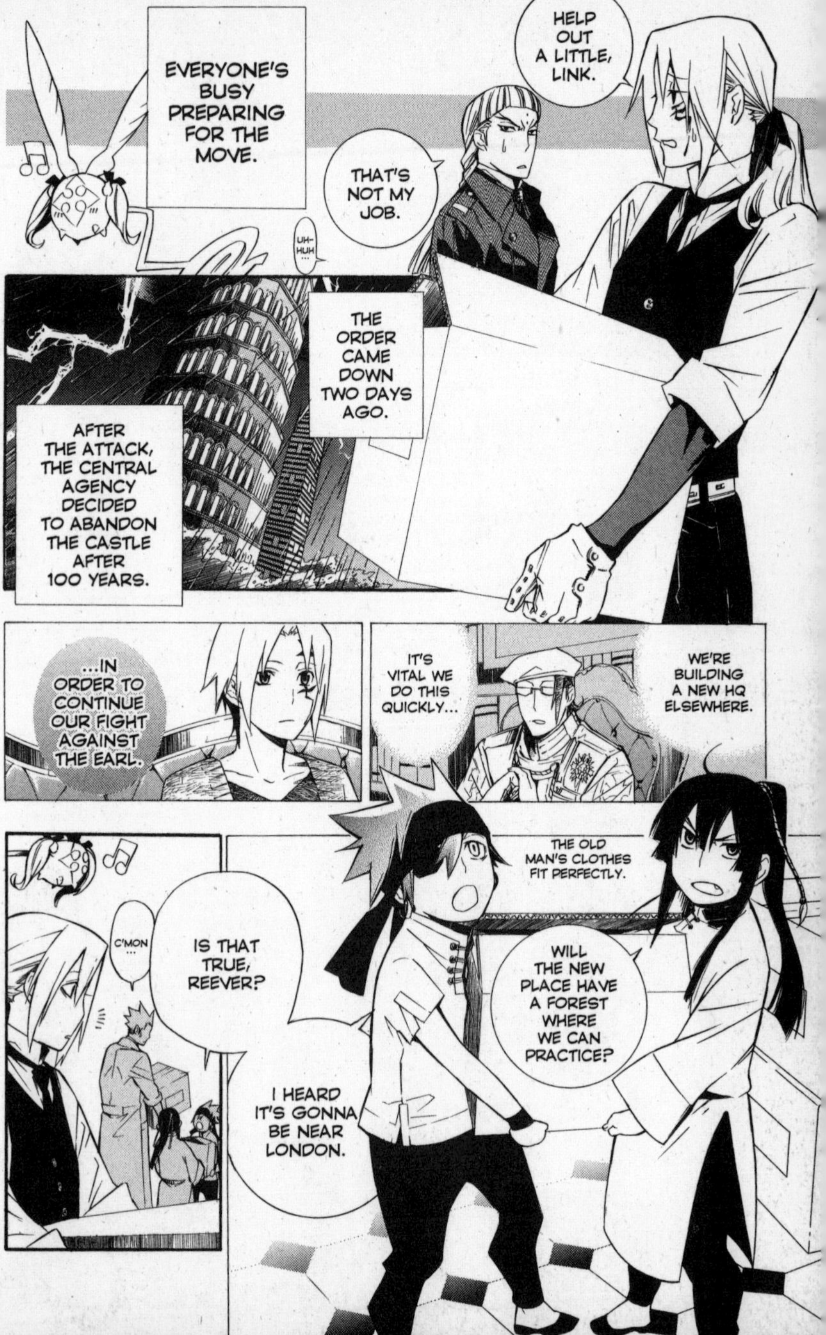
HELP OUT A LITTLE, LINK.
EVERYONE'S BUSY PREPARING FOR THE MOVE.
THAT'S NOT MY JOB.
UH-HUH...
THE ORDER CAME DOWN TWO DAYS AGO.
AFTER THE ATTACK, THE CENTRAL AGENCY DECIDED TO ABANDON THE CASTLE AFTER 100 YEARS.
WE'RE BUILDING A NEW HQ ELSEWHERE.
IT'S VITAL WE DO THIS QUICKLY...
...IN ORDER TO CONTINUE OUR FIGHT AGAINST THE EARL.
THE OLD MAN'S CLOTHES FIT PERFECTLY.
WILL THE NEW PLACE HAVE A FOREST WHERE WE CAN PRACTICE?
IS THAT TRUE, REEVER?
I HEARD IT'S GONNA BE NEAR LONDON.
C'MON...

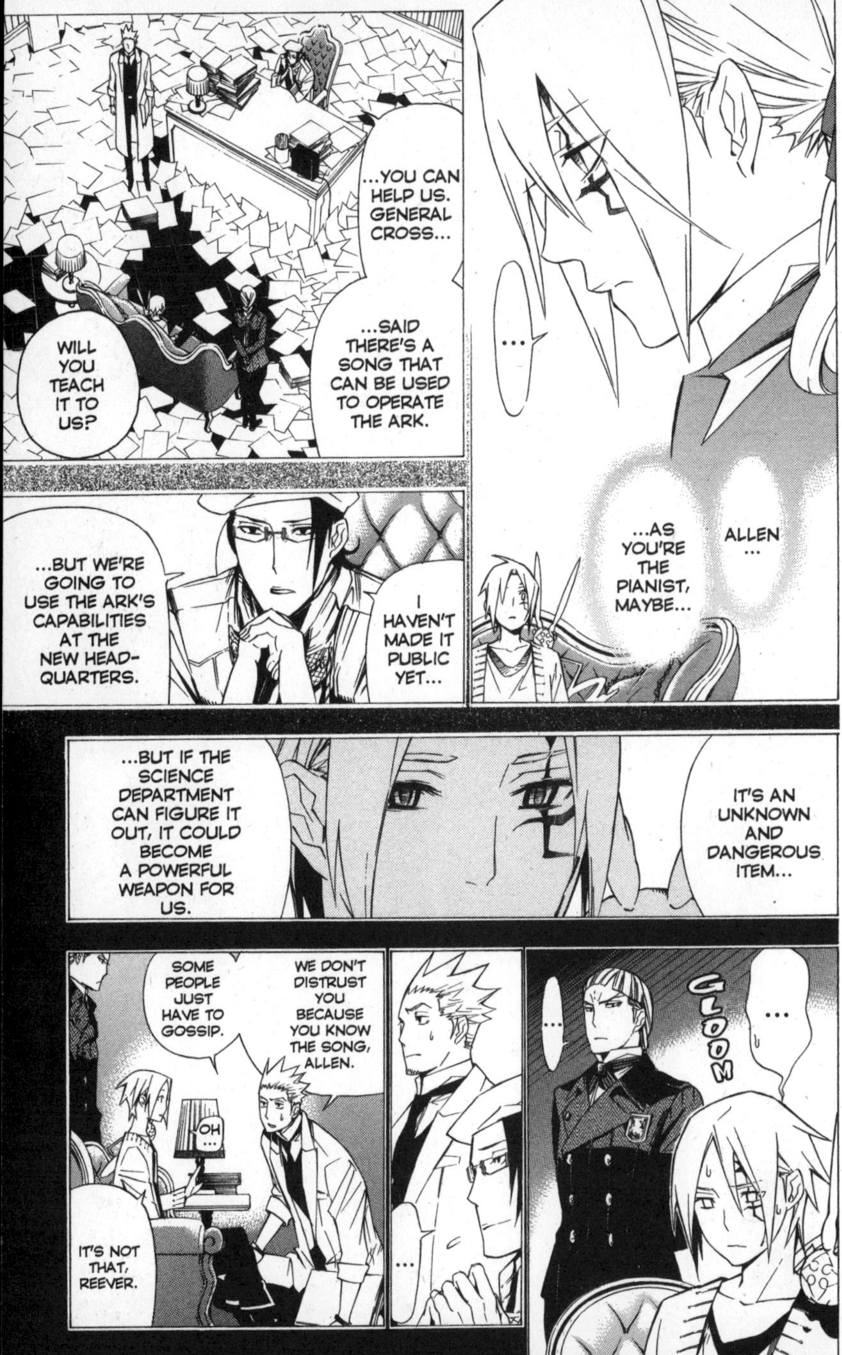

...
ALLEN...
...AS YOU'RE THE PIANIST, MAYBE...
...YOU CAN HELP US. GENERAL CROSS...
...SAID THERE'S A SONG THAT CAN BE USED TO OPERATE THE ARK.
WILL YOU TEACH IT TO US?
I HAVEN'T MADE IT PUBLIC YET...
...BUT WE'RE GOING TO USE THE ARK'S CAPABILITIES AT THE NEW HEAD-QUARTERS.
IT'S AN UNKNOWN AND DANGEROUS ITEM...
...BUT IF THE SCIENCE DEPARTMENT CAN FIGURE IT OUT, IT COULD BECOME A POWERFUL WEAPON FOR US.
...
GLOOM
...
...
WE DON'T DISTRUST YOU BECAUSE YOU KNOW THE SONG, ALLEN.
SOME PEOPLE JUST HAVE TO GOSSIP.
OH...
IT'S NOT THAT, REEVER.

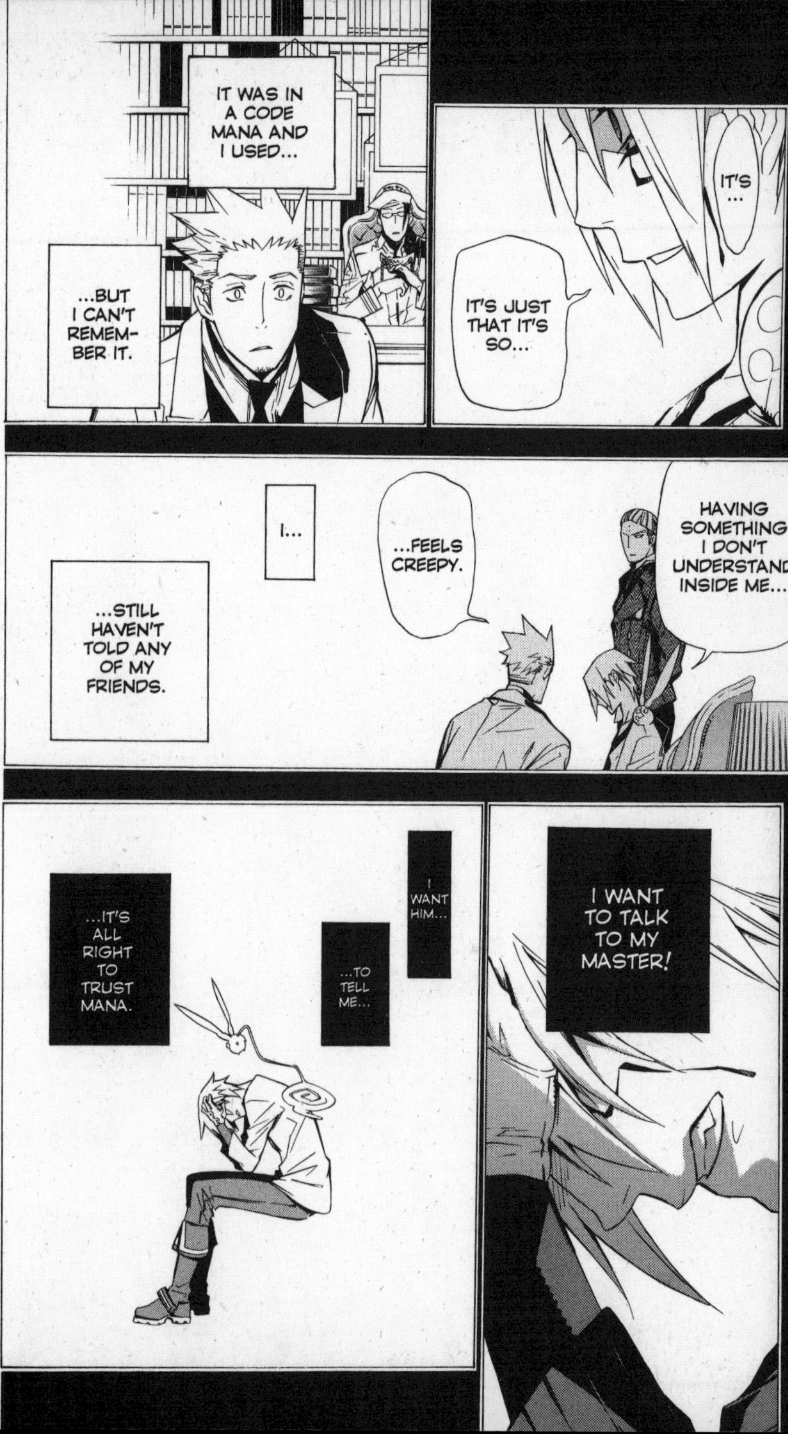
IT'S ...
IT'S JUST THAT IT'S SO...
IT WAS IN A CODE MANA AND I USED...
...BUT I CAN'T REMEMBER IT.
HAVING SOMETHING I DON'T UNDERSTAND INSIDE ME...
...FEELS CREEPY.
I...
...STILL HAVEN'T TOLD ANY OF MY FRIENDS.
I WANT TO TALK TO MY MASTER!
I WANT HIM...
...TO TELL ME...
...IT'S ALL RIGHT TO TRUST MANA.

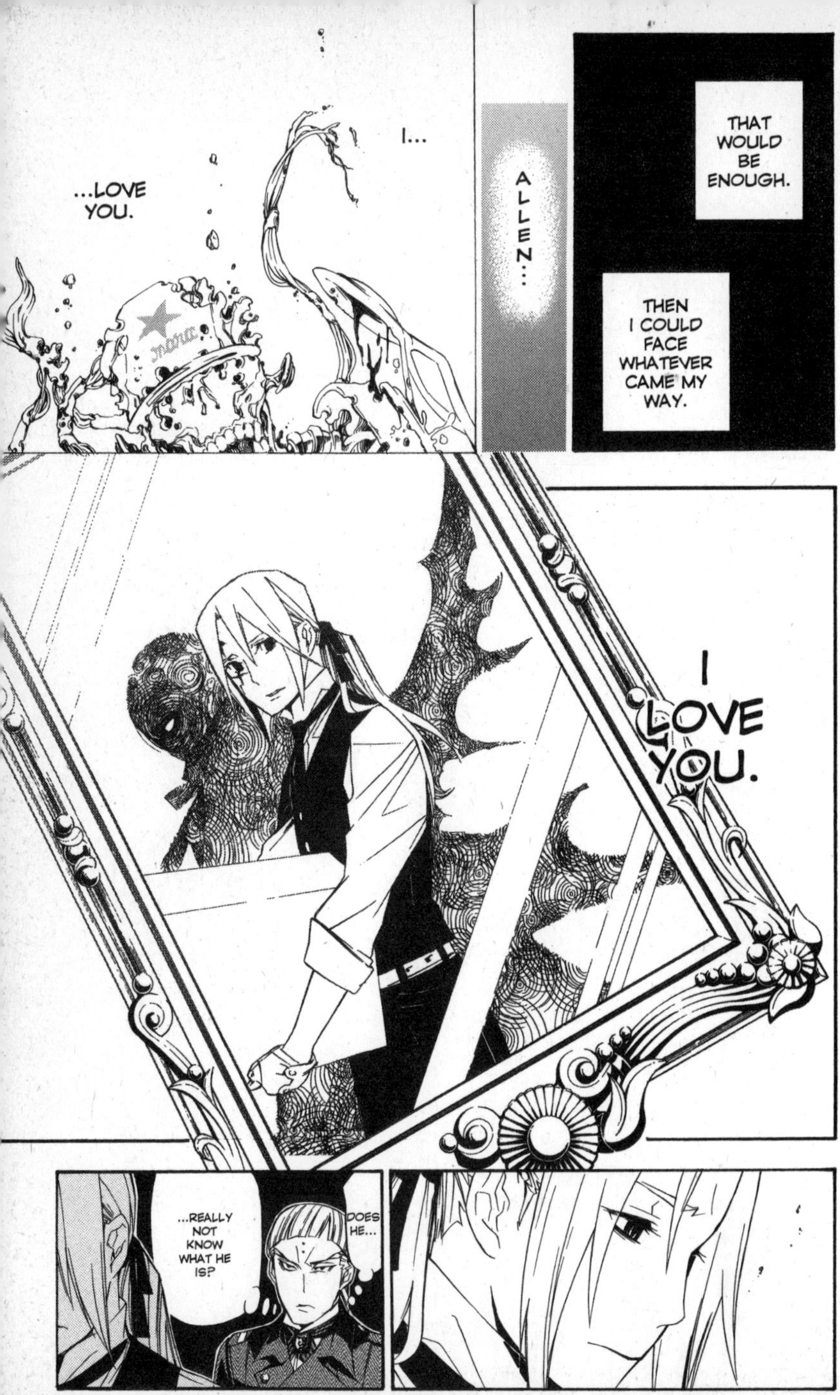
THAT WOULD BE ENOUGH.
THEN I COULD FACE WHATEVER CAME MY WAY.
ALLEN...
I...
...LOVE YOU.
I LOVE YOU.
DOES HE...
...REALLY NOT KNOW WHAT HE IS?

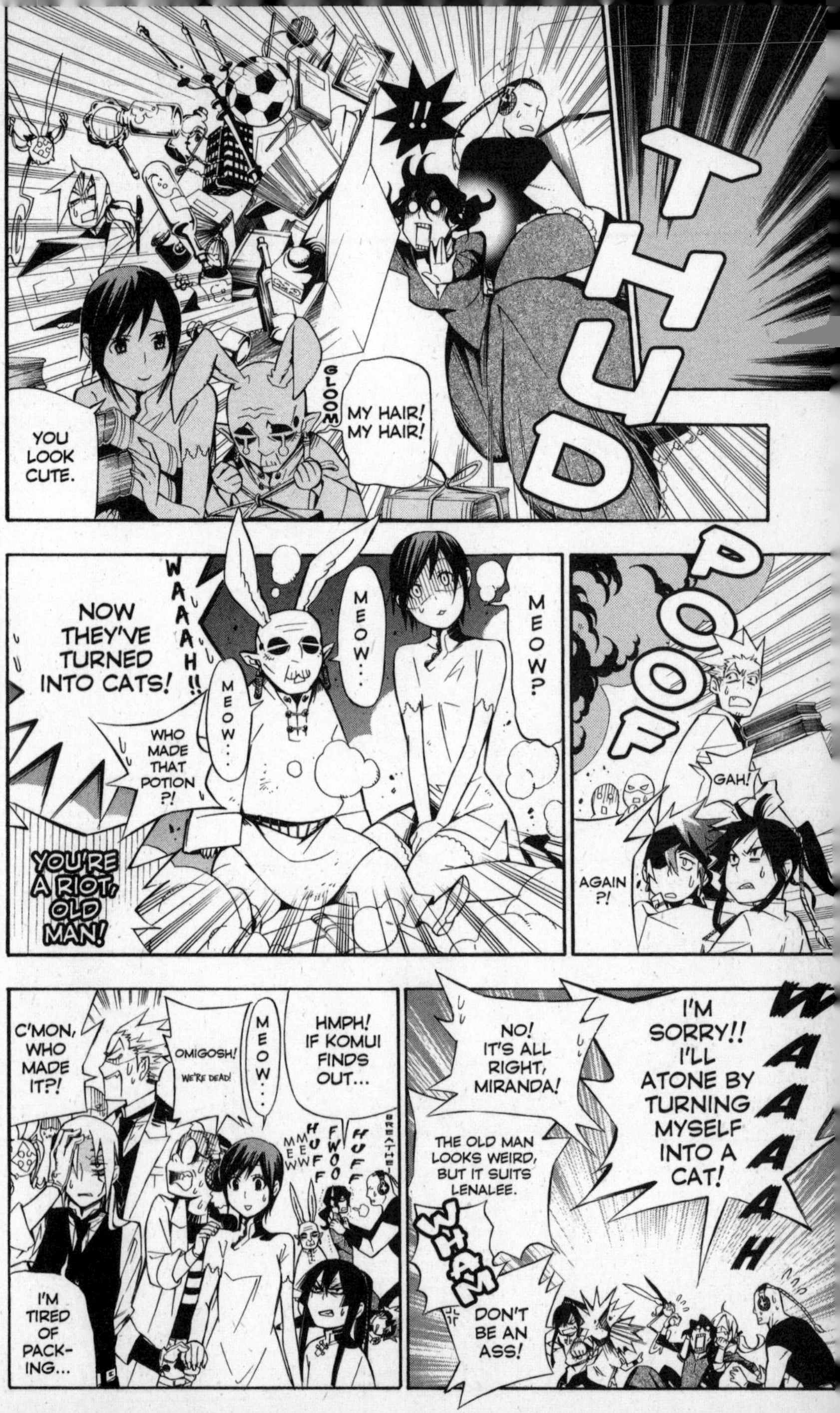
THUD
!!
MY HAIR! MY HAIR!
GLOOM
YOU LOOK CUTE.
POOF
GAH!
AGAIN?!
MEOW?
MEOW...
WAAAAH!!
NOW THEY'VE TURNED INTO CATS!
MEOW...
WHO MADE THAT POTION?!
YOU'RE A RIOT, OLD MAN!
WAAAAAH
I'M SORRY!! I'LL ATONE BY TURNING MYSELF INTO A CAT!
NO! IT'S ALL RIGHT, MIRANDA!
THE OLD MAN LOOKS WEIRD, BUT IT SUITS LENALEE.
WHAM
DON'T BE AN ASS!
HMPH! IF KOMUI FINDS OUT...
BREATHE
HUFF
FWOO
HUFF
MEW
MEW
MEOW...
OMIGOSH!
WE'RE DEAD!
C'MON, WHO MADE IT?!
I'M TIRED OF PACKING...

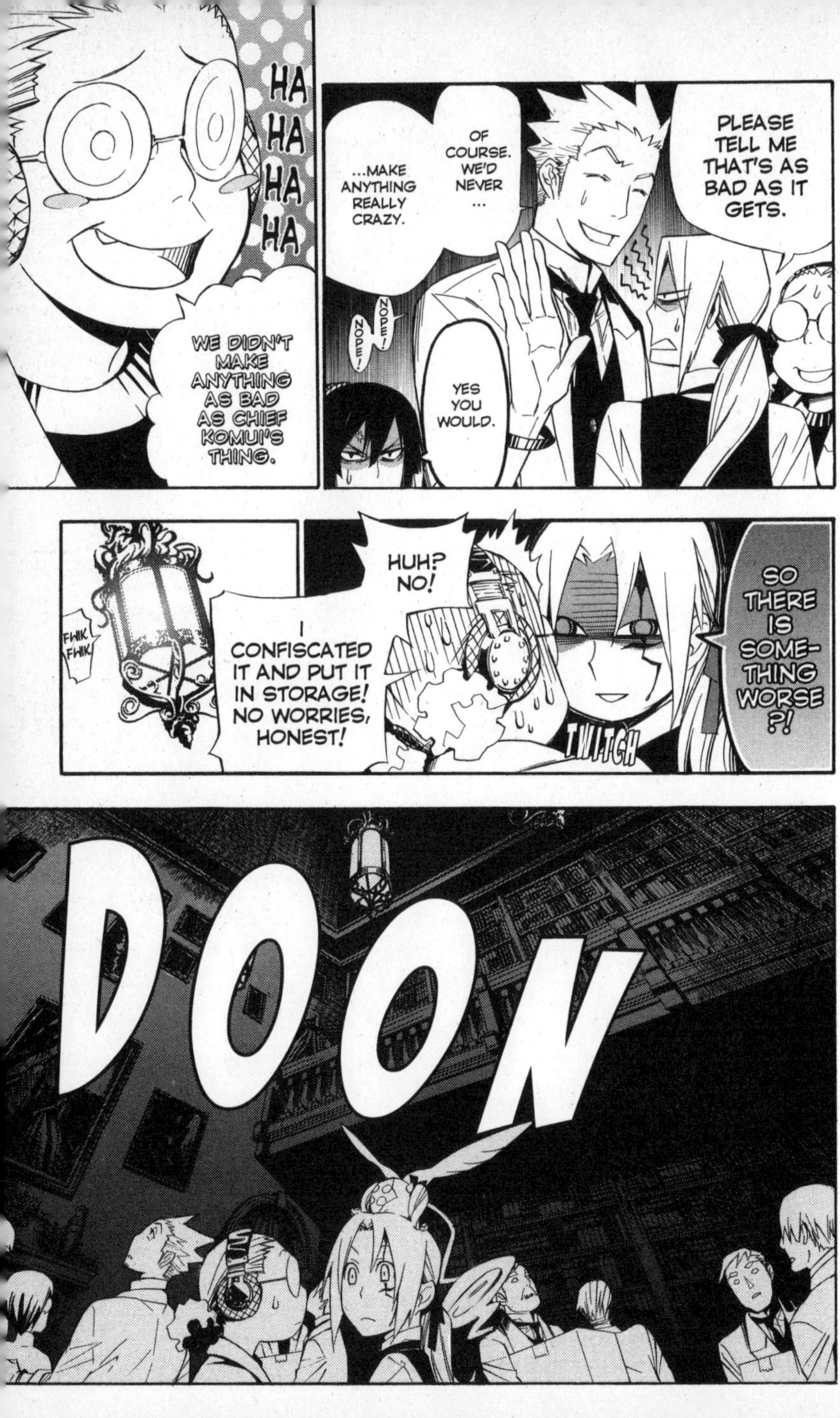
PLEASE TELL ME THAT'S AS BAD AS IT GETS.
OF COURSE. WE'D NEVER ...
...MAKE ANYTHING REALLY CRAZY.
NOPE! NOPE!
YES YOU WOULD.
HA HA HA HA
WE DIDN'T MAKE ANYTHING AS BAD AS CHIEF KOMUI'S THING.
SO THERE IS SOME-THING WORSE?!
TWITCH
HUH? NO!
I CONFISCATED IT AND PUT IT IN STORAGE! NO WORRIES, HONEST!
FWIK FWIK
DOON

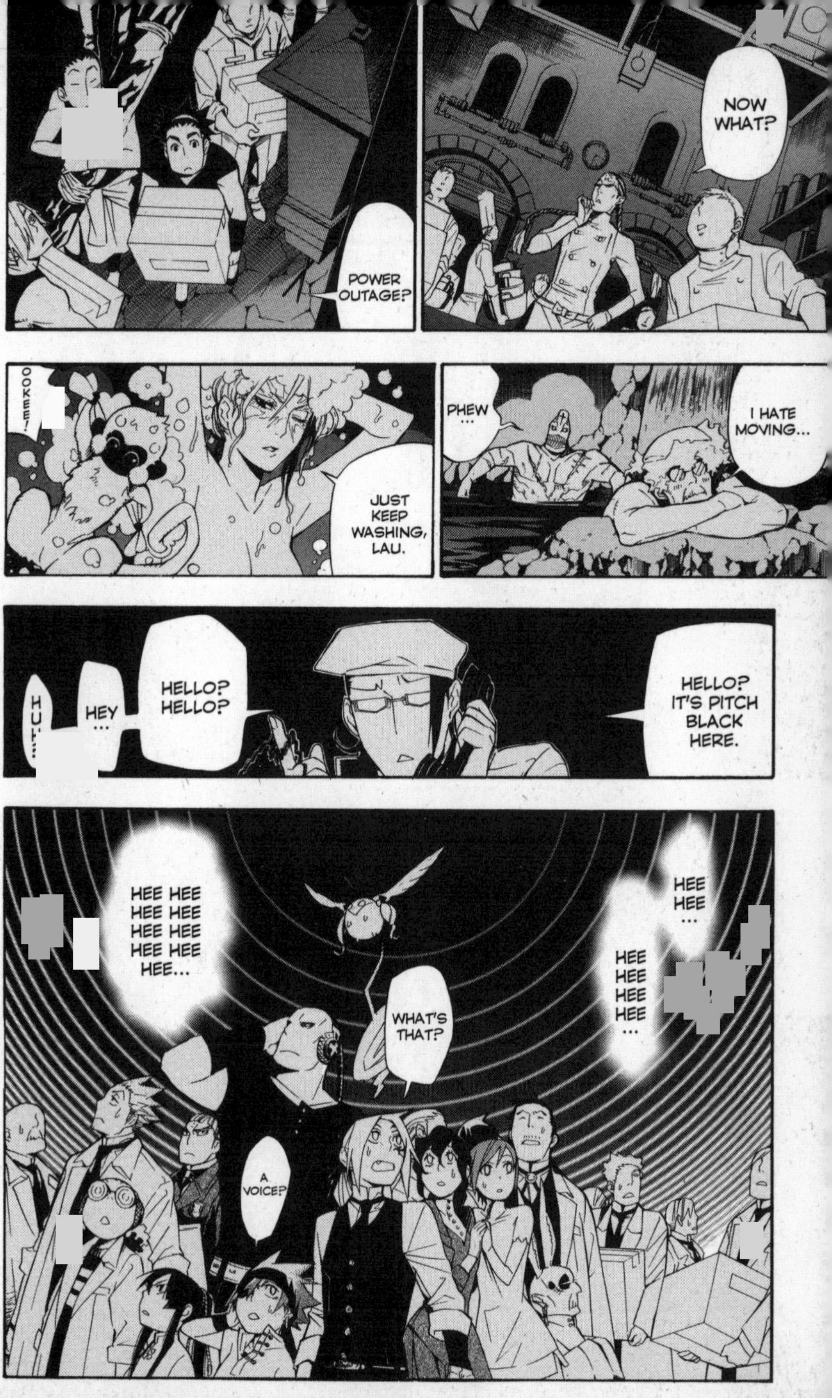
NOW WHAT?
POWER OUTAGE?
I HATE MOVING...
PHEW...
JUST KEEP WASHING, LAU.
OOKEE!
HELLO? IT'S PITCH BLACK HERE.
HELLO? HELLO?
HEY...
HUH
HEE HEE...
HEE HEE HEE HEE...
HEE HEE HEE HEE HEE HEE HEE HEE HEE...
WHAT'S THAT?
A VOICE?

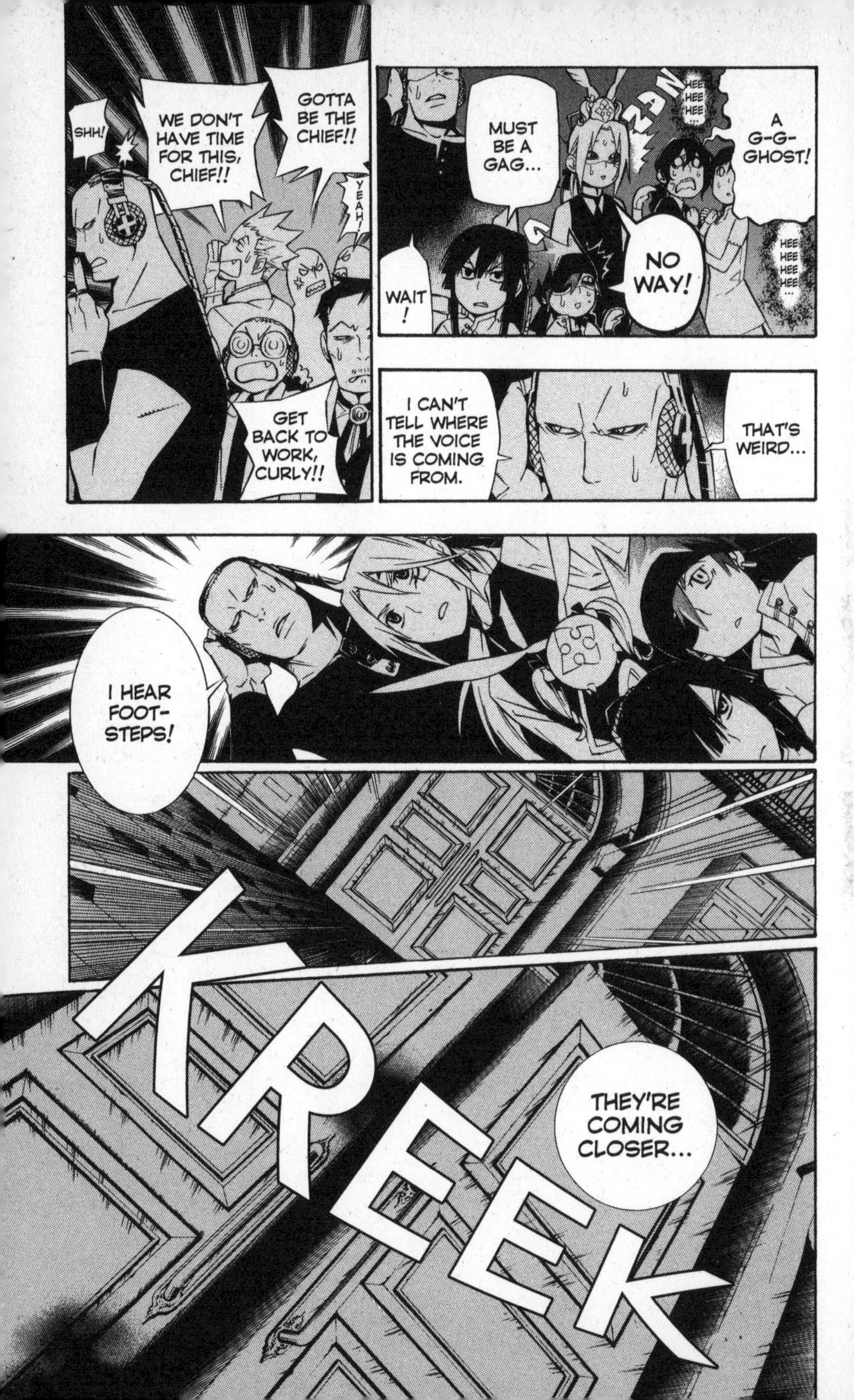
A G-G-GHOST!
HEE HEE HEE...
HEE HEE HEE HEE...
NO WAY!
MUST BE A GAG...
WAIT!
THAT'S WEIRD...
I CAN'T TELL WHERE THE VOICE IS COMING FROM.
GOTTA BE THE CHIEF!!
YEAH!
WE DON'T HAVE TIME FOR THIS, CHIEF!!
SHH!
GET BACK TO WORK, CURLY!!
I HEAR FOOT-STEPS!
THEY'RE COMING CLOSER...
KREEK

A PICTURE OF REEVER THAT
MY LITTLE BROTHER DREW.

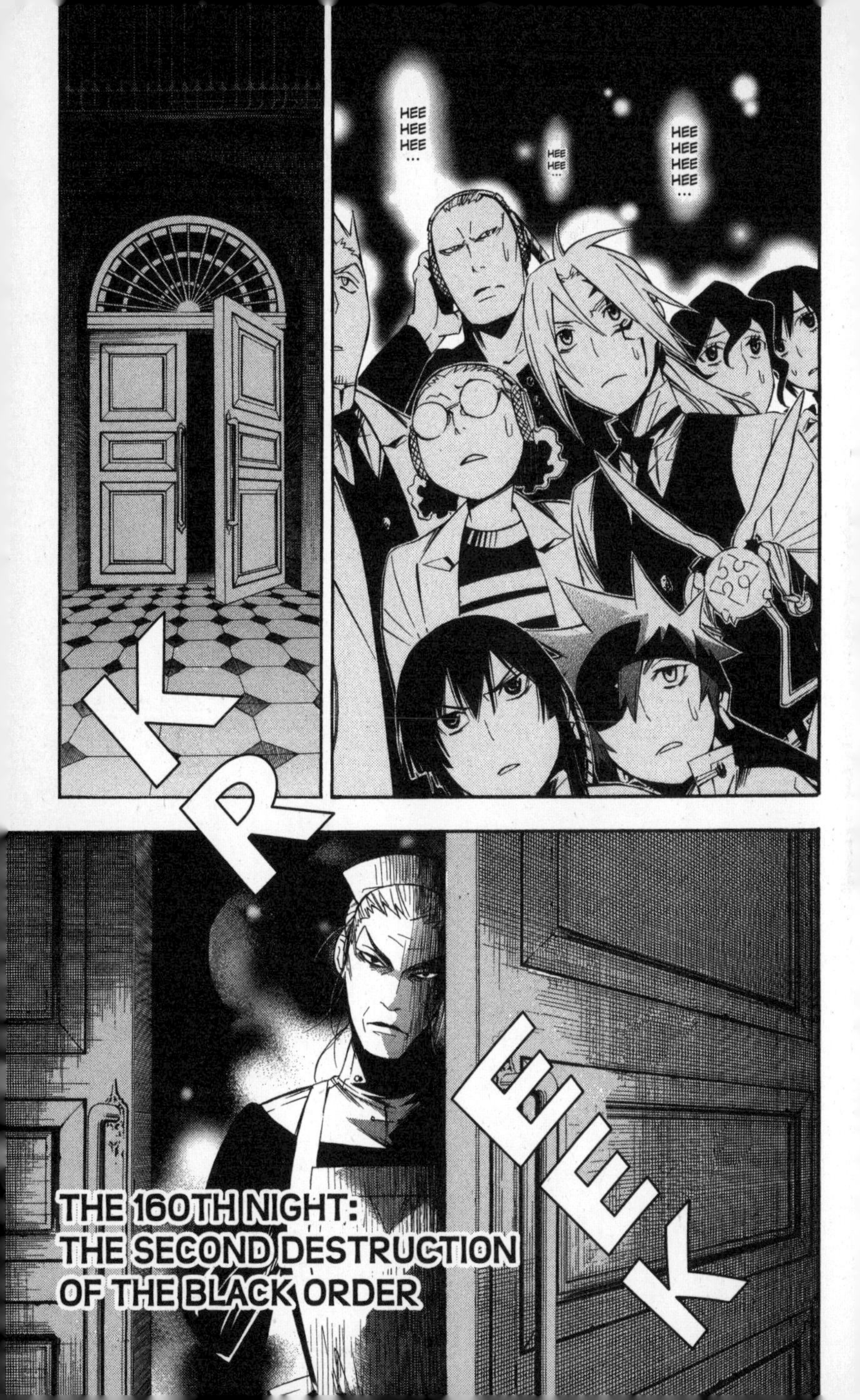
HEE HEE HEE HEE ...
HEE HEE ...
HEE HEE HEE ...
KREEEK
THE 160TH NIGHT: THE SECOND DESTRUCTION OF THE BLACK ORDER

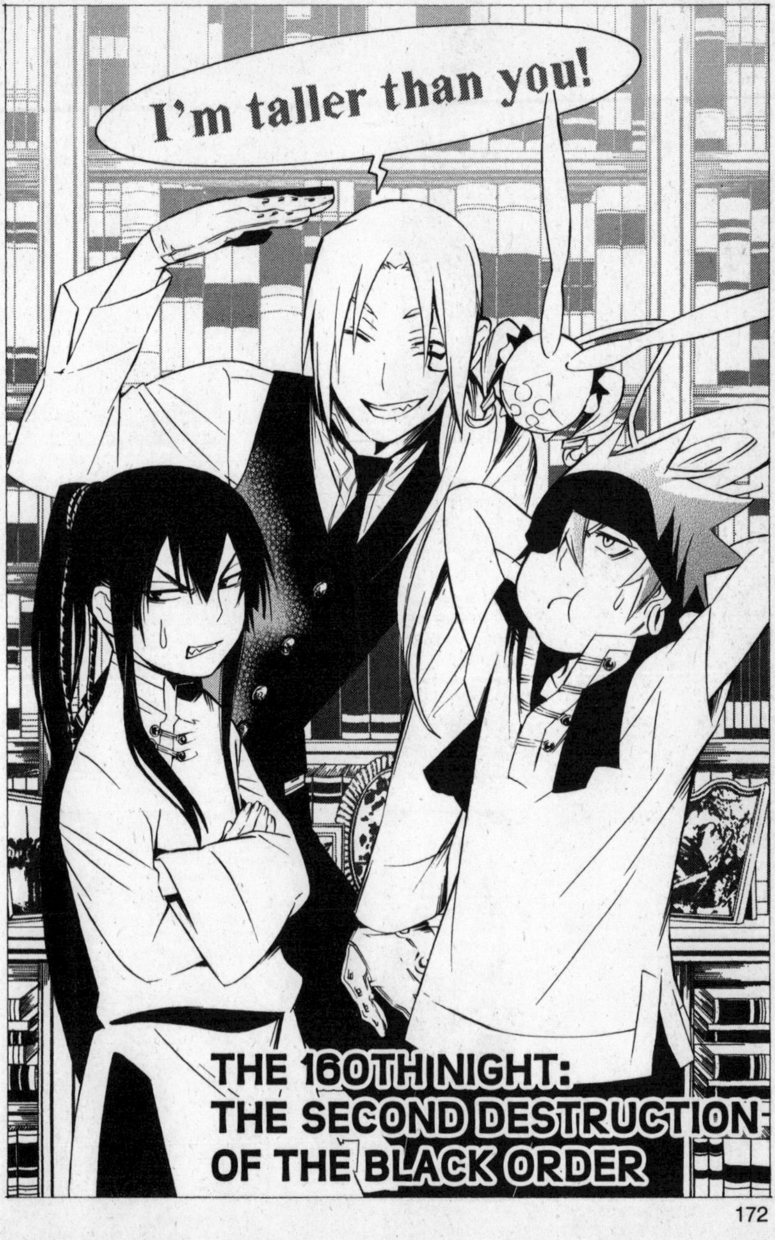
I'm taller than you!
THE 160TH NIGHT:
THE SECOND DESTRUCTION OF THE BLACK ORDER

READ THIS WAY

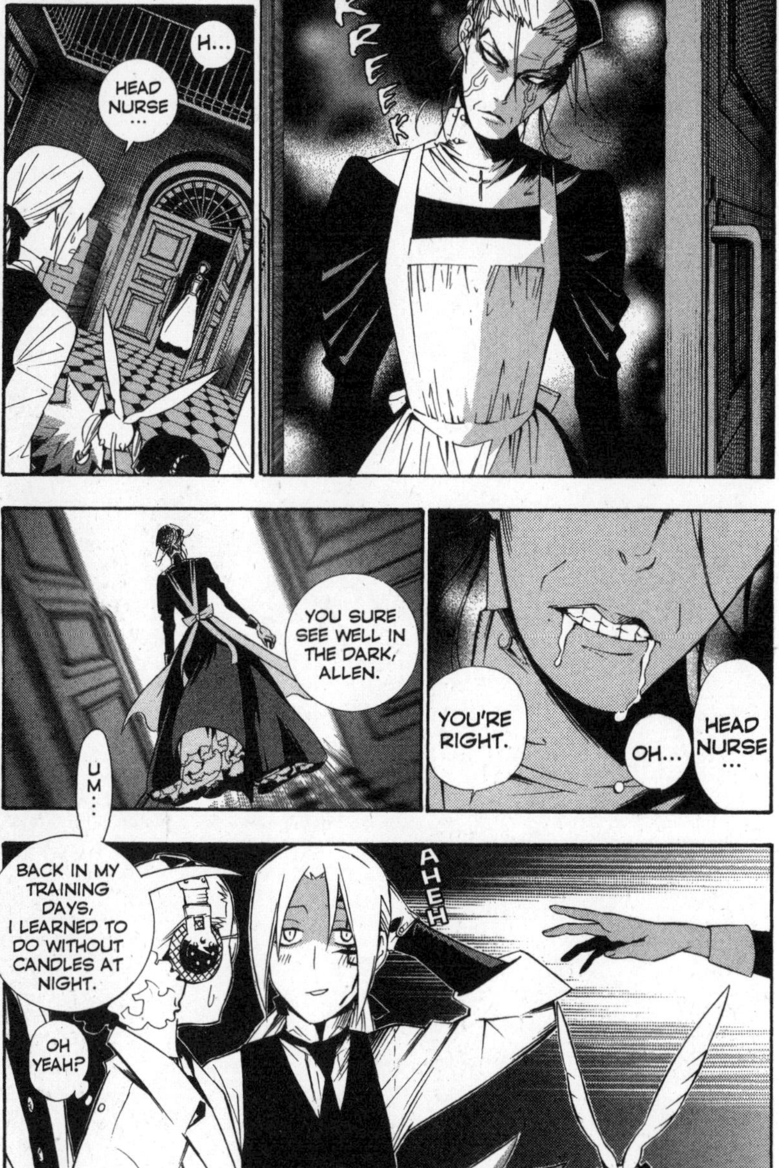
KREEK
H...
HEAD NURSE ...
HEAD NURSE ...
OH...
YOU'RE RIGHT.
YOU SURE SEE WELL IN THE DARK, ALLEN.
UM...
AHEH
BACK IN MY TRAINING DAYS, I LEARNED TO DO WITHOUT CANDLES AT NIGHT.
OH YEAH?

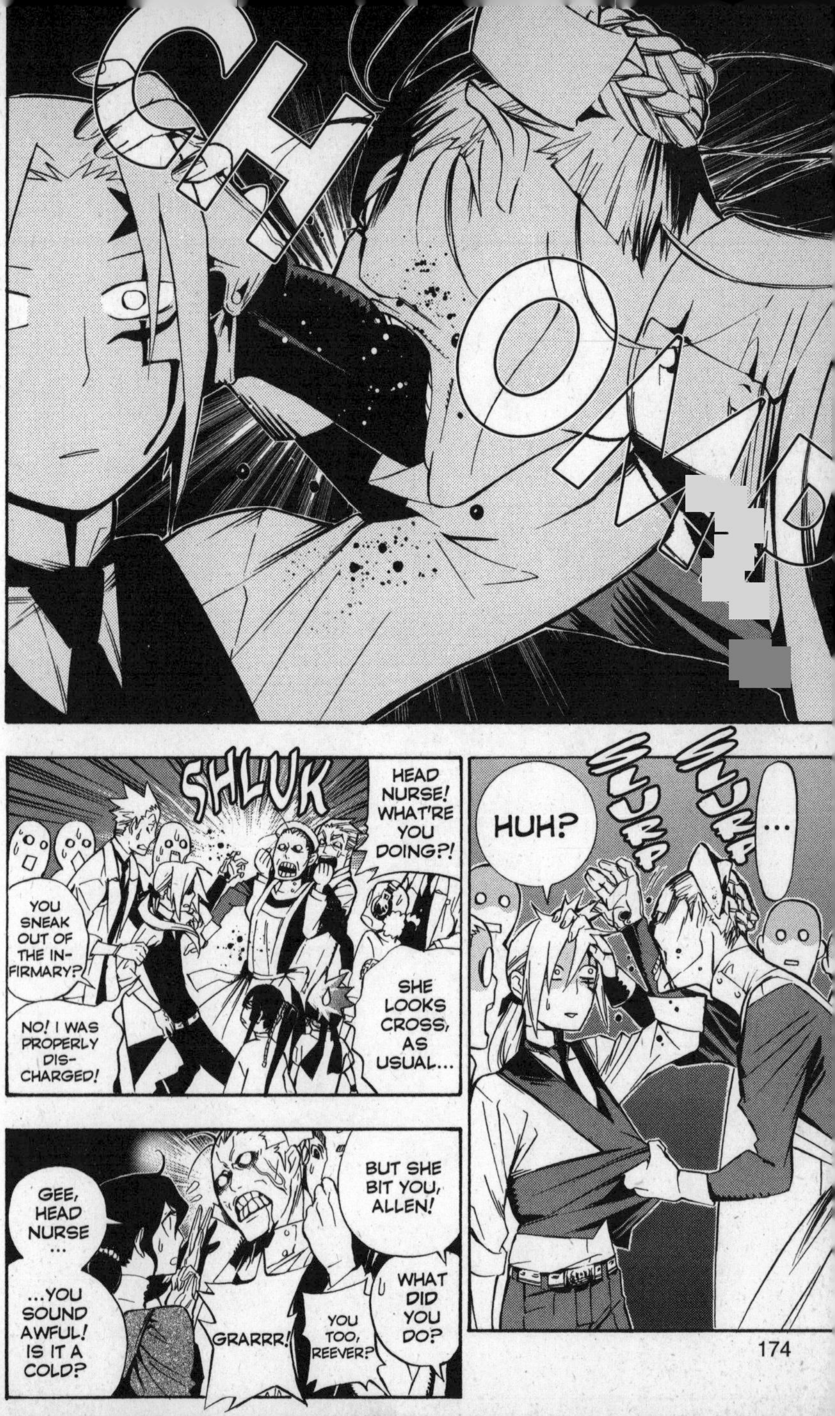
SLURP
SLURP
...
HUH?
SHLUK
HEAD NURSE! WHAT'RE YOU DOING?!
YOU SNEAK OUT OF THE IN-FIRMARY?
SHE LOOKS CROSS, AS USUAL...
NO! I WAS PROPERLY DIS-CHARGED!
BUT SHE BIT YOU, ALLEN!
GEE, HEAD NURSE...
WHAT DID YOU DO?
YOU TOO, REEVER?
...YOU SOUND AWFUL! IS IT A COLD?
GRARRR!

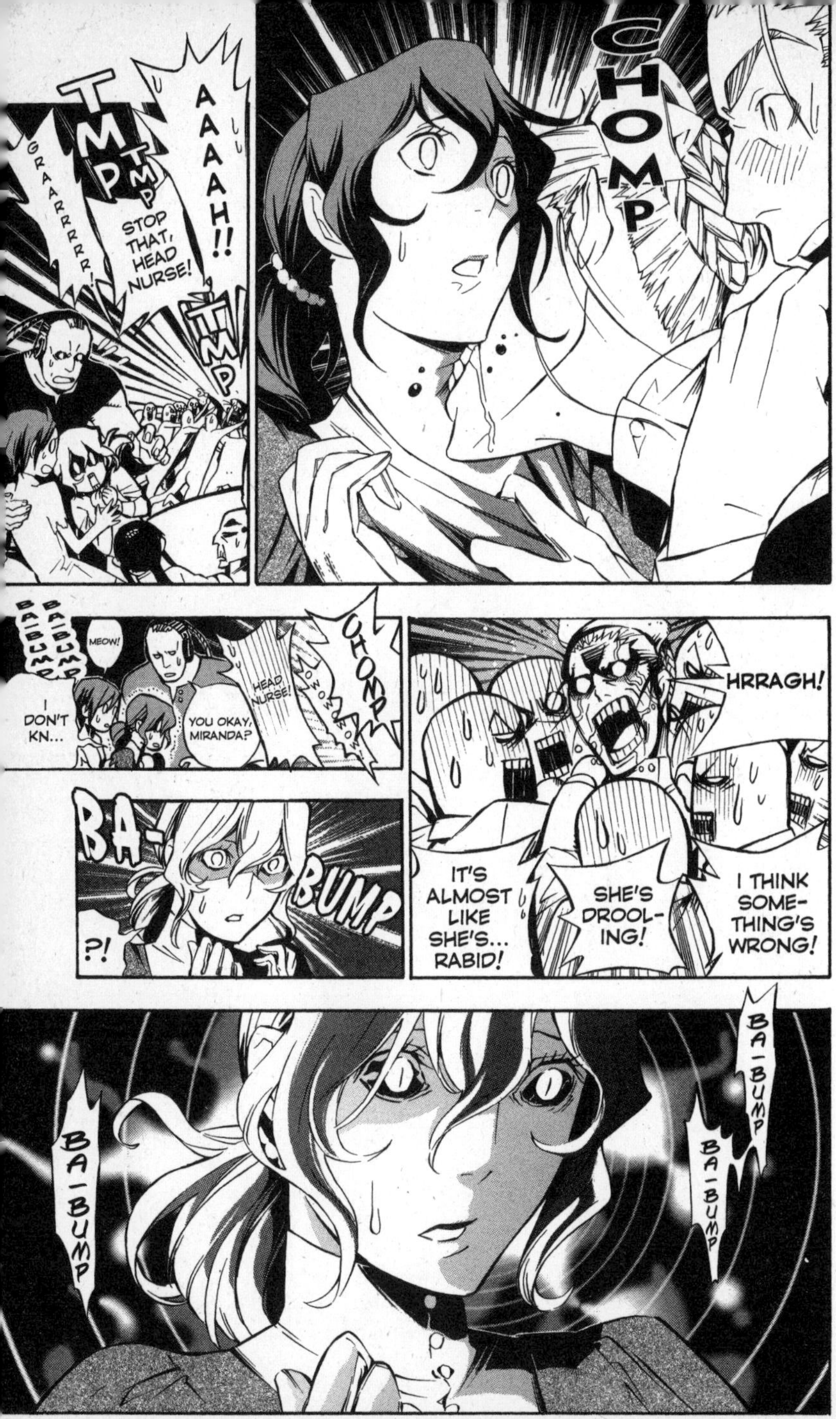
CHOMP
AAAAH!!
TMP
TMP
STOP THAT, HEAD NURSE!
GRAARRRRR!
TMP
HRRAGH!
I THINK SOME-THING'S WRONG!
SHE'S DROOL-ING!
IT'S ALMOST LIKE SHE'S... RABID!
CHOMP
NOW NOW NOW
HEAD NURSE!
YOU OKAY, MIRANDA?
MEOW!
I DON'T KN...
BA-BUMP
BA-BUMP
BA-BUMP
?!
BA-BUMP
BA-BUMP
BA-BUMP

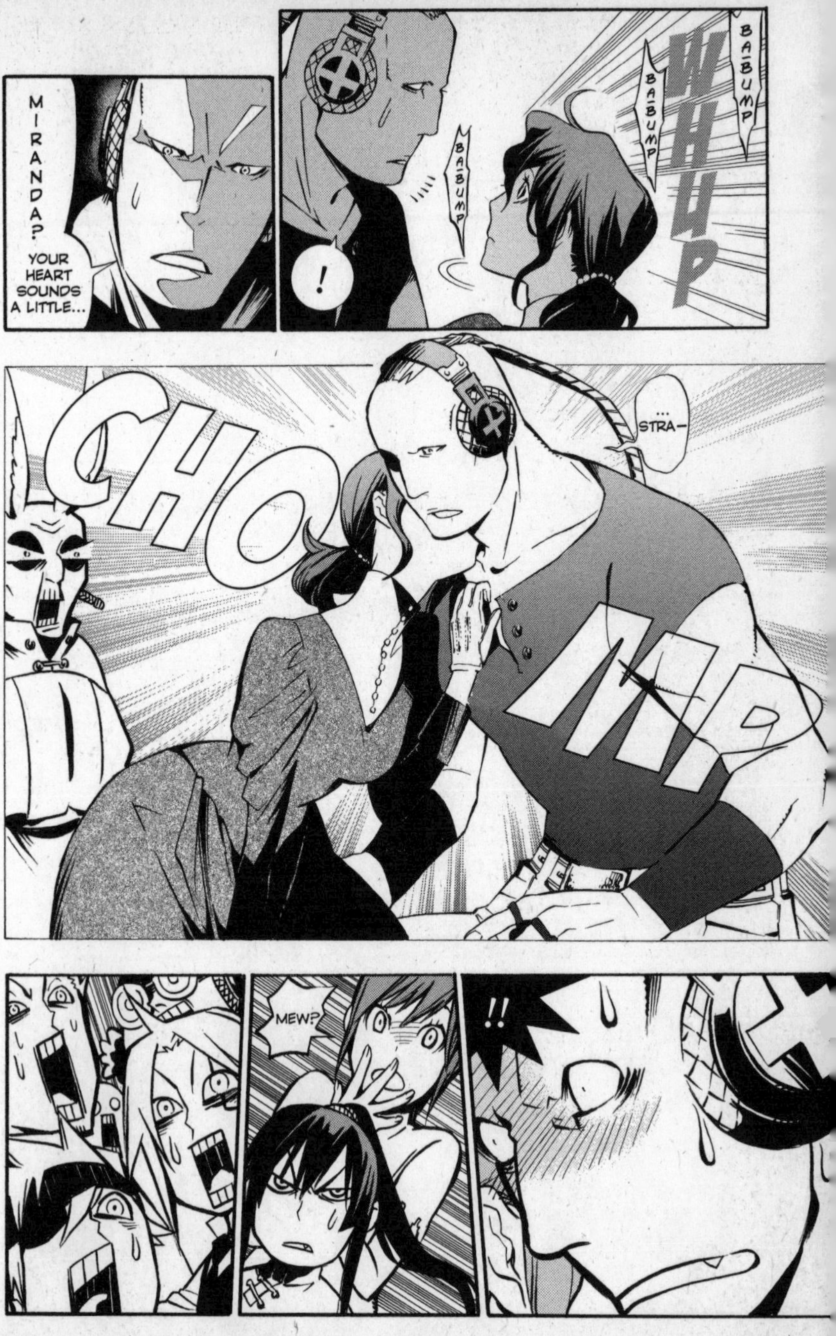
WHUP
BA-BUMP
BA-BUMP
BA-BUMP
!
MIRANDA? YOUR HEART SOUNDS A LITTLE...
... STRA—
CHOMP
!!
MEW?

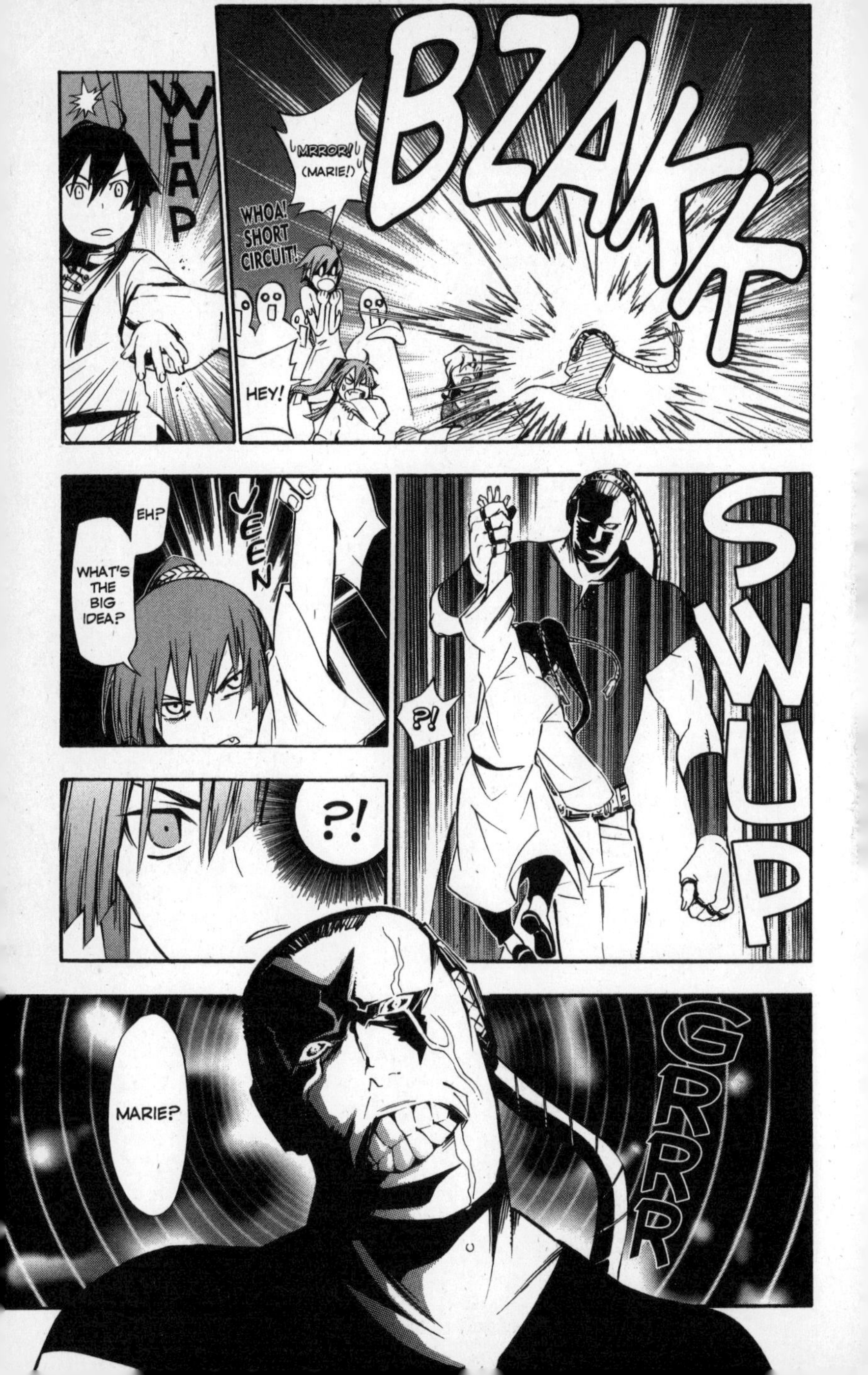
BZAKKT
MRROR! (MARIE!)
WHOA! SHORT CIRCUIT!
HEY!
WHAP
SWUP
?!
JEEN
EH? WHAT'S THE BIG IDEA?
?!
GRRRR
MARIE?

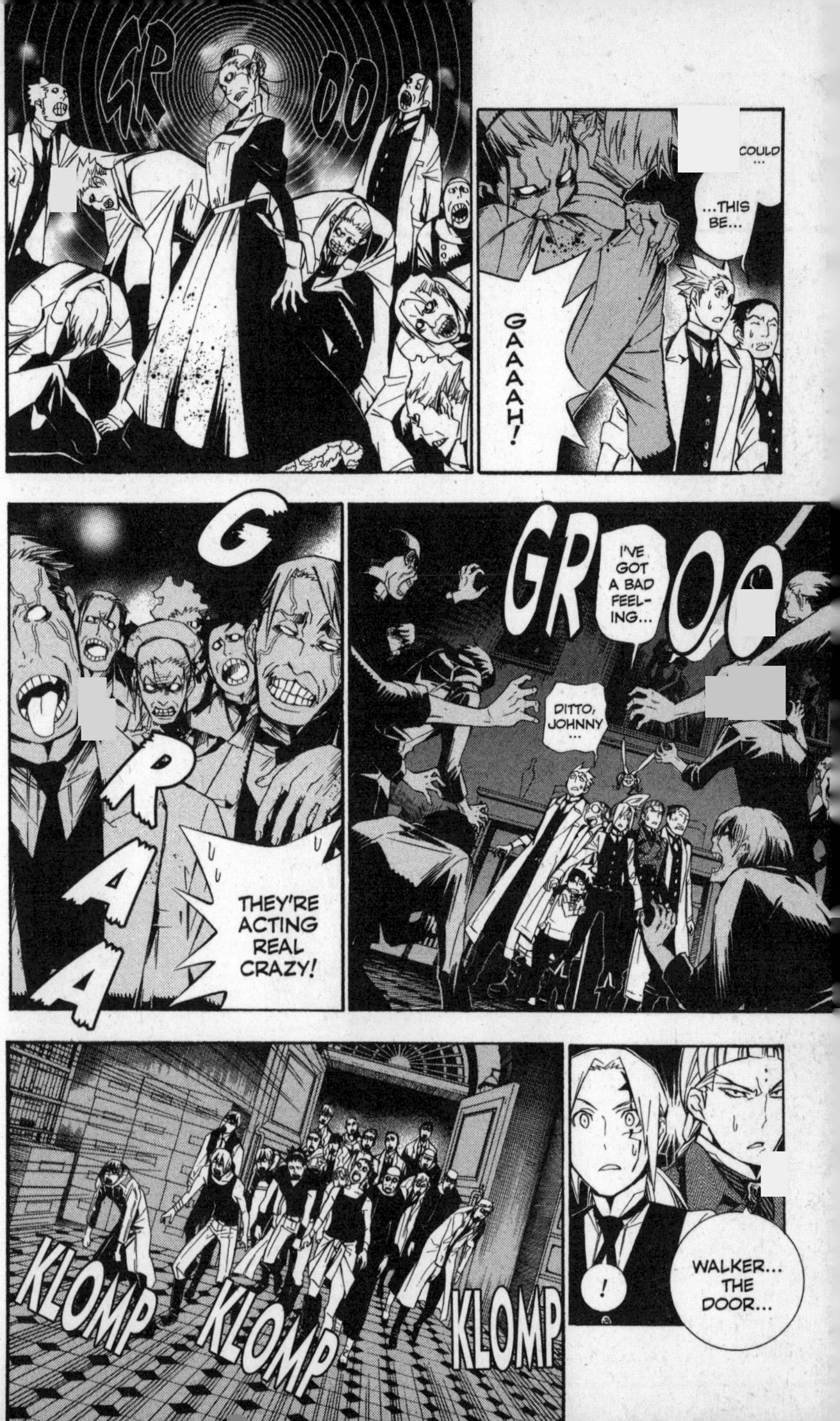
COULD...
...THIS BE...
GAAAAH!
GROO
GROO
I'VE GOT A BAD FEELING...
DITTO, JOHNNY...
GRAAA
THEY'RE ACTING REAL CRAZY!
!
WALKER... THE DOOR...
KLOMP
KLOMP
KLOMP

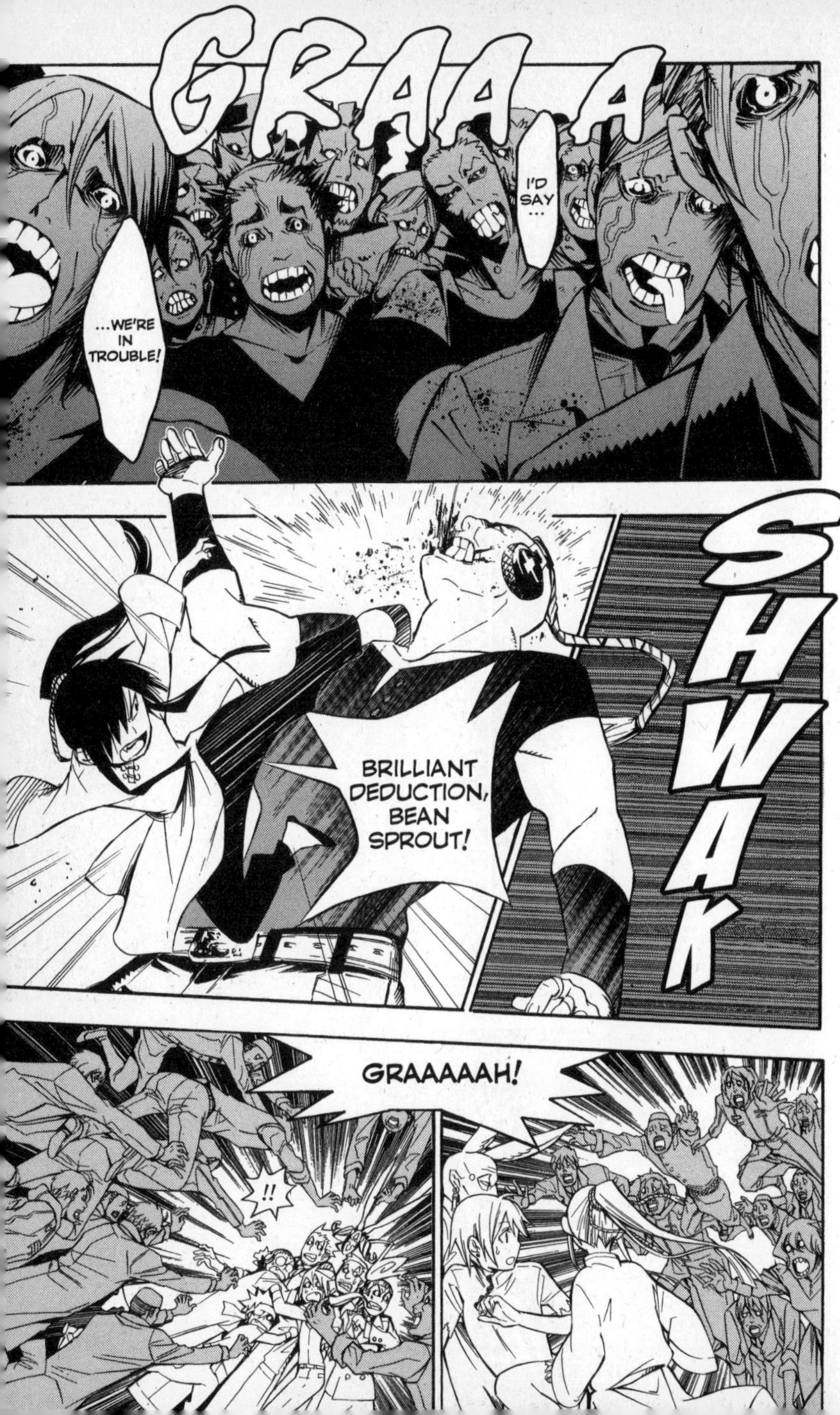
GRAAA
I'D SAY...
...WE'RE IN TROUBLE!
SHWAK
BRILLIANT DEDUCTION, BEAN SPROUT!
GRAAAAH!
!!

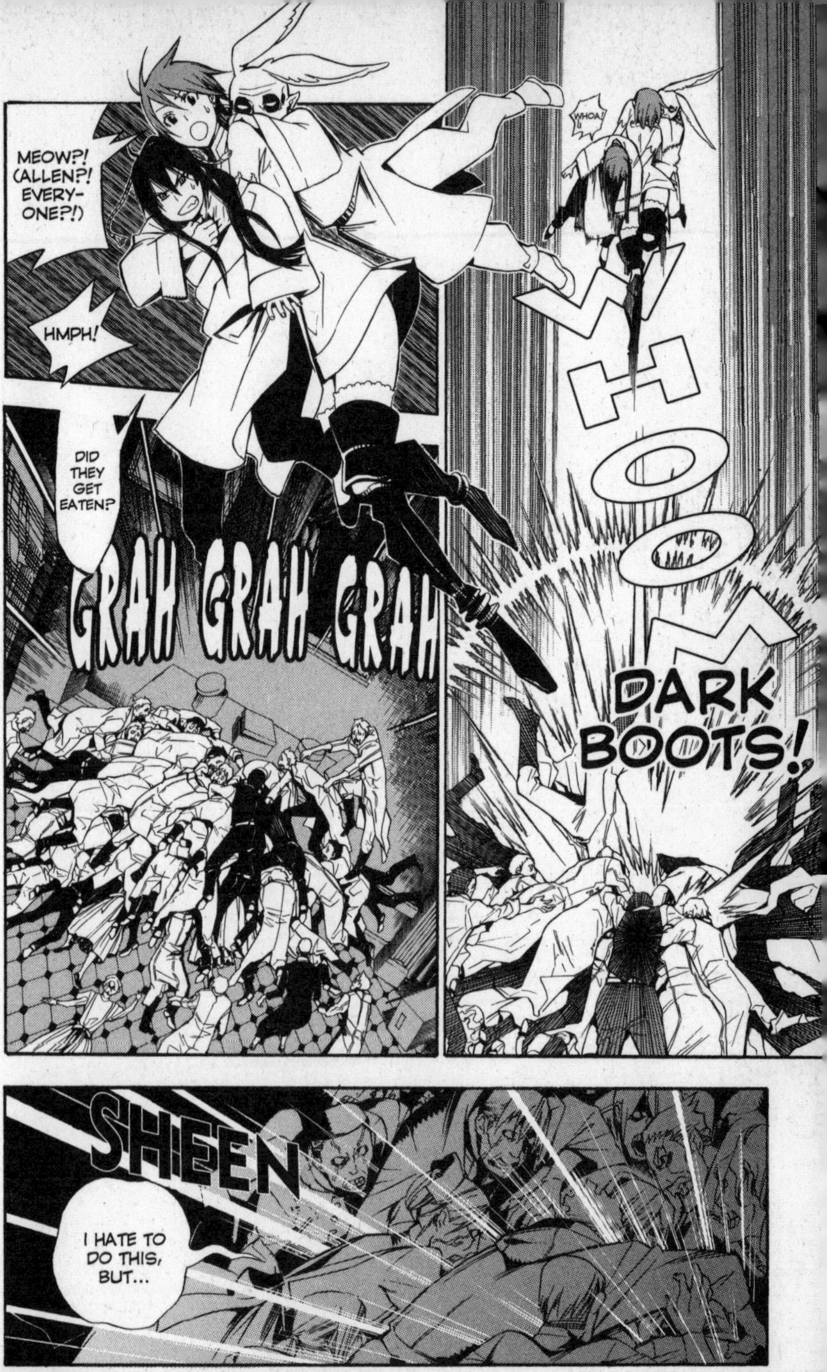
WHOA!
WHOOM
DARK BOOTS!
MEOW?! (ALLEN?! EVERY-ONE?!)
HMPH!
DID THEY GET EATEN?
GRAH GRAH GRAH
SHEEN
I HATE TO DO THIS, BUT...

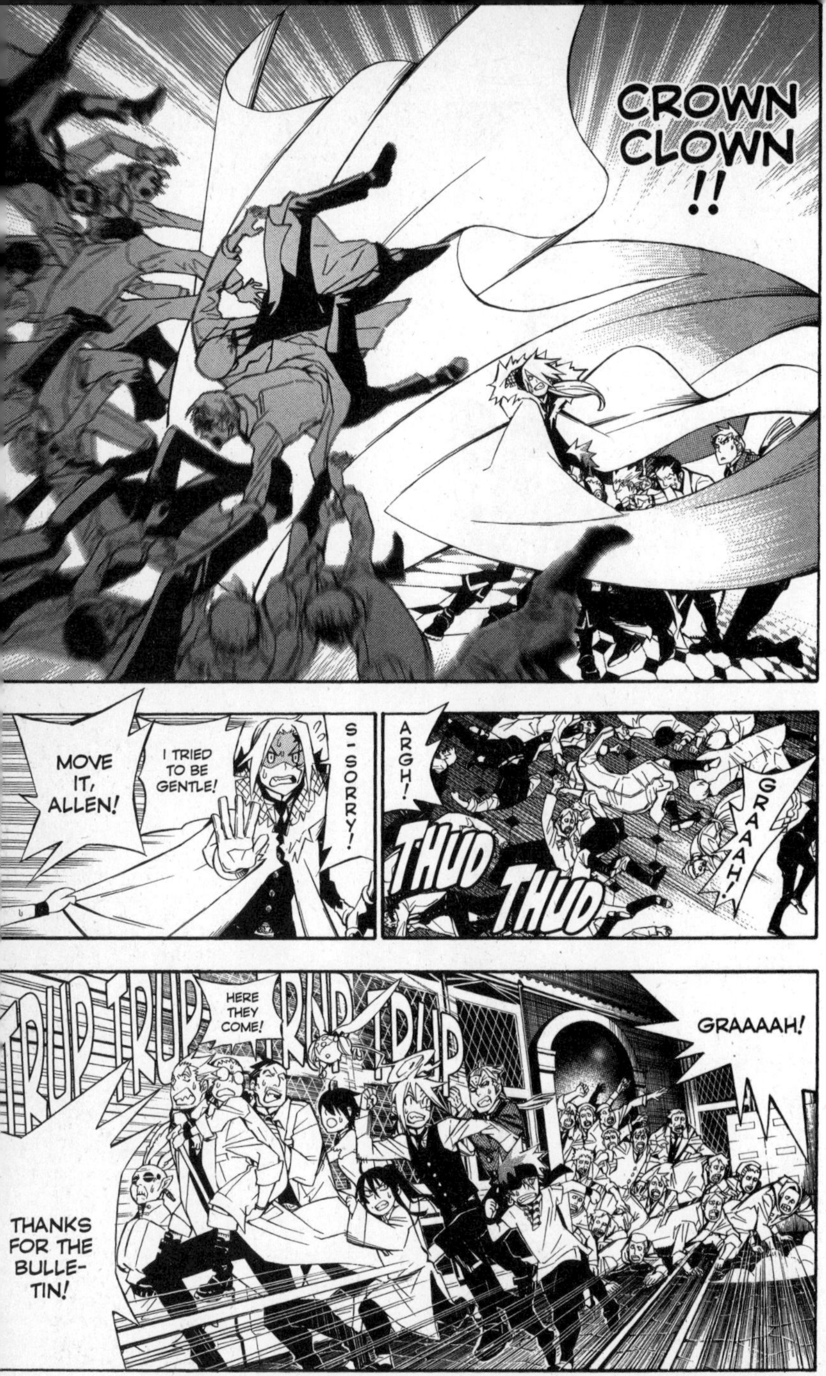
CROWN CLOWN!!
GRAAAAH!
ARGH!
THUD
THUD
S-SORRY!
I TRIED TO BE GENTLE!
MOVE IT, ALLEN!
GRAAAAH!
HERE THEY COME!
TRUP TRUP
THANKS FOR THE BULLE-TIN!

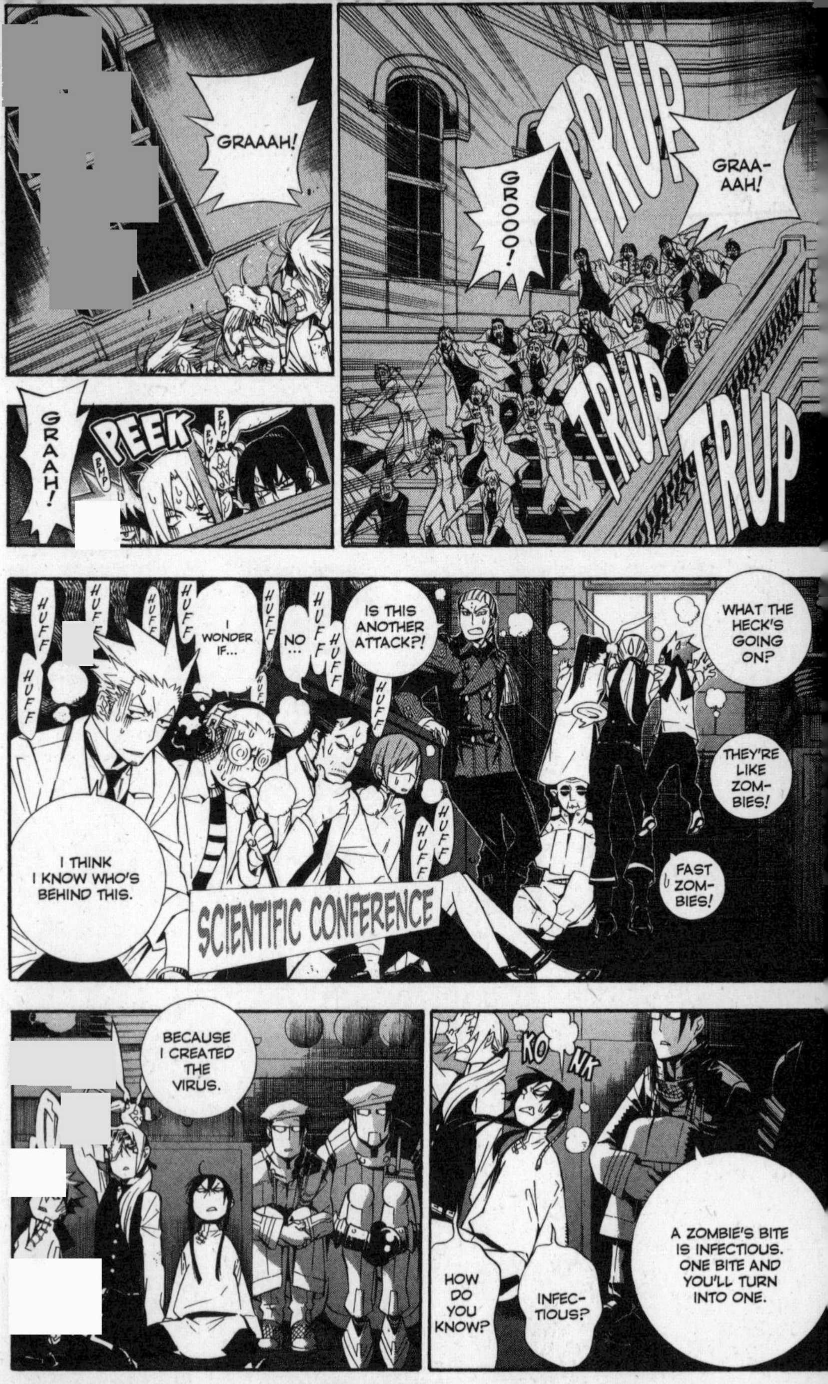
TRUP
GRAA-AAH!
GROOO!
TRUP
TRUP
GRAAAH!
GRAAAH!
PEEK
BMP
BMP
BMP
BMP
WHAT THE HECK'S GOING ON?
THEY'RE LIKE ZOM-BIES!
FAST ZOM-BIES!
IS THIS ANOTHER ATTACK?!
HUFF
HUFF HUFF
HUFF
NO...
HUFF
I WONDER IF...
HUFF
HUFF
HUFF
HUFF
HUFF
HUFF
I THINK I KNOW WHO'S BEHIND THIS.
SCIENTIFIC CONFERENCE
KONK
A ZOMBIE'S BITE IS INFECTIOUS. ONE BITE AND YOU'LL TURN INTO ONE.
INFEC-TIOUS?
HOW DO YOU KNOW?
BECAUSE I CREATED THE VIRUS.

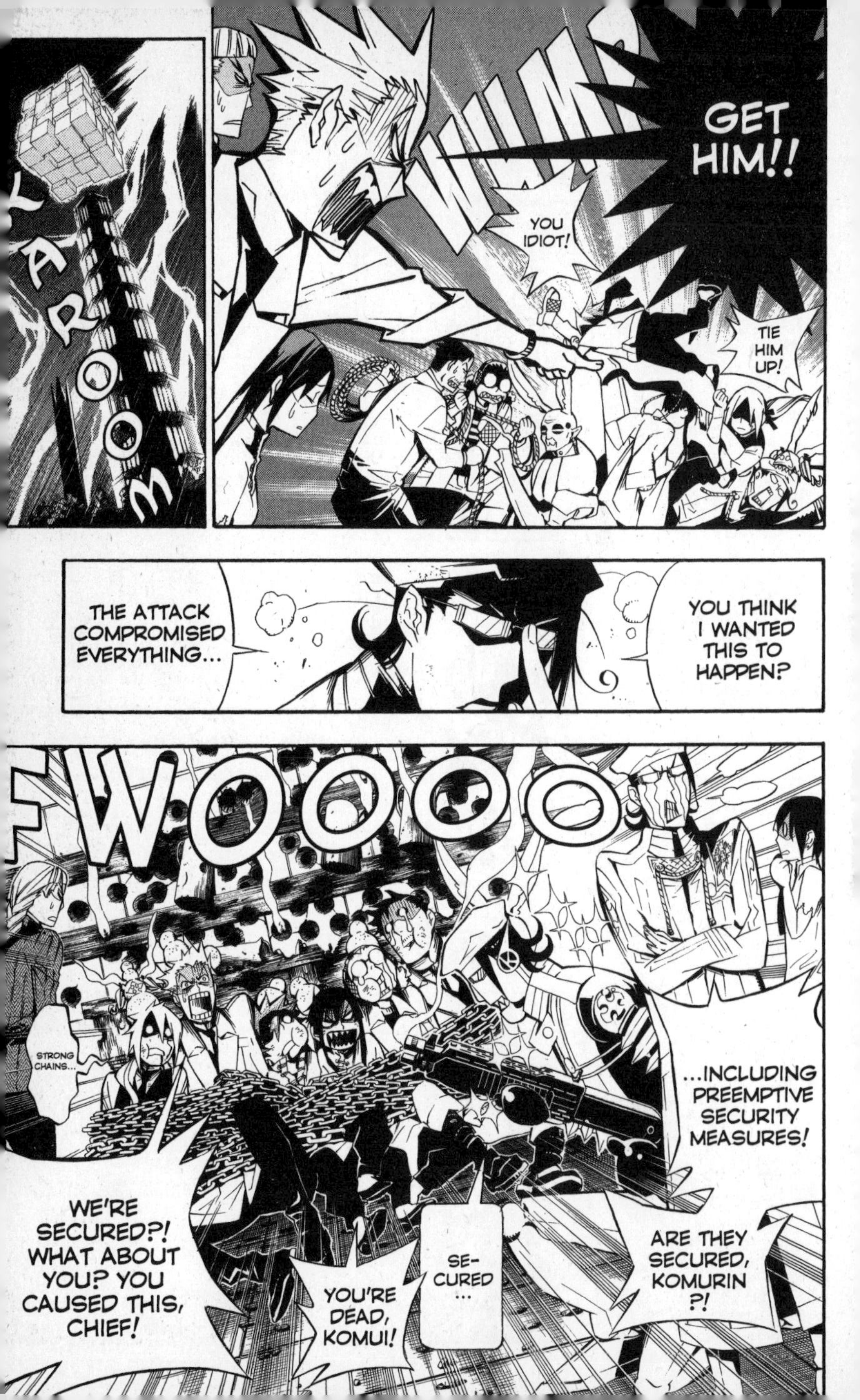
GET HIM!!
YOU IDIOT!
TIE HIM UP!
YOU THINK I WANTED THIS TO HAPPEN?
THE ATTACK COMPROMISED EVERYTHING...
FWOOOOO
...INCLUDING PREEMPTIVE SECURITY MEASURES!
ARE THEY SECURED, KOMURIN?!
SE-CURED...
YOU'RE DEAD, KOMUI!
WE'RE SECURED?! WHAT ABOUT YOU? YOU CAUSED THIS, CHIEF!
STRONG CHAINS...

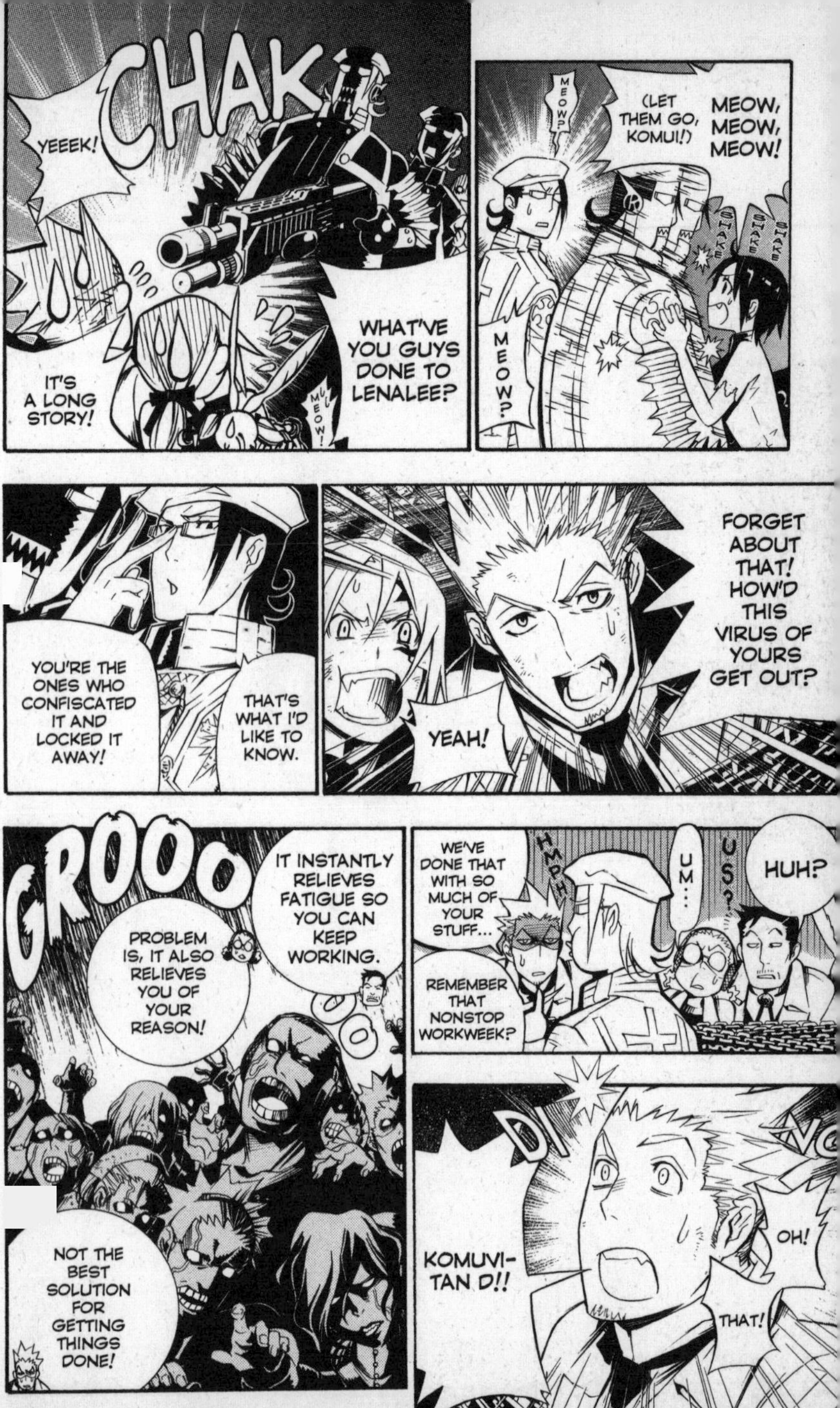
MEOW?
(LET THEM GO, KOMUI!)
MEOW, MEOW, MEOW!
SHAKE SHAKE SHAKE
MEOW?
CHAK
YEEEK!
WHAT'VE YOU GUYS DONE TO LENALEE?
MEOW!
IT'S A LONG STORY!
FORGET ABOUT THAT! HOW'D THIS VIRUS OF YOURS GET OUT?
YEAH!
THAT'S WHAT I'D LIKE TO KNOW.
YOU'RE THE ONES WHO CONFISCATED IT AND LOCKED IT AWAY!
HUH?
US?
UM...
HMPH
WE'VE DONE THAT WITH SO MUCH OF YOUR STUFF...
REMEMBER THAT NONSTOP WORKWEEK?
DING
OH! THAT!
KOMUVITAN D!!
GROOO
IT INSTANTLY RELIEVES FATIGUE SO YOU CAN KEEP WORKING.
PROBLEM IS, IT ALSO RELIEVES YOU OF YOUR REASON!
NOT THE BEST SOLUTION FOR GETTING THINGS DONE!

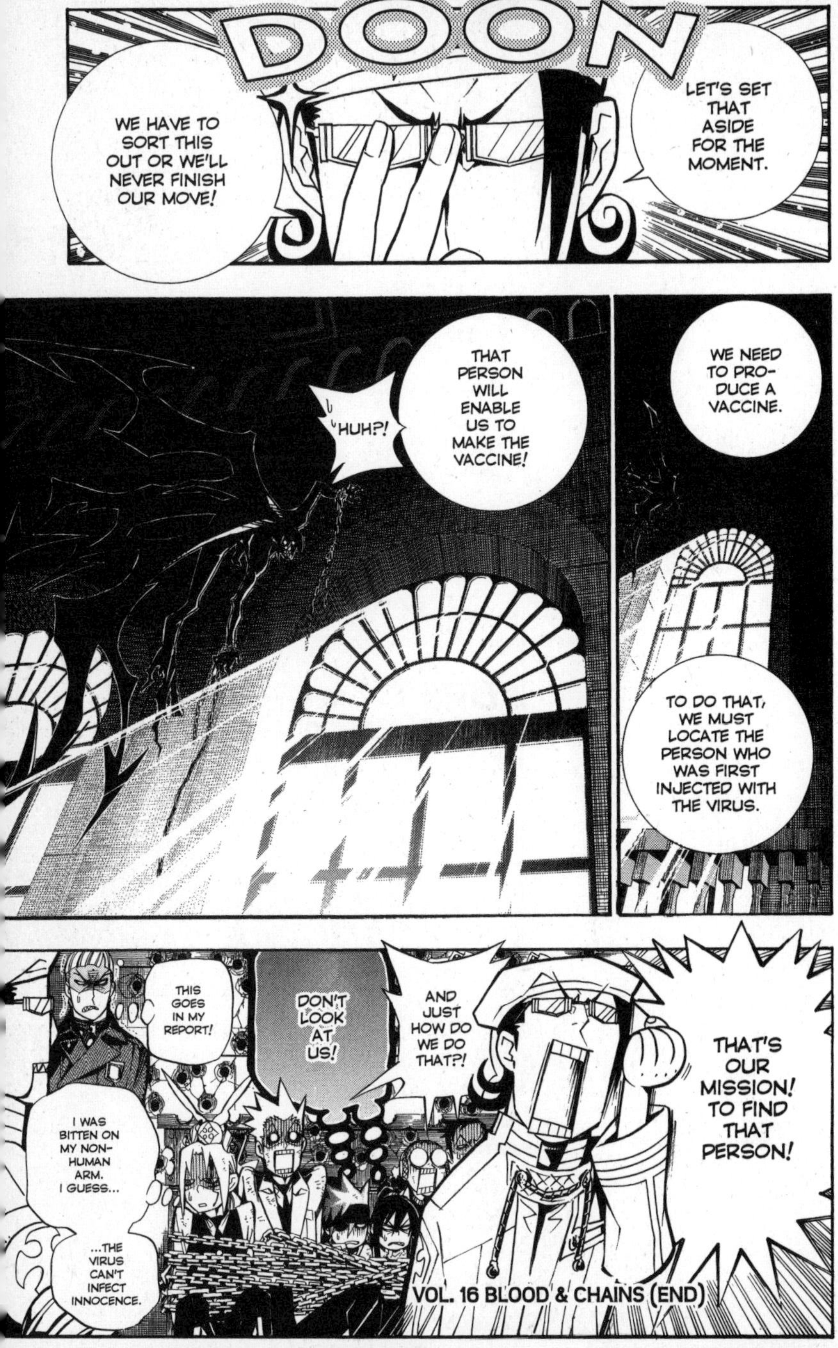
DOON
LET'S SET THAT ASIDE FOR THE MOMENT.
WE HAVE TO SORT THIS OUT OR WE'LL NEVER FINISH OUR MOVE!
WE NEED TO PRODUCE A VACCINE.
TO DO THAT, WE MUST LOCATE THE PERSON WHO WAS FIRST INJECTED WITH THE VIRUS.
THAT PERSON WILL ENABLE US TO MAKE THE VACCINE!
HUH?!
THAT'S OUR MISSION! TO FIND THAT PERSON!
AND JUST HOW DO WE DO THAT?!
DON'T LOOK AT US!
THIS GOES IN MY REPORT!
I WAS BITTEN ON MY NON-HUMAN ARM. I GUESS...
...THE VIRUS CAN'T INFECT INNOCENCE.
VOL. 16 BLOOD & CHAINS (END)

A PICTURE OF JOHNNY THAT MY LITTLE BROTHER DREW.

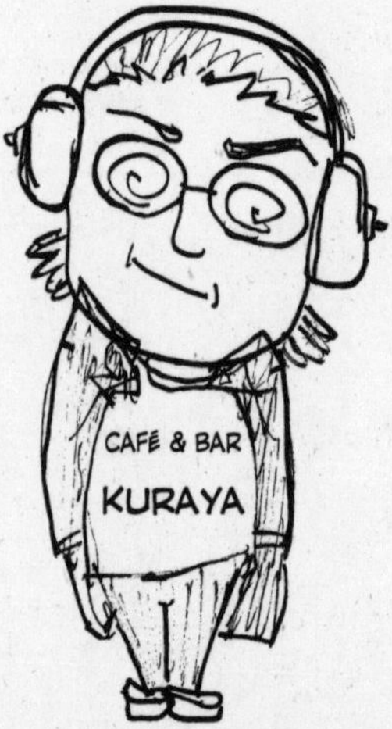
CAFÉ & BAR
KURAYA

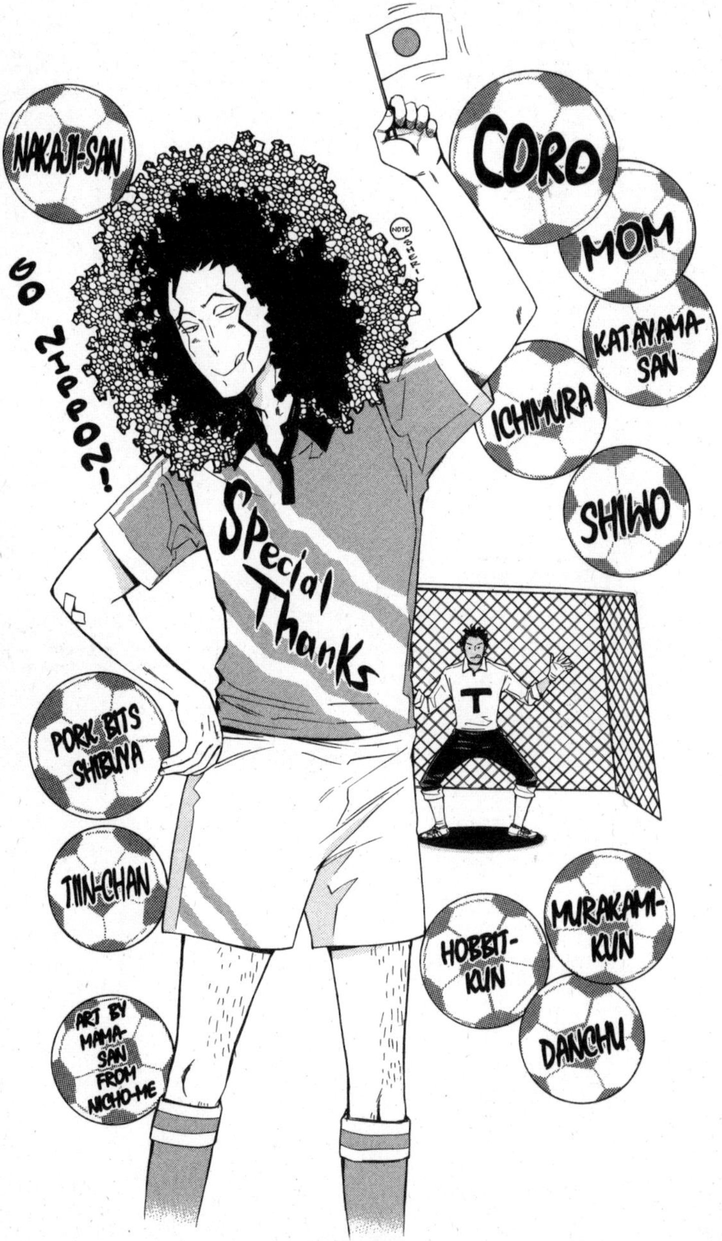
CORO
MOM
KATAYAMA-SAN
ICHIMURA
SHIWO
NOTE SHERI
NAKAJI-SAN
GO NIPPON!
Special Thanks
T
MURAKAMI-KUN
HOBBIT-KUN
DANCHU
PORK BITS SHIBUYA
TIIN-CHAN
ART BY MAMA-SAN FROM NICHO-ME

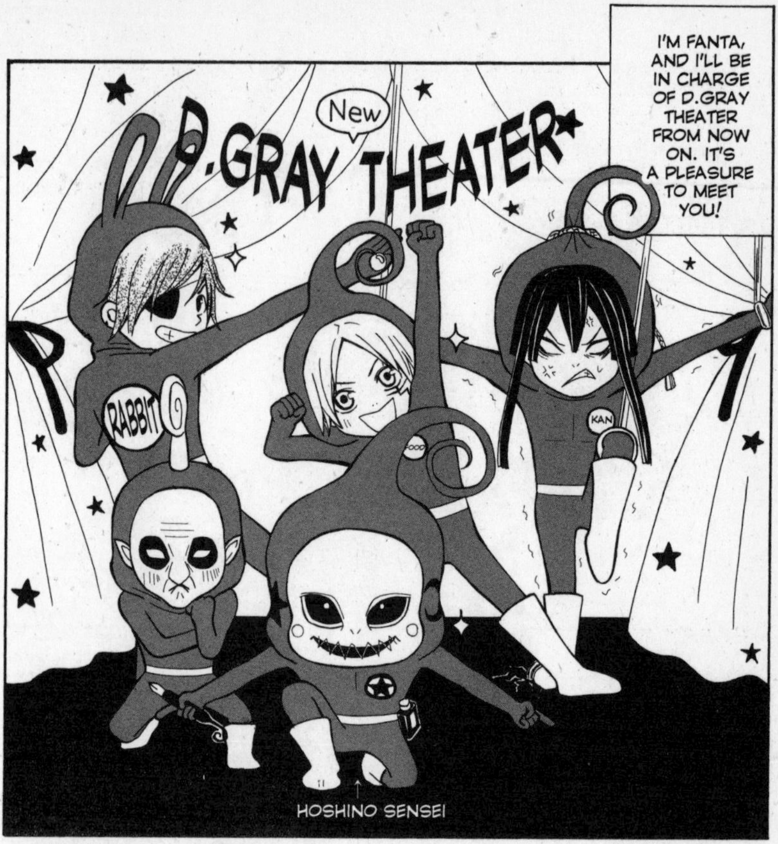
I'M FANTA, AND I'LL BE IN CHARGE OF D.GRAY THEATER FROM NOW ON. IT'S A PLEASURE TO MEET YOU!
New
D.GRAY THEATER
RABBIT
KAN
HOSHINO SENSEI

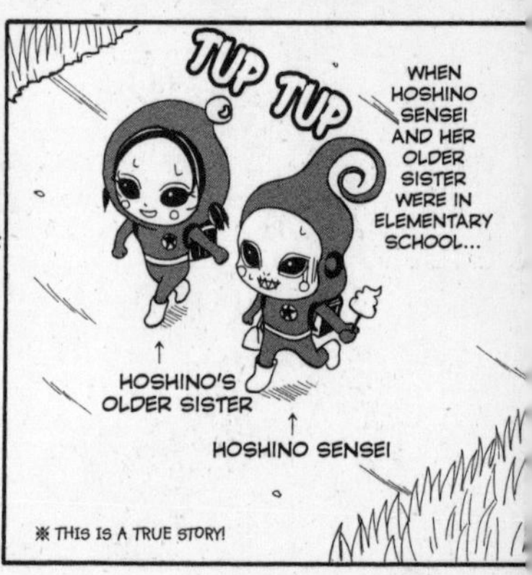
TUP TUP
WHEN HOSHINO SENSEI AND HER OLDER SISTER WERE IN ELEMENTARY SCHOOL...
HOSHINO'S OLDER SISTER
HOSHINO SENSEI
※ THIS IS A TRUE STORY!

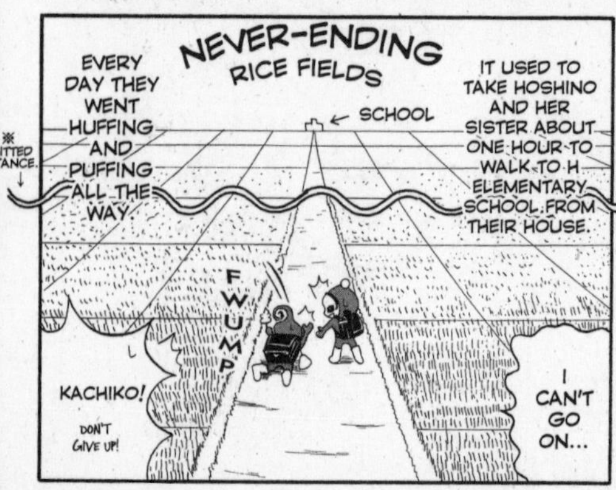
NEVER-ENDING RICE FIELDS
IT USED TO TAKE HOSHINO AND HER SISTER ABOUT ONE HOUR TO WALK TO H ELEMENTARY SCHOOL FROM THEIR HOUSE.
SCHOOL
EVERY DAY THEY WENT HUFFING AND PUFFING ALL THE WAY.
FWUMP
I CAN'T GO ON...
KACHIKO!
DON'T GIVE UP!

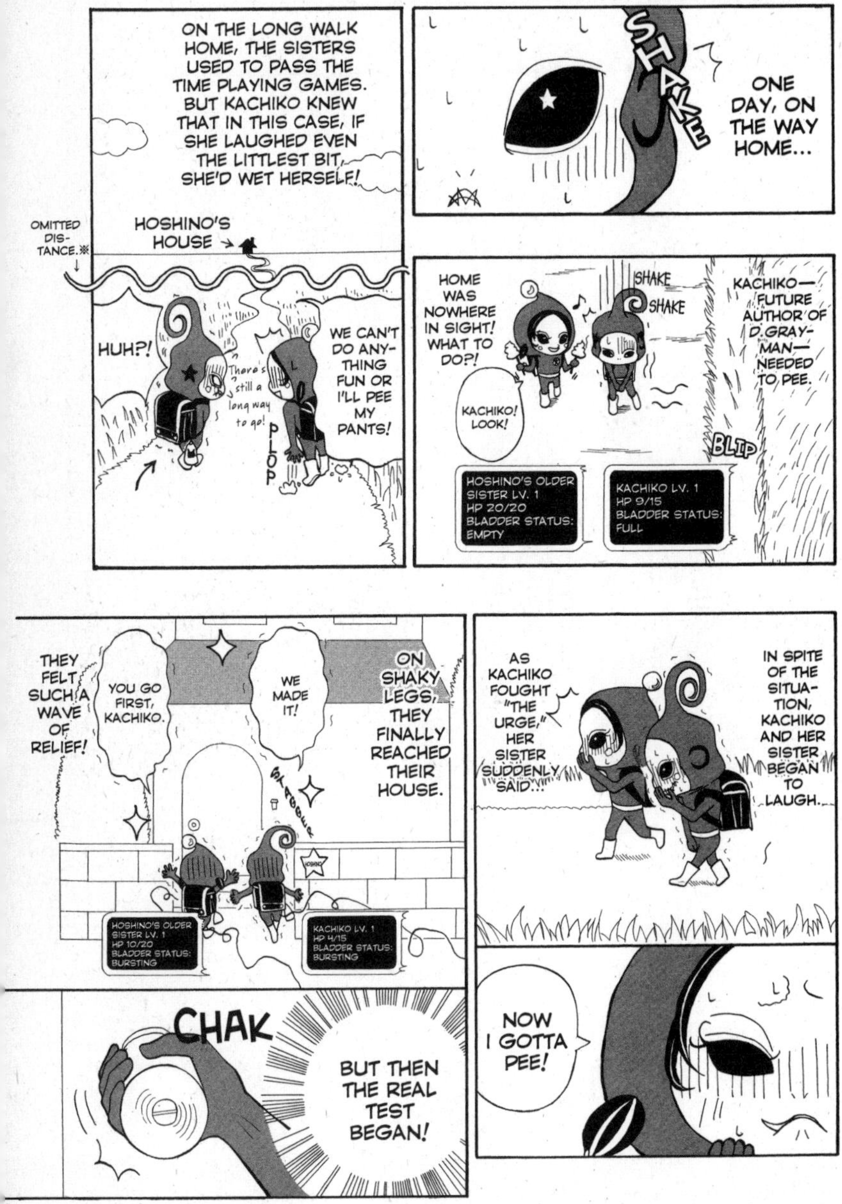

SHAKE
ONE DAY, ON THE WAY HOME...
KACHIKO—FUTURE AUTHOR OF D.GRAY-MAN—NEEDED TO PEE.
SHAKE
SHAKE
HOME WAS NOWHERE IN SIGHT! WHAT TO DO?!
KACHIKO! LOOK!
BLIP
KACHIKO LV. 1 HP 9/15 BLADDER STATUS: FULL
HOSHINO'S OLDER SISTER LV. 1 HP 20/20 BLADDER STATUS: EMPTY
ON THE LONG WALK HOME, THE SISTERS USED TO PASS THE TIME PLAYING GAMES. BUT KACHIKO KNEW THAT IN THIS CASE, IF SHE LAUGHED EVEN THE LITTLEST BIT, SHE'D WET HERSELF!
HOSHINO'S HOUSE →
OMITTED DIS-TANCE.※
WE CAN'T DO ANY-THING FUN OR I'LL PEE MY PANTS!
There's still a long way to go!
PLOP
HUH?!
IN SPITE OF THE SITUA-TION, KACHIKO AND HER SISTER BEGAN TO LAUGH.
AS KACHIKO FOUGHT "THE URGE," HER SISTER SUDDENLY SAID...
NOW I GOTTA PEE!
ON SHAKY LEGS, THEY FINALLY REACHED THEIR HOUSE.
WE MADE IT!
STAGGER
YOU GO FIRST, KACHIKO.
THEY FELT SUCH A WAVE OF RELIEF!
HOSHINO
KACHIKO LV. 1 HP 4/15 BLADDER STATUS: BURSTING
HOSHINO'S OLDER SISTER LV. 1 HP 10/20 BLADDER STATUS: BURSTING
BUT THEN THE REAL TEST BEGAN!
CHAK

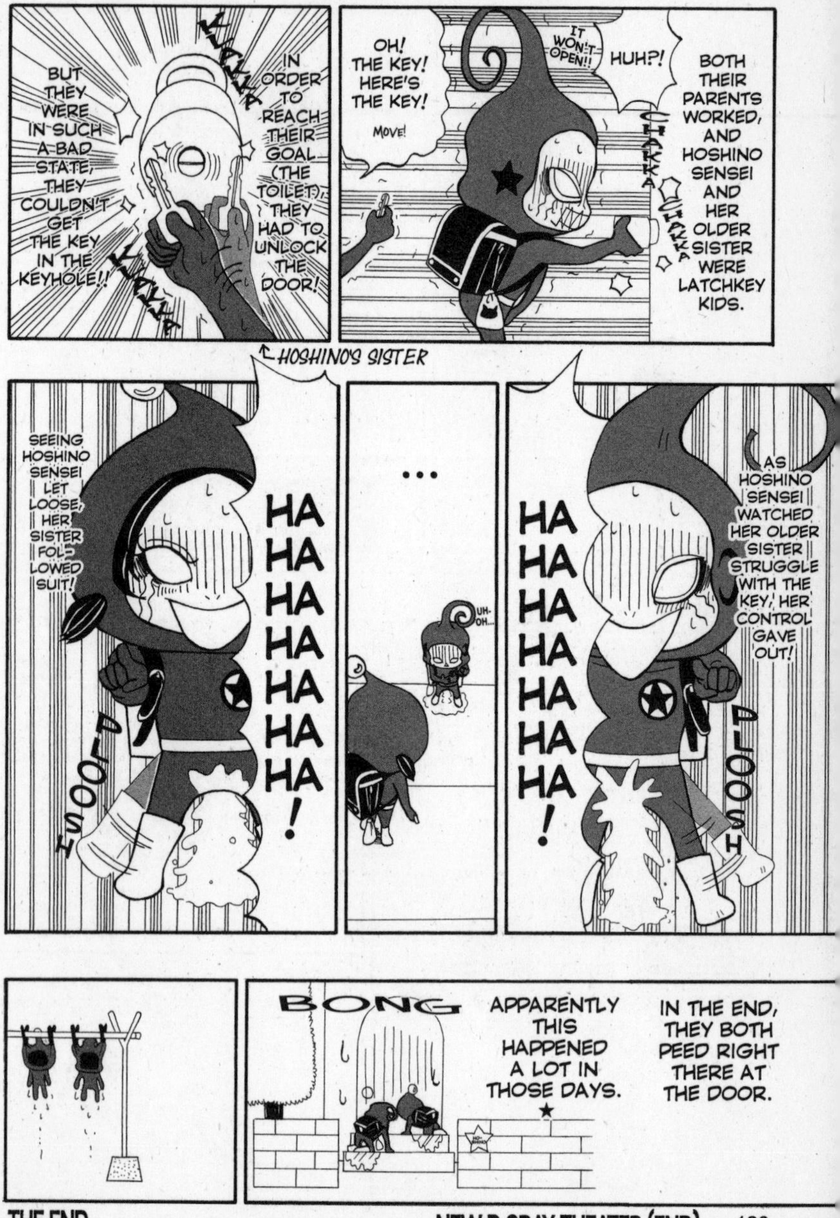
BOTH THEIR PARENTS WORKED, AND HOSHINO SENSEI AND HER OLDER SISTER WERE LATCHKEY KIDS.
HUH?!
IT WON'T OPEN!!
CHAKKA CHAKKA
OH! THE KEY! HERE'S THE KEY!
MOVE!
IN ORDER TO REACH THEIR GOAL (THE TOILET), THEY HAD TO UNLOCK THE DOOR!
BUT THEY WERE IN SUCH A BAD STATE, THEY COULDN'T GET THE KEY IN THE KEYHOLE!!
← HOSHINO'S SISTER
AS HOSHINO SENSEI WATCHED HER OLDER SISTER STRUGGLE WITH THE KEY, HER CONTROL GAVE OUT!
HA HA HA HA HA HA HA HA HA!
PLOOSH
...
UH-OH...
SEEING HOSHINO SENSEI LET LOOSE, HER SISTER FOL-LOWED SUIT!
HA HA HA HA HA HA HA HA HA!
PLOOSH
IN THE END, THEY BOTH PEED RIGHT THERE AT THE DOOR.
APPARENTLY THIS HAPPENED A LOT IN THOSE DAYS. ★
BONG

THE END

NEW D.GRAY THEATER (END)

BONUS

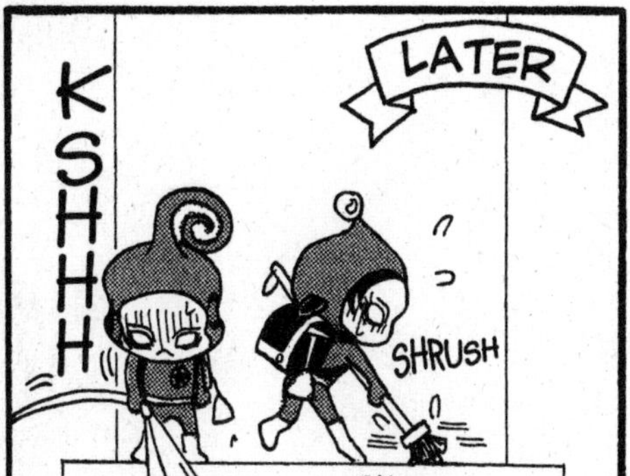
LATER
KSHHH
SHRUSH
SHRUSH

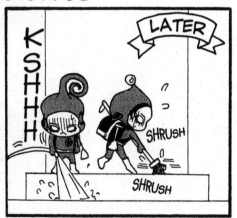

DESTROYING THE EVIDENCE ☆

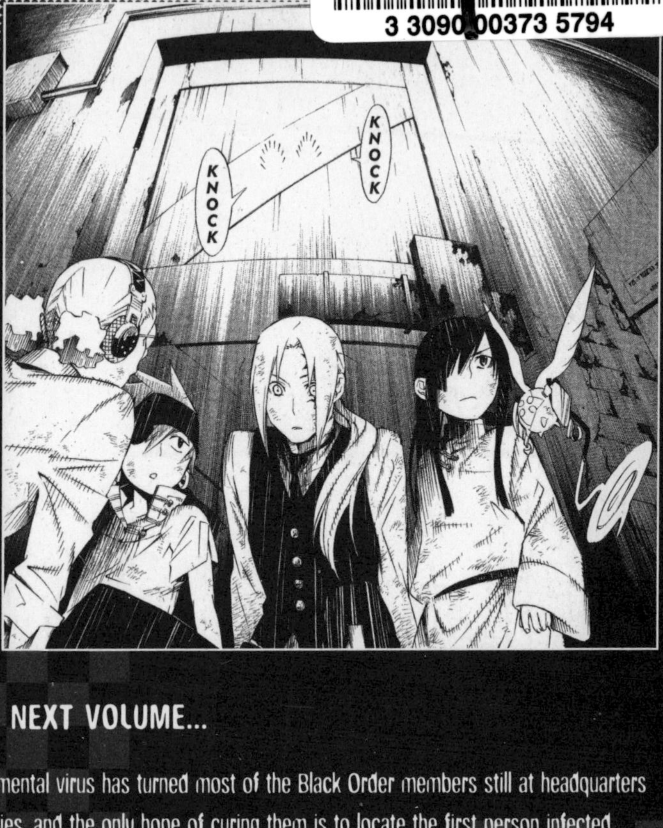
KNOCK
KNOCK

IN THE NEXT VOLUME...

An experimental virus has turned most of the Black Order members still at headquarters into zombies, and the only hope of curing them is to locate the first person infected. Unfortunately, Count Krory picks this moment to revive from his coma—and he's been infected with the same virus! Meanwhile, an almost-forgotten victim of Black Order experiments seizes the opportunity to exact a long-delayed vengeance!

Available May 2010!